Among the Powers of the Earth

Among the Powers of the Earth

THE AMERICAN REVOLUTION AND THE

MAKING OF A NEW WORLD EMPIRE

Eliga H. Gould

Harvard University Press

Cambridge, Massachusetts · London, England

2012

Library of Congress Cataloging-in-Publication Data

Gould, Eliga H.

Among the powers of the earth : the American Revolution and the making of a new world
empire / Eliga H. Gould.

p.   cm.

Includes bibliographical references and index.

ISBN 978-0-674-04608-5 (alk. paper)

1. United States—Foreign relations—1775–1783.   2. United States—Foreign relations—
1783–1815.   3. United States—International status—History.   4. United States—
History—Revolution, 1775–1783—Influence.   5. United States—Territorial
expansion.   I. Title.

E249.G68 2012

973.3'2—dc23   2011035333

For Nicky,

always

Contents

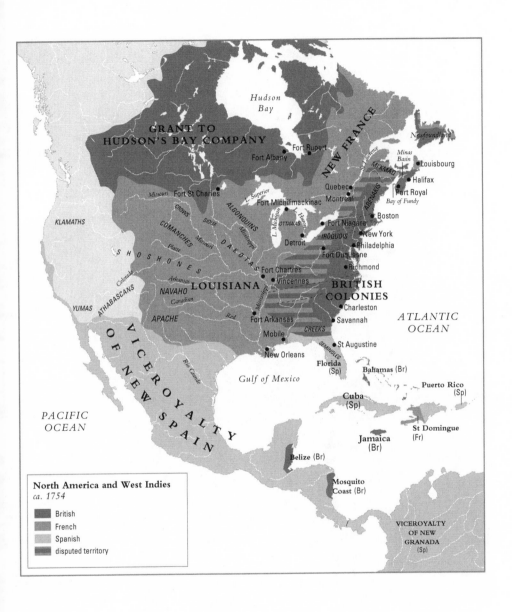

Hudson
Bay

GRANT TO
HUDSON'S BAY COMPANY
•Fort Rupert
Fort Albany•

NEW FRANCE

Newfoundland

Minas
Basin   •Louisbourg
                •Halifax
MI'KMAQ   Port Royal
Quebec•   Bay of Fundy
Montreal•

Missouri Fort St Charles•
Superior
Fort Michilimackinac
L. Michigan
ALGONQUINS
CROWS   SIOUX
COMANCHES   DAKOTAS
L. Huron
OTTAWAS
Fort Niagara•
Detroit•   IROQUOIS •New York
                      •Philadelphia
Fort Duquesne•

SHOSHONES
Platte
Colorado
ATHABASCANS
Arkansas
NAVAHO   Fort Chartres•
•Vincennes
LOUISIANA
Canadian
Red
APACHE   Fort Arkansas•
          Mobile•

KLAMATHS

YUMAS

BRITISH
COLONIES
•Richmond

•Charleston
•Savannah   ATLANTIC
            OCEAN
CREEKS

Rio Grande

VICEROYALTY
OF
NEW
SPAIN

PACIFIC
OCEAN

New Orleans•
SEMINOLES
•St Augustine
Florida
(Sp)   Bahamas (Br)

Gulf of Mexico

Cuba
(Sp)

Puerto Rico
(Sp)

St Domingue
(Fr)

Jamaica
(Br)

Belize (Br)

Mosquito
Coast (Br)

VICEROYALTY
OF NEW
GRANADA
(Sp)

North America and West Indies
ca. 1754

■ British
■ French
■ Spanish
■ disputed territory

North Atlantic
ca. 1763

Hudson Bay

RUPERT'S LAND

GRANT TO
HUDSON'S BAY
COMPANY

Newfoundland

Quebec

Halifax
Nova Scotia

Boston
New York

Philadelphia

Mississippi

Louisiana

St Louis

Ohio

Proclamation Line of 1763

**THIRTEEN
COLONIES**

Bermuda Is. (Br)

*West
Florida (Br)*
New Orleans

St Augustine

*East
Florida
(Br)*

*Gulf of
Mexico*

Bahamas (Br)

Cuba
(Sp)

Hispaniola

VICEROYALTY OF
NEW SPAIN

Belize
(Br)

Jamaica (Br)

St Domingue
(Fr)

Puerto Rico
(Sp)

*Caribbean
Sea*

Mosquito
Coast (Br)

VICEROYALTY
OF NEW
GRANADA
(Sp)

DUTCH
GUIANA

FRENCH
GUIANA

VICEROYALTY
OF BRAZIL (Port)

Amazon

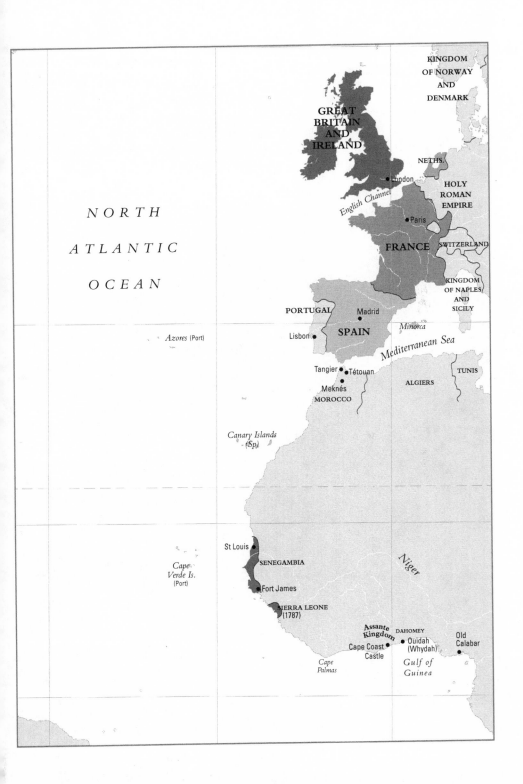

KINGDOM
OF NORWAY
AND
DENMARK

GREAT
BRITAIN
AND
IRELAND

NETHS.

●London

HOLY
ROMAN
EMPIRE

English Channel

●Paris

NORTH

ATLANTIC

OCEAN

FRANCE

SWITZERLAND

KINGDOM
OF NAPLES
AND
SICILY

PORTUGAL   Madrid
●

Azores (Port)

Lisbon●   SPAIN

Minorca

Mediterranean Sea

Tangier ● ●Tétouan
Meknés ●
MOROCCO

ALGIERS

TUNIS

Canary Islands
(Sp)

Cape
Verde Is.
(Port)

St Louis ●

SENEGAMBIA

Niger

●Fort James

SIERRA LEONE
(1787)

Assante
Kingdom   DAHOMEY
Cape Coast ●   ● Ouidah
Castle   (Whydah)

Old
Calabar
●

Cape
Palmas

Gulf of
Guinea

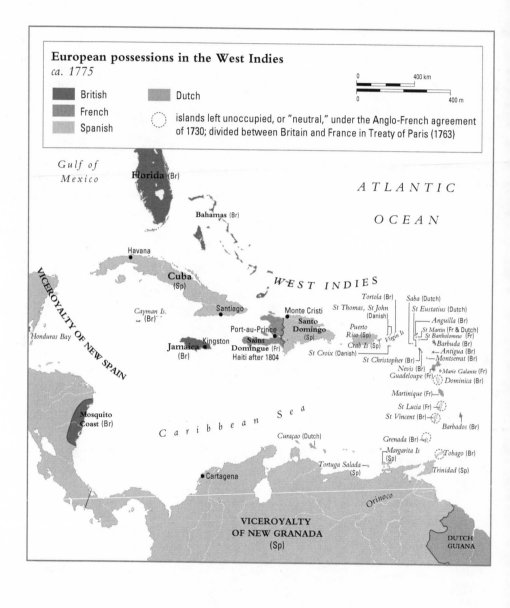

European possessions in the West Indies
ca. 1775

■ British   ■ Dutch
■ French
■ Spanish

○ islands left unoccupied, or "neutral," under the Anglo-French agreement of 1730; divided between Britain and France in Treaty of Paris (1763)

0 — 400 km
0 — 400 m

Gulf of Mexico

Florida (Br)

ATLANTIC

OCEAN

Bahamas (Br)

Havana

VICEROYALTY OF NEW SPAIN

WEST INDIES

Cuba (Sp)

Cayman Is. (Br)

Santiago

Monte Cristi

Tortola (Br)   Saba (Dutch)

St Thomas, St John (Danish)   St Eustatius (Dutch)

Anguilla (Br)

Santo Domingo (Sp)

Puerto Rico (Sp)   St Martin (Fr & Dutch) / St Bartholomew (Fr)

Port-au-Prince   Virgin Is   Barbuda (Br)

Honduras Bay

Kingston   Saint   Crab Is (Sp)   Antigua (Br)

Jamaica (Br)   Domingue (Fr)   St Croix (Danish)   St Christopher (Br)   Montserrat (Br)

Haiti after 1804   Nevis (Br)   Marie Galante (Fr)

Guadeloupe (Fr)   Dominica (Br)

Martinique (Fr)

Mosquito Coast (Br)

Caribbean   *Sea*   St Lucia (Fr)

St Vincent (Br)   Barbados (Br)

Curaçao (Dutch)   Grenada (Br)

Margarita Is (Sp)   Tobago (Br)

Tortuga Salada (Sp)   Trinidad (Sp)

• Cartagena

Orinoco

VICEROYALTY OF NEW GRANADA (Sp)

DUTCH GUIANA

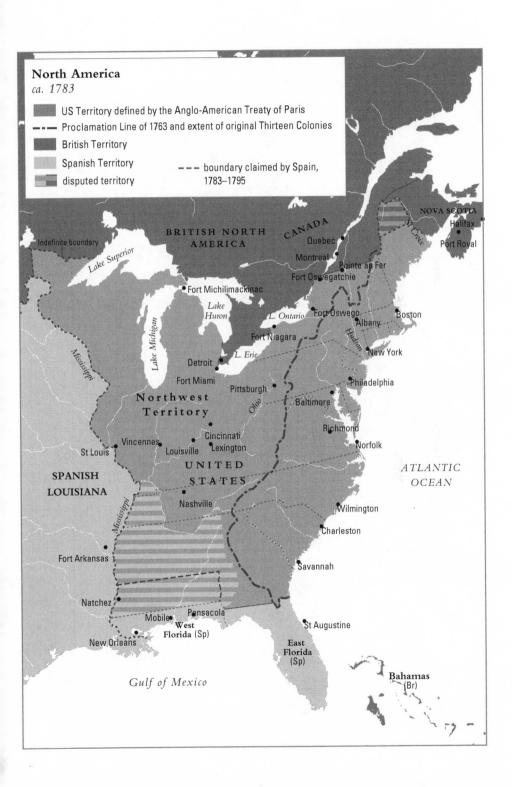

North America
ca. 1783

- US Territory defined by the Anglo-American Treaty of Paris
- –··– Proclamation Line of 1763 and extent of original Thirteen Colonies
- British Territory
- Spanish Territory
- disputed territory
- – – – boundary claimed by Spain, 1783–1795

Indefinite boundary

BRITISH NORTH AMERICA

CANADA

NOVA SCOTIA

Halifax

Port Royal

Lake Superior

Quebec

Montreal

Pointe au Fer

Fort Oswegatchie

St Croix

Fort Michilimackinac

Lake Huron

Lake Michigan

L. Ontario

Fort Oswego

Boston

Albany

Mississippi

Fort Niagara

L. Erie

New York

Hudson

Detroit

Fort Miami

Pittsburgh

Philadelphia

Northwest Territory

Ohio

Baltimore

Cincinnati

Richmond

Vincennes

Louisville

Lexington

Norfolk

St Louis

UNITED STATES

SPANISH LOUISIANA

ATLANTIC OCEAN

Mississippi

Nashville

Wilmington

Charleston

Fort Arkansas

Savannah

Natchez

Mobile

Pensacola

West Florida (Sp)

St Augustine

New Orleans

East Florida (Sp)

Bahamas (Br)

Gulf of Mexico

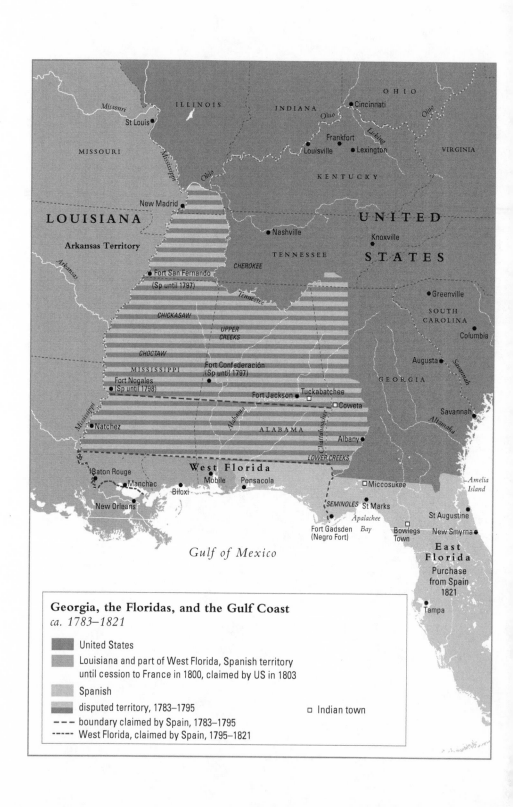

Georgia, the Floridas, and the Gulf Coast
ca. 1783–1821

■	United States
■	Louisiana and part of West Florida, Spanish territory until cession to France in 1800, claimed by US in 1803
■	Spanish
▨	disputed territory, 1783–1795
– – –	boundary claimed by Spain, 1783–1795
-----	West Florida, claimed by Spain, 1795–1821
□	Indian town

North America and West Indies
ca. 1821

US Territories

Adams-Onís (Transcontinental) Treaty line, 1821

British Territories

boundary Louisiana Purchase 1803

disputed and jointly occupied Anglo-American territory

Porcupine

Alaska
(Russia)

Indefinite boundary 1825

North-Western
Territory

*Hudson
Bay*

British North America

Rupert's Land

Newfoundland

Prince
Edward

New
Brunswick

Halifax
Nova Scotia

Oregon

Missouri

Great Lakes

Upper Canada

Quebec
Montreal

Maine

**Unorganized
Territory**

Michigan Territory

Platte

Boston

Detroit

New York
Philadelphia

Richmond

**VICEROYALTY
OF NEW SPAIN**
(to 1820)

Colorado

Arkansas

Canadian

Missouri

UNITED STATES

Mississippi

Arkansas Territory

Red

LA

Mobile

New Orleans

Charleston

Savannah

*ATLANTIC
OCEAN*

St Augustine

Florida

MEXICO
(Independent 1821)

Rio Grande

Gulf of Mexico

Bahamas
(Br)

Puerto Rico
(Sp)

Cuba (Sp)

DOMINICAN
REPUBLIC

HAITI

*PACIFIC
OCEAN*

Jamaica (Br)

Belize (Br)

**UNITED PROVINCES OF
CENTRAL AMERICA**
(1823)

REP. OF
GRAN COLOMBIA
(1819)

Among the Powers of the Earth

Introduction

A Nation among Nations

D URING THE SUMMER OF 1776, as Congress took the final, momentous steps toward declaring independence, John Adams began work on a "plan of treaties" to guide the new union in its relations with other governments. From the standpoint of the European rulers to whom it was addressed, much of what Adams wrote would have sounded familiar. Working with Benjamin Franklin, soon to embark for the court of Louis XVI, Adams and the members of his committee directed Congress to offer foreign nations, starting with France, a commercial treaty while avoiding a military alliance. Toward that end, the Model Treaty, as the plan came to be known, stipulated that any agreement be fully reciprocal, with trade on the freest possible terms in peacetime and a liberal definition of the goods that American ships could carry in times of war. In offering these terms, Adams laid down what, in many ways, are still the guiding principles of American foreign policy.[1] In one place, though, the treaty contained a provision that sounds jarring. Mindful that France and, in all likelihood, Spain would view an American overture as a chance to recoup losses suffered during their wars with Britain, Adams demanded that Europe's governments recognize the United States as the rightful successor to all of Britain's North American empire. This included Canada, which Continental soldiers had invaded the previous fall, as well as

Nova Scotia, Newfoundland, East and West Florida, and Bermuda. In the Union's opening bid for foreign recognition, Adams imagined a nation that has never existed—and presumably never will.[2]

This is a book about that nation, or, to be more precise, it is about the wider struggle to found that nation. For people in its vicinity, the American Revolution heralded two distinct but related changes. One involved the Union's quest to be accepted as a free and independent nation in Europe; the other, the right of its citizens to pacify and control what, from a European standpoint, was still a colonial periphery.[3] Today, no matter where within the United States they happen to live, Americans mark July 4, 1776, as the moment their history as an independent nation began. What we sometimes forget—though people at the time knew it—is that the United States could not become the nation that Americans imagined without the consent of other nations and people. In matters of religion and popular culture, in the goods that ordinary men and women bought and sold, in the rights that they claimed for themselves, and in their relations with others, including Indians, African Americans, and other Europeans, the revolution enabled the Union's citizens to begin making their own history, but the history that they made was often the history that others were willing to let them make. And that was only in places that acknowledged the authority of Congress. In much of North America, to say nothing of the Caribbean or the lands of Central and South America, Europe's colonial empires were as firmly ensconced as ever, and there were quite a few people, including quite a few on land claimed by the United States, who wished to keep things that way.[4] Because Americans were founding a nation among nations, they were doing so, at least in part, on someone else's terms.[5]

This paradox affected virtually every aspect of the United States' early history, starting with the search for recognition in Europe. As Adams and the other delegates in Philadelphia knew, the Declaration of Independence was only a beginning. For the former colonies to take their place among the powers of the earth, they needed European treaties that would turn the rights that Congress had unilaterally proclaimed into rights that other nations would respect.[6] No less important, if Americans were to have peace—including, ultimately, with the British subjects of George III—they had to show that they could fulfill the duties that European treaties entailed. To do this, they needed a government that could fend off threats from European armies and navies, they had to show that they were willing to enforce European agreements in their legislatures and courts of law, and they needed to comport themselves, in the words of Adams's friend, and sometime pastor, Samuel Cooper, before "the great theater of nations with advantage and glory."[7] Even the movement to withdraw from the African slave trade, which Congress sanctioned in 1776, highlighted the need for a treaty-worthy government with the stature to cooperate with Europe's other empires. Because the only way to achieve these goals was to conform to European norms and expectations, the revolution represented, on a rather elemental level, an attempt to remake the former colonies in Europe's image. Adams, for one, was well aware of this connection. In a letter to Harvard's John Winthrop, written as Congress was about to sever the last remaining ties to Britain, he predicted that one effect would be to force Americans to "compleat their governments." Once they did, he hoped that foreign courts would accept them as equals.[8]

In writing these words, Adams was thinking of Europe. In those areas of North America that were not part of the United States, Americans also sought European recognition. As was clear from the Model Treaty, however, the recognition that they sought was for peace based not on treaties between equals but on dominion over others. In both Europe and America, it was a commonplace that North America was an unusually wild and "savage land," as Samuel Cooper observed in 1780, an "immense part" of which "lies as nature hath left it."[9] For anyone who knew anything about how things actually worked, this conceit was a fiction. To look no farther than the continent's first inhabitants, Americans acknowledged their neighborhood's law-bound character through the treaties that they negotiated to acquire land from the Indians and the customs that they observed when they interacted with Native Americans in other areas, notably war and commerce.[10] Although the colonies that became the United States dwarfed the population of Britain's remaining possessions, much of what Cooper described as a lawless state of nature was likewise home to settlers from the British Isles and Europe, and it had a significant and growing population of Africans and African Americans. Because they were a maritime people, Americans also shared the coastal waters where they trawled for fish, the lanes through which they transported goods and slaves, and the seas where they preyed on foreign shipping. Regardless of their circumstances, the people whom Americans encountered in these places all had their own laws and customs, and they were able to compel Americans to accept the validity of those legalities.[11] Without always liking it, Americans recognized and acknowledged this reality too.

What Americans did not accept—though they often had no choice during the period covered by this book—was that anyone but Congress had a right to dominion over the lands and waters in the Union's vicinity. In making this claim, Americans recognized that Britain and Europe's other colonial powers already claimed jurisdiction over much of the extra-European world, including the coastal waters of North America and those parts of the continent that were in the possession of Indian nations. When it clashed with their own rights, Americans did not hesitate to dispute the presumption in this way of thinking. Often, though, Americans accepted the dominion of Europe's rulers, claiming it for themselves in order to extinguish the rights of others, whether the claimants were other European settlers or Indians and African Americans. This is what Adams was doing when he asserted the Union's right to all of British North America.[12] That he did so reminds us that the American Revolution was never just a struggle for the right of Americans to govern themselves. From the beginning, it was also a struggle for dominion over others. For that reason, the founding of the United States was a profoundly disruptive event, both for the Union's citizens and for people who were either unable to claim that status or who, in the case of the Loyalists, chose not to do so. As is clear from the terms with which Congress approached foreign governments in 1776, Americans believed that the only way to secure liberty for themselves was by making peace with others. But to a greater degree than we often realize, the peace that they sought reproduced key features of the European empires that they otherwise hoped to replace.

Because Americans only partly controlled their own destiny, their bid to join the powers of the earth was a protracted, drawn-out process. Focusing on the seven decades between the start of the French and Indian War in the mid-1750s and the articulation of what came to be known as the Monroe Doctrine, the following pages tell the story of this process as

Americans understood and experienced it. Throughout, a central concern is the law of nations, as the system of treaties and customs that Europeans used to wage war and make peace with other people was known. As most legal historians would agree, the law of nations had little in common with the municipal law that governments observed in relations with their own people. Under the common law of England, which formed the basis for the municipal law in all thirteen colonies that became the United States, courts and legislatures had the final say as to what was or was not legal. Although this authority was hardly absolute, writers often described the common law as a coherent body whose meaning could be clearly elucidated and whose rules were binding on all who came within its jurisdiction. The law of nations, on the other hand, was neither coherent nor binding. In *Commentaries on the Laws of England,* destined to be as influential in the United States as it was in Britain, William Blackstone wrote that because no nation could prescribe law to another, treaties rarely admitted of a single, universally agreed meaning, and the customs that governed war and commerce were equally protean. Faced with this paradox, Blackstone resorted to platitudes, defining the law of nations as "those principles of natural justice, in which . . . the learned of every nation agree."[13] He could just as easily have written that the law was whatever Europe's rulers said it was. Not surprisingly, the moments when Europeans failed to agree on what the law of nations meant were at least as common as the moments when they concurred.

If this was true in Europe, it was doubly so in America. In most of the world, Europe's rulers lacked the ability to force other people, including, often, their own subjects and allies, to accept the terms of their agreements with other rulers. To accommodate this reality, European treaties usually acknowledged a distinction between Europe and the world beyond. Sometimes they contained provisions that were theoretically binding both "within and without Europe" but that went into effect according to geographically specific timetables, with the subjects and allies of signatory nations who were in zones distant from Europe having more time to comply. On other occasions, treaty makers in Europe limited their efforts to one part of the world, or they agreed to settle their disputes with other Europeans with greater precision in some places, which were usually either in Europe or in close proximity to it, than in others.

In the century and a half after Columbus's voyages, the preferred device was to demarcate global "lines of amity" beyond which Europeans were free to disregard the terms of peace treaties that they had pledged to uphold in Europe. During the later seventeenth century, the main colonial powers gradually adopted a less chaotic system, whereby they made peace treaties that applied everywhere but left unresolved questions in particular regions for further discussion. Either way, peace in Europe was frequently the occasion for war elsewhere. In North America, this was how matters stood between Britain and France when the French and Indian War erupted in 1754, followed, two years later, by the Seven Years' War in Europe and the rest of the world. For Americans who remembered that event, the notion that Europe's colonial powers had the capacity to make peace in their neighborhood was a fantasy.[14]

Ironically, this was a point on which Britons and Americans agreed. As the book's opening chapters show, the British had a long history of attempting to pacify what would become the United States' neighborhood when Congress declared independence.[15] For most of the eighteenth century, Britain confined its peacemaking efforts to the seas and the suppression of smuggling and piracy. In the lead-up to the Seven Years' War, however, North America increasingly demanded equal attention. During the 1760s and 1770s, one lesson that people in both Britain and America took from the mid-century wars for empire was that the continent's interior had become too fully integrated with the rest of the European Atlantic for Britain to continue to make war on rivals there while remaining at peace with them in Europe. Although it has never received the scholarly attention that it deserves, the revolution's origins lay in a series of British attempts to make Americans more accountable to the Crown's treaties in Europe, starting with London's effort to regulate the wartime activities of colonial merchants and privateers in the West Indies, followed by what amounted to a massive initiative to bring peace to the eastern third of North America.[16] As also happened in Indian country, Americans rejected the specific terms of this peace, especially the ten thousand regulars that Britain stationed in the trans-Appalachian West and the colonial taxes that Parliament imposed to cover the costs. For the most part, though, they accepted the ends that Britain's reforms were meant to serve, and they believed that they needed to replicate the order that Britain was attempting to produce if they were to have peaceful relations in Europe. Although such ideas held little appeal for Indians, Loyalists or, often, African Americans, one way to read the claims in the Model Treaty is as an attempt to find what, to Americans, appeared to be a less threatening route to the peace that Britons and Americans both claimed to want.

Among other things, this convergence reminds us that the American Revolution was not just the first of the modern era's great liberationist events—the defining event, as many Americans still see it, when the people of the New World began to throw off the shackles of the Old—but also a crucial moment in the globalization of what was, at base, the public law of Europe's colonial powers. In claiming the rights of Europe's rulers for themselves, Americans sought wherever possible to avoid the main engines of Old World corruption: standing armies and navies, established churches, over-mighty executives, titled aristocracies, and other bastions of hereditary privilege. In an effort to play down the law's Eurocentrism, Americans also argued that the post-1776 law of nations was no longer the public law of Europe only but the public law of Europe *and* America, as Henry Wheaton, the United States' minister to Prussia and the country's leading nineteenth-century expert on the law of nations, wrote in 1845.[17] Still, Americans could go only so far in opting out of the obligations that being a treaty-worthy nation in Europe imposed. In the federal charters that they adopted for the Union, first in the Articles of Confederation and then in the Constitution of 1787, in their involvement with the growing antislavery movement in Britain and France, and in their relations with other nations and people, the Republic's citizens found themselves engaging with European laws and customs in ways that were at least as extensive as had been the case before 1776. Nowhere was the irony more apparent than in the fiscal burdens that accompanied independence. Although the American Revolution started as a colonial tax revolt, the costs of government for citizens of the United States far exceeded what Americans had borne as subjects of the British Empire, and in some states they approached five times what George III required of people in the Crown's remaining possessions.[18] Independence, it turned out, was not cheap.

Given the book's emphasis on legal geography, each of the following chapters deals with a different part of the Union's neighborhood. Perhaps

because it was so close to New England and an area that attracted so
many hyper-literate, memoir-writing Yankees, the part that has received
the most attention from historians is the northern region that stretched
from the Great Lakes, through the farmland of the Ohio and Saint Lawrence valleys to Maine and the Canadian Maritimes. Controlling this
area was one of Adams's goals in the Model Treaty, and it would remain
an American priority as late as the War of 1812.[19] However, because interactions here occurred across what, by the mid-1790s, was becoming a
clearly defined international border, this area was also unusual. By focusing on it to the exclusion of the Union's other borders, historians risk
overlooking two crucial facts. First, unlike the borderlands to the north,
where Britain retained the ability to defend and develop its colonial possessions, most of the territory that the Union acquired after 1783 was
under the dominion of Spain, where boundaries were much more porous
and fluid. Although the Louisiana Purchase (1803) was the most spectacular indication of this fluidity, with Napoleon doubling the size of the
United States with territory that he had recently seized from Spain, the
protean nature of the Union's borders was already evident in the Model
Treaty. On the Gulf Coast, the Union's rivals included Spain's decaying
but still potent empire, the Scottish-Bahamian merchant house of Panton,
Leslie, the short-lived Creek polity known as the State of Muskogee, the
even more transient Republic of West Florida—America's first "lone star"
state—and the Negro Fort at Prospect Bluff, so-called because of the escaped slaves who were mustered there when American gunboats destroyed
it in 1816. In the effort to turn the revolution's unfinished peace into a
lasting settlement, no part of North America was more important.[20]

If we hew too closely to the continent's interior boundaries, it can also
be easy to forget that Americans in 1776 were as preoccupied with the
sea as they were the land. As was clear from the Model Treaty's claims
on Newfoundland, Bermuda, and East Florida, none of which had much
value as agricultural settlements and which were important chiefly for
their ports and fisheries, the Union's neighbors to the east and south
were largely maritime, and they included places as distant as the sugar
islands of the Caribbean, West Africa's slave coasts, and the southern
cone of Spanish America.[21] Here the dominion that Americans sought
was not the exclusive dominion characteristic of territorial sovereignty

but a condominium based on mutually beneficial trade. Because the maritime nations of Europe were at war for most of the period covered by this book, the search for peace proved every bit as elusive on the high seas as it was on land. Not only did Britain claim wartime rights vis-à-vis other nations that, though temporary, threatened to bring American ships and sailors back under the Crown's maritime dominion, but the privateers and smugglers who swarmed the Union's waters also forced Americans to redouble their efforts to police their own coasts and ports.[22] As the book shows, these efforts included taking the first halting steps during the 1790s to end American involvement in the African slave trade, Congress's outright prohibition of slave imports in 1807, and the military operations that shut down the illegal slave trade on East Florida's Amelia Island and the Gulf Coast during the early 1820s. Although American antislavery drew strength from multiple sources, one of the most important was the widespread perception, which many slaveholders shared, that the traffic in human beings was piracy of a sort that no treaty-worthy nation should tolerate.

The Union's maritime borders are likewise crucial for understanding how the revolution worked to entrench slavery in the states where owning slaves remained legal. Because the slave trade depended, in part, on the conceit that captives brought to America had been legally enslaved according to the rules of war in Africa, those customs remained part of slavery's legality wherever slaves went.[23] As long as the trade continued, it was hard for planters in Virginia and the Carolinas to argue that slavery was consistent with the civilized laws of Western Europe, let alone the international peace that Congress proclaimed as its ultimate goal. Although hardly the outcome that slavery's opponents sought, ending imports into the United States had the effect of disassociating the right to own slaves in America from the warfare that the slave trade perpetuated in Africa. For this reason, many slaveholders, including four of the first five presidents of the United States, supported the effort to abolish the slave trade. In so doing, they helped turn human chattel from an anomalous, legally suspect form of property, one that jurists in Europe and America tolerated without fully endorsing, into what John C. Calhoun famously called the South's "peculiar institution," which was as legitimate as it was benevolent.[24] In the waters off their coasts no less than in the North

American interior, what Americans did beyond their borders had a major bearing on what they did at home.

Because of the problematic place that it occupies in histories of the revolution, a word is also in order about the word "nation." To look no further than the Declaration of Independence, Americans in 1776 could and did refer to themselves as a single people, and they were sufficiently well-versed in the classics to know that this usage was an English synonym for the Latinate "nation." In keeping with this, I have already referred at several places to the American Revolution as the founding of a nation, and I do so occasionally in the pages that follow.[25] Clearly, though, if by nation we mean a single, unitary, or monolithic nation-state, the United States did not qualify as one at the time of the revolution, nor would it qualify at any point before the Civil War (if then). This was because the Union within which the American nation found its expression was a constitutionally plural entity, a federal system of sovereign states where, in the words of the Tenth Amendment to the U.S. Constitution, all rights not explicitly granted to the central government were reserved to the states. Under the Articles of Confederation, which served as the original federal charter, the United States was not so much a nation as a perpetual league or treaty between independent states—each with its own "people"—and Americans sometimes described the Constitution that replaced it in 1789 as having elements of both a treaty and a national government. Before the American Civil War shattered this system in 1861, the law that adjudicated relations among its members was a branch of the law of nations, not the municipal laws and customs in Anglo-American common law, and it was widely recognized that one or more states might attempt to leave the Union and become free and independent states of their own, especially if a neighboring government, presumably Britain, France, or Spain, acknowledged their right to do so.[26] Nothing in the following pages should be read as taking issue with these insights.

This book does insist, however, that the nation that Americans created was an entangled nation.[27] Despite George Washington's famous warning against "entangling alliances" in his Farewell Address, the search for European treaties that the Model Treaty exemplified continued to bind Americans to other nations and people. In Europe, this was true whether the connections involved military alliances of the sort that both Washington and Adams dreaded—and that France insisted on as the price for recognition in 1778—or international confirmation of the commercial and territorial rights that the Model Treaty authorized Congress's emissaries to seek.[28] One of the book's central arguments is that the drive to be accepted as a treaty-worthy nation in Europe played a role in the making of the American republic at least as important as the liberal and republican ideologies that have framed scholarship on the American Revolution since the Second World War. Far more than liberalism or republicanism, the revolutionaries' emphasis on peace through treaty-worthiness explains why Americans ultimately opted for a national union that could represent the "one people" in the Declaration of Independence over a looser association among "the people of the different states," which is how the Union was envisioned under the Articles of Confederation.[29] As Americans knew from their own history as colonial subjects, and as we shall see in the chapters that follow on slavery and colonial and Indian warfare, the laws and customs that Americans wanted independence to secure were those that Europe's rulers generally reserved for nations that seemed comparable to their own. In order to be at peace with other European nations, in their own neighborhood no less than in the world beyond, Americans needed to have a nation that Europeans would recognize and accept.

Nor was the American republic's entangled history limited to Europe. Throughout the period covered by this book, connections of various sorts linked Americans to the slave factories of West Africa, the towns and villages of Indian country, the islands of the Caribbean, and the lands and waters of Spanish America. Sometimes Americans interacted with their neighbors on terms of equality; on other occasions, they did so in subordinate or inferior roles. Either way, the revolution proved to be a profoundly disruptive event, as the intrusion and growing authority of European notions of peace and treaty-worthiness created new hierarchies of value, new forms of dependency, and, often, new languages of exclusion. The victims of this loss of status were overwhelmingly people of color, especially the Indians whose colonial autonomy was gradually transformed into new categories of dependent nationhood and the African Americans whose servitude the revolution perpetuated. But at crucial moments, Indians and African Americans also encroached on and limited the ability of Americans to make their own history. And at times, the quest for peace exacted a cost among white settlers, notably the French Acadians whose removal from Nova Scotia in 1755 opens the book, and the tens of thousands of deracinated men, women, and children who made up the post-1783 Loyalist diaspora to Nova Scotia, Canada, and the Bahamas. Significantly, in the Articles of Confederation, Congress stipulated that the people of every state in the Union would be entitled to the benefits of citizenship in every other state—everyone, that is, except "paupers, vagabonds, and fugitives from justice."[30] In a sense, by creating a treaty-worthy nation for themselves, Americans helped create the condition of statelessness for others. Although we associate the problem of statelessness more with our own time than with the founders', it was in important respects one of the American Revolution's more unsavory legacies.[31]

Finally, let me be clear about the term "treaty-worthiness" and what I mean by the struggle to become a treaty-worthy nation. As the wording suggests, the book's focus is less on actual treaties that Americans made with other nations—though I do mention the provisions of specific agreements when they are relevant—and more on the broader process by which Americans sought to make themselves appear worthy of peaceful relations with other nations. Because the quest for treaty-worthiness affected every member of society, both in terms of the legal rights that belonging to a treaty-worthy nation conferred and the duties that it imposed, I have tried wherever possible to approach what we sometimes think of as a top-down subject from a bottom-up perspective, combining the experiences of people like John Adams with those of men and women who were neither rich nor powerful but who also had a stake in the outcome. By its very nature, though, treaty-worthiness was (and still is) a hierarchical construct, which held that some nations and people were more equal than others. This was amply clear from the tripartite division with which Americans imagined the Republic's international relations, starting with "sister nations" in Europe, as Thomas Jefferson wrote in his first address to Congress in 1801, followed by North Africa's Barbary States, and ending with what Jefferson called "our Indian neighbors."[32] In limning the relationships between these groups, Americans sometimes fell back on familiar, if old-fashioned, distinctions between Christians and non-Christians; on other occasions, they drew on emerging notions of racial difference; and they frequently used the ideas of civil society and civility that were currently popular in Europe.[33] However they defined their terms, it was clear both to Americans and, usually, to their neighbors that not all people were equally treaty-worthy and that international legitimacy was a thing of tremendous value, which could be lost as well as gained.

Because of this fluidity, much of what Congress hoped to achieve in the Model Treaty remained beyond the United States' grasp. During the late 1790s, differences over the Franco-American military alliance that Adams had hoped to avoid embroiled the French Republic and the United States in an undeclared naval war, while the North American space over which Congress claimed dominion in 1776 eventually became home to not one but two federal nations, each with a valid claim to be the legal successor to the British Empire. Although these facts are well-known, it is my hope that by looking at the nation's founding from what we might call the "outside in" perspective of the Union's relations with its neighbors, this book will convey a new and deeper understanding of what the revolution meant. As is clear from the fate of the North American union that Adams envisioned in 1776, the nation that Americans succeeded in founding was, from its very beginning, a protean and contingent polity. There was nothing preordained about the form that it would acquire by the time of Adams's death on July 4, 1826, nor could anybody have predicted the form that it holds today, let alone the form that it may assume in years to come. As historians have noted many times before, this was so partly because Americans themselves had different visions of what they wanted their nation to be. Even when they agreed among themselves, however, Americans could go only so far in deciding such matters on their own. In keeping with the ethnogenic myths that still shape the way historians usually write American history, we like to see the revolution as the moment when the American people, however the term is defined, began to make their own history. It would be more accurate to say that the revolution enabled Americans to make the history that other people were prepared to let them make.

CHAPTER 1

On the Margins of Europe

O N THE MORNING OF September 11, 1755, nearly three hundred British soldiers, most of them New England provincials under the command of Colonel John Winslow of Massachusetts, began loading groups of boys onto five ships anchored in Minas Basin, just south of the isthmus where Nova Scotia joins the North American mainland. The boys, some as young as ten, were part of a larger body of "French neutrals," or Acadians, being held in the village's Catholic churchyard. They and their families stood accused of abetting Britain's enemies in its undeclared war with France.[1]

Winslow did not relish the terms of his commission. Veteran of the Cartagena and Cape Breton expeditions of the 1740s and New England's most celebrated soldier, he told the Acadians that he found his task as "disagreeable . . . as I know it must be grievous to you who are of the same species."[2] If so, Winslow's feelings made no difference to the individuals in his custody. At first the boys refused to "go without their Fathers." But upon seeing the soldiers advance with fixed bayonets, they reluctantly "went off praying, singing and crying, being met by the women and children all the way." In all, over two thousand people left Minas, part of an estimated out-migration of seven thousand from western Nova Scotia and the Bay of Fundy. After the last transport sailed, Winslow's men torched both the village and the surrounding countryside.[3]

The Acadian removal, which aimed at nothing less than the displacement of an entire population and way of life, has long occupied a special place in the catalog of British imperial atrocities, most famously in the story of the star-crossed lovers in Henry Wadsworth Longfellow's poem *Evangeline*. According to an account in the French *Mercure de La Haye*, Winslow's soldiers "burned and destroyed [the Acadians'] houses, barns, farms and villages; their farm animals [were] driven into the woods where anyone who likes can take possession of them." "Thus," the correspondent wrote, "one of the most beautiful countries in the world is now ravaged and empty."[4] While proclaiming the removal's justness, British and American writers also noted the suffering that it caused. In Massachusetts, which received the largest number of refugees, Thomas Hutchinson was so moved by "the fatal Necessity of their Distress" that he took a woman, her four sons, and a grandson into his house.[5] Because they were shipped to places as distant as Europe and the West Indies— Britain's colonies on the North American seaboard all received exiles, as did England, France, and, eventually, Louisiana—it is hard to say how many died. If we include families who escaped by fleeing to the woods of Nova Scotia and the adjacent islands in the Gulf of Saint Lawrence, the best guess is that disease, starvation, and exposure together claimed around ten thousand lives.[6]

The operation that caused this tragedy was obviously an act of war, a nasty prologue to the conflagration that engulfed Europe and the rest of the world in 1756. In fighting that would spread as far as India and the Philippines, Britain vanquished the arms of both France and, ultimately, Spain, making its overseas empire, by some reckonings, the most extensive since the fall of Rome. Because of the unprecedented commitment of British blood and treasure, the Seven Years' War, or the French and Indian War, as the North American theater of the war is sometimes called, had particularly far-reaching implications for London's involvement in colonial governance and administration. In America the effects included expanding the navy's presence in the Caribbean, sending the army to serve in large numbers in North America for the first time in British history, and setting the stage for Parliament's ill-fated attempts at imperial reform during the 1760s and 1770s. Surveying the war in America in 1759, the English agronomist Arthur Young wrote that Britain appeared to be "turning over quite a new leaf in that part of the world," resolving its differences with Europe's other colonial powers "with the greatest nicety" and taking a more active role in the affairs of its own subjects.[7] Although these efforts were just starting to bear fruit, the determination to strengthen Britain's imperial power was already manifest in the ruthlessness with which Winslow's soldiers carried out their orders.

If it foreshadowed a more assertive British presence, however, the Acadian expulsion was also the product of a very different history. Although reminiscent of the duke of Cumberland's pacification of the Scottish Highlands in 1746, the fighting in Nova Scotia occurred in a region that was, at best, imperfectly integrated into the system of treaties that Europe's colonial powers used in relations with each other in Europe.[8] Not only were the Acadians effectively a people without a nation,[9] full subjects of neither Britain nor France, but they inhabited a borderland that lacked clear, internationally recognized boundaries. Significantly, when the last transport set sail in December 1755, Britain and France were still legally at peace. As such, the removal underscored the limits of European law and diplomacy throughout eastern North America and the extent to which places like Nova Scotia were on Europe's margins. In the retrospective words of Edmund Burke's *Annual Register,* the Seven Years' War—the first truly global war in European history—had its origins in a series of local disputes that had long seemed too unimportant "to call for a very laborious discussion" in Europe.[10] In a sense, Winslow's New Englanders and the boys of Minas were participants in two different wars: one driven by the increasingly global ambitions of Britain and France, the other the irregular, low-grade conflicts that had historically characterized relations between the rivals' subjects and allies in America. Each would play a crucial role in shaping the world that Americans inherited in 1776.

(1)

In both Europe and America, people often claimed that a distinguishing feature of European war and diplomacy was a propensity to temper the quest for power with the rule of law. According to the Protestant Swiss jurist Emer de Vattel, whose *Law of Nations* first appeared in French in 1758 and was probably the best-known treatise on the subject in America at the time of the revolution, the willingness of Europe's rulers to base their relations with each other on mutually agreed treaties and customs made it possible to think of Europe as a sort of "republic": a law-bound community of nations, as Vattel conceived it, whose members were united by "ties of common interest" and a shared commitment to "order and liberty."[11] Despite the insular, xenophobic strands of Georgian patriotism, even Britons sometimes spoke of Europe in such terms, describing it as a zone of law and civility—"the most civilized Quarter of the Globe," as an English pamphleteer wrote during the 1740s.[12] For many people, Europe's respect for the international rule of law was an important part of what it meant to live in a modern, enlightened age. "Europe hath for above a century past been greatly enriched by commerce and polished by arts," observed East Apthorp, the American-born vicar of Croydon, of what he took to be the prevailing trend in 1776. "Whoever compares the present age with the last, will discern an almost total change to have taken place in the manners, the customs, and the government of Christendom."[13]

Of course the Europe to which Apthorp referred was a republic in only the loosest, most general sense of the word. Because neither the Roman Catholic Church nor Europe's secular rulers had the capacity to force other nations to accept any one particular version of the law, Europeans interacted in an arena that lacked a common sovereign or an overarching legal authority. What Europe did have was a system of treaties, two of which—the treaties of Westphalia, which ended the Thirty Years' War in 1648, and Utrecht, which brought the European wars against France's Louis XIV to a close in 1713—had proved so durable that they had become a kind of public law. In Britain and Ireland this treaty-based law was widely credited with shielding the kingdoms' Protestants from the universal claims of the Catholic Church, as well as strengthening the constitutional rights that Parliament secured when it offered the English Crown to William and Mary in 1689 and the union with Scotland in 1707. Because the treaties of Westphalia and Utrecht also protected the liberties of Britain's neighbors, Catholic as well as Protestant, the effect was to give friends and enemies alike a reason to recognize each other's rights and to comport themselves in ways that were consistent with their agreements with other nations. This meant that wars between Europe's rulers, no matter how frequent they were or how long the fighting lasted, tended to be finite and limited, which combatants waged not for total victory or universal dominion but for goals that they believed their rivals would recognize in a peace treaty at the war's end.[14] Also, because the end of war was peace, governments at war had an interest in maintaining the rule of law. Writing in 1752, David Hume claimed that Europe's foreign wars had lost much "of their cruelty" as a result of these checks and balances, and belligerents had learned once their wars were over to "divest themselves of the brute and resume the man."[15] War, it seemed, had become the exception and peace the norm.

Then, as now, critics were quick to note that this image did not begin to capture the full reality of European warfare or the limited protections that European treaties often afforded people caught in its path. Because the law of nations only applied to things that treaty-worthy sovereigns did in the course of their interactions with each other, the acts of honor and humanity that rulers performed in its name were usually reserved for the regular forces of contending governments, not rebels, pirates, or, when they violated international agreements, civilians. To look no further than the duke of Cumberland's pacification of the Scottish Highlands in 1746, British forces committed horrific acts of violence without violating what they took to be the customary rules of war, let alone the conviction of apologists that their behavior was justified.[16] During the winter of 1757 and 1758, the German principality of Hanover, which George II ruled as a prince-elector of the Holy Roman Empire, experienced the full brunt of such tactics after the king repudiated a convention promising to withdraw the electorate from Britain's war with France. Claiming that the laws of war "authorized" him to retaliate against the Hanoverians for George II's failure to honor the convention, the duc de Richelieu, commander of the French army, allowed the soldiers under his command to loot and burn those areas that they occupied. Although Richelieu acknowledged the extraordinary nature of what he was doing and claimed that it was contrary to "the natural humanity of the French nation," as well as his own "personal character," he warned—accurately, as it turned out—that the destruction would not be limited to the king's personal estates but would include every town and village, "without sparing the smallest cabin."[17] In neighboring Hesse-Cassel, which Richelieu's soldiers also occupied but did not loot, the late 1750s produced the lowest birth and highest death rates of the eighteenth century, and farms and villages across Hanover were in ruins at the war's end.[18]

As the fate of Hanover and the Scottish Highlands suggests, Europe's treaty-based law was as much an instrument of war as it was of peace, and the need to uphold it formed an important part of the ethos of professional soldiers across Europe. In keeping with this, writers tended to differentiate the systematic violence of regular combatants—including, when the victims had broken an international agreement, against civilians—from violence that occurred without official sanction and to blame the worst excesses of war on mercenaries, privateers, and irregulars over whom European governments often had limited control. When allegations surfaced that the French had clubbed to death wounded English prisoners at the battle of Fontenoy in the Austrian Netherlands in 1745, a writer responded in the British press not by denying the charges but by blaming auxiliary units of Balkan *pandours* "and a few other Irregulars in *French* Pay," who allegedly killed their enemies before France's regulars "had Time to preserve them."[19] In his memoir of the Seven Years' War, the British army officer Sir Charles Hotham took a similar approach to French atrocities in Germany, praising the "humanity and benevolence" of officers who kept their troops in order and attributing the worst infractions to French partisans and to defeated and, often, disorganized and ill-disciplined regulars.[20] In the controversies that periodically swirled around the maintenance of a standing army in Britain, writers used similar terms to defend the king's own forces. "The Duty of a Soldier is honourable and honest," insisted the author of a British drill manual in 1756. "The Army despises those brave Indiscreets, who make their Valour Consist in doing Actions of Violence and Brutality. None are distinguished, none honored, none recompenced but the man of Worth, who regulates his Duty by *Religion, Humanity,* and *Justice.*"[21]

The result was a system that encouraged belligerents to think of war and the rule of law as mutually reinforcing categories. In the case of the time-honored right of occupying forces to "live off the land," eighteenth-century armies turned what had often been a license to plunder into a system of requisitioning supplies and contributions. In Germany and the Netherlands, military commissaries adopted the practice of negotiating treaties with local magistrates, whereby they agreed to refrain from forcible takings in exchange for payments that were not to exceed the district's peacetime revenue and officers undertook to discipline soldiers who violated such agreements by foraging on their own.[22] Often, the raising of contributions still carried the threat of violence. Upon entering Dutch territory in 1747, the colonel of France's Breton Volunteers threatened to visit several towns "with a Torch in my Hand" unless they supplied his troops with hay, oats, and straw, and it was well known that even well-regulated soldiers posed a heightened risk for crimes of all sorts, including theft, rape, and murder.[23] Yet because armies that rejected plunder in favor of treaties could raise larger supplies and devote fewer resources to maintaining order, they had an interest in recognizing distinctions between seizures that were necessary and those that were not, between public and private property, and between individuals who actively assisted the enemy and those who did not. In this spirit, France agreed to reimburse the neutral principality of Liége for expenses incurred during its invasion of the Netherlands in 1746, and it paid local villagers two and a half million florins, or two-fifths of the occupation's total cost, after the war was over.[24] No doubt with such agreements in mind the political economist Adam Smith told his students at Glasgow University: "When the Netherlands is the seat of war all the peasants grow rich."[25] Though speaking tongue in cheek, Smith captured what many saw as the regular and controlled character of war between treaty-worthy nations.

Although the main rationale of Europe's public law was to facilitate relations between nations, it also carried implications for how rulers interacted with their own subjects. One of the clearest signs involved the draconian codes that European governments used to discipline their armed forces.[26] In preparation for the unsuccessful British descent on the French port of L'Orient in 1746, General James St. Clair prescribed regulations that included dismissal for officers "seen drunk, whilst the Troops remain on the Territories of France"; death for officers and soldiers who plundered "without orders from the commander in chief"; and three hundred lashes for any enlisted man who left formation "to drink or . . .

ease himself" except in the company of a sergeant or corporal.[27] The soldiers were also subject to the articles of war used by the British army and navy, which Parliament broadened during the 1750s to include private ships of war and English and colonial militia. Although such rules often said as much about official intentions as they did about actual experience, discipline in the king's regular forces could be both swift and harsh. Speaking of a capital sentence handed down for plundering during the British expedition against Saint-Malo in 1758, one former soldier wrote that the officers on the court martial forced the three condemned men to throw "dice for their lives." "[T]he soldier whose chance was to die," the veteran recalled, "was . . . a man who had been near twenty years in the service, and was of extraordinary good character; but the commander was determined not to pardon the man on whom the lot should fall, as by his example others might be deterred from committing such irregularities for the future."[28] As with the municipal law that Europe's rulers used with their own people, the law of nations was, among other things, a brutally effective instrument of power.

During the middle decades of the eighteenth century, few places in Europe experienced this convergence between law and power more directly than the Scottish Highlands. Under the terms of the Anglo-Scottish union of 1707, the chieftains who controlled the Highlands remained legally autonomous, with one of the most important rights being the right to muster clansmen on their land for local wars and feuds. Following the last Jacobite rebellion in 1745, when Charles Stuart's Highland army reached Derby in the English Midlands, the British government made ending the clans' independence the cornerstone of a broader pacification. In the name of strengthening the Treaty of Union, Parliament enacted legislation that suppressed the clans' right to keep and bear arms; it outlawed the wearing of tartan, which was widely perceived as a military uniform; and it converted the Highlands' feudal tenures into commercial leaseholds.[29] During the Seven Years' War, the government countenanced a limited revival of the martial customs that these policies were meant to eradicate, with Highland lairds raising regiments among their tenants, dressed in the kilts and other regalia of the clans while subject to the same articles of war as the regular army. But the impact on Highland society was devastating. By the time Samuel

Johnson made his celebrated tour in the early 1770s, the region's vaunted independence was a distant memory. "There was perhaps never any change of national manners so quick, so great, and so general," wrote Johnson:

> We came hither too late to see what we expected—a people of peculiar appearance, and a system of antiquated life. The clans retain little now of their original character: their ferocity of temper is softened, their military ardour is extinguished, their dignity of independence is depressed, their contempt of government subdued, and their reverence for their chiefs abated. Of what they had before the late conquest of their country there remains only their language and their poverty.[30]

For all the talk about what Vattel called the "honour and humanity of the Europeans," governments across Europe embraced the treaties and customs that made up the law of nations for the simple reason that doing so served their own interests.[31] However, the idea of Europe as a law-bound republic resonated because of the elevated moral sentiments that the law of nations also evoked. In military and diplomatic encounters, which by definition occurred in the space between nations, moral sensibility alone often had to supply the compulsion that magistrates had the authority to enforce in disputes between members of the same nation. In a particularly vivid account taken from the capitulation of the British garrison on Minorca in 1782, the *Annual Register* made a point of noting the generosity of France's and Spain's soldiers as the ragged defenders left the citadel. Not only did the officers show their British counterparts every "kindness and tenderness," but, according to the anonymous writer, "the common soldiers of both armies, were so moved by the wretched condition of the garrison, that involuntary tears dropped from them as they passed."[32] Commanding officers tended to be especially important figures in such narratives. In the aftermath of Commodore George Anson's voyage round the world (1740–1744), during which his squadron plundered Spanish ships and possessions from the Straits of Magellan to the Philippines, British writers noted Anson's professionalism and attentiveness to European codes of war, as well as the diligence with which he insisted that the men under his command treat their enemies with honor and respect. According to a history by Richard Walter, who served as the expedition's chaplain, Anson was especially solicitous of Spanish prisoners on board his own ship, inviting "the principal persons among them" to dine at his table, forbidding members of the crew to "approach" two beautiful young women, and treating a Jesuit with such politeness that the priest began to reconsider "that article of his church, which asserts the impossibility of heretics being saved."[33] There was no reason, wrote a British pamphleteer in 1747, why nations should not wage war "with Politeness and good Manners, as well as . . . Humanity."[34]

By their very nature, the communities of trust upon which Europe's treaties and customs depended tended to be fragile and protean. Not surprisingly, women often served as particularly evocative harbingers of this fragility. In a play that the London bookseller Henry Dell based on the French siege of Minorca in 1756, Dell cast the travails of Maria, the beautiful daughter of a poor but ambitious British officer, at the drama's center, with two narrowly averted sexual assaults at the hands of French soldiers and a forced marriage to a British officer whom she does not love. As one of Maria's assailants warns her in the play's first act, "I know no law but the law of nature." Against this lawless backdrop, Dell portrayed the British and French commanders, General Blakeney and the duc de Richelieu, as exemplars of military professionalism and restraint, and he had each show Maria what Richelieu calls "respect and honour equal to [her] birth." In the end, their efforts are for naught, as Maria, despairing over the death of the man she loves, dies of wounds inflicted by the man she was supposed to marry. Yet even in death, Maria remained for Dell a symbol of the sentimental ties between law-bound enemies, as Richelieu rebukes her British father for his "love of gold." Given Richelieu's part in the devastation of George II's beloved German electorate in 1757, Dell was probably fortunate that the play was never staged. In the scene where the French commander accepts Blakeney's surrender, however, Dell had him treat his British counterpart with exquisite decorum and propriety. "*France* scorns to let him undistinguish'd pass," Richelieu tells his aides in a gloss on the honor that the rules of war prescribed for a worthy foe.[35]

When writers referred to the treaties and customs that made up the law of nations, they were thus using a term with two distinct though related meanings. On one hand, the law of nations was shorthand for the system that Europe's rulers used to manage relations with each other; on the other, it denoted a cosmopolitan world bound together by ties of commerce and sentiment. Either way, the law of nations was a European construct, "a system of artificial jurisprudence," in the words of William Paley, based on the treaties and diplomatic customs of Europe's leading powers.[36] As Anson's circumnavigation made clear, these treaties and customs were as binding in the waters of the Pacific as they were at Europe's center. In Britain this global scope was apparent in the administration of the Crown's overseas empire, including the treaty rights that Britain extended to possessions acquired from other Europeans, and the legal dominion that it exercised on the high seas.[37] For British settlers, the law's authority in the extra-European world derived added force from the doctrine that Britons who migrated overseas retained all the rights of natural-born subjects, and it was assumed that the European subjects of Europe's other colonial powers had comparable rights, especially in long-established colonies (like French Canada) where settlers had erected civil societies and lived under internationally recognized governments that replicated the conditions of civil society and government in Europe. As William Blackstone noted in *Commentaries on the Law of England* (1765–1769), the law of nations formed such a fundamental part of Britain's own constitution that it was "adopted in it's [*sic*] full extent" wherever English law was in force. Were the situation otherwise, wrote Blackstone, contracts between merchants would be worthless, treaties would lose their force, and Britain could expect neither friendship nor mercy from other governments; in a word, its people "must cease to be a part of the civilized world."[38]

One obviously would not want to read too much into such statements, not least because the treaties and customs to which Blackstone referred were so easily invoked to justify behavior that was anything but civilized. As General Wolfe informed the inhabitants of Canada before his forces invaded the province in 1759, the British government's aim was to check "the haughtiness of [the French] crown" in North America, not to wage war against "the industrious peasants, their wives and children, nor against the ministers of religion." As long as the Canadians took no part in the conflict, the British were willing to offer them "the sweets of peace amidst the horrors of war."[39] To his many admirers, Wolfe was a deeply compelling figure. Following his heroic death before the gates of Quebec, writers on both sides of the Atlantic dwelt in loving detail on his last letter to his mother, the tenderness that he showed his own soldiers, and his recitation below the heights of Abraham of Gray's "Elegy in a Country Churchyard," especially the prescient line: "The paths of glory lead but to the grave."[40] Yet when the city's defenses proved unexpectedly resilient during the summer of 1759—aided, Wolfe insisted, by provisions and other assistance from the surrounding countryside—he released himself from his earlier pledge and authorized what one of his officers called a campaign of "Skirmishing Cruelty and Devastation," destroying, by one reckoning, over "Fourteen Hundred fine Farm-Houses."[41] As a sergeant in Hopson's Grenadiers later wrote, British soldiers helped themselves to anything they could find: "Gowns, Shifts, Petticoats, Stockings, Coats and Waistcoats, Breeches, Shoes, and many other Articles too tedious to mention."[42] Wolfe also ordered a devastating bombardment of Quebec itself. In recounting the effects, a French witness described "large numbers of women with their children near the citadel, weeping, lamenting, and praying . . . gathering in groups to recite rosaries."[43] War, even when it was conducted according to European treaties and customs, was still war.

Nonetheless, Europe's treaty-based public law came to occupy a central place in the British imagination, if only as a description of how Britons everywhere wished to see their own history and the European history of which it was a part. It is no accident that Laurence Sterne's sentimental novel *Tristram Shandy*, the first two volumes of which appeared in 1759, had as a central theme the humanity and benevolence of soldiers like the narrator's Uncle Toby and his servant Corporal Trim. Nor is it surprising that John Winslow left such an affecting account of the part that he played in the Acadian removal. Even when belligerents observed the rules of war in the breach, writers insisted on their underlying vitality. In this spirit, the *Annual Register* noted with approval the stated determination of Britain's ally, Frederick II of Prussia, not to respond in kind to the barbarities committed by the Russian and Austrian armies in his province of Brandenburg during the summer of 1757. While the depredations of Prussia's enemies revealed their "true colours . . . to all of

Europe," Frederick's measured response showed that he recognized that illicit acts of war contributed "little to the end for which war is waged." Readers had every right to expect, the magazine concluded, that the Prussian king would show himself to be a worthy defender both of his own people's rights and of "the protestant religion and the liberties of Germany."[44] Although the writer was speaking of the plains of central Europe, such exhortations were no less applicable to the far-flung contests for empire in which Britain was engaged overseas.

(2)

If Europeans carried Europe's treaty law wherever they went, their interactions in the extra-European world were frequently with people who did not accept or, in some cases, even recognize that law. A major reason for this was that the peace treaties that functioned as a kind of public law in Europe often provided little guidance for Europeans elsewhere in matters such as which lands were under the dominion of which European ruler and where the boundaries between Europe's empires were. Until the peace of Westphalia in 1648, when the Spanish reluctantly agreed to allow the Dutch to participate in the exclusive dominion that Pope Alexander VI had given them after Columbus's first voyage, the areas not covered by European treaties included all of North America and the West Indies. Even after Europe's colonial powers began to recognize each other's rights in America, they continued to make peace in Europe while leaving their differences elsewhere to be settled at a later date. In the case of Acadia, the Anglo-French Treaty of Utrecht, which ceded the colony to Britain in 1713, left the boundaries of what was being ceded vague, saying only that France relinquished dominion over all lands and peoples within Acadia's "anciennes limites." On the eve of the Seven Years' War, Britain claimed that the cession included everything as far as the Saint Lawrence River, with a northern boundary that ran from a point opposite Quebec City to the eastern tip of the Gaspe Peninsula, while France confined the area under Britain's jurisdiction to the town of Port Royal and a narrow strip on Nova Scotia's Atlantic Seaboard. Between the two lines was the area where most Acadians lived.[45] Although Acadians did not reject the treaty's authority, their homeland's disputed boundaries made it hard to avoid the appearance that they did.

Compounding the shortcomings and failures of European peace treaties in America was a colonial typography that worked against the discipline that European armies used to compel soldiers to obey the rules of war in Europe. Although Wolfe's victory at Quebec was a notable exception, most American battles occurred on terrain that differed from Germany and the Netherlands, with battles that were often far removed from large towns and cities and lines of supply that were sometimes hundreds of miles long. Much of the fighting also occurred in dense brush and woodlands where soldiers were dispersed and hard to control and where European rules and discipline were of limited usefulness, and could be a positive hindrance. While the British adapted more quickly to such conditions than historians have sometimes realized, even Highland regiments, whose martial traditions supposedly made them well suited to fighting Indians, found that they had to allow their soldiers greater freedom on the battlefield or suffer the consequences. In 1755, following Major General Edward Braddock's crushing defeat in western Pennsylvania, critics blamed casualties that approached two-thirds of the expedition's thirteen hundred soldiers on Braddock's refusal to march in open formation and make better use of Indian scouts and colonial rangers. "The service here is not like that in Flanders or any part of Europe," reported Governor Edward Trelawny of Jamaica's long-running Maroon War in 1738.[46] With relatively minor changes, Trelawny could have said the same about any number of places on the North American mainland.

But the biggest difference between Europe and America was the difficulty that the British and their European rivals faced in their efforts to impose metropolitan notions of the law on their colonial subjects and allies. Although Britain's colonies of settlement all had legal systems based on English common law, the British Atlantic was a place of multiple legalities, some based on the legal systems of the colonies' European neighbors, others on African or Native American laws and customs.[47] There was nothing unusual about this diversity. Europe's legal pluralism was readily apparent from the Highlanders who rallied to Charles Stuart's Jacobite standard in 1745, the smugglers and privateers who made a mockery of Britain's maritime dominion in the English Channel, and the light troops and foreign auxiliaries that governments across Europe used to augment their regular forces. Not only did such groups generally operate according to their own legal norms, but their perceived barbarism and lack of refinement were also frequently depicted as being at odds with the moral sensibility upon which the law of nations depended.[48] As the British pacification of the Highlands showed, however, European governments had formidable military and fiscal resources at their disposal, enabling magistrates to administer uniform rules of justice in the nearest of Europe's hinterlands and clamping down on the ability of irregular and autonomous groups to challenge their monopoly on the use of violence. In the colonies, on the other hand, such resources tended to be much less developed or, in many places, entirely absent. This was true whether the groups in question were black and Native American auxiliaries, or provincial militia and privateers. Although the expanding colonial presence of the regular army and navy began to alter things in the Crown's favor during the late 1750s, it was striking just how successful Americans of all descriptions were in maintaining control over their own military and political affairs and how little power Britain had to make them change their ways.[49]

For observers versed in European war and diplomacy, no group exemplified these limits more fully than the Native American auxiliaries used by all the colonial powers. To Indians, Europe and America were separate creations, each with its own laws and customs.[50] Whether serving on their own or with European and colonial soldiers, native warriors were notoriously independent, practicing customs that were reputed to include torture, ritual dismemberment, and cannibalism. "The enemies we have to deal with," wrote the Swiss-born British officer Henry Bouquet during the early 1760s, "are infinitely more active and dangerous than the Hussars and Pandours" whom he had encountered in Europe.[51] In the words of William Currie, Anglican rector of Radnor Church near Philadelphia, Indians were "barbarous, cruel and inhuman"; their customs differed utterly from those of "civilized Nations, where Wars are managed by Rules."[52] Indians, of course, also managed their wars by rules, but their rules were often different. As the young George Washington discovered after negotiating a cease-fire with Ensign Joseph Coulon de Villiers Jumonville near the Forks of the Ohio in 1754, this autonomy was as true of Britain's own allies as it was of Indians in the service of France and Spain. In an event that haunted Washington for the rest of his life and that turned out to be the spark that ignited the Seven Years' War, a Seneca chief under his command named Tanaghrisson "split the Head of the French Captain" as Jumonville lay helpless on the ground, "took out his Brains and washed his Hands with them[,] and then scalped him"—all of which occurred after Jumonville had surrendered and therefore violated the rules of war as understood in Europe, but which neither Washington nor his officers seemed able to prevent.[53]

Given the central role that treaties played in Europe, some of the most vivid and highly publicized examples of the Indians' legal autonomy involved the surrender of European forts and garrisons. In Europe, sieges typically ended with carefully scripted capitulations (or "treaties"), whereby armed combatants and civilians were spared the loss of life and property that storming a fortified position usually entailed. In Henry Dell's play about the siege of Minorca, when one of General Blakeney's aides urges him to reject Richelieu's terms for surrender, the British commandant responds with a firm rebuke, reminding him of the bloodshed that would likely ensue: "Remember we are men and, and what is more, remember we are Christians."[54] To Indian warriors, however, agreements between European combatants often meant little, especially when they contravened indigenous military customs. Following the surrender of Fort Oswego in August 1756, Indians serving under the marquis de Montcalm allegedly "murther'd several [British] Soldiers, as they stood on the Parade, and scalped all our sick in the Hospital."[55] The same thing happened during the infamous massacre at Fort William Henry in 1757. In one of the more measured accounts, the *Boston Gazette* reported that Indians, furious over being deprived of the plunder that they had been promised by the French, "fell to stripping and plundering [the English prisoners] of all their Clothes, Arms and Baggage, killing and scalping everyone that resisted, not even sparing the Wounded or Sick, and privately carrying off Prisoners all such as they could." Surprisingly, in view of the Gallophobia that the incident unleashed in the colonial press, the paper also noted that the Indians who perpetrated the massacre did so "notwithstanding . . . the Opposition of the French." As Montcalm confided to his superiors in France, "what would be a violation in Europe cannot be regarded as such in America."[56]

Although observers sometimes described such encounters as acts of lawlessness, Indians could be as mindful as their European counterparts of the principles of military and diplomatic reciprocity and the benefits of following shared codes in interactions with others. "However savage they may appear," wrote William Bull of the Creek Indians on South Carolina's southern border in 1738, Native Americans were not "destitute of natural sense or the knowledge of their own interests." Indeed, as Bull conceded, Indians were often able to dictate the rules of engagement with the "English, French and Spaniards, notwithstanding the superior policy and refinements of those nations."[57] In the captivity narratives that became mainstays of popular literature on both sides of the Atlantic, a recurring theme was the need for Europeans to adapt to their captors' "customs and way of life," even when those customs seemed barbaric by European standards. In an account of his six-year captivity by Abenaki Indians during King William's War (1689–1697), John Gyles related numerous instances of "abusive and barbarous treatment," including the torture and murder of his brother James and the mid-winter abandonment of his closest friend, a young boy named John Evans from Cocheco (Dover), New Hampshire. On being sold to a French trapper on the Saint John River in present-day New Brunswick, Gyles gladly "threw away [his] greasy blanket and Indian flap" and put on European clothes. Yet Gyles was clear that the code that sanctioned such behavior also valued hospitality, courage, and discipline. In the case of favored captives like himself, it even afforded a degree of security. When his former Indian master visited him some twenty years later, Gyles claimed that he was pleased to see him and "made him feel very welcome." Until his death in the mid-1750s, Gyles put his knowledge of Indian ways to good use, serving the government of Massachusetts as an interpreter, diplomat, and soldier on the Maine frontier.[58]

As the treaties that they negotiated with Indians showed, Europeans readily acknowledged this capacity to engage in diplomatic relations. What the British and their European rivals refused to concede was that agreements with indigenous people in North America were comparable to the treaties that they made with each other in Europe. This was partly because Indians seemed to have so little regard for the moral sensibilities upon which European treaties depended. One oft-heard allegation involved native violations of European gender norms. In the narrative of his captivity, John Gyles recounted several instances when he was tortured by Abenaki women who "got together in a circle, dancing and yelling."[59] Although there are almost no firsthand accounts of rapes, Indians were also charged with acts against European women that included physical dismemberment and ritual cannibalism. According to Jonathan Carver, a Massachusetts soldier who witnessed the carnage at Fort William Henry in 1757, France's Indian allies killed indiscriminately: "men, women, and children were dispatched in the most wanton cruel manner, and immediately scalped." Another Massachusetts soldier claimed that the Indians tore "the Children from their Mothers Bosoms and their mothers from their Husbands."[60] In such circumstances, prescriptions against women taking up arms in their own defense often proved impossible to sustain. During the eighteenth century, one of the most famous women in New England was Hannah Emerson Duston, who was taken from her home in Haverhill, Massachusetts, in 1697. "Being where she had not her life secured by any law," explained Cotton Mather in one of several versions of the story, Duston and her two accomplices—a female servant and a young boy—used tomahawks to kill and scalp ten of their captors as they slept. Only two Indians escaped, one a "squaw" whom they "sorely wounded." The private, unauthorized nature of these heroics clearly troubled Mather, but he reasoned that, because Duston was protected by neither law nor government, she was justified in killing "the murderers by whom her child had been butchered."[61]

In explaining the differences between European and Indian treaties, writers also emphasized the Indians' "unsettled habitation" and the perception that Native Americans "lived by "hunting, fishing, and [gathering] wild fruits," occupying more land "than they are able to settle or cultivate." Not only did this lack of settled boundaries complicate efforts by European treaty makers to divide the land that Indians used into clearly bounded European dominions, but Europeans believed that their nomadic ways gave Indians no reason to acquire the habits of industry and trustworthiness that characterized even the "civilized empires of Peru and Mexico," let alone the treaty-bound governments of

Europe.[62] In his *Summary . . . of the British Settlements in North America* (1749), the Boston antiquarian William Douglass described Indians as primitives living in "small and distinct" tribes, only one stage removed from government by "distinct families," each *"Isolé"* from the others. "As China seems to be the elder brother of all the nations of mankind," wrote Douglass, "so America may with much propriety be called the youngest brother and meanest of mankind." Indians, he claimed, possessed "no civil government, no religion, no letters; the French call them *les hommes des bois,* or men-brutes of the forest."[63] Though willing to grant Indians some of the attributes of European sovereignty, even Cadwallader Colden thought that their form of government most closely resembled the "Ancient and Original Condition" of Europe's own monarchies and republics. "If I be not mistaken," Colden wrote in his history of the five Iroquois nations of New York, Indians were "living images" of "our Earliest Progenitors."[64] The result was an image of the North American interior as a place distinct from Europe's republic: one that was often beyond the reach of European treaties and where local customs sanctioned behavior on the part of both Indians and Europeans that would have been viewed with outrage had it occurred in Europe. Under such circumstances, Europeans claimed, war was the norm, and the peace that was the ordinary condition in relations between treaty-worthy nations in Europe became far more difficult to achieve.

Unlike Indians, British and European colonists in America were theoretically accountable to the metropolitan governments that they served, and Europe's colonial powers could—and did—hold each other responsible for perceived violations of European treaties and customs in the colonies that would have been considered violations in Europe. Nonetheless, Europeans in America were known to display many of the renegade tendencies that writers attributed to Indians. This was particularly true of colonial privateers. In the shipping lanes and coastal waters of North America and the West Indies, there was often little to distinguish the mores of marauders at sea from the customs of native warriors in the continent's interior. "Let us fall upon some Means," implored William Currie of Philadelphia following a Spanish raid on two Delaware plantations in 1747, "to keep off those Enemies of human Nature; I mean a lawless Crew of *French* and *Spanish* Privateers."[65] In a diatribe against

Pennsylvania's Quaker government for refusing to fortify the approaches to Philadelphia, Benjamin Franklin claimed that the same crew later murdered the captain of a British merchant ship, "tho' on his Knees begging Quarter." The captain's transgression, Franklin alleged, was that he had mounted a vigorous defense "for which every generous Enemy would have esteem'd him." As Franklin warned, no one wanted to be at the mercy of such unconstrained foes, and he painted a vivid picture of "the wanton and unbridled Rage, Rapine and Lust, of *Negroes, Mulattoes,* and others, the vilest and most abandoned of Mankind." "Your best Fortune," he promised his readers, "will be to fall under the Power of Commanders of King's [i.e., regular French or Spanish] Ships," who had the authority "to controul the Mariners; and not into the Hands of *licentious Privateers.* Who can, without the utmost Horror, conceive the Miseries of the Latter!"[66]

As these accounts suggest, writers feared the same qualities in privateers that they feared in Indians: their disregard for European treaties, their independence from the governments that they purported to serve, and their deficiency in the moral sentiments upon which the customary law of nations depended.[67] In the case of the Spaniards who raided the Delaware shore in 1747, Franklin attributed their "wanton" behavior, at least in part, to the multiracial composition of the "ragged Crew," but the same conduct appeared in accounts of white mariners. In New England, the transcripts of piracy trials—many involving former privateers—emphasized the democratic structure of private ships of war, the temptation for law-abiding sailors (especially young, unmarried ones) to adopt the mores of their outlaw captors, and the brutality and lack of accountability with which pirates were alleged to wage war against all humanity. In the words of a confession attributed to John Brown, a Jamaican convicted of piracy at Boston in 1717, "I know not where to begin. I may begin with Gaming! No, Whoring, That Led onto Gaming; and Gaming Led on to Drinking; and Drinking to Lying, and Swearing, and Cursing, & all that is bad; and so to Thieving; And so to This!"[68] As Philip Ashton recalled of being captured by Captain Ned Low off the coast of Nova Scotia in 1722:

[W]ho can express the concern and Agony I was in, to see my self, a Young Lad not 20 Years Old, carried forcibly from my Parents, whom I had so much reason to value for the tenderness I knew they had for me . . . ; confined to such Company as I could not but have an exceeding great abhorrence of; in Danger of being poisoned in my morals, by Living among them, and of falling a Sacrifice to Justice, if ever I should be taken with them.[69]

In the decade that followed the Treaty of Utrecht, Britain waged a largely successful war against colonial piracy, applying coercive resources on the high seas that far outstripped what it possessed in the North American interior, yet the Crown's maritime authority was anything but absolute. For every pirate who used his final words to ask forgiveness, there were many others, like John Quelch, who "seem'd to brave it out too much" and who, upon mounting Boston's gallows, "pulled off his Hat, and bowed to the Spectators."[70] On the Sunday before his execution in July 1726, William Fly, another pirate tried and convicted at Boston, refused to "come into publick" to hear a sermon by Benjamin Colman and, on the appointed day, "jumpt up into the *Cart*, with a nose gay in his hand, bowing with much unconcern to the Spectators as he pass'd along."[71] Onboard privateers, there was less room for open acts of defiance; there too, however, captains lacked the coercive powers available to commanders in the regular navy, making their ability to maintain discipline, at best, a negotiated authority.[72] "The Privateering Stroke," warned Cotton Mather in 1704, "easily degenerates into the Piratical."[73] Indeed, long after what one historian has called the "golden age of piracy" had ended, privateers remained objects of intense distrust, with many reputedly harboring plans to "turn pirates," as Admiral Vernon wrote after the crew of a privateer attempted to mutiny off Jamaica in 1740.[74] In 1757, when the depredations of British privateers in the West Indies threatened a breach with still-neutral Spain, Governor George Thomas of the Leeward Islands had two tried for piracy and hanged them "in View of all persons coming into or going out of the principal Harbour" of Antigua.[75] "I flatter myself," Thomas boasted to his superiors in London, "that His Catholick Majesty will have no farther Cause for Complaint, at least against any of the Privateers Commission'd by me."[76]

As with Indians in the continent's interior, the dependence of all the European powers on private ships of war ensured that, in many places, the waters of America continued to resemble what Cotton Mather called a "Commonwealth" of piracy and piratical depredation: places of private, unauthorized acts of violence, which were therefore only partly subject to European treaties and customs.[77] In the celebrated case of Captain Robert Jenkins, whose merchant vessel was stopped by a Havana *guarda costa* shortly after sailing from Jamaica in 1731, the Spanish commander allegedly strung him up by the neck, threatened to burn his ship if he did not divulge the location of its money, and severed his left ear, "bidding him carry it to his Master King George"; according to the *American Weekly Mercury,* Jenkins's captors also planned to scalp him, "but finding his Head close shaved, they forbore executing that Part of the Sentence."[78] Although the episode eventually supplied the name for the Anglo-Spanish war that commenced in 1739, perhaps the most striking part of Jenkins's story is the eight years that the British government waited to avenge his dismemberment. Noting the paucity of Spanish naval vessels capable of administering a more regular police in the Caribbean, Rear Admiral Stewart, commander of the British station at Jamaica, wrote in his report on the attack that "the Spanish method of guarding their coasts [by privateers] will keep that part of the world always in a state of war." Stewart also claimed that "the traders of Jamaica [were] as great rogues as the Spaniards"; that this "illicit trade [was frequently] carried on by armed sloops, or in convoy, in defiance of the law"; and that Britain's own mariners were often as "cruel to the Spaniards" and had "murdered seven or eight of them on their own shore." "Villany," Stewart concluded, "is inherent to that Climate."[79]

Taken together, Indians and privateers underscored the limits on Britain's ability to enforce its agreements with other European governments, one along the inland reaches of North America, the other in the coastal waters and shipping lanes of the Caribbean and the Western Atlantic. Settlers who occupied land that the British contested with one (or sometimes more) of their European rivals posed yet another set of constraints. Although the Acadians were the best-known example, they were hardly the only ones. On the coast of Central America, where several thousand British settlers conducted a highly profitable trade in logwood (used in the manufacture of dye) and mahogany during the eighteenth century, Spain's refusal to grant Britain legal jurisdiction with a

European treaty placed the inhabitants in what the king's advocate James Marriott called a legally ambiguous "family state." Because the logwood cutters were under the authority of neither Britain nor Spain, they were, in effect, subject "to no Jurisdiction at all"—"a collective body of fugitive persons composed of all nations," as Marriott wrote, who lived as "Outlaws with respect to the laws of both . . . Sovereigns." Although free as individuals to occupy land, erect houses, and establish families, "which is in effect colonizing," the settlers together constituted, at best, a "sort of colony," whose collective rights, according to Marriott, were "sometimes maintained by force, often interrupted and never allowed by the Court of Spain." In such circumstances, even law-abiding British subjects were no more likely to observe European treaties and customs than other people who lived beyond the reach and writ of government: "as they have a *natural* right," wrote Marriott, "to form themselves by an original compact into any model of government, so they may commit irregularities and outrages on the Neighboring Settlements of the Crown of Spain, without the Crown of Great Britain by the law of nations being responsible for it."[80]

Although Marriott's purpose was to show that Spain had an interest in a treaty that would allow Britain to form "some sort of Civil Government" on Honduras Bay, his thinking about the detrimental effects of the logwood cutters' liminal status was typical.[81] As Jamaica's Governor Trelawny wrote in 1749, the British settlements on the coast of Central America tended to be havens for "Marooners [and] Men of desperate fortunes, whose debts will not let them stay under any established Government." Trelawny also claimed that the logwood cutters had a history of "exciting the Indians . . . to rob & plunder the Neighboring Spaniards[,] committing all manner of Barbarities."[82] In the words of Boston's William Douglass, the logwood cutters' "maroon, licentious, lawless life" made their settlements a natural "receptacle" for men who might otherwise be drawn to "the more wicked life of piracy."[83] Following his escape from Ned Low's pirates, Philip Ashton painted a similar picture of the key where he made landfall in Honduras Bay, remarking on the "great Civility" of the logwood cutters who gave him shelter, while concluding that "they were after all Bad Company." "[T]here was," Ashton wrote, "but little difference between them and the Pirates, as to their Common Conversation; only I thought they were not now engaged in any such bad design as rendred [*sic*] it unlawful to Joyn with them, nor dangerous to be found in their Company."[84]

As with the unruly mores that writers attributed to privateers and Indians, this picaresque history placed the logwood cutters on the margins of Europe's treaty-based republic, and it limited their sentimental resonance, not only with the neighboring Spaniards, to whom they seemed like so many "Contraband Traders [and] lawless Vagabonds," but also with the British public.[85] On repeated occasions during the European colonial wars of the 1740s and 1750s—often, as in 1754, when Britain and Spain were officially at peace in Europe—Spanish forces attacked the British settlements scattered along the coast, seizing the inhabitants' belongings, burning their houses, and removing them and their families into Spanish territory. When Phillipe Remires d'Estines, captain-general of Jucatan, forced several hundred Honduras Baymen and women to abandon their estates in 1764 for a narrow strip along the Valis River, the settlers' committee petitioned Governor William Lyttleton of Jamaica, writing that they were unable "to maintain themselves and their families" in their present circumstances, and that they had no "means of preserving themselves from famine."[86] Under pressure from London, Spain eventually relented and allowed them to return, but more than a few people in Britain and the colonies thought that "Don Remires . . . [had] acted as a faithful servant to his master." On receiving the logwood cutters' petition in 1764, Governor Lyttleton responded somewhat casually that "he did not apprehend that the Spaniards intended any violence." Quoting the seventeenth-century adventurer William Dampier, a writer in Britain reminded readers of Benjamin Martin's *General Magazine* that the British logwood settlements "had [their] rise from the decay of privateering"; that the logwood cutters "had not forgotten their old drinking bouts and would still spend 30 or 40 l. at a sitting . . . carousing and firing of[f] guns"; and that their manners were so "debauched" that even "sober men who came into the bay to cut wood . . . could never settle themselves under any civil government, but continued in their wickedness."[87]

With relatively minor adjustments, the writer could just as easily have been speaking of how the British viewed the neutral French whom

Winslow's soldiers expelled from Nova Scotia in 1755. Although the Acadians were several times more numerous than the logwood cutters and they practiced settled agriculture, their refusal to accept the jurisdiction of English law or to swear unconditional oaths of allegiance after France's cession of the colony in 1713 placed them in a similarly vulnerable situation. Under a "treaty" that Governor Philipps negotiated in 1730, the Acadians agreed to accept a special oath in French in exchange for verbal assurances that they would not be required to bear arms on George II's behalf. Nonetheless, the neutral French remained in the eyes of their British masters a "very ungovernable people," resolving their public and private disputes according to the "Laws of Paris"; continuing to pay quit rents to the French authorities on nearby Cape Breton Island; and giving shelter to Catholic missionaries like the incendiary Father Jean-Louis Le Loutre, who was widely suspected during the 1740s and 1750s of encouraging the Mi'kmaq Indians to wage a *"guerre eternelle"* against Nova Scotia's Protestant settlers.[88] In the words of William Shirley, governor of Massachusetts and one of the removal's main architects, the neutral French were *"English* Subjects by Virtue of the Treaty and their Oath of Allegiance," but under the "Influence and Command" of France.[89] As a British pamphleteer wrote of the Acadians' political condition in 1755:

> There is, in fact, no civil Power, either legislative or executive. The *French* Missionaries, who are not only sent by the Bishop of *Quebec,* but absolutely under his Directions in their several Districts and Villages, act as sole Magistrates or Justices of the Peace. . . . [A]ll Complaints may, if the Parties think proper, be brought before the [British] Commander in Chief and Council of *Annapolis;* [but it is] a Liberty, which, if we consider the State of this People, their Prejudices to the *English,* we may be certain, is not often made use of.[90]

As was true of descriptions of Indians and privateers, such generalizations obscured a more complex reality. During the 1740s, efforts by British Governor Paul Mascarene, himself a Protestant French refugee born the same year that Louis XIV revoked the Edict of Nantes (1685), to cultivate the Acadians' goodwill prompted many to observe a careful neutrality during the Anglo-French War of 1744 to 1748. When several hundred French and Indian soldiers occupied Minas in 1744, the inhabitants' deputies asked them to leave, insisting that they "live[d] under a mild and tranquil government" and that they had "good reasons to be faithful to it."[91] As John Gyles recalled of the Acadian trapper who purchased him from the Abenaki Indians in 1695, "I had not lived long with this gentleman before he committed to me the keys to his store, etc." "[M]y whole employment," Gyles wrote, "was trading and hunting, in which I acted faithfully for my master and never knowingly wronged him of the value of one farthing." During the English siege of the French fort at nearby Nashwaak (present-day Fredericton, New Brunswick) in 1696, Gyles went so far as to post a note in English at the behest of the trapper's wife, "entreat[ing] . . . the English not to burn my [sic] house or barn nor destroy my cattle" and assuring the soldiers that the family had "shown kindness to the English captives as we were capacitated." In exchange, the trapper's wife promised to encourage her husband to repatriate Gyles, which the trapper eventually did, even offering to pay the cost of Gyles's passage to Boston.[92]

If Gyles and the French trapper's family were able to form their own circle of trust, the ambiguities inherent in the Acadians' position under the Treaty of Utrecht nonetheless made such circles hard to sustain, especially as the clouds of war gathered during the early 1750s. Despite nearly a century of settled agriculture, the Acadians' neutrality placed them in a legal situation that had more in common with that of pirates, logwood cutters, and Indians than with settled European colonists. As Dr. Johnson remarked in 1756, the most that could be said of the Acadian removal was that Britain had "distressed some private families."[93] Not coincidentally, one of the charges leveled against the Acadians in 1755 was that they had repeatedly aided and encouraged the Mi'kmaq in hostile acts against British colonists, burning houses, plundering farms, and treating "English Prisoners . . . with more severity, than the French King's Subjects themselves did."[94] According to Wilhelm Van Alzenheim, George II's resident at Frankfurt, even would-be immigrants from Europe were familiar with such stories, preferring a settled colony like Massachusetts to a disputed borderland where, according to reports in the German press, the inhabitants were "in the Utmost danger" from the

French and Indians.[95] As the Talbot County, Maryland, planter Edward Lloyd wrote shortly after four ships carrying a thousand neutral exiles arrived in the Chesapeake Bay in December 1755, the Acadians were "all rigid Roman Catholicks, and so attached to the French King, that sooner than deny his power over them, they have quitted all that they had in the World." "[W]e have as much reason here," he concluded, "to be apprehensive of them as Enemies, as they [had] at Hallifax."[96]

(3)

When Lloyd penned these words, Britain and France were still at peace. By general agreement, the war that officially commenced with the British declaration on May 17, 1756, had its origins in a series of conflicts "beyond the Seas," as the French polemicist Jacob Nicolas Moreau wrote in 1757, while emissaries of the two governments "seemed wholly taken up with a System of Pacification" in Europe.[97] In keeping with attitudes toward acts of war by and against people on Europe's margins, the public statements of both nations—those of France were reprinted, often in translation, in Britain and the colonies—made only passing reference to engagements like the one between Winslow's New Englanders and the boys of Minas. Instead, publicists concentrated on the belligerents' regular armies and navies. According to the British declaration, the government of George II was responding to a string of French encroachments, starting with the 1754 attack by "a body of *French* Troops, under the Command of an Officer bearing the *French* King's Commission," on Virginia's stockade at the Forks of the Ohio (modern-day Pittsburgh).[98] From France's standpoint, the key event was Admiral Boscawen's bombardment and subsequent capture of the French transports *Alcide* and *Lys* off Newfoundland during the summer of 1755, minutes after being hailed in French and English and giving a misleading reply to the question "Are we at Peace, or War?"[99] Unlike the intermittent, low-grade conflict in Nova Scotia, which remained largely "hidden" from Europe's view, the fighting between British and French regulars was a matter of the first importance to governments everywhere.

As the speed with which the Seven Years' War turned into a global conflict showed, however, it was increasingly difficult for Britain and

France to remain at peace in any part of the world while their colonial subjects and allies committed hostilities in North America. This was especially true of engagements where regular European officers were present, as George Washington discovered after his Seneca guide killed Ensign Jumonville in 1754. In leading Washington and his provincial soldiers to the French encampment in southwestern Pennsylvania, Tanaghrisson apparently hoped to involve Britain in a Seneca effort to restore the Iroquois confederacy's influence over the Ohio valley Indians, and all the evidence suggests that it was he who killed the French officer, not the young colonel from Virginia or one of his soldiers.[100] Nonetheless, French publicists insisted that Jumonville was "murdered by the English."[101] "Did they not," wrote Robert Martin Lesuire in a satire on the war, "assassinate Mr. De Jumonville, who came to treat with them?"[102] Upon surrendering Fort Necessity to Jumonville's brother two months after the engagement, Washington inadvertently appeared to confirm this version of events by accepting a capitulation that described Jumonville's death as an "assassination." As Adam Stephen, one of Washington's officers, explained, it was raining so hard during the negotiations that Washington was forced "to take the Sense" of the French articles from a Dutch translator and an illegible transcript "on wet and blotted Paper." "Every Officer then present is willing to declare," Stephen insisted, "that there was no such word as *Assassination* mentioned. The Terms expressed to us were, 'the Death of Jumonville.' If [the word assassination] had been mentioned, we could have got it alter'd."[103] As it was, Washington turned an unauthorized act by a renegade Indian into one for which Britain could be held accountable in courts throughout Europe.

This changing relationship between Europe and America was destined to have three far-reaching effects, each of which would play a central role in shaping the world that Americans sought to join in 1776. First, the war forced Britain to begin searching for ways to reduce the autonomy of the king's American subjects and, in so doing, to bring them more directly under the control of the British Crown and, ultimately, Parliament. In Nova Scotia and the Ohio valley, this shift was already well under way by the time war was officially declared in 1756, and was evident in the large numbers of regular soldiers that the government began sending to the mainland colonies in 1755, the military law that

Parliament adopted for American rangers and provincials who served under British officers, and the growing interest in tightening the reins of empire once the war was over. No less important, in the waters of North America and the Caribbean, Britain embarked on an unprecedented effort to regulate the activities of colonial merchants who traded illegally with the enemy and privateers who raided the ships of neutral and friendly powers. Although the exigencies of war supplied the initial rationale for most of these measures, the government kept many of them in place once the war was over, with one of the principal goals being to make Britons in America more accountable to the Crown's treaty obligations in Europe.[104] To a very real degree, the American Revolution had its origins, not in the growing distinctiveness of the colonies that became the United States or their sense of being places apart from Britain, but in the bonds that tied them as never before to Europe's diplomatic republic.

Although the consequences were not fully apparent in 1755, the second effect of North America's growing importance was a new determination on Britain's part to extend European treaty law over the continent's interior, including, especially, Indian country. As it had many times before, this determination often manifested itself in plans to acquire native land for settlement by colonists from the older colonies on the Atlantic Seaboard and Britain. Following Blackstone's logic in the *Commentaries,* British and Anglo-American settlers would bring the common law of England with them and, in so doing, create enclaves where the law of nations held sway with the same force as in Europe. With increasing frequency, though, British officials sought to place Native Americans directly under the Crown's protection, at times with the goal of safeguarding them from land-hungry settlers. The government's appointment of Sir William Johnson in 1756 as superintendent for Indian affairs north of the Ohio River and Edmund Atkin as superintendent in the south were important watersheds in this regard, breaking the colonies' longstanding monopoly on the management of Indian relations and enabling Britain to take a much more direct role in handling dangerous allies like the Seneca chief Tanaghrisson. Not coincidentally, in the years before the American Revolution, Britain gained a reputation for being a far more reliable friend of the Indians than settlers in the colonies that became the United States.[105] But the Crown's growing presence also had the effect of expanding Europe's republic to include areas that had long been on Europe's margins. Without that prehistory, Congress's bid to join the powers of the earth would have been far more difficult to sustain.

In 1755, of course, the Declaration of Independence was still well in the future. For people like the Acadians, the most immediate effect of the collapsing boundaries between Europe and America was to expose them to the sort of war-without-restraints that Europe's rulers reserved for groups who violated European treaties and agreements in Europe. Given their familiarity with French and Indian warfare, American rangers like Robert Rogers's backwoods New Englanders, who served in the regular army during the war, often took the lead in this process. In a passage as remarkable for its dispassionate tone as for the callousness of what it described, a soldier submitted the following report of Lieutenant Moses Hazen's mid-winter raid on an Acadian settlement in the Saint John valley in 1759:

> [T]he whole of the inhabitants being gone off, he [i.e., Hazen and his rangers] burned one hundred and forty-seven dwelling-houses, two Mass-houses, besides all their barns, stables, granaries, &c. He returned down the river . . . where he found a house in a thick forest with a number of cattle, horses, and hogs; these he destroyed. There was fire in the chimney; the people were gone off into the woods; he pursued, killed, and scalped six men, brought in four, with two women and three children; he returned to the house, set it on fire, threw the cattle into the flames, and arrived safe with his prisoners.[106]

Though chilling, such accounts were hardly unusual. Nor were they limited to the French. In preparation for the notorious raid by Rogers's rangers on the Abenaki mission village of Saint Francis in November 1759, the officers and enlisted men were told to "remember the barbarities that had been committed by the enemy's Indian scoundrels on every occasion."[107] According to Robert Kirk, a Highland soldier who participated in the expedition, the rangers set "fire [to] the town . . . and kill[ed] everyone without mercy," including women, children, and the elderly: "those whom the flames did not devour were either shot or tomahawk'd."

"Thus," Kirk wrote, "the inhumanity of these Savages was rewarded with a calamity, dreadful indeed, but justly deserved."[108]

For regular British soldiers like Kirk, the results occasionally seemed to anticipate a new kind of war, one based not on the subjugation of hostile populations—or at least not on subjugation alone—but on eradication and removal.[109] In the British destruction of French and Indian villages during the late 1750s, there was often little evidence of the desire for a negotiated settlement that was supposed to inform war between regular belligerents in Europe. Instead, the goal involved what, speaking of the Indians who took up arms during Pontiac's War in 1763, General Jeffrey Amherst, commander in chief of the British army in North America, called the extirpation of "this execrable race."[110] In this, the war in Indian country and the unsettled districts of Canada and Acadia differed in crucial ways from what the soldiers of Britain and France did in Scotland and Hanover, and it was likewise different from Wolfe's devastation of the countryside around Quebec. There, the objective was to cow and reduce to obedience civilians who had violated the law of nations, whether by breaking an agreement with another government or by rebelling against their own sovereign, and to dissuade people elsewhere from following their example. In Indian country and Acadia, by contrast, the goal seemed to be the elimination of Britain's enemies. Significantly, in the capitulation for the surrender of Canada in 1760, Britain agreed to extend the full rights of war to all of France's subjects in the province— all, that is, except the Acadians. With them, Britain intended to do as it pleased.[111]

Not everyone welcomed such tactics. During the summer of 1759, after learning that colonial rangers had murdered two French boys because they were "making too much noise," Malcolm Fraser of the 78th Highland Regiment responded with a sweeping condemnation of "that cowardice and barbarity which seems so natural to a native of America, whether of Indian or European extraction."[112] Despite his willingness to devastate the Saint Lawrence valley, Wolfe also betrayed some uneasiness, prohibiting "the inhuman practice of scalping, except when the enemy are Indians, or Canadians dressed like Indians."[113] Following the return of peace in 1763, the government would move more forcefully in this direction, softening Amherst's desire to extirpate Britain's indigenous enemies with a policy of paternal benevolence. As Wolfe's order in 1759 suggests, however, anyone who appeared to be an Indian in wartime— including, presumably, anyone who was an Indian—merited different treatment.[114] After British soldiers captured a Canadian *habitant* during the summer of 1759, "quite naked, painted red and blue, with feathers attached to his head," John Knox, an Irish lieutenant in the British army, wrote that wearing Indian dress was "not uncommon among the natives of this country, when detached on any enterprise with the savages."[115] In support of his point, Knox related the story of a group of thirty Canadians under the command of their priest, whom a detachment of regulars ambushed and scalped. The reason, Knox explained, was that the Canadians had "disguised themselves like Indians," which freed the British to wage war on them without restraint.[116]

As the Acadians discovered, they had more in common with Canadians dressed as Indians than they did with law-abiding *habitants*. According to Nova Scotia's Chief Justice Jonathan Belcher, Britain was justified in expelling the neutral French because they had acted the part of "rebels." By classifying them as rebels, Belcher created a misleading impression that they were unambiguously British subjects—a status that Acadians themselves rejected by refusing to bear arms on behalf of Britain and that France disputed by claiming as its own territory the districts where they lived. In most other respects, the Acadians were full subjects of neither government. According to the British, they inhabited land to which they had no title, they observed Catholic rites without a legally established clergy, and they had a history of fighting alongside Britain's enemies, most recently at the siege of Fort Beauséjour (1755) near Minas. Naturally the French made no objection on this last point, yet they too regarded the Acadians' neutrality with suspicion. "Let us hope," wrote an officer who witnessed the removal from the French garrison at Louisburg on Cape Breton Island, "[that] the ill-treatment they are experiencing will make them realize how much it is to their advantage to be subject to us."[117] As the neutral leader Jean Baptiste Galerm lamented after arriving at Philadelphia in 1756, France seemed to be no more troubled by his people's fate than Britain.[118]

Although it would be anachronistic to think of the Acadians as "stateless," they clearly showed what could happen to a people who lived according to their own laws and customs in what Sir James Marriott called a "family state" but without the high dominion that only Europe's rulers could provide. Significantly, when the Acadians finally did penetrate Europe's consciousness, they did so not as wronged subjects of the French crown but as exemplars of what the abbé Raynal, in a deliberate inversion of the European conjunction between law and sovereignty, called the ravaged innocence of a quasi-socialist "society of brethren, every individual of which was equally ready to give and receive what he thought the common right of mankind." "Such are the effects," wrote Raynal in his *History of the Indies* (1770), "of national jealousies, and of the rapaciousness of government."[119] By the time that Henry Wadsworth Longfellow published *Evangeline* in 1847, the Acadians' character as a people without a nation had become their chief claim to virtue: "They dwelt together in love these simple Acadian farmers," wrote the poet of the tragedy that befell his young heroine and her lover Gabriel, victims of "the tyrants of England." Significantly, Longfellow described with equal feeling the fate of Father Leblanc, whom the French had imprisoned forty years before "as the friend of the English." " 'Man is unjust, but God is just,' " the neutral priest is quoted as saying.[120] Clearly, the New England bard felt the same way.

In writing these words, Longfellow made extensive use of the journal that Winslow kept during the removal. In 1755, however, Winslow and his soldiers were engaged in a war that had yet to be recognized as such in Europe, one that pitted them against a people whose rights under Europe's treaty-based republic were too ambiguous and poorly defined to make them a compelling part of the war's larger narrative. As his journal makes clear, Winslow was keenly aware of this fact. Having served in the regular army during the 1740s, he thought of himself as a professional soldier. Both the journal and his surviving letters are full of references to the removal as a "troublesome jobb," which was "very disagreeable to [his] natural make & temper" and which military duty alone could compel him to perform.[121] Yet in the event that he encountered resistance from either the Acadians or their Mi'kmaq allies, Winslow's instructions empowered him to engage in scorched earth tactics, taking "an eye for an eye, a tooth for a tooth and . . . life for life from the nearest neighbors where such mischiefe is performed."[122] Although the law of nations was as binding at Minas Basin as in the Netherlands, the hostile entities with which Winslow's superiors envisioned him interacting were fundamentally different from the subjects of treaty-worthy governments that were central to the operation of the law of nations in Europe. His personal qualms notwithstanding, Winslow was free to use all the power at his disposal, secure in the knowledge that the victims' suffering would go unavenged and, to the best of his knowledge, unheard.

CHAPTER 2

The Law of Slavery

FOUR YEARS AFTER LEAVING her native Scotland, Lady Isabella Hamilton seemed unaltered by life in the West Indies. "Tho' the lily has far got the better of the rose," wrote her visiting friend and countrywoman Janet Schaw, "she is as beautiful as ever." Noting that Lady Belle had lost none of her wit and vivacity, Schaw was pleased to see that her friend was popular with the other planters on Saint Kitts, and the successful law practice of her husband, William Leslie Hamilton, allowed her to lead a life of stunning opulence. "The elegance in which they live is not to be described," wrote Schaw of the couple's spacious residence at Olivees. "The drawing room and bed-chambers are entirely fitted up and furnished in the English taste," and the great hall, which Schaw estimated as being "between fifty and sixty feet long," was finished in mahogany, with "eight windows and three doors all glazed." Perched on a hill overlooking the port of Basseterre, the house afforded sweeping views of "the sea, shipping, town and a great part of the Island," while a "constant sea-breeze" cooled the interior.[1] It was all very much to the Scottish traveler's liking.

As Schaw's journal also made clear, however, there was one thing about Lady Belle's situation that struck her as both exotic and unsettling. On arriving at Olivees, Schaw observed that her friend "had standing by her a little Mulatto girl not above five years old, whom she retains as a pet. This brown beauty was dressed out like an infant Sultan, and is a fine contrast to the delicate complexion of her Lady." Schaw's other impressions of West Indian slavery were equally vivid. At various points, she remarked on the whipping of naked field hands, female as well as male; the danger of slave revolt at Christmas (when "the good Buccara God" briefly stayed the overseer's hand); and the sexual "indulgence" of planters toward "young black wenches" who—Schaw insisted—"lay themselves out for white lovers," producing "crouds of Mulattoes, which you meet with in the streets, houses and indeed everywhere." Writing as a "humane European," Schaw took a critical view of these and other signs of slavery's deleterious effects, invariably in ways that kept a healthy distance between the mores of her native Scotland and those of the world that she was visiting. But she also insisted that Europeans needed to accept the Caribbean on its own terms. This was especially true of slavery's unforgiving law, which she was sure British Americans "would be as averse to . . . as we are, could it be avoided." Because slavery was so different from the free labor of metropolitan Britain, the rules were necessarily different too.[2]

In this, Janet Schaw's views were utterly typical. Spanning the opening weeks of 1775, Schaw's visit to Olivees came at a fluid moment in the history of British slavery. Bolstered by the moral confidence that the Seven Years' War inspired among Britons everywhere—and aided in some quarters by hostility to slaveholders who denied Parliament's rights of taxation in North America—antislavery sentiments long, if vaguely, held by people in Britain were showing signs of becoming a coherent movement to abolish slavery.[3] Of the factors that contributed to this development, none was more decisive than the 1772 case of James Somerset, an enslaved African American whom Chief Justice Lord Mansfield ruled could not be deported to Jamaica after leaving the service of his master in London. As an intimate of Mansfield's sister in Edinburgh, Schaw may have been aware of Somerset's case, including the misleading but widespread belief that the Scottish-born chief justice had declared slavery illegal in England. Given the breadth of her reading, Schaw could also have been familiar with Sir William Blackstone's claim that slavery was so abhorrent to English law "that a slave or negro, the instant he lands in England, becomes a freeman."[4] In North America and the West Indies, such notions were sufficiently prevalent during the mid-1770s that blacks fleeing slavery occasionally attempted to board ships for Britain, "imagin[ing] they will be free."[5] Although slavery was not actually illegal in England, the common law was increasingly hostile to the system that bound slaves to a life of servitude.

Nothing in Janet Schaw's remarks indicates that she thought this hostility should—or even could—be extended to the colonies, nor did most British jurists think otherwise. Instead, slavery flourished on Europe's legal margins in many of the same ways as Britain's wars with the French and Indians. In the treaties that functioned as a kind of public law in Europe, Britain and Europe's other colonial powers recognized the right of Europeans to own slaves in Africa and America, and Parliament authorized British merchants to participate in slavery and the slave trade as well. On this basis, the notorious *asiento de negros* in the Anglo-Spanish Treaty of Utrecht allowed Britain's South Sea Company to transport nearly seventy-five thousand "black slaves" to Spanish America between 1714 and 1739, doing so with the full consent of both Parliament and Europe's other rulers.[6] Yet as was true of French and Indian warfare, slavery also had its own laws and customs. According to writers on the law of nations, these differences were partly the result of an African culture where prisoners of war and criminals had many fewer rights than in Europe. In Britain, slavery's legal diversity was also protected by the empire's loose-knit structure and the freedom that colonies like Jamaica and Virginia had to enact laws authorizing chattel servitude, regardless of whether the institution was legal in England. Because slavery was a permanent feature of colonial society, these departures could not be excused by the exigencies of war or the lawlessness of a remote hinterland. As Janet Schaw discovered, slavery's anomalies were there for all to see.

(1)

Although colonial slaveholders were well aware of the anomalous character of the institution upon which their wealth depended, few doubted (at least in public) that the principles of Britain's "matchless constitution" were as suited to the slaveholding societies of British America as they

were to the free soil of England.[7] "The form of government here," wrote
the absentee planter Edward Long in his influential *History of Jamaica*
(1774), "resembles that of England almost as nearly as the condition of a
dependent colony *can* be brought to resemble that of its mother country."
"Here, as in England," insisted Long, "we have coroners, constables, and
justices of the peace." English models also pervaded the upper reaches of
the judiciary, including the court of common pleas, the court of exche-
quer, and the court of king's bench, and they formed the basis for Jamaica's three-part legislature, which consisted of a royal governor, an appointed council, and an elective lower house or assembly. According to
Long, Jamaica's assembly, in particular, was "an epitome of the [British]
house of commons, called by the same authority, deriving its power from
the same source, instituted for the same ends, and governed by the same
forms." As Long conceded, neither the British government nor Jamaica's
governors necessarily accepted this analogy, but the island's planters did.
"It will be difficult to find a reason," wrote Long, "why [the assembly]
should not have the same privileges and powers, the same superiority
over the courts of justice, and the same rank in the system of our little
community, as the house of commons has in that of Britain."[8]

As a former vice admiralty judge and speaker of the Jamaica house,
Long had a vested interest in taking such a broad view of colonial rights,
but he was hardly alone. As the Virginia patriot Richard Bland insisted in
his defiant response to Parliament's various attempts at colonial taxation
in 1766, Britons in America had the same "right to the liberties and
privileges of *Englishmen,* as if they were actually resident within the
kingdom."[9] Even colonists who chose to remain loyal to the Crown in
1776 tended to conceive of their rights in liberal terms. Speaking of a series of "encroachments" by the Barbados assembly on the governor's
prerogatives during the late 1780s, one official claimed that the islanders'
sense of entitlement was so extensive that the king's friends were at the
mercy of a "democracy," with the lower house claiming rights that exceeded even those of "the House of Commons in England."[10] *"Americans,"*
wrote John Randolph of Virginia in 1774,

> are descended from the Loins of *Britons,* and therefore may, with
> Propriety, be called the Children, and *England* the Mother of them.

We are not only allied by Blood, but are still further united, by the extensive Trade and Commerce carried on between us. Our Manners are similar; our Religion and Language the same. There is no Diversity between the Laws of each Country, but such as local Circumstances have occasioned.[11]

Although poor and middling whites in America did not generally use this sort of elevated language, they were no less attached to—or likely to defend—what they regarded as their fundamental rights as British subjects. On the North American leg of her journey, Janet Schaw found the sense of entitlement among lower-class whites as striking as she did the practice of owning slaves in the West Indies. "[T]here is a most disgusting equality," she wrote of the "American clown[s]" whom she encountered near Wilmington, North Carolina, in February 1775. "I am sorry to say," she added, "that I cannot look at them without connecting the idea of the tar and feather."[12] On repeated occasions during the 1760s and 1770s, crowds animated by such principles intervened in the controversy over Parliament's right to levy taxes in America, and not just in the thirteen colonies that eventually declared independence. During the Stamp Act Crisis, several British islands in the West Indies experienced riots similar to those that convulsed New York, Boston, and Philadelphia. In October 1765 a crowd at Basseterre "broke open" the house of the deputy stamp distributor for Saint Kitts, seizing the stamps and "commit[ting] them to the Flames." On attempting to apprehend the perpetrators, the stampmaster William Tuckett claimed that he could easily have been "murder'd" but for the timely intervention of "some Negroes who knew me." After returning to his own house, Tuckett was "waited upon by 500 white people" who forced him to accompany them back to Basseterre, subjected him to "many gross Insults," and compelled him to resign his office.[13] Although the governor of the Leeward Islands, George Thomas, posted a reward in hopes of punishing the ringleaders, his efforts were for naught. "Where there is so general a discontent," Thomas explained, "I have little hopes of a Discovery."[14]

As incidents like these suggest, Britain's colonists in America claimed rights every bit as extensive as those enjoyed by their fellow subjects in England. Indeed, in many respects, the rights that they claimed were broader. Nowhere was this more evident than with slavery. As slavery's defenders admitted, there was something grotesque in the spectacle of American planters "clamouring with so much vehemence for what they den[ied] to so many thousand Negroes, whom they hold in bondage." "'Give freedom . . . to others,'" Edward Long imagined a critic saying, "'before you claim it for yourself.'"[15] As the standoff on the North American mainland deepened, the British government's apologists were only too happy to use this point to blunt the claims advanced by the American Congress. "[H]ow is it," asked Samuel Johnson in his oft-quoted polemic on colonial taxation, "that we hear the loudest yelps for liberty among the drivers of negroes?"[16] Johnson wrote as a ministerial supporter and opponent of the American cause, but such questions resonated with Britons more favorably disposed to their fellow subjects. In late 1775, David Hartley, a pro-American member of Parliament, suggested using the regulation of slavery as a way to avert American independence. In exchange for having their fiscal autonomy restored, colonial assemblies would acknowledge Parliament's imperial sovereignty by "admit[ting] and register[ing]" a British act that guaranteed slaves throughout the empire a jury trial. As an English friend explained the measure to Benjamin Franklin:

> It is not an unreasonable request to make to America, that they shd treat an act of Parliament flowing from general principles of humanity and justice, with a different reception, to what has been given to acts of grievance. . . . The object . . . [is] to correct a vice, which has spread thro the continent of North America, contrary to the laws of God and of man, and to the fundamental principles of this Constitution, from which yours are derived.[17]

What neither Hartley nor Franklin's correspondent seemed prepared to concede was that the right to own slaves was part of the liberty that Congress was seeking to defend. Slaveholders themselves often found this fact embarrassing. Henry Laurens, future president of Congress and one of South Carolina's wealthiest planters, declared to a friend in 1774 that slavery was so "repugnant" that only "dire necessity could drive [him] to it."[18] Even Long, not usually at a loss for words, confined himself to pointing out that chattel servitude had been "tolerated both by the *Ro-mans* and the *Athenians:* yet no people were ever more jealous of their liberty."[19] There was no question, however, that slavery had its origins in the same colonial autonomy that made the British government's centralizing reforms of the 1760s and 1770s appear so threatening. In tacit recognition of this fact, radical patriots in Britain and America, many of whom opposed both slavery and Parliament's colonial taxes, generally favored antislavery schemes that would allow American planters to emancipate their bondsmen and women voluntarily. In this vein, Benjamin Rush of Philadelphia argued in a 1772 tract calling for gradual emancipation that free blacks in America would work much more efficiently and at far lower costs to planters than slaves. "I cannot entertain a doubt," wrote Rush, quoting the French naturalist and colonial intendant Pierre Poivre, "that our West-India colonies, had they been distributed without reservation among a free people, would have produced double the quantity that is now procured from the unfortunate negroes."[20] Although the wealth of West Indian planters like the Hamiltons raised questions about whether this was true, the great hope was that colonial slaveholders would recognize the superiority of free labor on their own rather than being forced to abolish slavery by a reform-minded British Parliament.

Not surprisingly, given the problems that state-sponsored abolition raised for men like Rush, some of the most forceful statements connecting African slavery and colonial liberty came from the pens of British conservatives. In *Taxation, No Tyranny,* Johnson left no doubt that the answer to his question about liberty and "the drivers of negroes" was to be found in the same exaggerated sense of right that led Americans to deny Parliament's fiscal sovereignty. "These lords of themselves, these kings of *Me*, these demigods of independence," wrote Johnson: "That they inherit the right of their ancestors is allowed; but they can inherit no more."[21] Although Edmund Burke did not share Johnson's views on taxation, he, too, thought that for slaveholders in Virginia and the Carolinas the "haughtiness of domination combines with the spirit of freedom, fortifies it, and renders it invincible."[22] According to Josiah Tucker, it was no accident that George Washington and Henry Laurens, two of "the greatest *American* Champions for the unalienable Rights of Mankind," had shown "by their own Example, that they have no Objections against Slavery, provided they shall be free themselves, and have the Power of enslaving Others."[23] For this reason, some people predicted that the British West Indies would follow the example of the rebellious colonies to the north. In the words of Tucker:

> were the planters in Jamaica . . . to set up an independent Government, and to elect a King of their own,—there is no doubt to be made, but that they would tie up his Majesty's Hands as much as possible, and make him little more than a Cypher. . . . [T]hey would expect to be at full Liberty . . . to whip and scourge their poor Negroes, according to their own brutal Will and Pleasure.[24]

Far from being an anomaly at odds with Britain's empire of liberty, the right to own slaves was among the fundamental rights of Englishmen in America.

Burke, Tucker, and Johnson all spoke as men of letters who knew more about British politics than they did about conditions in America, yet in their remarks on slavery and liberty, they were on solid ground. On the eve of Mansfield's decision in *Somerset*, the colonial right to own slaves was so well established that many people assumed that it applied to masters who brought household slaves with them to England. This is what Charles Stewart, Somerset's owner, did when he left Virginia in 1769. One reason the case turned out to be so important was that slaveholders in Britain, including Edward Long and Henry Laurens, expected Stewart to win, and the West India lobby paid the costs of Stewart's defense. By refusing to allow Somerset to be sent to Jamaica, Mansfield disappointed these hopes; however, he did not directly challenge the right to own slaves in England. He also upheld the rights of slaveholders in America, writing that slavery's "odious" character did nothing to alter the fact that the institution was positively "authorized by the laws and opinions of Virginia and Jamaica."[25] In this, Francis Hargrave, the barrister who helped Somerset gain his freedom, fully concurred. Not only was slavery "ancient and . . . almost universal," wrote Hargrave, but its roots in "most of our American colonies" were so deep that there was "little probability of ever seeing it generally suppressed."[26] As Long remarked in his *Candid Reflections* on the case, Parliament had repeatedly recognized the rights of colonists in this regard, "declar[ing] *Negroes* to be the same in the hands of the owner, as lands, houses, hereditaments, or other real estate." "Our law, I grant, favours liberty," wrote Long of the hostility to slavery in England. But courts throughout the empire had an obligation to dispense "equal justice" to the planter "who has at least an equal pretension to be favoured by the laws of his country."[27] Most jurists, including Mansfield, seemed to agree.

Nonetheless, Mansfield drew a line between English common law and the positive law on which the institution depended in America.[28] Before *Somerset,* English law was, at best, ambivalent over what Blackstone called "pure and proper slavery."[29] As Chief Justice Holt wrote in a 1706 case involving the collection of a debt in London from the sale of a slave in Virginia, commercial law in England took "no notice of a negro."[30] The same was true of criminal law. English magistrates, wrote Sir John Fielding in 1768, had "nothing to do with Blacks" except when they broke the law "by the commission of Fraud, Felony or breach of the Peace."[31] This silence meant that Americans who brought slaves with them to London could not use the courts to impose special penalties to keep them from escaping. Often, masters responded by granting slaves "half-freedom," allowing them to live on their own while remaining part of their master's household. For slaves who refused such terms, an owner's only recourse was to send them to America where the punishment for running away included whipping, branding, and—for repeat male offenders—castration. By holding that such deportations required "positive laws" that England lacked, Mansfield restricted the rights of English masters in this regard. No less important, he opened the way for courts to begin limiting their rights in other areas. While skirting the question of whether, without positive authorization, the law permitted slavery in any form in England, *Somerset* ultimately emboldened some justices to disregard the rights of slave owners in England altogether. One was Mansfield's arch-nemesis John Wilkes, who freed a London slave in 1774, advising the plaintiff to sue his former master for back pay.[32] As Somerset told a relative in England shortly after his release, "Lord Mansfield had given them their freedom."[33]

Under such circumstances it was hard to argue that the slaveholding colonies in America were as seamlessly part of English society and Britain's matchless constitution as West Indian planters like Edward Long and slave owners in Congress claimed. Mindful, perhaps, of the controversy over the question of whether Britain's colonists were entitled to the same rights as Englishmen in matters of taxation, Mansfield avoided making a definitive statement on whether the laws that authorized colonial slavery had their roots in English common law. Nonetheless, by characterizing America's slave codes as "odious," he suggested that such laws were, at best, corrupt variants of the law of England. Significantly, more than a few Americans agreed. In remarks on the origins of slavery in Virginia, St. George Tucker, a Bermuda native who became professor of law at William and Mary during the 1790s, readily conceded that the colony's original English settlers did not bring with them "any prototype of that slavery which has been established among us." Instead, slavery had developed "like a leprosy," starting with the Dutch who brought the first Africans to Virginia in 1619 and spreading to every English colony in America.[34] In *A Summary View of the Rights of British America* (1774), Thomas Jefferson took the same view, insisting, somewhat implausibly, that the "abolition of domestic slavery [was] the great object of desire" in all the colonies where the institution was currently established. Jefferson also claimed that Americans would already have withdrawn from the slave trade if not for the opposition of British ministers who preferred "the immediate advantage of a few African corsairs to the lasting interests" of the colonies. Although both claims were questionable, they left no doubt about slavery's foreign origins. According to Jefferson, chattel servitude formed no part of the "system of laws under which [Americans] . . . lived in the mother country" but had come from somewhere else.[35]

As the course of events would show, this construction of slave law posed more of a threat to planters in the British Caribbean than it did to slaveholders in the colonies that became the United States. In the West Indies, Mansfield's declaration that slavery derived its legitimacy from positive laws that England lacked meant that the colonial statutes and decisions that authorized the institution could be changed, whether by courts and legislatures in America or by Parliament.[36] During the eighteenth century's final quarter, as Britain's willingness to condone slavery's legal anomalies waned, British Americans increasingly had to contend with instructions like those in a 1790 report by the king's law officers on

British Honduras, which held that the government of a "modern settlement" could not deny "free persons of Colour" the rights and privileges
of British subjects, regardless of the existence of such race-based distinctions "in most of the British Colonies."[37] To many people it seemed
to be only a matter of time before Parliament abolished slavery altogether.
In the colonies that became the United States, on the other hand, the legitimacy that *Somerset* bestowed on the positive law of chattel servitude
eventually became one of slavery's principal bulwarks, both in relations
between slave and free-soil states within the American union and in relations with other nations, especially Britain. Although the Crown used
antislavery as a weapon to retaliate against patriot masters during the
Revolutionary War, Britain had no choice but to recognize the positive
rights of American slaveholders once the war was over, and other nations
eventually followed suit. As long as every government—or federation of
governments—was free to decide for itself whether to allow its citizens to
buy and sell other human beings, there was nothing that any other nation or government could do about it.

Even as it undercut the rights of slaveholders in England, Mansfield's
decision in *Somerset* thus represented a partial victory for slaveholders in
America. It was, however, a victory that exacted a high cost, which was to
place slavery's odious law beyond the pale of English common law. "He
that admits no right but force, no justice but superior violence," wrote
Thomas Day in a public letter to Henry Laurens in 1776, "arms every man
against himself, and justifies all excesses."[38] Day was a staunch abolitionist, but his views were hardly exceptional. According to the West Indian
planter Bryan Edwards, the "leading principle" upon which colonial slave
law depended was "fear" backed by "a sense of that absolute coercive necessity, which . . . supercedes all questions of right."[39] On the Christmas
Day that she spent on Antigua in 1774, Janet Schaw confided in her journal
that she found the holiday unsettling for two reasons. The first was the
"universal Jubilee" occasioned by the popular belief that "the good Buccara God" would hurt any master who used "the inhuman whip" against
his slaves during the festivities; the second was the resulting danger of
insurrection. "It is necessary," wrote Schaw, "to keep a lookout during
this season of unbounded freedom; and every [white] man on the Island is
in arms and patrols go all round the different plantations as well as keep

guard in the town."[40] In the words of Ottobah Cugoano, a member of London's free black community who had worked as a field hand in Grenada, "the poorest in England would not change their situation" with that of a slave in the colonies.[41] Although British Americans were free to sanction slavery, the only way to do so was with laws and legislation that departed from English norms. "The law of England abhors and will not endure the existence of slavery," wrote Blackstone in the first volume of the *Commentaries*.[42] Clearly, the law was different in America.

(2)

Despite slavery's basis in the rights of Americans as British subjects, the common law's ambivalence toward chattel servitude was well known even before *Somerset* cast doubt on the institution's legality in England, followed in 1778 by *Knight v. Wedderburn,* which abolished slavery outright in Scotland. By contrast, slaveholders had broad rights under the treaties and customs that together comprised the European law of nations. In the case of the Spanish *asiento* in the Treaty of Utrecht, the governments of Britain and Spain affirmed the right to buy and sell slaves in unambiguous terms. Under the agreement, the British South Sea Company was allowed to ship forty-eight hundred "black slaves" annually to designated ports in Spanish America. In return, the Spanish crown, which received £34,000 from the company each year for the privilege, had the right to inspect the cargo for smuggled goods and "old or defective" captives, and both parties pledged to observe commercial and diplomatic reciprocity in their relations with each other. Although Britain withdrew from the arrangement in 1750—having insisted on its renewal at the peace that ended the War of Jenkins' Ear in 1748—the growth of antislavery opinion in England did little to disrupt this pattern.[43] In the Anglo-American treaty that ended the Revolutionary War in 1783, the emissaries of George III agreed that the king's forces would withdraw from the United States without "carrying away any Negroes or other property of the American inhabitants," and Britain made similar concessions in the agreements that brought the Napoleonic Wars to a close in 1814 and 1815.[44] By that time, the slave trade (though not slavery) was illegal throughout the British Empire, and Britain was pushing other governments to follow its example. But when they chose to exercise it, the members of Europe's diplomatic republic still had the right to traffic in human beings.

Nor was this simply a matter of positive treaty law. According to writers on the law of nations, the unwritten rules and customs that people in the extra-European world observed in matters of war and commerce also sanctioned slavery. Here, jurists assumed that slavery, though a "disgrace," in the words of Vattel, "happily banished from Europe," was legal in Africa and America.[45] " 'Tis found in three quarters of the globe," insisted William Wallace, one of the barristers who represented Charles Stewart, Somerset's owner, in 1772: "In *Asia*," Wallace claimed, slavery comprehended "the whole people; in *Africa* and *America* far the greater part."[46] According to Anna Maria Falconbridge, estranged wife of the English abolitionist Alexander Falconbridge, Africa, in particular, was a place where "three-fourths" of the inhabitants "come into the world, like hogs or sheep, subject, at any moment, to be rob'd of their lives by the other fourth." Under such conditions, it was hard to argue that "the Slave Trade [was] inconsistent with any moral, or religious[,] law." Rather than "invading the happiness of Africa," wrote Falconbridge, slavery tended

> to promote it by pacifying the murdering, despotic chieftains of that country, who only spare the lives of their vassals from a desire of acquiring the manufactures of this and other nations, and by saving millions from perdition, whose future existence is rendered comfortable by the cherishing hands of Christian masters.[47]

Whatever one made of slavery's status under English law, it clearly had deep roots in the customs of Africa and America.

The effect was to strengthen slavery's protected status under Europe's own treaties and international customs. For many people, of course, the claim that the slave trade had a pacifying effect on Africa would have been hard to accept, as would Falconbridge's contention about the benevolence of masters in America. According to Ottobah Cugoano, field hands caught eating sugarcane on Grenada were sometimes "struck over the face to knock their teeth out"; others "had their teeth pulled out" as a preventive measure. As for the slave trade, merchants who trafficked along the coasts of Africa were "depredators, plunderers and destroyers of nations."[48] Significantly, in the influential report that the Lords of Trade issued in 1789, one of the central questions was how far Europeans in Africa were responsible for the perpetual warfare that writers like Anna Maria Falconbridge used to justify the slave trade. According to Thomas Poplett, a British officer who spent the American Revolutionary War at Goree, roughly a quarter of the slaves shipped to America were "prisoners made in the Wars" that European traders "stirred up" in order to "purchase Prisoners on both Sides." Based on his years in the trade, the English hymnist John Newton was less certain whether Africa's rulers "entered into [wars] for the Purpose of making Slaves," but he, too, thought "it probable."[49] As James Swan, a Scottish-born merchant living in Boston, argued in a pamphlet that appeared in the wake of *Somerset,* the slave trade, which apologists blamed on Africa's warlike character, was in fact one of the chief causes of war on the subcontinent, with European slave traders "inciting" the rulers of the principal kingdoms "to war one with another." The result, wrote Swan, was to turn Africa's kings from "protectors of their people" into oppressors.[50]

If Europeans were responsible for the slave trade's violence, most people agreed that the customs of both Africa and America sanctioned slavery. Of particular significance was the perception that those customs afforded captives few of the safeguards that prisoners were entitled to claim in times of war in Europe. By general agreement, slavery had its origins in what Blackstone called the "right of slaughter," by which a "conqueror" gained the "right to the life of his captive." Because the law of nations permitted victors in certain circumstances to kill a defeated enemy, a combatant who spared his opponent's life allegedly had a "right to deal with him as he pleases," including, if he wished, to enslave him. Blackstone himself found this right "repugnant to reason, and the principles of natural law," but many jurists accepted it, especially those steeped in the seventeenth-century natural law tradition of Locke, Grotius, and Pufendorf.[51] According to Hugo Grotius, slavery was justifiable under the law of nations because it gave captors an incentive "to forbear . . . killing their Prisoners, either in the Fight, or some Time after."[52] In a similar fashion, the English barrister Charles Molloy, whose 1676 digest of maritime law was being reprinted a hundred years later, reported that a captor's dominion over prisoners of war was so extensive that it included a right to enslave their children.[53] Even John Locke, who regarded "perfect" slavery as "nothing else but the state of war continued between a lawful conqueror and a captive," thought that a master to whom a prisoner had "forfeited" his life might "delay to take it, and make use of him to his own service, and he does him no injury by it."[54]

As part of this rationale, jurists made clear that slaughtering and enslaving prisoners of war had become obsolete "in War between Christian Princes," as Charles Molloy wrote in his digest of maritime law.[55] According to Blackstone, slavery's obsolescence in Europe was grounded in natural law and the "plain" fact that war, which was only justifiable as an act of self-defense, conferred no right over prisoners except "to disable them from doing harm to us by confining their persons." "[T]herefore," Blackstone reasoned, "it gives no other right," let alone "a right to kill, torture, abuse, plunder, or even to enslave, an enemy, when the war is over."[56] For others, especially jurists who accepted a latent right of slaughter, slavery's disappearance from Western Europe had to be explained in historical terms and the gradual introduction of what Vattel called "humane and salutary customs."[57] Either way, whether based on natural law or the refinement of manners, the effect was to situate the strictures against "pure and proper slavery" in countries like England within a more general set of European prescriptions.[58] Although Vattel maintained that it was lawful to enslave prisoners of war if they were "guilty of some crime deserving of death," he assumed that such circumstances were only likely to arise in wars with "savage nation[s], who observe no rules, and never give quarter." "Let us in this particular bestow on the European nations the praise to which they are justly entitled," wrote the Swiss jurist. "Prisoners of war are seldom ill treated."[59] In the words of an apologia that Dr. Johnson wrote for the London-based Committee for Cloathing French Prisoners of War in 1760, "the relief of enemies has a tendency to unite mankind in fraternal affection; to soften the acrimony of adverse nations, and dispose them to peace and amity: in the meantime, it alleviates captivity, and takes away something from the miseries of war."[60] Under such a humane regime, slavery lost its underlying purpose.

While affirming these enlightened principles for themselves and their European neighbors, the British were sure that they did not always apply to captivity elsewhere. Slavery's defenders could thus argue that Europe's hostility to enslaving prisoners of war was exceptional and the European treaties that sanctioned slavery a recognition of how things worked in the world beyond. In this spirit, Edward Long admitted that under some circumstances it might be advisable to prohibit slavery in a "free country," but he insisted that there were many places, including, presumably, Jamaica, where slavery was "*inevitably* necessary."[61] While hoping to purge British America of slavery's taint, Philadelphia's Benjamin Rush also placed limits on abolition's reach. "It has been said," he wrote, "that we do a kindness to the Negroes, . . . as we thereby save their lives, which had been forfeited by their being conquered in war." As an argument for slavery's lawfulness in America, such reasoning struck Rush as absurd, yet he conceded that Africans might take a different view. For those who did, the most that an enlightened European could do was refrain from giving encouragement: "Sooner let them imbrue their hands in each others blood, or condemn one another to perpetual slavery," he wrote of Africa's supposed proclivity for endless warfare, "than the name of one christian, or one American, be stained by the perpetrators of such enormous crimes."[62] Despite blaming the slave trade on the "artifice" of European merchants, even Cugoano thought that the problem stemmed in part from the fact that slavery—albeit of a less exploitative and onerous variety—was legal in Africa.[63]

If so, Africans were hardly unique. As Anthony Benezet observed in 1760, the African slave trade resembled nothing so much as the Indians' "Captivity of our People" in outlying districts like western Pennsylvania. Although no longer sanctioned "by the Christian Powers of Europe," wrote Benezet, the "inhuman practice" of enslaving enemies was still common among "the Nations of Asia and Africa, and . . . we find it also practised by the Natives of America."[64] In stories of Indian captivity and redemption, writers frequently highlighted these commonalities by using the same legal terms and idioms found in descriptions of the slave trade. Recalling her abduction by Abenakis in 1754, Susannah Johnson of Charlestown, New Hampshire, wrote that for settlers along the Connecticut River's upper valley, "reports of captured families and slaughtered friends" were a daily fact of life.[65] Although Johnson never used the word "slave" to describe her captivity, she repeatedly referred to herself as the "property" of her "master," explaining that Indians bestowed ownership on whoever "first laid hands on a prisoner."[66] Even after she was adopted by an Abenaki family in the Jesuit mission village at Saint Francis, she continued to think of herself as a chattel servant, a perspective that her captors eventually confirmed by selling her to the French at Montreal. Nor did the "bondage" of Johnson and her family end with their "deliver[ance]" from the Indians. Although they were "purchased by gentlemen of respectability," they remained subject to their new masters' will and pleasure. "Mr. DuQuesne [governor of Quebec] bought my sister," wrote Johnson, "my eldest daughter was owned by three affluent old maids by the name of Jaisson, and the other [daughter] was owned by the mayor of the city." In his letter authorizing funds to purchase their liberty from the French, New Hampshire's governor Benning Wentworth acknowledged this reality by referring to Johnson and her fellow captives as prisoners "detained in servitude."[67]

For abolitionists like Anthony Benezet, the hope was that stories of the bondage that Indians imposed on their own "Flesh and Blood" would encourage readers to "extend [their] Thoughts to others," yet stories like Susannah Johnson's could be put to very different uses.[68] Indeed, one effect of captivity narratives was to emphasize the extent to which slavery was both ubiquitous and legal.[69] During the Anglo-French controversy over who was to blame for the start of the Seven Years' War, Governor Thomas Pownall of Massachusetts argued that one of France's infractions had been to encourage the Indians to make slaves of "British subjects in time of peace" and to force them to purchase their liberty in the same way that "a Negro slave might do."[70] As Susannah Johnson admitted, the Indians "never treated [her] with cruelty to a wanton degree," and she doubted whether had she "fallen into the hands of French soldiery" she would have received the same treatment.[71] On the other hand, she also recognized that there was no guarantee that her captivity would end with her redemption, allowing her to look back on her abduction as a temporary, or even an edifying, interlude. As Elizabeth Hanson of Dover, New Hampshire, wrote in the story of her captivity in 1724, her elder daughter, Sarah, experienced a different fate from Johnson when her Indian mistress took such a liking to her that she refused to ransom her with the rest of the family and instead kept her as a wife for her son.[72] At various points in her narrative, Johnson feared that the same fate might befall one of her children, and she wondered whether she would ever taste freedom again. "My fellow prisoners were as gloomy as myself," she wrote of the mood during her confinement at Saint Francis.[73] As Johnson and her fellow captors knew, it was entirely possible for Americans to be slaves.

The accounts of Europeans held captive on Africa's Barbary Coast provided similar evidence of slavery's continuance in the world beyond Europe. Unlike captives redeemed from Native Americans, which typically occurred after a few months and rarely more than a year later, European prisoners in the Muslim principalities of North Africa often endured years, if not decades, of captivity.[74] Although the numbers paled in comparison to those for the Atlantic slave trade—in the 1760s alone, more than 400,000 slaves left West Africa for British America, against perhaps 20,000 Britons (and possibly ten times as many Europeans) who experienced some form of North African servitude between 1600 and 1750—the enslavement of whites in the Maghrib betrayed many of the characteristics associated with black slavery in America: exposure to a sophisticated, highly commodified market, total physical (and sexual) subjection to a master's will, and the premise that a conqueror's powers over prisoners of war were unlimited.[75] "It will be needless to recount the barbarous treatment [that] we met with," wrote a British sailor of his captivity in Morocco sometime before 1721. In retaliation for the resistance that the author and his shipmates made before their surrender, the governor of the port of Tétouan subjected the crew to a hundred "bastinadoes" on the soles of their feet. They were then marched to the inland city of Meknés, where they were taken to a plaza fronting the royal palace, "stripp'd naked as we were born," and forced to stand "with every Part of our Bodies open to the View of such as come thither to be made Purchasers." According to the anonymous narrator, the only men spared this fate were two "very handsome Lads, of about 17 Years of Age," whom Morocco's ruler, Moulay Ismaïl, retained "for his own brutish Lusts."[76]

As with the redemption of Indian captives, Britain's response to such incidents suggested that it viewed them as legitimate acts of enslavement. Speaking of the Barbary corsairs, Vattel thought that the "Christian nations" of Europe would be "justified in forming a confederacy . . . to destroy [these] haunts of pirates," yet the strongest maritime powers, including Britain and France, generally preferred to engage North Africa's rulers diplomatically, negotiating treaties and subsidies for the protection of their subjects and dispatching consuls to oversee their enforcement.[77] Because Britain's agreements only protected its own nationals, one effect was to condone the enslavement of weaker rivals, especially Italians and, after 1783, Americans.[78] Furthermore, by paying tribute and ransoming captives, Britain appeared to accept the slavery of its own subjects. As Thomas Troughton of the privateer *Inspector* recalled after his ship ran aground in Tangier Bay in 1746, the surviving crew initially hoped for assistance from the local inhabitants, "as the Emperor of *Morocco* was . . . under a Treaty of Peace with the *British* Court." Because Britain owed money on a ransom that was negotiated a decade earlier, however, Troughton and his shipmates spent nearly five years as slaves, all with the consent of the local British consul and, during a brief stopover, the captain of a visiting British warship.[79] The crew of the British naval vessel *Litchfield* experienced a shorter but similar period of slavery after their ship sank off the Moroccan coast in 1758. On the pretext that Morocco was "neither at war [n]or peace with *England*," the emperor Sidi Mohammed forced the crew "to work the same as the other Christian slaves" until the British government complied with his demands. According to James Sutherland, one of the ship's officers, the men "were allow'd to sit down an hour and a half in the middle of the day; but had many a stroke from their drivers, when they were doing their best to deserve better usage."[80]

According to Vattel, the most disturbing part of such accounts was the complicity of the European powers "most able to chastise" the perpetrators.[81] Given their lurid style, their voyeuristic, quasi-pornographic obsessions, and the exotic barbarism that they attributed to their Moorish tormentors, stories of European captives in North Africa often said as much about the public for which they were written as they did the experiences of those who wrote them. Among other things, they dramatized their authors' suffering; often they justified a decision to collaborate or convert to Islam; occasionally they cast doubt on the morality of other forms of slavery. "The reader will here find how far human nature may be degraded," wrote the translator of Jean Louis Marie Poiret's *Travels through Barbary:* "the ferocity of these Arabs, must indeed shock every person of feeling or delicacy."[82] Whatever other purpose they served, though, the stories of British captives showed that North Africa's Muslim rulers regarded slavery as legal according to their own version of what Vattel, in his tripartite schema, called the "customary" law of nations.[83] No less important, Britain's diplomatic conventions suggested that it recognized slavery's legality as well. As Vattel admitted, the Barbary corsairs' "piracies" could not "be considered . . . regular acts of war," yet the "effects" of their depredations, including, presumably, the Europeans whom they captured and enslaved, were "lawful" property.[84] It was hard to miss the implications for African American slavery. "I have often heard," wrote Joseph Morgan in his *History of Algiers*, "that our *American* Planters, tho' they have no Gallies, are passable good *Algerines*."[85]

Despite the slave trade's greater geographic reach and the larger numbers involved, British writers used the same logic to justify the shipment of millions of African slaves to America. In 1750 Parliament explicitly recognized the slave trade's legality, authorizing merchants from any British port to ship "Negroes at reasonable Rates" to the colonies, while forbidding the use of "Fraud, Force, or Violence . . . [to] carry away from the Coast of Africa, any Negro or Native of the said Country."[86] The prohibition on acts of fraud and violence probably reflected a desire to avoid antagonizing rulers like the king of Barra, whose resentment over several unauthorized captures prompted the Company of Merchants Trading to Africa to threaten slave ship captains in 1751 with penalties of £100 for every captive so detained.[87] But affirmations of the slave trade's legality were also meant to reassure people in Britain and America that the trade was, in fact, sanctioned by the Africans with whom it originated. According to an officer with the Royal African Company during the late 1740s, no British merchant ever knowingly purchased a "Negro without just Cause, and conformable to the Laws of the Country [i.e., Africa]." However unjust and repulsive the activities of slave traders might be under English law, it was "Negroes [who] prescribe Laws to the Europeans," not the other way around.[88] Francis Moore, chief factor for the African Company at James Fort on the Gambia River, placed a similar emphasis on African law in a published account of the trade during the 1730s. Although Moore conceded that local traders sometimes tried to sell "stolen" captives to British merchants, the company's policy was to limit its purchases to prisoners of war and criminals. If

Moore or his agents suspected that a captive had been enslaved by any other method, they sent "for the Alcade, or chief Men of the Place, and consult[ed] with them about the Matter."[89]

As an indication of the force that such arguments carried in Britain, abolitionists hesitated to question, at least in public, the premise that it was lawful to purchase slaves who had been legally enslaved in Africa. Instead, they sought to prove that most slaves were victims of "panyaring" (or kidnapping) raids that Africans themselves regarded as illegal. As Ottobah Cugoano recalled of his captivity near Ajumako in modern Ghana, "I was snatched away from my native country, with about eighteen or twenty more boys and girls, as we were playing in a field." The gang's pretext, he wrote, was that "we had committed a fault against their lord, and . . . must go and answer for it."[90] According to the testimony in Thomas Clarkson's 1789 pamphlet calling for the trade's abolition, such abductions were not unusual. One witness told Clarkson that, on learning that a group of "natives" at Cape Palmas—on the border between modern Liberia and Côte d'Ivoire—planned to attack a neighboring village, he asked "if the inhabitants had done them any injury." "They replied, no; but that there was a considerable number of fine stout young men belonging to it who were *good for trade*. This was their only reason."[91] Another of Clarkson's interlocutors recalled accompanying the king of New Town (in modern Nigeria) up the Calabar River "to trade for slaves":

> In the day time, we called at the villages as we passed, and purchased our slaves fairly; but in the night we made several excursions on the banks of the river. The canoes were usually left with an armed force: the rest, when landed, broke into the village, and, rushing into the huts of the inhabitants, seized men, women, and children promiscuously. We obtained about fifty negroes in this manner.[92]

Although chilling, stories of nighttime deception left open the possibility that slaves in Africa could still be purchased "fairly" by the light of day.

Defenders of the slave trade frequently carried matters further, claiming that many allegations of fraud were the work of armchair humanitarians in Britain who "measure Right and Wrong by the Standard of their own Laws."[93] In his *Observations* glossing the Lords of Trade's 1789 report, the English pamphleteer John Ranby corrected several witnesses for what he saw as a tendency to speak of "panyaring" in West Africa as though it were the same as "kidnapping" in England. "We confine the meaning of both these words," wrote Ranby, "to the seizing [of] any person, *not being an enemy,* by force or fraud." Africans, on the other hand, used both to describe "enemies, seized or taken in any other manner than openly in the field of battle." When witnesses testified that men, women, and children had been reduced to slavery by panyaring, often what they were actually describing was the covert but legal enslavement of prisoners of war.[94] Perhaps with an eye to Britain's tacit acceptance of white slavery in the Maghrib, observers also noted that many native traders in the African interior were Muslims "perpetually at war with" their non-Muslim neighbors. Drawing on evidence collected during his three-year residence at Sierra Leone in the 1780s, the British naval officer John Matthews argued that the "prisoners made in these religious wars furnish a great part of the slaves which are sold to the Europeans." "I have reason to believe," Matthews insisted, that most would "be put to death if [their captors] had not the means of disposing of them." When the American Revolutionary War briefly interrupted the slave trade during the late 1770s, the inland kingdoms to Sierra Leone's east responded—or so Matthews claimed—by resuming the practice of slitting the throats of prisoners " 'as they used to do before white men came to their country.' "[95]

From observations like these, it required little effort or, presumably, imagination to argue that the merchants who shipped slaves to America were engaged in acts of Christian charity and redemption. "Pray do not . . . suppose me a friend to slavery, or wholly an enemy to abolishing the Slave Trade," wrote Anna Maria Falconbridge of her gradual turning away from the abhorrence with which she had once regarded the African trade. "I wish freedom to every creature formed by God, who knows its value."[96] As the Liverpool captain Robert Norris told the Lords of Trade in 1789, captives in Dahomey, the native kingdom that dominated the Bight of Benin for much of the eighteenth century, were ritually sacrificed on "Days of Ceremonial" to inspire the king's subjects and tribute-paying allies "with Awe and Terror." "The Roof of the Palace," Norris told his interlocutors, "is decorated with a prodigious Number of human Heads; and when the King means to make War, it is an Expression in use to say, *The Palace wants Thatching.*"[97] John Matthews painted a similar picture of the kingdoms in the vicinity of Sierra Leone, writing that "death and slavery" were the "punishments for almost every offence," whether murder, petty theft, or witchcraft, as well as the fate of most prisoners of war.[98] "I believe we may safely conclude," wrote Matthews, "that slavery can never be abolished in a country like Africa, consisting of a prodigious number of small independent states, perpetually at variance, and under no restraining form of government, where the people are of a vindictive and revengeful spirit."[99] Because the law in Africa was so different, there was no reason the merchants who traded there should not have a different law as well.

Although the British campaign to abolish the slave trade did not become a full-fledged movement until the late 1780s, the trade's legality was already on people's minds at the time of *Somerset*. For the most part, those who questioned the right to own slaves in England recognized, in Mansfield's words, "that there have been, and still are[,] slaves to a great number in Africa." Despite the absence of positive "laws and opinions" authorizing slavery in England, the British also accepted that Africans were "goods and chattels" in Jamaica and Virginia and that they could be bought and sold on that basis throughout the British Atlantic.[100] In subsequent cases, Mansfield did his best to avoid further entanglements in slavery's extra-European law. In 1773 he was asked to rule on a habeas corpus petition alleging that Little Ephraim Robin John and Ancona Robin Robin John, two Africans being confined on a Virginia-bound ship at Bristol, had been illegally enslaved on the Calabar coast in 1767. The brothers were relatives of Old Calabar's king, Grandee Ephraim Robin John, and they had been slave traders before they were abducted during a battle onboard a British slave ship. In their affidavit, the Robin Johns insisted that they were "free men" when they boarded the ship and were the captain's guests, which made their enslavement illegal under both African law and parliamentary statute. Had they not agreed to settle out of court, Mansfield could have found himself in the awkward position of having to decide as a matter of English law exactly what constituted a legal act of enslavement in Africa. Instead, forestalling what could have become another precedent-setting decision, the captain responsible for the brothers' abduction agreed to pay their current owner

for their liberty. Because the Robin Johns regained their freedom by being purchased, the case had no impact on slavery's status in England,
nor did it affect the legality of buying slaves in Africa and America. Fit-
tingly, the two princes returned to Old Calabar and the business in
which they had been engaged when they were captured.[101]

(3)

Although the law of nations provided a much more solid foundation for
slavery than English common law, it nonetheless highlighted the extent
to which even genteel settings like the Hamiltons' plantation at Olivees
were, in subtle but unmistakable ways, places of chronic war and violence. As Janet Schaw's journal made clear, this reality was not always
apparent to the casual observer, nor did it prevent slaveholding Americans
from embracing European norms of civil society in other areas. "The
people in town live very well and are extremely polite and hospitable,"
wrote the Scottish traveler of Basseterre's white inhabitants. "The stores
are full of European commodities, and many of the merchants very rich.
They are a people I like vastly, and were there nothing to make me wish
otherwise, I would desire to live forever with them."[102] Despite slavery's
dependence on African customs, the same mimetic impulses were also
evident among blacks who wished to remake themselves along English
lines. This, in fact, was one of *Somerset*'s central lessons. Although never
more than a small minority of the empire's total black population, African men and women—whether in the larger towns and cities of Britain
or in the ports of North America and the West Indies—who converted to
Christianity, who learned to read and write, and who had access to
blacks in the same position could sometimes lay claim to English legal
rights as well. Whatever one makes of the authorial provenance of Olau-
dah Equiano's famous narrative, one way to read it is as an extended
essay on the rule of law post-*Somerset,* with the rights of free blacks in
England serving as a beacon for African men and women throughout the
British Atlantic.[103]

In the colonies, however, slavery condemned the vast majority of
blacks to what Locke called "a state of war continued" by other means.[104]
"The *end* or *object* of civil society," wrote Vattel, was to ensure that every

citizen had a right to "the peaceful possession of property," that every-one had an equal chance "of obtaining justice," and that all were pro-tected against "external violence."[105] Because slaves were, by definition, noncitizens, they were excluded from all of these benefits, which made them unable to participate in the reciprocal relationships on which civil society in England depended. "In modern times," wrote David Hume of the free-soil nations of Western Europe, "a bad servant finds not easily a good master, nor a bad master a good servant; and the checks are mu-tual." In places where slavery was still common, such checks were non-existent. Nor were slavery's effects limited to the economy and domestic relations between masters and servants. Speaking of the impact on colo-nial war and defense, Hume insisted that slavery turned "every man of rank" into "a petty tyrant"—"educated amid the flattery, submission, and low debasement of his slaves." Naturally the people subject to such "unbounded dominion" thought only of how best to make their escape.[106] In the words of a pamphlet sometimes attributed to Edward Trelawny, governor of Jamaica during the late 1730s and 1740s, slaveholding colo-nies were for this reason unusually vulnerable to foreign invasion. "A free Negroe that has fifteen or twenty Acres of his own," surmised Tre-lawny (or whoever wrote the pamphlet), "will defend it with his Life against the *French* or *Spaniards*." A slave, by contrast, had "nothing to lose [during an invasion] if the Enemy prevails, and if he goes over to him may get his Liberty." For colonial slaveholders, the implications were clear: "you will be in Danger of every Slave's turning against you," or at least every slave "that is not well watch'd and kept under by good Discipline."[107]

Even as the buying and selling of human beings remained legal under European treaty law, slavery's presence in British America ensured that the colonies with the largest numbers of slaves remained, in unmistak-able ways, on Europe's legal margins. In the Caribbean, where blacks outnumbered whites in some islands by a factor of ten to one, Jamaica and the Leeward Islands were swept by recurring acts of slave resistance during the 1760s and 1770s, some rumored, others terrifyingly real. The West Indies also contained large and powerful communities of escaped slaves or "maroons," all of them fiercely independent and many—as the war against the Black Caribs on Saint Vincent in 1772 and 1773 showed—

capable of holding their own against British regulars. Given this dynamic, Caribbean planters tended to take a far less hostile view of the
British government's expanding presence, especially in matters involving the army and navy, than their fellow subjects to the north. In 1770,
the same year as the Boston Massacre, Saint Kitts requested two hundred regulars to help keep order among the island's "turbulent and savage"
slaves.[108] Nor was the threat of slave revolt limited to the West Indies. As
the Anglican missionary Charles Woodmason wrote in a sermon that he
intended to deliver in 1767 to the Scots-Irish settlement at the Waxhaws
in South Carolina, the colony's whites had "an *Internal* Enemy [of] Not
less than 100 M [100,000] *Africans.*" Rather than sparring over doctrine,
Woodmason cautioned, Presbyterians and Anglicans would be well advised to "live like Brethren in Unity," lest their slaves surprise them and
"begin [their] Friendships towards each other in one Common Death."[109]
Despite relatively small black populations, even the northern colonies
were susceptible to such fears. In 1741 New York magistrates, convinced
that they had discovered a plot on the part of local slaves and freemen to
torch the city, arrested twenty whites and 152 blacks. After gaining more
than eighty confessions—many through torture—they executed thirty-
four, thirteen of whom (all black) were burned at the stake.[110]

In the West Indies, one result of this climate of fear was to give slave
owners and the governments that represented them an interest in limiting the impact of European warfare on the main slaveholding colonies.
Even when it was nothing more than rumor, the mere threat of a slave
revolt often led British slaveholders to cooperate with slaveholders in
other European colonies. During the wars of the 1740s and 1750s, officials in the British West Indies entered into conventions with their
French counterparts whereby each agreed not to steal the other's slaves
or to plunder and burn their plantations. Speaking of one such agreement
in 1757, George Thomas, governor of the Leeward Islands, reported that
planters in the islands' coastal districts were able to live in complete
"tranquility," while the Anglo-French war raged in their neighborhood.[111] British planters also recognized that in the event of an invasion
their best hope was often not to help the king's forces defend their colonies but to negotiate generous terms of surrender. When British forces
occupied Saint Bartholomew in 1744, that was more or less what the

island's French inhabitants did, declaring themselves subjects of the British Crown, accepting a British offer of toleration, and, no doubt, assuming that nothing would happen to threaten their rights as slave owners.[112] According to Edward Long, most planters in Jamaica supported having British regulars stationed on the island because they feared an insurrection by their own slaves, not because they worried about a French or Spanish invasion.[113] No matter what other issues divided them, fear of slave revolts was one thing that planters everywhere had in common.

When it suited their purposes, of course, Britain's European rivals were free to use the threat of slave revolt, not as a basis for intercolonial diplomacy but as an instrument of war. Until Cuba emerged as a major slaveholding colony after the Seven Years' War, Spain posed a particular threat in this regard, especially along "frontiers" where the two empires had overlapping maritime and territorial claims.[114] Drawing on the doctrine of Christian liberty, which held that slaves who converted to Christianity were entitled to freedom, Spaniards in Florida and the Caribbean routinely offered freedom to blacks fleeing slavery in British territory, especially if the fugitives were Catholic. British records are full of complaints like the one lodged against a priest on Puerto Rico for giving "spiritual advantage to slaves, who are quite insensible of them, except as procuring their manumission." "I pray leave to assure you," insisted the Leeward Islands' Governor Thomas to his Spanish counterpart in 1751, "that not a single Slave has deserted us in search of the Roman Catholick Religion, or of Christianity of any Denomination whatsoever."[115] Nonetheless, it was clear that British slaves were aware of the possibilities for freedom in Spanish territory. During the Stono Rebellion of 1739, many of the slaves who sought to escape the plantations of South Carolina for Florida were "Angolans" who observed the Catholic rites and catechism of their native Kongo. Of those who managed to elude capture, several eventually joined a Spanish company of black soldiers and took up arms against their former masters.[116] In 1741 five of the New York slave conspiracy's ringleaders were black sailors whom the British had taken from a Spanish corsair. Among other things, they were charged with being Spanish "Emissaries" who had been commissioned *"to burn all the Magazines and considerable Towns"* of British North America.[117]

Faced with such threats, British officials responded by forming their own alliances with slaves and free blacks. Among these were communities of maroons, many of them escaped slaves originally from Africa, who populated the mountains and inland forests of the larger sugar islands. During the final years of Jamaica's long-running First Maroon War (1665–1740), Coromantee warriors led by Captain Cudjoe and an *obeah* priestess known as Nanny devastated large parts of the colony, threatening a general slave insurrection and forcing the colonial government, amid looming war with Spain, to sue for peace.[118] In the Trelawny Town Treaty, which brought the war to a close in 1739, Governor Edward Trelawny turned the maroons into military adjuncts of the colonial government. During the Tacky Slave Rebellion of 1760, maroons served the colony with distinction, prompting the Jamaica assembly to grant the principal towns a subsidy of several hundred pounds "to encourage their future service."[119] At no point, however, could planters on the island take the maroons' loyalty for granted. During the early 1770s there were complaints of maroons plundering goods from neighboring plantations, while Thomas Thistlewood suspected the Leeward Maroons of abetting the Hanover slave revolt of 1776.[120] Significantly, in the ceremony that finalized the Treaty of 1739, Governor Trelawny acknowledged Captain Cudjoe's power and autonomy by taking a Coromantee oath, whereby the two men sealed their friendship by drinking from a cup filled with rum and blood from each other's veins.[121] Although the governor clearly had the advantage, his ability to uphold the rule of law in Jamaica's maroon towns remained entangled—and intermingled—with the maroons' own laws and customs.

Because of this dynamic, British and colonial officials repeatedly had to reach similar accommodations with slaves whom they recruited for their own military forces. Invariably, the price included manumission. One of the most famous units—and certainly the most controversial—was the "Ethiopian Regiment" that Virginia's governor Lord Dunmore raised in 1775 from the slaves and indentured servants of patriot masters. As was evident from the "Liberty to Slaves" emblazoned on the regiment's uniforms, Dunmore's action was partly meant as a reproach to Virginia planters who, in the words of the English polemicist John Lind, had "taken up arms in support of . . . [the] *self-evident truths*—'that all men are *equal*,'" yet Dunmore was also employing a time-honored method of ensuring the soldiers' loyalty.[122] Despite objections from southern planters, Congress eventually approved the use of black soldiers in the Continental army, many, like the First Rhode Island Regiment, consisting of emancipated slaves, as well as free blacks, mulattoes, and Indians.[123] Speaking of the black soldiers that the Jamaica assembly authorized him to raise for the British assault on Spanish Portobello in 1741, Governor Trelawny observed that the only way to secure their fidelity was "to promise liberty to such of them as do not desire to return to their masters, and to assure them that they shall not be employed but as soldiers in his Majesty's service." The reason, Trelawny explained, was that the British intended to use them as rangers or "Hussars . . . before and on the flanks of the main body." In such open and dispersed formations, black soldiers could easily desert to the Spanish if they had not already been freed by the British.[124]

Although Trelawny's purpose was to find recruits for the British army, his observation is a salutary reminder that slavery's character as a perpetual state of war was more than a pithy aphorism coined by jurists and philosophers in Europe. To a degree that Americans found impossible to ignore, any community that depended on the labor of enslaved men and women was, at best, an "imperfect" civil society, one where many—if not most—of the inhabitants were legally people who had no stake in the society's well-being. As was clear from Lord Dunmore's Ethiopian Regiment, the civic incapacity of slaves was, in many ways, a legal fiction, one that disguised the fact that African Americans, especially second- or third-generation Creoles, were as integral to political, military, and economic life in the colonies as white settlers. If there had been any blacks on hand to hear the sermon that Charles Woodmason intended to deliver to the Scots-Irish congregation at Waxhaws Church in South Carolina, many would have had ties to the community that were deeper than those of a natural-born Briton like Elizabeth Jackson, widowed mother of the future president of the United States and a recent immigrant to the district from Ireland. Unlike Elizabeth Jackson, however, enslaved African Americans were captives whose loss of freedom was legally permanent, whether as a result of being taken prisoner in Africa or by virtue of having an ancestor who had been condemned to such a fate. As such, they were legal outsiders in many of the same ways as Indians, Acadians, and pirates. But there was one crucial difference. Slaves were outsiders at the center of the wealthiest and most influential of Britain's American colonies.

When Janet Schaw crossed the Hamiltons' threshold at Olivees in 1775, this was a reality that British planters were increasingly reluctant to admit. Wherever possible, slavery's apologists depicted the institution as one of paternalistic benevolence where "Christian masters," in the words of Anna Maria Falconbridge, were restrained by a combination of factors, including "the fear of reciprocal injury," the "laws of the land," and their own "religious tenets."[125] Mindful, in particular, of the need for reciprocity, proslavery writers liked to claim that slaves took a similar view of their situation. According to Falconbridge, the slaves whom she met on Jamaica showed little evidence of wanting to change their status, including slaves who had saved enough to consider "ransoming themselves."[126] Writing to her daughter in England on the occasion of her thirteenth birthday, Jamaica's Ann Gardner Brodbelt assured the girl that the day had been "noticed . . . by the negroes" on the family plantation, "who celebrated [it] with much cheerfulness, and were all united in their good wishes to you."[127] During a visit to the Hamiltons' boiling house with Lady Belle, Janet Schaw related a similar story, reporting that the mere sight of her friend's face was "pardon" to several slaves who had been "condemned to the lash." "Their gratitude" on that occasion, wrote Schaw, "was the only instance of sensibility" that she observed among the island's black majority.[128]

As Schaw's words suggested, however, it was clear that the gratitude of the individuals whom Lady Hamilton pardoned was the product of a coercive and violent reality, one that, according to knowledgeable people in both Britain and America, far outstripped the violence that was also part of the law's coercive apparatus in England. During the summer of 1775, while on the North Carolina leg of her American travels, Schaw was horrified to learn—in a probable echo of Lord Dunmore's offer of freedom to the slaves of patriot masters in Virginia—that the king had issued a proclamation "promising every Negro that would murder his Master and family that he should have his Master's plantation." Although Schaw viewed the rumor as a patriot lie being spread to discredit the government's supporters, she thought the odds "ten to one" that slaves in Wilmington, where she was staying, would "try the experiment." "In that case," she wrote, "[white] friends and foes will all be one," regardless of their position on the looming war with Britain.[129] Whatever slavery's defenders might say, the laws and customs that justified slavery in America gave enslaved African Americans little reason to accept the law of their masters—or rather, little reason apart from fear of the lash and the other coercive measures sanctioned by colonial slave codes. In British America, this was already a lived reality, and there was no reason to think that it would not continue to be a reality in the colonies that became the United States.

CHAPTER 3

Pax Britannica

PAUL WENTWORTH WAS SAID to be one of the cleverest men in England. A gifted linguist and shrewd diplomat, the Barbados native had been, by turns, a merchant in Portsmouth, New Hampshire, a planter on the Demerara River in Surinam, and a wealthy speculator and man of fashion in London. For all these reasons, he seemed like a natural choice to lead Britain's last-ditch effort to dissuade Benjamin Franklin, Congress's emissary in Paris, from concluding an alliance with France.[1] But even Wentworth was unprepared for what the famously urbane American had to say when the two met in early 1778. While welcoming Britain's offer to negotiate and conceding that, reunited, "Britain and America [could] be the greatest Empire on Earth," Franklin spent much of the interview lecturing Wentworth about the "Barbarities inflicted on his Country." To Wentworth's surprise and indignation, Franklin nearly "lost his Breath in relating the burning of Towns, the neglect or ill-treatment of Prisoners," and the "system of devastation and Cruelty" that had characterized Britain's operations since the first shots on Lexington Common. At one point, Franklin even spoke of "English men [as] Barbarous!" "I told him," Wentworth reported, that "I could not wait upon him for that sort of instruction, and must beg to moderate him by calling his attention to the Humanity, the Benevolence, [and] the reputation" of Britain's goals.[2]

Although history confirms many of Franklin's allegations, Wentworth's response is a reminder of the rectitude with which the British viewed their conduct during the American Revolution. From the government's standpoint, Britain was engaged in a "just and lawful war"—as the historian Edward Gibbon wrote in 1779—whose moral and legal underpinnings ought to be obvious to impartial observers everywhere.[3] In particular, the government claimed to be fighting to uphold the law of nations in both Europe and America. Despite the looming breach with France and, eventually, Spain and the Dutch Republic, Britain insisted throughout the Revolutionary War that the war was a struggle for the welfare of "the great European republic," as the Presbyterian minister Alexander Carlyle assured his parishioners at Inveresk, Scotland, in 1776.[4] As Wentworth's interview with Benjamin Franklin made clear, people who thought this way invariably took as a given the benevolent nature of Britain's authority over its own subjects and allies. Often, though, the government's defenders went further, maintaining that the war was also a war for peace with others. "Our fleets and armies are great and formidable," wrote the English minister Ebenezer Radcliff. "[T]o lay waste and destroy . . . with any other view, but to procure peace and good government, is unbecoming a brave people."[5] As the Irish naval chaplain Thomas Lewis O'Beirne insisted in a sermon at St. Paul's Chapel in New York, shortly after the cataclysmic fire that destroyed much of the city in September 1776, Britain's was "the cause of peace, loyalty, and sound reason."[6]

To a savvy politician like Franklin, such professions would surely have sounded hollow, partaking of the self-justifying rhetoric that great powers always used to cloak their real ambitions. In at least one respect, however, observers who insisted on the peaceful nature of Britain's objectives were very much on target. To a greater extent than is often realized, the revolution's origins lay in a novel series of attempts to pacify Britain's empire in North America and the West Indies. Mindful that the global cataclysm of the Seven Years' War had started in America and that the colonists who initiated hostilities had at times acted on their own authority, the British government determined during the early 1760s that the only way to ensure that the hard-won peace endured was to extend Britain's military-fiscal state to include both the older colonies of settlement and the possessions that Britain had recently acquired from France and Spain. By pursuing this goal through the creation of a peacetime army of ten thousand regulars and by using the ill-fated project of parliamentary taxation to help cover the costs, Britain eventually drove the colonies that became the United States to rebel. However, the government's actions affected other parts of the British Empire as well, including Britain's relations with other Europeans and with blacks and Indians. Without the reforms of the 1760s and early 1770s, a host of related changes, including, notably, the growth of antislavery in Britain and a new sense of British responsibility in the world beyond, would have been far less potent, and it would have been harder for Congress to bid for European recognition. For all these reasons, the years before the American Revolution marked a new phase in the expansion of the public law of Europe. By attempting to bring the extra-European portions of their Atlantic empire more fully within Europe's republic, the British helped initiate a transformation that proved much longer-lived than the North American empire that they briefly ruled—and that even the Union's citizens would find difficult to resist.

(1)

Insofar as there were precedents for the British reforms that started the revolution, they were to be found not on the North American mainland but in what William Blackstone called Britain's "maritime state."[7] Under the seventeenth-century Navigation Acts, Britain monopolized the colonies' trade, requiring that the most valuable exports—especially rice, indigo, tobacco, and sugar—be shipped through British ports and carried in British or colonial ships. Although the purpose of these regulations was to protect the maritime industries that kept the Royal Navy supplied with ships and sailors, the need to enforce them required Britain to maintain some twenty vice-admiralty courts in the colonies, which heard maritime causes from Newfoundland to Barbados. The men who presided over these courts were often local merchants with ties to the ports where they lived. But they took their instructions from England, and they decided cases without juries, with duties that included condemning wartime prizes, safeguarding the pines that the navy used to mast its vessels, and enforcing the laws governing smuggling, salvage, bottomry, shipboard wages, collision, and piracy.[8] On land, an American could spend a lifetime without encountering an agent of the British government, let alone worry about Britain's relations with other European nations. The ocean, however, was another matter. As Benjamin Franklin told the House of Commons in 1766, "the sea is yours": "You maintain by your fleets, the safety of navigation in it, and keep it clear of pirates; you may have therefore a natural and equitable right to some toll or duty on merchandizes carried through that part of your dominions."[9]

Britons and Americans viewed the oceans over which Britain exercised this dominion as a law-bound space, and they assumed that European treaties and customs operated with as much force and authority on the high seas as they did on land. During the later seventeenth and eighteenth centuries, Europe's rulers devoted considerable time and effort to defining their maritime rights in America, far more so, in fact, than they did territorial questions such as the location of boundaries in Acadia or Indian relations in the Ohio valley. At the peace of Utrecht in 1713, for example, Britain left the terms of the Acadian cession vague, passing in a few words over the question of what was and was not being transferred. On the other hand, the *asiento* agreement with Spain, which authorized the British South Sea Company to make an annual shipment of slaves to Spanish America, consisted of forty-two articles, with provisions that governed everything from the age and sex of the captives that the company was licensed to sell in Spanish ports to the duties that Spanish officials had a right to levy in return.[10] Utrecht also turned out to be a decisive moment in the European campaign against piracy, with Britain and France jointly pledging to punish the pirates of both nations and make a "terror and example" of them to others.[11] Although piracy did not entirely disappear, merchant ships throughout Britain's Atlantic empire were able to dispense with the weight and cost of carrying artillery for self-defense, and the price of insuring cargos on transatlantic voyages steadily fell.[12] For a businessman like Franklin, this alone was reason to be a loyal and dutiful subject of the Crown.

If Britain had a long history of upholding the maritime law of nations in American waters—a history, according to the future earl of Liverpool Charles Jenkinson, that helped "preserve the Freedom of Navigation for

all nations"—the rights that it claimed under that law expanded considerably in the two decades before the revolution.[13] This was partly because
Britain's naval capacity was so formidable, nearly equaling the combined tonnage of its two nearest competitors, France and Spain, and
making the North Atlantic a virtual British lake.[14] During the mid-century
wars with France and Spain, Britain devoted an unprecedented share of
this capacity to America. In keeping with the maritime strategy established during the wars against Louis XIV, the largest ships of the line,
especially the triple-deckers meant for regular, set-piece engagements,
remained in European waters, controlling the Western Approaches to
the English Channel and cruising in the Mediterranean. From the mid-
1740s onward, though, the purpose of this strategy shifted from a purely
European set of objectives to intercepting enemy ships headed for North
America and the West Indies and acting as a vanguard for the navy's stations in the colonies. Following the outbreak of the Seven Years' War, the
king's ships performed this service with devastating efficiency, strengthening the British army on the North American mainland and giving
Britain's cruisers a free hand in the Caribbean.[15] In making the case for
the new strategy in 1758, Jenkinson, for one, claimed that trade with
America had become too important for Britain to tolerate "usurpations"
there by its European rivals.[16] America, agreed another writer, was "the
only *real Seminary* of Commerce and Navigation in the Universe."[17]

Britain's changing priorities also reflected a more general shift that
took place in British thinking about the maritime law of nations. At the
heart of this change lay the vexed question of whether the ships of neutral powers had a right to trade with Britain's enemies in time of war. In
what became known as the Rule of the War of 1756—so-called because it
was first articulated during the Seven Years' War—Britain began seizing
neutral ships that traded with the French, targeting in particular ships
flying the flag of the Dutch Republic but also the merchantmen of Swe-
den, Denmark, and, at times, Spain. In the case of the Dutch, the new
rule allowed British warships and admiralty courts to disregard provisions in the Anglo-Dutch Treaty of 1674 that protected the Netherlands'
carrying trade in America and to seize as lawful prize any Dutch ships
found "carrying on that trade of the King's enemies, which is not allowed them in time of peace."[18] Because these rights only applied to

wartime commerce, Britain insisted that they were consistent with its peacetime commitment to the principles of free navigation, but the Rule of 1756 had the effect of giving Britain's maritime forces the same extensive rights over civilian property at sea as regular soldiers who occupied hostile and neutral territory on land. As the German-born financier Nicolas Magens wrote of Britain's maritime rights in 1755, the main purpose of "Sea-Battles" was not "so much to kill People, as to be Masters of Trade, whereby People live; and by stopping their Supplies, to compel our Enemies in the End to live in Friendship with us." "What signifies our being Masters at Sea," Magens wondered, "if we shall not have Liberty to stop [neutral] Ships from serving our Enemy?"[19]

Not surprisingly, the Rule of 1756 was deeply unpopular in Europe, with much of the controversy centering on Britain's apparent disregard for the treaty rights of one of its oldest allies. During the American Revolution, Admiral George Rodney showed how extensive the rights that Britain claimed were when he sacked the Dutch entrepôt of Saint Eustatius in the West Indies in February 1781, weeks after Britain declared war on the Dutch Republic for trading with the Americans and supplying Congress with gunpowder and other war materiel. (Franklin, for one, sent his dispatches from Paris to Congress via the island.) In an episode that triggered riots in Amsterdam, a parliamentary inquiry at Westminster, and multiple lawsuits in England, several of which were still pending at the time of Rodney's death in 1792, the admiral's forces stripped everything of value that they could find on the rocky outcropping, even ransacking graves. The island's 350-member Jewish community, some of whom were British subjects, suffered especially. On Rodney's orders, husbands and fathers were separated from their families, their clothes were ripped open "to search for concealed money," and they were banished, often with no idea of where they were headed. Convinced that Loyal American and British merchants on the island had also been trading with the Americans, Rodney had his officers confiscate their property as well. Only the island's sugar planters were left unmolested, but they were minor players in an economy driven almost entirely by foreign trade.[20] "[W]hether the acts were defensible or not," wrote the *Annual Register* in 1781, it was painful to recount the details of an affair that had incurred "the odium of all Europe."[21]

Targeting the seaborne trade of neutral governments was a dangerous and costly policy, one that left Britain increasingly isolated in Europe and that led to the formation of an anti-British League of Armed Neutrality by Russia and the Baltic powers in 1780, but it was also consistent with the rights that Britain claimed over people who could not claim the protection of European treaties and customs. Significantly, during the Seven Years' War, and again during the American Revolutionary War, Britain insisted that the Dutch and other nominally friendly merchants who traded with the enemy were little better than vagrants and renegades on land, whose ambiguous nationality and allegiance enabled them to engage in covert acts of war while claiming the rights of peace.[22] Speaking in 1781 of the polyglot community of British, French, Dutch, and North American merchants who used Saint Eustatius as a base for illicit trade, the *Annual Register* claimed that the island's "checkered and transient inhabitants" were so involved "in traffic and gain, that when Holland herself was engaged in a war," they traded with the Republic's enemies as if there had been "no rupture with the parent state."[23] Admiral Rodney used similar terms to describe the British and Loyalist merchants whom his forces apprehended on the island, noting the "respect and humanity" that "a declared enemy" was entitled to claim while insisting that "a perfidious people, wearing the mask of friendship, [but acting as] traitors to their country, and rebelling against their king, deserve[d] no favour or consideration."[24] This of course was how the British had described the Acadians in 1755, and it carried similar implications in the Caribbean. As Lord Germain reminded the House of Commons during the first of Parliament's two inquiries into the island's capture in 1781, most of the merchants who "call[ed] themselves inhabitants" were actually English; if anyone deserved "exemplary punishment and severity," it was they. "[T]hese very people," noted Germain in a pointed retort to the ministry's critics, "pretend to [to be] . . . subjects of and seek protection from the very kingdom, which, by their unnatural and illicit commerce, they had attempted to ruin."[25] With such people, Britain could do as it pleased.

Given the enormous sums involved—some estimates put Rodney's share of the spoils from Saint Eustatius at more than £100,000—the government obviously had less-than-elevated reasons to condone the admiral's actions. Yet Germain's words underscored the extent to which "the Ocean [was] the public Road of the Universe," as Charles Jenkinson remarked in 1758, where the seaborne merchants of one nation had little trouble adopting the emblems of another. The result was to prolong the duration of Britain's wars and to delay the return of peace.[26] In the years before the revolution, some of the most convincing evidence of mercantile double-dealing came from colonial vice-admiralty judges such as Jamaica's Edward Long and New York's Lewis Morris, father of the revolutionary leader Gouverneur Morris. As Morris noted in a prize case that came before his court in 1758, Dutch merchants and seamen resorted "to all possible Arts for concealing the true Proprietors of the Cargoe" on board their ships. Often, according to Morris, "the Covering [was] so well laid on, that a Detection of the enemys Property [eluded] . . . the severest searching into the Ships Documents, or the Strictest Examination of the Crew."[27] In an indication of how difficult foiling such schemes could be, Captain John Gardner of the Dutch schooner *Koninghen Esther*, who was a natural-born Englishman from Newcastle-upon-Tyne but who had become a naturalized Dutch subject with a wife and children on Curacao, testified in a prize case from the late 1750s that before his ship was condemned on Jamaica it was stopped on the high seas by a Rhode Island privateer, "who detained her for the Space of about three Days, and searched her as thoroughly as possibly [*sic*] in every part." Although the ship's officers "examined the whole Cargo," along with the ship's crew and papers, the commander eventually let the vessel go, convinced that nothing was amiss.[28]

In the name of limiting the duration of its wars with other nations, and in so doing to hasten the return of peace, Britain thus sought to clamp down on illicit trade of all descriptions, including, often, the trade of its own subjects. To be sure, it could be hard to differentiate smuggling by British and colonial merchants from the commerce of others. At times, Britain's merchants evaded wartime embargos by becoming naturalized subjects of neutral governments or by hiring ships and seamen from other countries to give "a foreign Name" to enemy property. After one of his cruisers detained a Danish vessel off Jamaica with a cargo of French goods in 1761, Rear-Admiral Charles Holmes wrote that the captain, though a natural-born Dane, was "no more than a Machine to blind the

Government [to the] . . . shameful and criminal" activities of a cabal of merchants from Dublin and New York.[29] Merchants in ports throughout the British Atlantic also freighted enemy goods in their own ships, using neutral entrepôt like Saint Eustatius and Monte Cristi, the Spanish way station across the border from French Saint-Domingue, to make it look as though they were carrying property to and from the territory of nations with which Britain was at peace. "I have got from the Governor . . . a Certificate that the Cargoe [that] I bought from [a French coasting vessel] was purchased from Spaniards," wrote Richard Mercer, one of several British agents at Monte Cristi, of a scheme to disguise a shipment of French sugar by sending it to North America in the hold of a New York privateer.[30] According to Edward Long, most of the British trade at Monte Cristi during the early 1760s was conducted on behalf of French planters on Saint-Domingue. "[B]y this means," wrote Long, North American merchants and ship owners "thought it no injury to their consciences to swear positively, 'That they did, dispose of, or deliver their outward cargo *to Spaniards,* and did receive the proceeds or homeward cargoe *from Spaniards* also,'" even though the cargo was invariably French.[31]

If the illicit trade of Britain's own merchants was entangled with the trade of its rivals, however, the government's treatment of the two was noticeably different, with merchants who could prove that they were the subjects of another European government often having the better claim to protection. During the late 1750s, Britain was particularly attentive to Spain's neutral rights. Among the beneficiaries was Felipe Ybañez, a ship captain from Trinidad, Cuba, whose cargo was seized by a New York privateer in 1756. Although in the view of one historian Captain Ybañez was clearly "evading the laws of his own country," and he may have been a pirate, fears in England that Spain would become involved in the war that had just been declared against France repeatedly prompted British officials to take the Spaniard's side.[32] On learning that *La Virgen del Rosario,* Ybañez's ship, had been plundered, the governor of Jamaica wrote his counterpart at New York, Sir Charles Hardy, asking him to apprehend the offending captain when he returned to his home port.[33] For his part, Ybañez noted that Lord Holdernesse, the British secretary in charge of colonial affairs, had written Governor Hardy describing the seizure of his ship's cargo as "contrary to all Humanity and Good Faith," and Ybañez claimed that several British officials encouraged him to contest the action.[34] Responding to complaints by Spain's envoy in London, Lord Holdernesse pressed matters still further, instructing the governor of New York to begin proceedings for piracy against Richard Haddon, captain of the schooner that made the capture.[35] Although Judge Morris did not find sufficient evidence in the ensuing case to support such a "heavy charge," he agreed that the "Seizure had been Irregularly Made." In June 1761 Morris ruled that Haddon had violated his original instructions, thereby forfeiting the £1,500 bond for good behavior that all captains were required to post when they accepted the command of private ships of war.[36]

Occasionally, this determination to extend the protection of British laws and institutions to law-abiding foreigners like Felipe Ybañez—if that is what Ybañez was—encroached on the rights of British subjects in other areas as well, especially in matters touching on servitude and slavery. Because the Admiralty regarded the Royal Navy's regular warships as English territory, naval commanders were not above admonishing their own officers that "the laws of this country admit of no badges of slavery," as Vice-Admiral Francis Holburne wrote on learning that John James, master of the *Northumberland*, was keeping a slave as his personal servant from his days as a Boston ship captain.[37] With growing frequency, colonial vice-admiralty judges extended the same consideration to black seamen on board the vessels of other nations, doing so with particular alacrity if a European government seemed likely to vouch for their status as freemen. In a 1746 case involving a cargo of slaves captured with a French sloop, the vice-admiralty court at Newport, Rhode Island, condemned every captive in the ship's hold except a "Negro named Henry who pretends to be free." Because Henry lacked papers to support his claim, the judge ordered the prisoner to "remain in [his] Captors hands," but he also gave him "three years to prove his freedom."[38] Fifteen years later, in deciding the fate of a "Spanish Negro" named Joseph, Judge Richard Morris of New York did not insist on even these conditions, accepting a shipmate's testimony that Joseph was "a free man" and therefore not "liable to Condemnation."[39] By 1760, when George Thomas, governor of the Leeward Islands, decided not to free the multiracial crew of a Martinique privateer who had refused quarter to several people on board a British vessel, the action seemed sufficiently unusual to warrant a special letter to William Pitt, explaining why he had condemned twenty of the crew "to be better instructed in the laws of war and humanity" through hard labor and servitude. "[S]uch savages," wrote Thomas, had no right "to the benefits of a cartel," but presumably the case was otherwise with law-abiding freemen.[40]

The liberation of blacks who could show that they were free and law-abiding subjects of a European government partook of the same logic that gave Britain an increasingly free hand with white merchants and sailors who lacked that status: both showed the growing authority of European treaties and customs in American waters, as well as Britain's willingness to enforce them. In explaining his seizure of commercial property on Saint Eustatius, Admiral Rodney was clearly mindful of the distinction between law-abiding subjects and pirates, vagabonds, and smugglers, referring to the Dutch entrepôt as a den of "Robbers, Adventurers, Betrayers of their Country[,] and Rebels to their King."[41] Although Rodney's treatment of the island's Jews suggested anti-Semitic motives, he may also have assumed (mistakenly) that Jewish merchants were a nationally unaffiliated community whose plight would go unnoticed in Europe. Significantly, in their efforts to gain compensation, traders like Abraham Mendés sought to avoid any hint of statelessness, identifying themselves—as Mendés did on behalf of himself and his two brothers—as "natural born subjects of the States General in Holland" and explaining that they had been settled as merchants on the island since 1756 and that they had no connections with other nations, including the United States. Although they had little else in common, Mendés and his brothers followed the same strategy as the free blacks whom colonial vice-admiralty judges released from captured ships, arguing that they were free-born subjects of a European government and that they were "peaceably employed in a fair and lawful commerce."[42] In the words of a petition from a committee of Jewish merchants contesting Rodney's order of banishment, theirs was a religion that valued peace and obedience to the law. "It is the peculiar happiness of those who live under the British constitution," wrote the committee,

> to be indulged with their own sentiments in matters of religion, . . .
> and it is the peculiar happiness of the Hebrew nation to say, that

their religion teaches peace, and obedience to the government under which they live; and when civil dissensions have threatened to subvert the constitution, the Hebrew nation have ever preserved a peaceful demeanor, with true loyalty to the King, and a firm and steady attachment to the laws and constitution.[43]

Because Saint Eustatius was a conquered island subject to military law, the situation of the British and Jewish merchants whose property Rodney seized differed from that of merchants in ports like New York and Boston, yet Britain showed a similar determination and, at times, ruthlessness toward the latter group. Indeed, Britain's willingness to continue its efforts against the clandestine trade of merchants in North America ultimately played a crucial role in the coming of the American Revolution. Because the British believed that smuggled goods accounted for "about a Third of [the colonies'] actual Imports" in peacetime, American merchants and seamen often seemed to be no more trustworthy or mindful of the law than the Dutch.[44] In the words of an opinion upholding the imprisonment of Peter Dorey, captain of the sloop *Polly,* for making a false declaration to port officials, New York's vice-admiralty court held in 1772 that shipmasters were "so much Citizens of the World that they cannot be considered as tied to this or any other province."[45] "[W]herever the Acts of Navigation are disregarded," concurred Thomas Whately in his defense of the Grenville ministry's reforms, Britain's colonies in America were "no longer *British* Colonies, but Colonies of the Countries they trade to."[46] Thus the governor of Massachusetts, Francis Bernard, reported shortly after detaining a Mississippi trader in 1761 for smuggling that the ship's master had started his voyage by sailing to Monte Cristi, where he freighted a load of Saint-Domingue sugar to Jamaica; there, "in conjunction with an English Renegade" from Saint Thomas, who had been "pass[ing] for a Dane," the captain fitted out the ship with naval stores for New Orleans; finally, before returning to Boston, he entered into a partnership with "a Frenchman who has been very much versed in trade with the English and is"—Bernard claimed— "familiarly known in Rhode Island." The scheme's sole purpose, warned the governor, was "to buy Shipping and freight it with provisions, naval stores and ammunition" for Britain's enemies.[47] Although subjects of the British Crown, such people were in effect the subjects of whichever government they served, and they were engaged in acts of war against their own nation.

In the years before the revolution, the British did not always agree on how to manage this entangled commerce to their own advantage. Following the advice of writers like the Scottish political economist Adam Smith, should the government reduce—if not repeal—Parliament's restrictions on colonial trade, secure in the knowledge that Britain's flourishing merchant marine would keep the Royal Navy supplied with ships and sailors? Or, as ultimately happened, should Britain hew to mercantilist orthodoxy and enforce the Navigation Acts in America with greater vigor? Despite his wartime efforts to prevent North American merchants from trading with the enemy, Edward Long, for one, appeared in his *History of Jamaica* to advocate a degree of commercial freedom with the neighboring ports of Spanish America. He did so, however, largely because Spain's own restrictions tended "to operate against our vital interests" and because he believed that the benefits of such a policy would accrue entirely to Britain.[48] For the most part, Britons were sure that the commercial inroads of foreign rivals threatened their maritime supremacy, and they believed that the only way to meet that threat was by stopping what George Grenville and Charles Jenkinson called the "contraband Trade" of their own people.[49] Writing in 1774, William Allen spoke for people throughout the British Atlantic when he claimed that anyone who purchased "contraband Goods . . . strengthens the Hands of an implacable Enemy," including both France and "those Pack-Horses of the World, the Dutch." "[T]hese silent Sons of *Mammon*," wrote Allen in a pointed jab at colonial smugglers who did business with merchants on Saint Eustatius, "supply half *America* . . . with Spice, Linen, Tea, &c." In the hands of fair traders, such goods "would naturally flow in the Channel of Commerce to the Mother Country."[50] Only by remaining vigilant against such abuses could the British hope to ensure lasting peace.

With the goal of safeguarding the treaty rights that they had expended so much blood and treasure to acquire, the British embarked on a series of sweeping reforms in the Seven Years' War's aftermath to strengthen their maritime empire in America. The salient features included enhancing the powers of vice-admiralty judges, trebling the number of customs officials in colonial ports, establishing a new commission at Boston to enforce the Navigation Acts, and creating a naval "sea guard" of forty-four vessels to intercept merchant ships as they entered or left American harbors. In the main, these plans were meant to pay for the expanded navy and army that Britain's new possessions in America seemed to require. Given the rapid recovery of French naval power after 1763 and the Spanish Bourbon Reforms of Charles III, which it was widely feared had the potential to turn Spain's American dominions into a serious rival to Britain's own empire, the ministers who sponsored these measures were keenly aware that empires of the sea were inherently transitory constructs, which could be lost as quickly as they had been gained. Speaking of the need for an enlarged "Peace Establishment" in 1766, Thomas Whately, for one, insisted that "the Extent of our Dominions, the Encrease of our Power, the Resentment of our Enemies, and the Jealousies of our Neighbours [all] require it."[51] In the words of a sermon that John Bonar, chaplain of the *Cereberus,* preached at Spithead on the occasion of the king's review of the fleet in 1773, "to see our Navy here, in [this] quiet Harbour, give peace to Europe; and keep the World in Awe, by the bare Remembrance of their former Exploits," was every bit as stirring as the trophies that Britain's fleets brought home in "time of War." "Happy People!" Bonar exclaimed, "who, when the Clouds of War begin to gather all around, are saved from the breaking of the Storm . . . by their rapid [and] formidable preparations against it."[52]

If the British believed that they needed to protect the recent peace from European rivals, though, proponents of the new measures just as often had as their object Britain's own colonists, especially the merchants and seamen whose protean loyalties threatened Britain's ability to maintain its postwar supremacy. Because Britain's maritime reforms were largely a matter of enhancing powers that the government already possessed, they did not arouse the same principled opposition as Parliament's novel attempts, starting with the American Stamp Act in 1765, to fund a standing army of ten thousand regulars with direct colonial taxation. Still, the government's reforms were deeply unpopular. For wealthy merchants like South Carolina's Henry Laurens or John Hancock of Boston, the experience of having their ships seized by the Royal Navy's smuggling cutters was often decisive in tipping them toward radical patriotism, and the new regulations did nothing to curry favor with ordinary jack-tars, many of whom had cut their political teeth resisting the navy's wartime press gangs during the 1740s and 1750s. During the Stamp Act crisis, the initial opposition to the tax in New York was largely the work of former privateer captains like Isaac Sears, and merchants and seamen alike were well represented in the crowds that gathered up and down the North American seaboard.[53] As Joseph Harrison, beleaguered collector of customs for the port of Boston, reported in June 1768, shortly after discovering John Hancock's sloop *Liberty* with an undeclared cargo of Madeira wine in its hold and a customs official locked in its cabin, the "running of Goods and Smuggling"—activities that merchants like Hancock had once carefully hid from view—had "become public Virtue and Patriotism." "Hancock and Liberty [is] the Cry here, as Wilkes and Liberty is in London!" wrote Harrison.[54] In the name of achieving lasting peace, Britain was charting a course that seemed likely to produce another war.

(2)

During the 1760s and early 1770s, the western Atlantic was already a recognized part of Europe's diplomatic republic. Although the Crown's maritime authority was far from absolute, Britons and Americans alike viewed the waters of North America and the Caribbean as an area where war between Europe's colonial powers was the exception and peace the norm and where, in theory if not always in practice, Britain had the authority to compel its own subjects to respect European agreements and where it could force other nations to do the same. In North America's interior, on the other hand, things were different. Although Europe's colonial powers could—and increasingly did—hold each other accountable for the actions of their subjects and allies, there was little agreement over where the boundaries of their possessions were, nor did they always control the resulting conflicts. At the peace of Aix-la-Chapelle (1748), which ended the series of European wars that started with the War of Jenkins' Ear in 1739, Britain and France acknowledged this fact, referring their North American differences to a special commission and turning a blind eye to hostilities while the delegates negotiated. To do otherwise, wrote

Charles Jenkinson in 1758, would have been to allow "trifling" disputes in the colonies to dictate the course of war and peace in Europe. Because the "rights of the European Kingdoms" were so uncertain, colonial wars in America often lasted for years, "while the Mother Countries . . . lived, if not in Friendship, at least in Peace."[55] The most expedient way to maintain that peace was for Europe's colonial powers to overlook treaty violations on the North American mainland in the same way that they did the activities of merchants who traded with whomever they pleased in the Caribbean.

As with the war at sea, however, the Seven Years' War suggested that Europe and America had become too integrated for this bifurcated geography to remain viable. Not only did the war's global scope belie the trivial nature of disputes in Acadia and the Ohio valley, but the fighting drew territory as far west as the Mississippi River into the vortex of Britain's European diplomacy. Reflecting in 1759 on the new proximity of the North American mainland to Europe, Arthur Young concluded that Britain could no longer afford to follow the time-honored practice of "stop[ping] the encroachments of the French for a time," while the two nations left their colonial differences "to be adjusted by commissaries." For any peace to be lasting, the British government would need to take a much more direct role in colonial affairs and insist on defining "the exact bounds of each nation . . . with the greatest nicety."[56] Following the conquest of Canada in 1760, Benjamin Franklin made the same point with respect to the likely consequences of the province's annexation by Britain. "[I]f peace be an advantage," wrote Franklin, giving Britain dominion over all of France's possessions in North America must eventually "be such to all *Europe*":

> The present war teaches us, that disputes arising in *America,* may be an occasion of embroiling nations who have no concerns there. . . . Injuries are . . . committed on both sides, resentment provoked, the colonies first engaged, and then the mother countries. And two great nations can scarce be at war in *Europe,* but some other prince or state thinks it a convenient opportunity, to revive some ancient claim, seize some advantage, obtain some territory, or enlarge some power at the expense of a neighbor. The flames of war once kindled, often spread far and wide, and the mischief is infinite.[57]

Clearly, it was in everyone's interests for Britain to make peace on terms that would be as enduring in North America as they were on the high seas and in Europe.

Superficially, this was what Britain's emissaries at the peace of Paris in 1763 achieved, substituting internationally recognized boundaries for disputed borderlands throughout North America and spelling out the colonial rights of the signatory nations in clear and unambiguous terms. Although the commercially vital port of New Orleans eluded Britain's grasp, the settlement abolished France's empire on the North American mainland, dividing its possessions between Britain and Spain, with the Mississippi serving as a "natural" boundary between their respective dominions. Because Britain gained all of Spanish Florida, the peace also broke Spain's monopoly on the Gulf of Mexico, and it resolved the territorial rivalry over the "neutral islands" in the Caribbean by confirming Britain's title to Saint Vincent, Dominica, Grenada, and Tobago, while ceding Saint Lucia to France. Without question, Britain was the main beneficiary of these terms, but defenders of the peace claimed that Europe's other colonial powers would benefit as well. As George Johnstone, governor of British West Florida, wrote on welcoming Spain's governor, Antonio de Ulloa, to Louisiana in 1766, settling "the Boundary Line of Empire by notorious Limits" augured well for both nations. "The last War," explained Johnstone, started with a dispute over the rights of Britain and France "on the Ohio or Belle Riviere." The recent treaty "rendered any Disputes on that Subject impossible."[58] In early 1764, when Spain deported a group of British logwood cutters from their settlements on Honduras Bay, despite treaty provisions acknowledging their right to be there, and when France did the same thing to a group of salt workers from Bermuda on Turks Island in the Bahamas, the most striking feature of the two incidents was how quickly they were resolved.[59]

Even as they welcomed the new clarity on such matters, Britons assumed that the settlement's durability would depend on how well the government dealt with three challenges, all related to Britain's authority on the North American mainland. As the Honduras and Turks Island incidents showed, the first involved the need to check violations of the recent treaty by France and Spain, whose governments resented Britain's triumph and who, it was generally believed, would seize the first opportunity to avenge their losses. To counter such threats, the king's ministers insisted that the Crown needed to retain the ability to use force without depending on either the colonies or the king's Indian allies. During the brief French and Spanish confrontations in 1764, the Grenville ministry did this by dispatching ships of the line from their normal posting in the English Channel to compel the Bourbon powers to pull back their forces.[60] But for the first time in the history of British America, the government also decided to keep a standing army of ten thousand regulars in Canada, the two Floridas, and North America's Indian country. To some observers, the new establishment suggested that the government regarded the peace as little more than an "armed truce," as William Pitt—now in opposition—warned the House of Commons in 1764, yet most Britons, including Pitt, assumed that without such a force, the peace would be "hollow and unlikely to be permanent." Even some colonists admitted the need for regular troops. As John Dickinson observed in his *Letters from a Farmer in Pennsylvania* (1768), Britain's military policies, despite creating a pretext for parliamentary taxation, "seemed to have something gentle and kind in [their] intention, and to aim only *at our welfare.*" "In this age," wrote an English pamphleteer in 1766, "all the kingdoms in Europe maintain a standing military force." To ensure that France and Spain respected the peace, "America must have a considerable share" of such forces too.[61]

As happened on the high seas, one consequence of the army's new presence in North America was to compel a heightened respect on the part of British Americans for the rights of Britain's European neighbors, especially when those rights were sanctioned by a European treaty. During the Louisiana revolt of 1768, when the French Superior Council of New Orleans evicted the Spanish administration of Antonio de Ulloa, the conspiracy's leaders went out of their way to create an opening for British intervention, arguing that because the Spaniard had failed "to take possession of the colony with the usual formalities"—including proclaiming Spanish sovereignty with an artillery salute in New Orleans and lowering the French fleur-de-lis—Spain's attempts to alter the colony's laws were "encroachments" on the rights of people who were still legally "subjects of France."[62] Among those who thought they saw an opportunity for British expansion was West Florida's lieutenant governor Montfort

Browne, who claimed that the people of New Orleans hoped "to become British subjects" and urged London to intervene. As Frederick Haldimand, commander of the British garrison at Pensacola, informed the conspirators, however, the likely European repercussions of even a temporary British occupation of the province made such a step impossible.[63] Following the example of France, Britain watched as a Spanish force under the Irish general Alejandro O'Reilly re-occupied the province, abolishing the Superior Council and French law, trying the revolt's French leaders for treason, and executing five, including Pierre Marquis, a Swiss colonel of the provincial militia, who was charged with plotting to turn the colony into an independent republic.[64] "Permit me . . . to offer my congratulations on this occasion," wrote General Thomas Gage, commander of British forces in America, on learning of O'Reilly's arrival in New Orleans. Although the general made no mention of the revolt, he must have hoped that Spain would show similar restraint should his soldiers encounter similar difficulties in Boston.[65]

In many places, of course, the British army's position in the North American interior was no more secure than Spain's. During a visit to Pensacola in 1764, Lord Adam Gordon, colonel of the sixty-sixth regiment of foot in the West Indies, was shocked to discover that the three battalions assigned to East Florida and the Illinois territory could barely muster five hundred effectives, a third of their peacetime establishment. "Some of the Regiments are commanded by a Captain," wrote Gordon, adding that "the [number] of Absent Officers is too great [for] a Country . . . so little reconciled to our Constitution and Government."[66] In his *Concise Account of North America* (1765), the former ranger Robert Rogers expressed similar concerns, warning that the "British Empire in North America [had] become so extensive" that it was unreasonable to expect "any one man . . . to give a just account of its several parts."[67] Despite agreements with native leaders that they would "not Keep anything a secret from each other," British officials complained repeatedly that they were unable to prevent France and Spain from maintaining a presence among the Indians of the Gulf Coast and the Mississippi valley.[68] On learning in 1772 that Scutchabee, headman of a Lower Creek town on the Chattahoochee River, had accepted an invitation from the governor of Havana to visit Cuba, David Taitt, the local British agent, was unable to do more than extract a promise from the Creek leader that he would report "every thing that passes between him and the Governor" and that he would "hide nothing from his [British] Father."[69]

Not surprisingly, given Britain's attitudes toward seaborne trade, British officials viewed with particular concern the European traders who resided in Indian country, often taking Indian wives and living in Indian villages. As was clear from John Fitzpatrick, an Irish merchant who moved to Manchac in British West Florida after being expelled from New Orleans in 1769, Indian traders could be wealthy, and some were men of considerable refinement. During the two decades that he spent at Manchac, Fitzpatrick maintained an extensive circle of correspondents, using fellow merchants throughout North America and the Caribbean to keep abreast of the latest developments and acquiring a library that, at the time of his death in 1791, included Voltaire's *Universal History,* Tobias Smollett's *Roderick Random,* and the works of Alexander Pope.[70] But Indian traders could also be as protean in their loyalties as their counterparts on the seas, and they were often objects of official suspicion and distrust. In Fitzpatrick's case, following the Spanish invasion of West Florida in 1778, British soldiers looted his warehouse. He responded by placing himself and his common law French Creole wife under the protection of Spanish Louisiana's governor Bernardo de Galvéz, writing that Manchac's "remaining Inhabitants[,] heretofore English," had all been "obliged to turn Spaniards."[71] As Harry Gordon, the army's chief engineer for North America, wrote of Britain's position at Fort Chartres on the east bank of the Mississippi in the mid-1760s, the British had undisputed "Superiority over the French" in the region, yet French and Spanish merchants from Saint Louis and New Orleans continued to trade with Indians in the fort's vicinity, making Britain's garrison hardly worth the trouble and expense. "Coop'd up," lamented Gordon, "We make a foolish figure, [and] hardly have the Dominion of the Country."[72]

If Britain's was a hollow empire, the garrisons that Gordon visited nonetheless pointed to a new, more centralized form of empire, one that gave less agency to colonial soldiers and officials and that, in some places, did not even depend on American settlers.[73] It was also, the British claimed, an empire that was better able to meet its obligations to Europe's other colonial powers. Although the Privy Council opened both East and West Florida to British settlement in 1763, a particularly striking sign of this was the government's willingness to allow law-abiding foreigners to remain in both colonies.[74] Speaking of French squatters on what, until 1763, had been the legally vacant islands of Saint Vincent and Dominica, Thomas Whately wrote that their property was "not rightful" because the French king lacked the right to "grant where he had not Dominion." Given Britain's uncontested title to both islands under the recent peace, however, Whately saw no harm in the "Experiment" of allowing them to remain.[75] No doubt such promises rang hollow for Acadians who had been expelled from Nova Scotia and who began moving by the thousands to Spanish Louisiana in the mid-1760s, turning the area around New Orleans into a *"nouvelle l'Acadie."*[76] In the Quebec Act of 1774, on the other hand, Parliament took significant strides in the direction of greater tolerance, granting French Catholics freedom of religion and allowing the Catholic Church to continue collecting tithes. "The people of this Province," wrote Lord Adam Gordon as he journeyed up the Saint Lawrence valley in 1765, "seem not at all dissatisfied with their new Masters." Although Gordon acknowledged that the French did not yet understand (or like) "our Forms of Civil Government," he was sure that most of Quebec's inhabitants would eventually "become useful Subjects, in Peace and War, if properly moulded."[77]

If Britain's relations with other Europeans bespoke a new commitment to European treaty law in the colonies, a similar determination was evident in the response to a second set of challenges involving Indian relations. As was clear from Pontiac's War—the Indian uprising that convulsed the Ohio valley and Great Lakes region between 1763 and 1766—the end of the Seven Years' War was a catastrophe for Native Americans, destroying the check that France had placed on British ambitions in the North American interior and opening enormous new tracts of indigenous land to white settlement. No less significant, Pontiac's War showed that Britain lacked the resources to compel the Indians to accept the new order, as native war parties seized nearly every British outpost from Fort Pitt in western Pennsylvania to Detroit. Although the British army used provincial auxiliaries to restore order in 1763 and 1764, one effect was to strengthen the case for keeping regulars in North America, most of whom were initially used to garrison strongholds in Indian country. The war also forced the British government to create what amounted to an Indian protectorate west of the Appalachians, temporarily prohibiting settlement on native land in the Royal Proclamation of 1763 and leaving responsibility for Indian diplomacy with two Crown-appointed superintendents. To colonial speculators like George Washington, whose Ohio valley incursions had started the Seven Years' War a decade earlier, these polices amounted to little more than a "temporary expedient to quiet the Minds of the Indians," but there were people who thought they saw the makings of what one historian has called an enduring "Pax Britannica in North America."[78] According to Lord Egremont, even the king hoped to "conciliate the Affections of the Indian Nations, by every Act of strict Justice."[79] "Such an instance of our goodwill," wrote Henry Ellis, Georgia's former governor, of Britain's new Indian policies in 1763, will "fix them more firmly in our Interest, than all the Talks we can give them, or all the Presents we can bestow on them."[80]

In seeking to placate the Indians, the British were clearly seeking to restore local peace, but they were also attempting to bring them within the terms of the peace settlement in Europe. In his request to New England's governors for provincial troops in December 1763, General Gage explained that the soldiers would be used to punish native warriors who had rallied to Pontiac's standard and to "obtain a peace which shall be lasting and durable."[81] Although Gage made no mention of France or Spain, one oft-heard concern was that the continuation of even low-grade hostilities in Indian country would create an opening for Britain's European rivals. In his *History of the Late War* (1772), Thomas Mante, a former army officer and sometime French spy, attributed Pontiac's War in part to the intrigues of French merchants, many of whom, he claimed, encouraged the Indians to consider the British "in the light of masters, and even tyrants, rather than friends."[82] For anyone who remembered the international consequences of Jumonville's death in 1754, there were also reasons to fear that Britain's Indian allies might commit unauthorized hostilities against other Europeans. When a band of Creek hunters "barbarously murdered" several French castaways on East Florida's Gulf Coast in 1766, the British governor James Grant took care to show the survivors every civility, securing the release of three prisoners who were still being held captive in Creek towns and arranging for a ship to take the captain's wife and the rest of the crew to New Orleans. No less important, Grant sent word to the local Creek headman that the "Great King [was] at Peace with the French and Spaniards, and that he [would] be very angry at his Indian Children, if they kill any of them."[83]

As such encounters made clear, Britain was able to go only so far in forcing Indians to honor the Crown's agreements with other European nations. On receiving a request in the early 1770s from a French army officer for help recovering a slave who had fled to the Chickasaws near Manchac, John Fitzpatrick readily agreed, noting that the officer had "used [him] with the greatest politeness" during his own Indian captivity in 1764 and that he had been waiting for a chance to "return" his generosity.[84] But Fitzpatrick must have realized that there were no guarantees that his efforts would meet with success. Although Britain's Indian treaties routinely included clauses promising "to restore Negroes and Deserters," the decentralized structure of indigenous society meant that to be successful, intermediaries had to negotiate with "a number of Leading Men," each of whom had "Weight in the direction of their Affairs."[85] Complicating such proceedings further, Indians often accepted runaway slaves as adopted family members, granting freedom to any who took Indian wives. According to the naturalist William Bartram, practically every Indian town that he visited during the 1770s contained black fugitives, and they invariably "were free and in as good circumstances as their masters."[86] "Daily are the Depredations which they commit," wrote West Florida's governor, William Johnstone, of his relations with the Creek Indians in 1766, accusing the residents of Creek towns of stealing cattle, "harboring Slaves and Deserters," firing on "the crew of a Spanish Vessel" in Pensacola Bay, and shooting "one Mr. Gray thro' the Leg." "In short," Johnstone warned, the Indians' "Contempt for the English Nation is such, that the common Name they now give them is that of 'Fowl,' saying, 'that they can equally knock off the Head of the one Animal as of the other, with Impunity.'"[87]

Nor were breaches of the peace limited to Native Americans. In the decade that followed the end of the Seven Years' War, poor, land-hungry American settlers flooded into the Ohio valley, creating a new white population of nearly fifty thousand by the time the first shots were exchanged on Lexington Common. In some places, the newcomers occupied land that had been purchased through the regular channel of Indian treaties and diplomacy. Often, though, they went wherever they pleased, planting farms "without any title whatsoever" and inviting charges of barbarism and lawlessness.[88] When a group of settlers shot and killed a young Seneca man on the Susquehanna River in 1769, Sir William Johnson wrote that they had done so "without the least provocation." There were also reports of settlers who disguised themselves as Indians and robbed other whites. Because such acts of impunity were rarely punished, the people who committed them had little reason to stop. Speaking of the Seneca who had been murdered on the Susquehanna, Johnson warned that it was not the only such incident and that acts of violence on the part of the region's "infatuated and lawless inhabitants" were common. Once again, this was how the British had described the Acadians during the 1750s, and it was not so different from the terms used to describe merchants who traded with Britain's enemies and privateers who seized neutral ships. Although backcountry settlers could be even more violent, they, too, had their own law, and they were only partly accountable to the government that they claimed to serve. With good reason, Indians complained that it was often impossible for them to "have any great dependence on the white People."[89]

Even so, the years before the revolution showed a new willingness in some quarters to make peace with Native Americans by treating them as part of what Edmund Burke, speaking of Britain's responsibilities in India, called a benevolent, law-bound "federal trust."[90] During Pontiac's War, as Indian raids prompted thousands of settlers to flee previously secure towns like Carlisle, Pennsylvania, colonial newspapers dusted off the old jeremiads, denouncing "savages" who killed "defenceless frontier Settlers without Mercy," but not everyone accepted such conventions. When the Scots-Irish "Paxton Boys" murdered two groups of Christian Indians in December 1763, hacking the second group to pieces while they prayed at a Lancaster, Pennsylvania, workhouse, colonial authorities placed the rest of the community under the protection of a body of Highland soldiers and sent a delegation, including Benjamin Franklin, to persuade the self-appointed militia to disband. In an anonymous pamphlet, Franklin made clear that the massacre's Irish perpetrators were the true savages, not their helpless victims. "If it be right to kill

[such] Men," asked Franklin in a none-too-subtle reference to the posse's Celtic features, why not avenge their barbarous deeds by allowing the victims' own kith and kin to do the same to "all the freckled red-haired Men, Women, and Children" that they could find? Colonel Henry Bouquet, the Swiss-born ranger who helped end the insurrection with his victory over the Indians at Bushy Run in 1764, had nothing but disdain for men like the Paxton Boys, writing that they were cowards who "found it easier to kill Indians in a Goal [i.e., jail], than to fight them fairly in the Woods."[91] In Robert Rogers's play *Ponteach,* which the former ranger wrote after moving to London, the most unsavory characters are a pair of Indian-hating woodsmen bent on "hunt[ing] the savage Herd where-e'er they're found" and a Scottish trader named Mc-Dole, who thinks it "no Crime to cheat and gull an *Indian.*"[92] Britain, on the other hand, held out the possibility of peace based on paternal benevolence and the rule of law.

Although Britain's new humanitarianism did not always make a difference in Indian country, it occasionally did. In West Florida the ministry dismissed Governor Johnstone in 1767 on charges that he had "commenced hostilities against the [Creek] Indians without any directions" from Whitehall. British governors, explained Lord Shelburne, were expected "to make the Indians sensible that they owe their peace to His Majesty's clemency and his desire of protecting not of destroying them."[93] In disputes between Indians and settlers, British officials occasionally went even further, holding whites, especially poor whites, accountable to indigenous customs. When an East Florida "cracker"—an ethnic pejorative that became popular during the 1760s—murdered an Indian on the Saint Johns River in 1769, James Grant, the colony's governor, had the settler put to death "in the presence of the murdered Indian's father and a number of other Indians." Such methods troubled Grant, but the consequences would have been much worse, he told his superiors in London, had he not given the Indians "blood for blood according to their idea of the law."[94] Speaking of his first encounter with Pontiac near Detroit in 1760, Robert Rogers wrote that the Ottawa chief did not think of "himself as a conquered Prince, [but] . . . expected to be treated with the respect and honour due to a King or Emperor, by all who came into his Country." While Indians in general were vengeful and "easily induced . . . to make wars," Rogers insisted that Pontiac's reason for going to war in 1763 was "to make a peace" that would be as "honourable to himself" as it was "to the King of Great Britain." "Were proper measures taken," Rogers observed, "this Indian might be rendered very serviceable" to Britain's interests in North America.[95]

As events would show, of course, the most serious threat to Britain's effort to craft a lasting peace in North America came not from France or Spain, or from Indian friends and foes, but from the resistance that greeted Parliament's attempts to check the autonomy of the colonies on the Atlantic seaboard. Despite the hostility toward what Hector St. John de Crévecoeur called "half civilized, half savage" settlers in Indian country, the British continued to think of their North American empire as a settler-based dominion, one where federal trusts of the sort that Burke associated with Britain's empire in South Asia were the exception rather than the norm. In the Proclamation of 1763, the government opened the most accessible of Britain's new territories—Quebec, the two Floridas, and Grenada—to British settlement, and it did the same in separate enactments to the "unoccupied" Caribbean islands of Dominica, Tobago, and Saint Vincent.[96] At the Treaty of Fort Stanwix in 1768, Britain took additional steps in this direction, negotiating a controversial agreement that made Cherokee land in Kentucky available to settlers from Pennsylvania and Virginia, and the government eventually approved a new colony for the district to be named Vandalia in honor of George III's German queen.[97] Speaking of Jamaica's plan to colonize the disputed island of Rattan in Honduras Bay, Edward Long wrote that it was "astonishing" that Britain would allow any place where British settlements could flourish "to remain unexplored, unpossessed, uninhabited." Only through "colonizing and trade," wrote Long, could Britain hope to counter the "growing and united power of France and Spain." Trade and settlement, he claimed, were "the only solid foundations on which we can build a successful opposition in this part of the world."[98]

If the settler empire remained paramount, however, the regular army that the Crown needed to enforce European treaty law in North America's interior created obligations that, proponents argued, could only be met through parliamentary taxes, and such levies were at odds with the rights of self-government that Britain's colonists viewed as their birthright.

Although Parliament's attempts at colonial taxation have sometimes been taken as a sign that Britain was treating Britons in America "differently from ordinary men and women who happened to live in England," apologists for the Stamp Act and its successors generally viewed the new measures in exactly the opposite way, that is, as a means of incorporating Americans into the national system of revenue as it existed in Britain.[99] In Thomas Whately's classic formulation, Parliament was justified in taxing the colonists because it "virtually" represented "all *British* Subjects," regardless of where within the king's dominions they lived. "[E]very Member of Parliament," Whately explained, "sits in the House, not as Representative of his own constituents, but as one of that august Assembly by which all the Commons of *Great-Britain* are represented." Because the British Empire was a community defined by long-distance warfare, one where professional soldiers and sailors did most of the fighting and where most people were armchair patriots, the British argued that the only way for Americans to fulfill their military and fiscal obligations was by contributing to the national revenue in the same way as men and women in Britain. "There were twelve millions of people in England and Ireland who were not represented" in the House of Commons, noted Lord Mansfield during the debate over the Stamp Act, yet each paid taxes levied in Parliament. By taxing the colonists without their consent, agreed the attorney general Fletcher Norton, "we use North America as we use ourselves."[100]

Had Parliament's reforms succeeded, the consequences would have been nothing short of momentous, placing the British army on the same permanent footing in the colonies as the Royal Navy, strengthening the Crown's capacity for independent action in North America's interior, and limiting the autonomy and stature of the colonies' own institutions. To many Americans, the last of these was the most objectionable part of the new measures, far more so, in some ways, than the threat to the abstract right of no taxation without representation. "Americans," insisted the Massachusetts House of Representatives in an open letter to Lord Chancellor Camden in 1768,

> have ever been considered by the nation as subjects remote; and succeeding kings . . . have always directed their requisitions, to be laid before the representatives of their people in America. . . . Must it

not then be grievous to subjects, who have in many repeated instances afforded the strongest marks of loyalty and zeal for the service of their sovereign, to be now called on, in a manner, which implies a distrust of a free and willing compliance?[101]

John Dickinson expressed the same concerns in his *Letters from a Farmer in Pennsylvania,* warning that once Parliament began funding the ordinary functions of government in America with taxes that it raised on its own authority, the colonies' assemblies would cease to enjoy even the "puny privileges of French parliaments." "Some few of them may meet of their own accord, by virtue of their charters," Dickinson speculated. "But what will they have to do when they are met?"[102] As Franklin lamented in 1774, the British Empire might have endured indefinitely had Parliament left the assemblies' fiscal rights undisturbed and allowed "the King's subjects in those remote countries the pleasure of shewing their zeal and loyalty."[103]

What neither Franklin nor Dickinson seemed to realize was that the fiscal autonomy that each viewed as fundamental to the constitution of Britain's settler empire was ultimately what the proponents of colonial taxation most dreaded. In particular, defenders of Grenville's reforms insisted that however remote and autonomous the older colonies might have been when they were first settled, Europe and North America were now too unified for Americans to fulfill their military and fiscal obligations to the Crown through any means other than paying taxes levied by Parliament. As late as the commencement of hostilities on Lexington Common, ministerial writers were still noting occasions during the 1740s and 1750s when colonial assemblies had refused to allocate funds for their own defense, when the assistance that the colonies did provide was inadequate, and when provincial soldiers deserted or refused to follow orders. In the words of a pamphlet sometimes attributed to the Irish barrister William Greatrakes, Americans had rejected every chance to "associate and unite" for their own defense, "from the peace of Utrecht to the war of 1756."[104] "We boast of our bountiful compliance with the requisitions made during the last war," agreed the Maryland Loyalist Jonathan Boucher in 1774, but even then "there . . . was more than one rich province that refused to comply, although the war was in the very bowels of the country."[105] As William Knox warned in 1768, the only alternative to raising a parliamentary revenue in America was military vulnerability, followed, he feared, by renewed war:

> If the national expence be reduced by the disbanding troops, suffering the navy to rot in harbor for want of repairs and mariners, dismantling fortresses, or suffering magazines to be exhausted; or, should the colonies be left without protection and a force sufficient to secure the fidelity of our new subjects; this would only be to invite hostility, and expose the nation to insult, perhaps destruction. Present safety cannot be had without an expensive peace established.[106]

Peace and taxation, it seemed, were synonymous.

Although neither the Americans nor their British "friends" allowed such claims to go unanswered, Britain's reforms amounted to nothing less than a series of attempts to remove the last vestiges of the conditions that had once placed British America "beyond the line." In part, these plans reflected the widespread belief that North America had become such an integral part of Europe's diplomatic republic that Britain needed to maintain the same vigilance in America—based on the same regular military and naval establishments—that it did in Europe. For this reason, the British assumed that they were also justified in holding Britons in America accountable to the same obligations as their fellow subjects in Europe, including the obligation to abide by European customs and conventions in relations with foreign powers and the municipal duty to pay taxes levied by Parliament. Not surprisingly, a recurring theme in the British response to the American Revolution was that by disputing these obligations, the colonists were bent on returning both themselves and the rest of Britain's Atlantic empire to what Thomas Whately, speaking of the period before the first Navigation Act (1651), described as a chaotic world of "adventurers" and "fugitives." In *Taxation, No Tyranny*, Samuel Johnson had nothing but scorn for the pretensions of the American Congress, mocking those who would "quit the comforts of a warm home for . . . something which they think better." "These surely are brave words," commented Dr. Johnson, but they were not, he implied, words that the British government needed to take all that seriously.[107] If Americans did declare their colonies to be independent states, it was they, not the British, who would have to make their way as strangers amid the "states of the world," as John Dickinson warned his fellow delegates to the Continental Congress in Philadelphia on July 1, 1776, and it was they, in all likelihood, who would find themselves braving "the storm in a skiff made of paper."[108]

(3)

Although American independence was clearly a risky project, one that left its proponents vulnerable to charges of wishful thinking, if not reckless enthusiasm, the idea that Britain's reforms would lay the basis for lasting peace turned out to be equally fantastic. Among other things, the American Revolution showed just how dangerous the illusions spawned by imperial greatness could be, including illusions of peace and pacification. "History proves, that great conquests have always been ruinous to free governments," lamented Alexander Carlyle in 1776. "Was it for us," he asked his parishioners at Inveresk, "to extend our dominions from pole to pole, and to all the shores that are washed by the Indian or Atlantic oceans?"[109] Based on Parliament's failure to raise a significant revenue in America, Adam Smith was even more pointed, arguing in *Wealth of Nations* (1776) that the colonies for which Britain had expended so much blood and treasure during the 1740s and 1750s were not true "provinces of the British empire" but, rather, "a sort of splendid and showy equipage of empire." In an oft-quoted passage, Smith concluded:

> The rulers of Great Britain have, for more than a century, amused the people with the imagination that they possessed a great empire on the west side of the Atlantic. This empire, however, has hitherto existed in imagination only. It has hitherto been, not an empire, but the project of an empire; not a gold mine, but the project of a gold mine; a project which has cost, which continues to cost, and which, if pursued in the same way as it has been hitherto, is likely to cost, immense expence, without being likely to bring any profit.[110]

Britain's empire was an empire of the imagination.

If so, it was still a force to be reckoned with. Historians have long recognized the decade before the revolution as marking the origin of the great humanitarian movements that helped define the next century (or more) of Britain's imperial history: the abolition of slavery, the implementation of free trade, the protection of aboriginal rights, and the reform of British India. Each of these initiatives sprang from its own sources, yet all partook of a common desire to pacify the British Empire, purging it of what Richard Watson, bishop of Llandaff, in 1784 called the use of "unjust force" and bringing the government of its outlying regions within the ambit of European norms and institutions.[111] "He that admits no right but force," wrote Thomas Day in condemning the African slave trade in 1776, "arms every man against himself, and justifies all excesses."[112] William Bolts used nearly identical terms in his discussion of the East India Company's administration of justice in Bengal, urging that "despotism and arbitrary violence are not more pernicious to individuals than they are unpropitious to trade."[113] In neither Africa nor India did the absence of peace threaten to involve Britain in another European war, as hostilities in North America clearly did. To a remarkable degree, though, the pacific claims that were so conspicuous during Paul Wentworth's interview with Benjamin Franklin continued to animate imperial policy, even as the full extent of Britain's folly in America became apparent.

Of the various consequences of this transatlantic quest for peace, none was of greater moment than to endow Britain and Europe's other colonial powers with ultimate legal and moral authority in North America and to bring the colonies more fully within Europe's ambit. For groups as historically marginal as black sailors in the Royal Navy and Iroquois warriors in Indian country, Britain's expanding sense of trusteeship compelled officials in the colonies to recognize that, on some level, they had an obligation to safeguard the rights of all the Crown's subjects and tributary allies, including indigenous peoples and slaves. Increasingly, however, a different fate awaited rootless people like the English renegade whom the governor of Massachusetts, Francis Bernard, discovered commanding a vessel in Boston Harbor in 1761 and who claimed to be a Dane because he had lived "a good deal at St. Thomas's."[114] Although the army and navy officers who fought to uphold the British government's authority in North America between 1775 and 1783 did not always choose to act on such perceptions, the revolution had the potential to place even the wealthiest and most refined of the king's American subjects in the same legally vulnerable situation as Governor Bernard's ersatz Dane, inviting enormities like the burning of Charlestown during the battle of Bunker Hill, the near starvation of American soldiers and seamen being held on prison brigs in New York Harbor, and all-out war and depredations on American trade. In lecturing Wentworth about Britain's "system of devastation and cruelty," Franklin knew whereof he spoke. But would the union of states that critics disparaged as a "pirate republic" be any different?

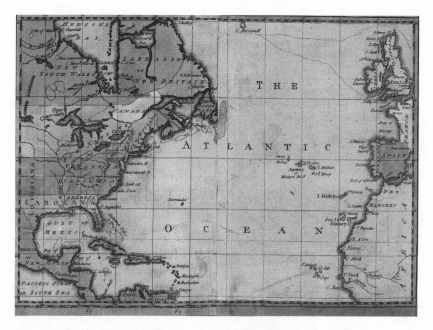

A detail from a map projection from 1755 captures the growing sense of the North Atlantic as a geographically unified space. By the 1750s, British mapmakers usually depicted the Atlantic Ocean as a single body of water, as opposed to two separate oceans. (Library of Congress)

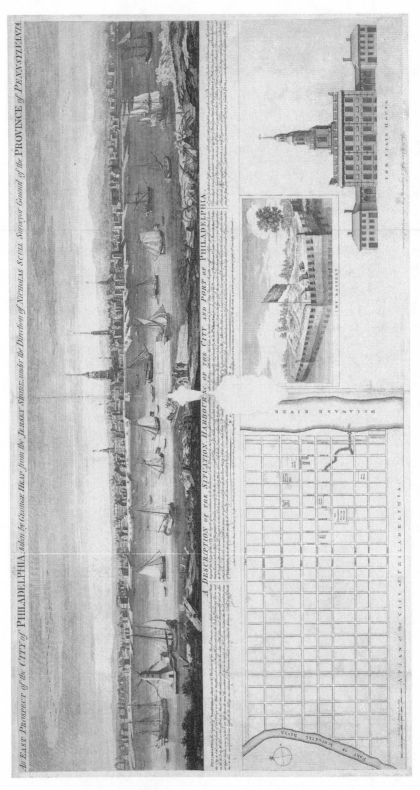

The city of Philadelphia, 1768. Depictions of European cities in America typically emphasized their maritime character, including their connections to seaborne trade routes and their importance in naval warfare. At the time of the revolution, Philadelphia was the largest city in British America. (Library of Congress)

A lighthouse damaged by a British attack in 1758. Britain captured Louisburg, which guarded the entrance to the Saint Lawrence River, from France in 1745 and again in 1758, the second time for good. (Library of Congress)

A view of Havana's harbor after a British bombardment. Following Spain's entry into the Seven Years' War in 1761, Britain seized Havana but returned it in 1763. (Library of Congress)

As is clear from Benjamin West's famous tableau of William Penn's treaty with the Indians in 1681, Europeans regarded Native Americans as worthy treaty partners. But they also assumed that Indians observed their own codes of conduct, which often differed from those that Europeans observed in conflicts with each other. (Library of Congress)

In this nineteenth-century engraving, the marquis de Montcalm attempts to prevent France's Indian allies from killing British American soldiers and civilians after the surrender of Fort William Henry in 1757. The depiction of Montcalm's humane gesture is all the more striking in view of the Gallophobia that swept British America during the Seven Years' War. (Library of Congress)

Throughout the Seven Years' War, Robert Rogers was instrumental in teaching the king's regulars what, in the British army, came to be known as "bush fighting." During both the Revolutionary War and the War of 1812, Americans accused the British of inciting their Indian allies to acts of brutality against soldiers and civilians. Yet Americans also employed so-called Indian tactics. (Library of Congress)

James Fort, in Accra on the Gold Coast, was one of several slave factories that the Royal Africa Company operated on the west coast of Africa during the first half of the eighteenth century. Operating under parliamentary statute and European treaty law, British and American traders at such outposts purchased slaves from African merchants for transportation to the colonies. (William Smith, *Thirty Different Drafts of Guinea* [London, n.d., 1727])

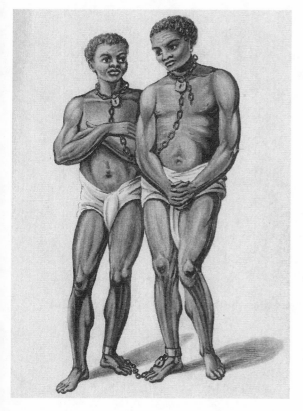

Captured Africans in chains, Sierra Leone, 1805. Although slavery was of dubious legality in Britain and Western Europe, jurists believed that it was legal to buy and sell prisoners of war, witches, and murderers in Africa, all of whom would have been put to death had they remained in their own country. (Boston Public Library, Department of Rare Books & Manuscripts)

Leonard Parkinson, a maroon leader in Jamaica. Slavery's origins in the rules of war were evident in the persistent fear on the part of white slaveholders of black insurrection. (Houghton Library, Harvard University—Hyde Collection [1600–1800])

A depiction of a delegation of Black Caribs signing a treaty with the British military on Saint Vincent in 1773. Although the American Revolution was the most famous aftershock of Britain's victory during the Seven Years' War, it was by no means the only one. On what had been the neutral West Indian island of Saint Vincent, Black Caribs—so called because they were descended from escaped slaves who intermarried with the island's indigenous people— responded to threats to their land with an insurgency that Britain settled through force of arms and diplomacy. (Harvard College Library, Widener Library, SA 1027.93.3(1) 1801)

Britannia, with olive branch and staff topped with liberty cap. To ensure that the peace of 1763 endured, Britain embarked on a far-reaching imperial reform. In America the new measures included cracking down on colonial smuggling, creating a ten thousand-strong peacetime standing army, and taxing the colonists in Parliament to help cover the costs. Although such policies were widely unpopular with Americans, many Britons saw the reforms as a natural consequence of Britain's new obligations, and there were widespread hopes that a strengthened British Empire would bring lasting peace to both Europe and America. (Library of Congress)

In a map cartouche from 1777, British merchants and Indians exchange goods in what, in the aftermath of the Seven Years' War, the British hoped would be an era of peace and mutually beneficial trade. (Library of Congress)

In "The Congress or the Necessary Politicians," an English cartoonist shows two delegates in a privy to ridicule Congress's pretensions. One has been using a sheet of resolutions to clean himself, while the other reads—but does not appear to understand—Samuel Johnson's *Taxation, No Tyranny* (1775). (Library of Congress)

This engraving of the burning of New York depicts the sinister consequences of the alleged political self-indulgence and irresponsibility of the American revolutionaries. In the foreground, groups of Continental soldiers cudgel people attempting to douse the flames, while two black men, at the lower left, abscond with a chest. (Library of Congress)

The *Jersey*, the most notorious of the derelict hulks where Britain housed American prisoners of war in New York Harbor. Because Americans were rebels, Britain was accused of denying them the protections to which European combatants were entitled under the customary rules of war. (*The United States of America: A Pictorial History* (New York: Imperial Publishing Company, 1906–09), vol. 2)

With General Burgoyne's surrender to the Continental army at Saratoga in 1777, Congress took an important step toward being accepted in Europe as an independent sovereign. In early 1778 France signed a treaty with the United States, recognizing American independence and entering the war against Britain. (Library of Congress)

A map of the West Indies from 1783. Despite Britain's recognition of American independence in 1782, none of Europe's colonial powers viewed the loose-knit union of states as an equal with the same rights and responsibilities as sovereigns in Europe. During the 1780s, Spain closed the Mississippi River to American ships and goods, Britain excluded Americans from the West Indian carrying trade, and British soldiers continued to garrison forts in what was now the Northwest Territory of the United States. (Library of Congress)

A triumphal arch erected for George Washington in Trenton, New Jersey. During Washington's journey to New York, where he was inaugurated as president in April 1789, citizens feted him with dinners, parades, and musket and artillery salutes. To strengthen the Union and enhance its status in Europe, the Constitutional Convention that met at Philadelphia in 1787 framed a national government with many of the powers that Americans had found so objectionable in the hands of the British Crown and Parliament. (Library of Congress)

The Massachusetts ship captain Paul Cuffe, whose visit to England and Sierra Leone in 1812 is commemorated in this engraving. During the Revolutionary War, slaves sought freedom by fleeing to the British army, and several thousand Black Loyalists left at the war's end for England, Nova Scotia, and, eventually, Sierra Leone. Although the revolution prompted Congress and the northern states to take the first steps to abolish slavery, Britain remained a beacon of liberty for blacks in the United States. (Library of Congress)

A print celebrates the Haitian Constitution of 1801. For both blacks and whites, Toussaint Louverture and the former slaves who seized French Saint-Domingue during the 1790s posed a grave threat to slaveholders. Despite assisting Louverture during the Franco-American Quasi-War of 1798–1800, the United States refused to recognize Haiti's independence in 1804, even though the black republic's declaration was modeled on the one that Jefferson wrote in 1776. (Library of Congress)

The Creek leader Se-loc-ta fought as an ally of the United States during the War
of 1812. For Native Americans, the peace that ended the Revolutionary War was a
catastrophe, as Britain ceded millions of acres of Indian land to Spain and the
United States. Although the Indians' response to this betrayal varied, the result
everywhere was a conflict between the historic independence of North America's
native people and the novel claims of sovereignty being advanced by Congress
and the states. Many Indians sided with nativists like the Shawnee prophet
Tenskwatawa and his brother Tecumseh and with Josiah Francis, leader of the
Red Stick Creeks. (Library of Congress)

Andrew Jackson parades after his victory in 1814 over Creeks allied with Britain in Alabama. Americans eventually turned Europe's troubles to their advantage, acquiring Louisiana from France in 1803 and Florida from Spain between 1819 and 1821 and inflicting crushing defeats on the Indians. During the treaty that followed Jackson's triumph, the Creeks ceded half of their remaining homeland to the United States. (Library of Congress)

In James Gillray's famous cartoon, drawn the same year that Admiral Nelson destroyed the French and Spanish fleets at Trafalgar, William Pitt and Napoleon divide the world. Napoleon takes Europe, while the British minister helps himself to the Western Atlantic, including North America. Although the heaviest fighting occurred in Europe, the French Revolutionary and Napoleonic Wars were global conflicts that repeatedly threatened to embroil America. (Library of Congress)

A cotton plantation on the Mississippi. Napoleon's defeat at Waterloo in 1815 opened the way for Americans to realize the peace that had been the Union's goal since 1776. Among the chief beneficiaries were southern slaveholders who turned millions of acres in Georgia, Alabama, and Mississippi—much of it seized during Andrew Jackson's wars with the Indians—into cotton plantations like the one pictured here. (Library of Congress)

Emanuel Leutze, *Washington Crossing the Delaware*, 1851. Although he spent part of his youth in America, Leutze trained as an artist in Germany, where he was living when he painted his famous tableau of Washington's sneak attack on the Hessian garrison at Trenton in 1776. The painting became one of the most recognizable depictions of the Revolutionary War. James Monroe is the standard-bearer in Washington's boat. (Library of Congress)

CHAPTER 4

Independence

B Y THE TIME André Michaux arrived at Mansker's Station, he must have realized that his mission to Kentucky and Tennessee had been a failure. Over the last three years, the renowned botanist and secret emissary for the French Republic had visited the leading men of both states, hoping to find allies for France's war in Europe. In 1793, on the first of his two journeys, he had even approached George Rogers Clark, hero of the American Revolution, with the offer of a commission to seize Spanish Louisiana with an army of Kentucky adventurers. Ultimately, however, his efforts had been for naught. Despite the treaty that they signed in 1778, Americans did not intend to fight on France's behalf. Now, on a windswept February evening, ten miles from Nashville and with the return journey to South Carolina still before him, Michaux had no choice but to accept the hospitality of Kasper Mansker, a local Indian fighter who claimed to be an "enemy of the French because, he said, they have killed their king." Although Michaux's journal is silent as to why Colonel Mansker would hold such views, he was so taken aback that he refused to dine with him, "believing that a Republican should not be under obligations to a fanatical partisan of Royalty." Because of the drenching rain, Michaux spent the night in the main house, yet he kept his debts to a minimum. "I slept on my Deerskin," wrote Michaux of the evening's arrangements. The next morning he took care to pay his host for the corn that "he supplied me with to cross the Wilderness."[1]

Without question, Michaux had reason to leave Mansker's house feeling embarrassed, yet the mission that brought him there was not as far-fetched as it seemed. Like the other states in the American union, Kentucky and Tennessee were sovereign and independent republics during the mid-1790s, and they had the potential to be autonomous, albeit distant, players in relations with Europe's colonial powers. As Michaux knew, some of the people whom he visited thought that Kentucky and Tennessee might be better off under the protection of another government. Among the members of this group was a young attorney named Andrew Jackson, whom Michaux met during his second trip.[2] Despite receiving only passing notice in Michaux's journal, the future president was already making a name for himself, and he was closely allied with William Blount, the Tennessee governor who later resigned from the U.S. Senate amid revelations that he had conspired to seize Louisiana and the two Floridas for Britain. Although there is no evidence that Jackson was involved in this scheme, his patriotism was nearly as opportunistic. In 1789 he had gone to Natchez in Spanish West Florida and sworn allegiance to Spain's Charles IV (to avoid paying duties on goods shipped through New Orleans), and he remained convinced, or so he wrote a friend in 1794, that unless Congress started tending to the needs of Americans in the West, Tennessee might be compelled "to break or seek a protection from some other Source than the present."[3] Had Michaux's plan succeeded, Jackson was just the sort of restless young man who might have been tempted to join the expedition.

Despite the Union's secession from Britain, the revolution did nothing to check the forces that were drawing Americans more closely into Europe's orbit. As signified by the "decent respect to the opinions of mankind" that Congress professed in the Declaration of Independence, one of the United States' founding goals was to win acceptance as a full-fledged member of Europe's diplomatic republic. On this basis, Americans intended to do all the things that "Independent States may of right do," including "levy War, conclude Peace, contract Alliances, [and] establish Commerce."[4] Because of these aspirations, however, the revolution forced Americans to confront many of the problems that had vexed the

British Empire before 1776. Foremost among these was the question of whether Americans could gain the recognition of Europe's leading powers while remaining true to what admirers on both sides of the Atlantic called a "republican empire"—a loose-knit confederation where authority was shared equally among the Union's sovereign parts and where, in the words of the Tenth Amendment to the U.S. Constitution, all "powers" not delegated to the central government were to be "reserved to the States respectively, or to the people."[5] For people during the 1780s and 1790s, the great question was whether these two imperatives really were compatible. Could the United States claim the same treaty rights as George III had possessed in eastern North America before the revolution, even as Americans rejected the unitary sovereignty that jurists like Vattel viewed as being essential for making a "figure . . . in the universal society of nations"?[6] And could the new Union withstand the centrifugal tendencies that had undone the British Empire, or would the former colonies eventually sink into a renewed condition of dependency, proxies for the imperial powers of Europe and easy marks for foreign agitators like Michaux? "It will not be an easy matter to bring the American States to act as a nation," wrote the English politician Lord Sheffield in 1784.[7] Despite the stirring words with which Congress declared independence, it was by no means clear that the pessimists were wrong.

(1)

In proclaiming their nascent statehood, Americans accepted that their new governments would need to conform to the norms of Europe's colonial powers, especially the norms enshrined in the public law of European treaties and diplomatic customs. Although the Declaration of Independence was an act of secession from Britain, it was an act of secession that Congress undertook as the "most effectual" means for "forming foreign Alliances" in Europe.[8] "It is not choice . . . but necessity which calls for Independence," observed Richard Henry Lee in laying his momentous resolution before Congress on June 7, 1776. "No state in Europe will either Treat or Trade with us so long as we consider ourselves Subjects of G. B."[9] Lee's fellow Virginian Thomas Jefferson, often depicted as the founding father of American isolationism, also acknowledged the need for the United States to cultivate treaty relations with the leading states of Europe, especially those "having American territory."[10] Following Thomas Paine's advice in *Common Sense,* most Americans assumed that once they had secured their independence from Britain, they would be well advised to steer clear of "European wars and quarrels," yet few people—least of all Paine—thought it possible, or even desirable, to sever all ties.[11] As Secretary of State Edmund Randolph reminded the British ambassador in 1794, Americans were "without the European circle," but their "frequent correspondence with Europe" meant that they were entitled to the same rights and privileges as other Europeans. To suggest otherwise, Randolph insisted, would be to deny them the "modern usage of nations" because the United States "[were] sovereignties of a recent date, and in the Western hemisphere."[12]

As these words suggest, Americans recognized that independence was a condition that required the consent of other governments, not something that they could achieve unilaterally (or solely on their own terms). Although this was true of all nations, two things made the United States especially dependent on the good opinion of Europe's imperial powers. The first was the Union's origins in what the English historian Edward Gibbon called the "criminal enterprise" of rebellion.[13] In *Common Sense,* Thomas Paine warned that as long as "we profess ourselves the subjects of Britain, we must, in the eye of foreign nations, be considered as rebels." For Europe's rulers to recognize a band of outlaws who were, by their own admission, at a war with their lawful king would be "dangerous to *their peace,*" wrote Paine, adding that Britain's archrivals, France and Spain, were unlikely to come to the colonies' assistance "until we take rank with other nations."[14] Nor was the declaration enough to dispel the taint of rebellion. Even after the former colonies proclaimed themselves sovereign states, their independence was, at most, a "pretended independence" without the external validation of European recognition.[15] On learning of Congress's manifesto as he approached New York in July 1776, Ambrose Serle, General Howe's private secretary, called the delegates' repudiation of British sovereignty an act of "madness" and "villainy" and the declaration itself an "impudent, false and atrocious Proclamation."[16] In an unofficial response penned at the North Ministry's behest, John Lind, an English jurist and associate of Jeremy Bentham, used similar terms. The American declaration, Lind insisted, was nothing more than an "audacious paper," one beneath the dignity of the king's ministers to acknowledge, let alone refute.[17]

Although British officers sometimes overlooked such principles and granted Continental soldiers the rights of war, they claimed that they were entitled to treat Americans who supported independence as lawless combatants, who were neither bound nor protected by the customs of European nations. In his account of the failed negotiations that preceded General Howe's invasion of New York in August 1776, Ambrose Serle placed much of the blame on George Washington and his insistence on being treated as the commander of a regular army with the same rights as the army of a sovereign nation in Europe. Washington, wrote Serle, was a "little paltry colonel of militia at the head of a banditti [of] rebels"; only criminal self-delusion could explain the general's refusal to accept that fact and recognize Howe as "the representative of his lawful sovereign."[18] Following the Continental army's evacuation of New York in September, similar allegations appeared in British accounts of the fire that destroyed much of the city. Although neither Washington nor Congress publicly authorized the destruction, British writers were quick to fault the Americans, noting in particular the involvement of Isaac Fellows, a Continental officer from Connecticut, who was arrested for arson, as well as numerous people "with large bundles of matches" and a carpenter named Wright White, who slashed leather fire buckets with his cutlass and cudgeled a woman attempting to douse the flames.[19] "This was not the sudden act of a vanquished and flying enemy," insisted Thomas Lewis O'Beirne in the sermon that he preached to the British officer corps at St. Paul's Chapel on the morning after the fire was quelled, but a deliberate plot on the part of "base incendiaries . . . wearing the mask of peace."[20] In the words of Myles Cooper, rector of King's College (present-day Columbia University), Americans, like all rebels, were a most "ungenerous enemy," who wreaked destruction "without any prospect of advantage to themselves, [but] for the sole purpose, it should seem, of doing injury to others."[21]

In the face of these accusations, Americans sought to show that in matters of humanitarianism and civilized warfare they were the equals of their former countrymen, if not their betters. Following the Continental

army's retreat across New Jersey in late 1776, Washington's officers issued a manifesto denying British allegations that they intended "to burn
and destroy" Philadelphia. Any such attempt, insisted Major-General
Israel Putnam, would be treated as a "crime of the blackest dye" to be
punished by death "without ceremony."[22] Americans also took exception
to Britain's initial refusal to grant Continental prisoners the customary
privileges of war, a stance—as Washington complained to General Gage in
August 1775—that led to housing American officers in a "common gaol"
as though they were "felons" and to denying the sick and wounded medi-
cal attention.[23] Mindful of Washington's threat to retaliate against British
officers in American custody, Lord Howe eventually instructed his forces
to treat Continental officers as ordinary prisoners of war. In British-
occupied New York, officers holding commissions from the Continental
Congress were allowed to wear their uniforms in public and those of the
highest rank—notably General John Sullivan of New Hampshire—were
given parole so that they could return home "to procure . . . necessaries"
for themselves.[24] Still, not all British commanders shared Howe's moderate views, and even high-ranking Americans remained vulnerable to captors who viewed them as "rebels . . . in arms against their sovereign." "I
think it is rather imprudent to give these fellows so much liberty," wrote
Captain Frederick Mackenzie of the Continental officers whom he saw
strolling about the streets of New York in 1776. "They publicly avow their
principles, and instead of appearing sensible of the crime they have committed, seem to glory in the cause in which they are engaged."[25]

Because of such attitudes, Americans in British custody continued to
endure substandard conditions, especially the thousands of soldiers and
sailors who were held on derelict transport ships at New York, Charleston, and Halifax, Nova Scotia. According to Ebenezer Fox, a sixteen-
year-old Continental soldier from Massachusetts, life on board the *Jersey* in Brooklyn's Wallabout Bay was terrible, so much so that even the
"portholes were closed and secured," and prisoners were only allowed
above deck once a day. Another prisoner recalled that the daily "saluta-
tion" from the *Jersey*'s guards was, "Rebels! turn out your dead!"[26] Although Britain also kept French, Spanish, and Dutch prisoners in such
hulks, Americans assumed that as putative rebels they were the main
objects of this refusal "to respect the law of nations."[27] "Our unhappy

countrymen [have been] stifled in their own filth, and die by [the] hundreds under the hands of their cruel, merciless keepers, and under the immediate eye of British officers," claimed a writer in the *Connecticut Gazette,* adding that the "barbarism" on Britain's ships exceeded that of Calcutta's notorious Black Hole.[28] At New York, whose waters contained the largest number of prison ships, malnutrition and disease accounted for death rates that approached 80 percent, but conditions elsewhere were no better. According to Robert Mills, who wrote a history of the revolution in South Carolina during the 1820s, a horrific fate awaited prisoners on board the British hulks at Charleston:

> The condition of these unfortunate men was truly deplorable. They were crowded in these ships in such numbers, that [many] were obliged to stand up, for want of room to lie down. The sick could obtain no relief, and in consequence of this cruel treatment, upwards of eight hundred of these brave men (nearly a third of the whole) expired, in the short space of thirteen months' captivity. Out of 1900 taken at the surrender of Charleston, on the 12th of May, 1780, and several hundreds more, taken afterwards at Camden and Fishing Creek, . . . there were only 740 restored to the service of their country, when a general exchange took place.[29]

Although the Americans' treatment of British prisoners was often little better, such experiences underscored the high cost of engaging in what, according to the law of nations, were illegal acts of rebellion and irregular warfare. During the bitter fighting that characterized the final campaigns in the Lower South, the British sought to emphasize these costs by arming Loyalist militias, burning the houses of the king's enemies, encouraging the slaves of patriot masters to flee to British lines, and denying quarter to American soldiers. In one of the most notorious engagements of the war, Loyalist troopers from Banastre Tarleton's British Legion chased a regiment of Virginia Continentals across South Carolina during the spring of 1780, catching their beleaguered prey at the Waxhaws, where they killed or wounded two-thirds, many "after they had ceased to resist and [had] laid down their arms."[30] In the account that he sent to his superiors at Charleston, Tarleton claimed that the regiment's colonel received and "positively rejected" a British demand for his surrender, but most Americans viewed the slaughter as an unprovoked massacre, the enormity of which was only magnified by Sir Henry Clinton's subsequent commendation of Tarleton's conduct.[31] "The enemy seemed to have laid aside . . . every principle of humanity and justice," Robert Mills recalled in his history of the campaigns of 1780 and 1781, adding that the partisan warfare that "Tarleton's Quarter" helped trigger in the Carolina backcountry was, if anything, even worse. Speaking of the tit-for-tat violence and civil strife that engulfed the region, Mills wrote that "the ties of nature were . . . dissolved; countrymen, neighbors, friends, and brothers, took different sides, and ranged themselves under the opposing standards of the contending factions." In the name of subduing rebellion, or, for patriots, winning independence, "private revenge was gratified, many houses were burnt, and many people inhumanly murdered."[32]

For Americans who lived through it, this devastation became one of the war's enduring legacies, endowing the quest for national independence with vivid tales of personal suffering. Andrew Jackson, for one, never forgot the privation that he and his family endured at the hands of the king's soldiers. "[I]t was a time of great trials," recalled Susan Alexander, one of the family's neighbors at the Waxhaws.[33] Though only thirteen when Charleston fell to the British, Jackson's trials included hiding from Tarleton's soldiers, joining a unit of backcountry partisans as a courier, contracting smallpox in a British jail, and losing both his brothers and his mother, Elizabeth, who died from cholera while ministering to relatives on a prison ship at Charleston.[34] As Jackson recalled years later, Tarleton passed so close to where he was hiding at one point that "I could have shot him," but the defining moment, of which the future president was inordinately proud, came when a British officer slashed his left hand and forehead after Jackson refused to clean his boots.[35] Such experiences left Jackson with a lasting hatred of everything that Britain stood for during the revolution, as well as a deep-seated sympathy for anyone willing to follow the Americans' example. Despite the oath that he took to the Spanish king in 1789, he had no trouble viewing the French Revolution as a comparable "revolution in favour of human rights," nor did he question that France's ensuing war with Britain was a continuation of America's own struggle to emancipate "liberty . . . from the despotism of Kings." "Should Boneparte make a landing on the English shore," wrote the junior senator from Tennessee in 1798, "Tyranny will be humbled, a throne crushed and a republick will spring from the wreck."[36] Having fought for the same goals, Jackson wished the Corsican every success.

(2)

Although Britain's recognition of the United States in 1783 freed Americans from the charge of rebellion, they continued to face a second, equally intractable set of problems in that neither Britain nor Europe's other powers accepted them as treaty-worthy equals. Not surprisingly, these problems were especially striking in relations with London. Because of differences over compensation due to Loyalists and British merchants who had lost property, officials in Canada refused to honor the Anglo-American Treaty of Paris, garrisoning posts in what was now the Union's Northwest Territory and assisting hostile Indians. At the same time, Britain proved unwilling to negotiate a commercial treaty that would place the Republic's trade on the same footing as other nations in Europe. Although the younger William Pitt, who formed his first government in 1783, sponsored legislation that would have permitted Americans to keep the privileges that they had enjoyed as British subjects, his opponents carried the day, ensuring that Americans would be subject to the same prohibitions under the Navigation Acts—especially the prohibition on carrying goods to and from the British West Indies—as foreigners. To soften the effects, the Privy Council issued a series of orders establishing liberal rules for trade between metropolitan Britain and the United States, yet these regulations did not have the permanence of an act of Parliament, let alone an international treaty.[37] As Thomas Jefferson observed in 1793, Britain's refusal to give Americans the "security" that it extended to "the navigation of others" meant that the largest and most valuable portion of the Republic's foreign trade existed at the "sole discretion" of the Crown and could be withdrawn at any moment "on that single will."[38] Although no longer subjects of George III, Americans were also not yet fully independent.

This posed especially serious problems for merchants whose liveli-hoods depended on a quick resumption of the West Indian carrying trade. Because the North American seaboard remained the closest and cheapest source of beef, grain, and fish, governors in the British Caribbean occa-sionally suspended the prohibition on American ships, both to keep the cost of provisions low and—during the hurricanes that devastated Brit-ain's islands in 1784, 1785, and 1786—to avert starvation. American mer-chants also benefited from what Jamaica's Archibald Campbell called "malcontents" among the islands' planters and merchants, many of whom were Loyalists "connected by relationship and trade with the people of North America" and who resented "being proscribed by proclamation."[39] According to Phineas Bond, who served as British consul in Philadelphia during the mid-1780s, the city's merchants sometimes sent goods to Brit-ish ports through Dutch Saint Eustatius, or they partnered with British merchants to supply their ships with "double papers"—an "ingenious col-lusion," noted Bond, that enabled them to avoid paying duties in either British or American ports.[40] Either way, Captain Horatio Nelson, who briefly commanded the Leeward Islands naval station in 1785, did not ex-aggerate by much when he complained that Americans were engrossing "nearly the whole trade between the British colonies and the United States." For the future hero of Trafalgar—and, no doubt, for many of his fellow officers—it was more than he could bear "to see American ships and vessels with their colours flying in defiance of the laws, and by permission of the officer of the customs landing and unloading in our ports."[41]

Nonetheless, as Americans were well aware, commerce based on smug-gling, clandestine arrangements, and the whim of British governors was not the same thing as a regular, legally sanctioned trade. When officials in the British Caribbean lifted the restrictions on American goods, they generally did so on short notice, which meant that merchants in North American ports had no way of knowing in advance "whether the trade is open or shut at Jamaica or Barbadoes." "If they send a vessel to Jamaica and the ports are shut," wrote Jacob Crowninshield of Salem, Massachu-setts, "the voyage is ruined." "Fish in a warm climate will spoil in a few weeks, and beef and pork cannot long be preserved." Even when an island's ports were open, British planters often met their obligations to American merchants with rum and molasses, which lost their value more quickly

than sugar or coffee, and there was always the risk of seizure by an over-
zealous officer like Captain Nelson. When that happened, British vice-
admiralty judges sometimes condemned both the cargo and the vessel,
even though "no attempt has been made to smuggle."[42] "We suffer very
much in this State from the unequal trade [that] we now have with the
British," wrote Stephen Higginson of the impact of Britain's restrictions
on Massachusetts in 1789.[43] Under such conditions, the most that Americans could hope for was what Crowninshield called a "languid palsied
trade, half shut, half open, never free." "All that is wanted," Crowninshield lamented, "is to open the trade to American vessels." "[L]et the
commerce be free for 5 or 6 years and it will be seen which is the best
system."[44]

Although the absence of a commercial treaty bore especially hard on
merchants in New England, it was not the only area where Britain's acceptance of American sovereignty was less than complete. Following the
outbreak of war with France in 1793, Britain closed French ports in Europe and the West Indies to neutral vessels, a significant and growing
number of which flew American colors. To bolster its naval resources,
Britain also brokered a truce between Portugal and Algiers, allowing the
North African corsairs that the Portuguese navy had kept bottled up in
the Mediterranean to resume making raids on the shipping of Britain's
rivals in the Atlantic. Although neither measure specifically targeted the
United States, Americans perceived both as a direct assault on the Republic's sovereignty, a further indication—if such were needed—of Britain's refusal to make real peace with the former colonies and accord
them equal rank with other nations. By the spring of 1794, American
seamen were once again languishing on British prison ships in the West
Indies, and the travails of Americans who had been taken as captives along
the Barbary Coast, allegedly with Britain's blessing, would come to assume near-mythic proportions in the national memory. "God have mercy
upon our poor countrymen," declared an American at Lisbon of the
depredations on American shipping. "I now see no other alternative but
[renewed] war with the English or humbly begging them to take us under
their protection again as subjects or slaves."[45]

Nor was the Union's exposure to British arrogance limited to the high
seas. At Detroit and the other British-occupied posts in the Northwest

Territory, all of which stood on land that Britain had ostensibly ceded to the United States in 1783, British officers and traders continued to supply Indians with arms and ammunition, helping to subvert the various treaties that Congress attempted to negotiate with the king's former Indian allies between 1784 and 1789. Strengthened and emboldened by this assistance, Indians under the leadership of the Miami chief Little Turtle inflicted humiliating defeats on the U.S. Army in 1790 and 1791, on the latter occasion killing or wounding nearly three-quarters of a twelve hundred-strong force led by General Arthur St. Clair, governor of the Northwest Territory.[46] "Peace can neither be honorable expedient or permanent under present circumstances," wrote General Anthony Wayne of the activities of Britain's Indian agents within the Union's borders in 1792: "altho' they may not *directly*—I am confident that they *indirectly* stimulate the savages to continue the War, nor can all the sophistry of British Embassadors Agents or state spies convince me to the contrary until they surrender up those posts."[47] In the words of Pittsburgh newspaperman Hugh Henry Brackenridge, the Indian war in the Northwest Territory was not "a war . . . with Indians merely; it [was also] a war with the British king, under cover": "Have we felt the jaw of the lion," asked Brackenridge, in a none-too-subtle reminder of Britain's actions as an avowed enemy between 1776 and 1783, "and shall we be still lashed with his tail?"[48] Not surprisingly, some people, Brackenridge among them, wondered whether another declared war might be preferable to an unfinished peace.

Although the low-grade hostilities with Britain posed grave dangers, relations with Spain in the former British colony of West Florida were no better. Although France reluctantly supported the claims that Congress advanced in the Model Treaty on the two Floridas, recognizing both as integral parts of the United States in the Franco-American Treaty of 1778, Spain did not. Shortly after Spain entered the war, forces under Bernardo de Gálvez crossed the Mississippi River from Louisiana and seized the British posts at Baton Rouge, Mobile, and Pensacola. In the treaty that it negotiated in 1783 with Spain, Britain agreed to give both Floridas to Madrid; however, in the West Florida cession, Britain used a northern boundary that lay a hundred miles north of the parallel where its treaty with Congress placed the Union's southern limits. Although Spain had the better title—the more southerly line in the American treaty had only briefly been used in 1763, whereas the Spanish line had been West Florida's northern border for nearly twenty years—Congress refused to budge, reasoning that settlers from the United States would eventually be more than a match in the disputed territory for Spain's overstretched resources.[49] Spain's response was to treat the Union as a hostile power, closing New Orleans and the Lower Mississippi River to American navigation in 1784, requiring Americans at Vicksburg and Natchez, which the United States claimed under the Anglo-American Treaty of Paris, to take oaths to the Spanish king, and extending its territorial claims to include parts of Georgia, Kentucky, and Tennessee. The Spanish also sought alliances with the region's Indians, many of whom, especially the twenty-to-forty thousand-strong Creek Nation, had reasons of their own to dislike the Americans.[50]

The result was a veritable war of all against all, in which Spain and the United States engaged in low-grade hostilities against each other— often with Britain and, sometimes, France lurking in the wings—while vying for the allegiance of Indians, Loyalists, and Americans in territory that each government claimed.[51] In the confrontations that resulted, people like Andrew Jackson were no longer rebels, but they often had equally ambiguous relationships with the rival governments, opening them to charges of being little better than what the Articles of Confederation classified as "paupers, vagabonds, and fugitives from justice." Writing from Lexington, Kentucky, in 1792, the French émigré Berthélemi Tardiveau warned the governor of Louisiana that Americans were a restless, untrustworthy people. "Isolated among strangers," wrote Tardiveau, "they are as docile and as submissive to authority as those who boast less of their independence. As soon as they are in a group, however, they become dangerous; soon they want to run things."[52] In recognition of this danger, Spain promised American settlers who transferred their allegiance "a refuge under the [Spanish] king's protection," as James White of Knoxville wrote in 1789.[53] For Americans who refused, however, the alternative was commercial "strangulation" and, often, military conflict.[54] Although the governments of Spain and the United States managed to avoid open warfare, Spain's Indian allies were less restrained, engaging in running hostilities that included a brief Creek war against squatters from Georgia in 1786 and a Cherokee attack on

Nashville.[55] As a correspondent in the *Knoxville Gazette* wrote in 1792, there was no question that Spanish officials at Pensacola had armed the Indians, "advising and stimulating them to go to war with the frontier inhabitants of the United States."[56]

In many ways Spain's North American empire was less formidable than it seemed. As would become painfully clear during the Nootka Sound crisis of 1790, when Britain and Spain nearly came to blows in North America after a Spanish naval officer arrested a group of British traders on Vancouver Island in the Pacific Northwest, one of Spain's problems was that its empire was so vast, stretching from Alaska to the Florida Keys while lacking the resources necessary to turn this sprawling dominion into a unified empire.[57] Even so, as Americans were well aware, Spain was still a major power, backed by the third-largest navy in Europe—at a moment when the United States possessed no navy at all— and the near certainty that Britain and France would actively oppose an attempt to seize West Florida by any force but their own. From Saint Louis, New Orleans, and Pensacola, Spanish officials continued to encroach on the authority of the United States, and they were able to fan disaffection as far as the headwaters of the Ohio in western Pennsylvania. Whatever he thought of Spain's long-term prospects, Berthélemi Tardiveau acknowledged this reality at the end of his letter to the Louisiana governor by asking that he be permitted "as a Spanish subject" to ship Kentucky tobacco through New Orleans "without paying the duty exacted from this produce when it comes from abroad."[58] As the Irish adventurer John O'Fallon observed shortly after arriving at Lexington in 1790, it was well known that the people of the "Western Country" would never place any trust in Congress. Unless the United States managed to open the Mississippi to American shipping, their only hope was to "confederate, independently, among themselves," and form an alliance based on principles of free trade with whatever "European power" controlled New Orleans.[59]

As André Michaux began his travels through Kentucky and Tennessee in 1793, sentiments like these would certainly have been on his mind, yet the United States' relations with France were often no better. To be sure, Americans remained grateful for France's early embrace—a gratitude readily apparent in the paired portraits of Louis XVI and George

Washington that adorned homes and public spaces during the 1780s and the optimism with which Americans greeted the onset of the French Revolution in 1789. Nonetheless, there was a pervasive sense that the alliance with France had done little to offset the commercial advantages that Americans lost when they ceased to be British subjects, and some feared that the French viewed the Treaty of 1778 as a way "to depress and fetter us so as to keep *America* dependent on [their] nation."[60] Following France's declaration of war against Britain, the National Convention's overtures to the United States only deepened these apprehensions, culminating in the Washington administration's formal request in August 1793 that France recall its rabble-rousing ambassador Edmond Charles Genêt. Although Jefferson's letter affirmed the administration's support for "liberty and . . . the French cause," affronts to American sovereignty such as Michaux's proposed expedition against Louisiana—for which Citizen Genêt was the chief author and instigator—could only end by embroiling the United States with Spain, and Americans had no desire for "another expensive and ruinous war" with Britain. "I do not wish . . . to behave unjust or dishonourable to the French nation," wrote a Cincinnati newspaper editor in 1793. But if the people of Kentucky and Tennessee attacked Louisiana at France's behest, Americans could be sure that "the arms of both kingdoms [Britain and Spain]" would be turned against them.[61]

When they declared independence, Americans had hoped to gain all the rights that independent nations enjoyed in Europe. Nearly twenty years later, fully realizing these hopes seemed to be a very long way off. Despite the Anglo-American peace treaty of 1783, neither Britain nor Europe's other governments accepted the Union as a treaty-worthy sovereign with rights comparable to their own. In an essay that he wrote for the *Leiden Gazette* while in England in 1784, Thomas Jefferson observed that the image of the United States that most Europeans encountered in the British press was little better than a caricature. All too often, wrote Jefferson,

> America is a scene of . . . riot and anarchy. Wearied out with contention, it is on the verge of falling again into the lap of Gr[eat] Br[itain] for repose. It's [*sic*] citizens are groaning under the oppression of

heavy taxes. They are flying for refuge to the frozen regions which still remain subject to Gr. Br. Their assemblies and congresses are become odious, in one paragraph represented as tyrannizing over their constituents, and in another as possessing no power or influence at all.

"[N]othing," Jefferson assured the *Gazette*'s readers, could be "less true," yet he realized that Britain was where Europeans generally obtained their information about the former colonies. In the absence of compelling evidence to the contrary, the most that Americans could hope for was that "Europe [would] be as wise and just now" as its people had been during the Revolutionary War and that they would discount the truth of such "fabricated papers" and judge the facts for themselves.[62]

(3)

The problem was that the British image was not as far-fetched as Jefferson would have liked. Although British writers betrayed "ill humor" toward their erstwhile fellow subjects, many correctly perceived that what Lord Sheffield called the "unsettled" condition of the American union was one of the chief obstacles to equality with the nations of Europe. "No treaty can be made with the American states that can be binding on the whole," wrote Sheffield in 1784. "We might as reasonably dread the effects of combinations among the German as among the American States, and deprecate the resolves of the Diet, as those of Congress."[63] As Jefferson noted in the *Leiden Gazette*—which, if not a direct response to Sheffield's *Observations,* was an attempt to refute writers who shared Sheffield's views—the Union's weakness did not mean that the states were in social or political anarchy, nor did the absence of a strong central government directly threaten the postwar revival of the American economy. However, when it came to persuading Spain to open the Mississippi to American shipping or to obtaining concessions in the British Caribbean and removing British soldiers from U.S. territory, the Union's unsettled state posed difficulties that were both real and urgent and made it nearly impossible to form lasting treaty relationships with other nations.

Whatever they said for the benefit of readers in Europe, Americans readily acknowledged this reality to each other. Although the Articles of Confederation, which was ratified by the last of the thirteen states in 1781, gave Congress exclusive authority over the Union's relations with other governments, only state legislatures could impose taxes for revenue. As a result, the states controlled the most fundamental attribute of sovereignty. Furthermore, because members of Congress voted with their state delegations rather than as individuals, with a majority of nine delegations required to enact legislation and conduct other business, the states had an effective veto over everything else Congress did. Without "additional powers of government," warned South Carolina's Charles Pinckney of the resulting weakness in an open letter to the Continental Congress in 1786, "we cannot exist as a nation, and . . . all the treaties [that] you may form must be ineffectual."[64] Upon preparing to resign the command of the Continental army in June 1783, George Washington used nearly identical language, writing in his *Circular to the State Governments* that "it is only in our united character as an empire, that our independence is acknowledged, that our power can be regarded, or our credit supported." "The treaties of the European powers," added Washington, "will have no validity on a dissolution of the union; we shall be left nearly in a state of nature."[65] Although Americans found it hard to agree over how, exactly, this situation ought to be remedied, it was clear that under the Articles of Confederation, the "sovereignty of the United States"—in the sense that sovereignty was understood by governments and jurists in Europe—"reside[d], not in Congress collectively, but [in] the States individually."[66]

Not surprisingly, this arrangement complicated the efforts of Congress to honor agreements with other governments, especially the provisions in the Treaty of 1783 that covered the tens of thousands of displaced Loyalists.[67] In exchange for British recognition, the American commissioners accepted language that allowed both "real British subjects" and Loyal American refugees to collect outstanding debts and recover estates that had been confiscated during the Revolutionary War, and the treaty obligated the United States to repeal all laws that were not "perfectly consistent" with a "spirit of conciliation" between the two nations. Because the United States lacked the power to enforce these terms, however, the

most that could be promised was that "Congress [would] earnestly recommend [them] to the legislatures of the respective states."[68] In New
York, where British forces remained ensconced on Manhattan until 1783,
the legislature responded by openly defying Congress with a Trespass
Act that targeted New Yorkers who had "voluntarily put themselves . . .
in the power of the enemy" during the occupation.[69] Virginia, whose
planters owed more than £2 million to British merchants, was equally
truculent, pegging the rights of British creditors to compensation for
slaves that the British army had "stolen" during the war. "Vengeance
unrestrained, and undistinguished, hath been let loose upon us in all her
horrors!" wrote an American who favored a more conciliatory stance in
1784: "But it is peace!—Let our injuries and our resentments be buried
forever in the definitive treaty!"[70] Among those who urged compliance
with the treaty in New York was an up-and-coming attorney named Alexander Hamilton, but even Hamilton's considerable rhetorical gifts
were for naught. Ten years later, most grievances involving British creditors and the Loyalists were still unresolved.

Britain was quick to seize on these diplomatic shortcomings, using
the question of Loyalist compensation, in particular, as a pretext for
maintaining garrisons in the Northwest Territory and refusing to negotiate a commercial treaty. "Things cannot long remain as they are," wrote
the British consul and former Loyalist Phineas Bond from Philadelphia
in 1787. Because the American republic consisted of "thirteen different
States, each claiming and exercising sovereign and independent powers,
with various forms of government," Congress was by its very nature a
body of "great mutual jealousies and interests . . . clashing and interfer-
ing with each other."[71] Even Britons who considered themselves friends
of America noted the Union's weakness. In moving that the House of
Commons support the Shelburne ministry's peace terms on February
17, 1783, Thomas Pitt, for one, assured the chamber that by promising
that Congress would recommend the Loyalists' grievances "to the different provinces," the American peace commissioners had done all that
they could. What more could Britain expect from the Americans, asked
Pitt, "than to pledge themselves strongly to recommend their case
and claims?"[72] In his pamphlet defending the provisional treaty, the English dissenting minister Andrew Kippis said the same thing. "The

point of a full and complete restitution was urged again and again," wrote Kippis.

> But it was not in the power of the American Commissioners to pro-
> ceed farther than they did; neither is it in the power of Congress to
> do more than *earnestly to recommend* the Loyalists to compassion
> and favour. Each particular State in America is sovereign and su-
> preme in itself, with regard to legislative and judicial authority; and,
> therefore, cannot be controuled in the exercise of its jurisdiction
> over its own subjects.[73]

As these words suggest, the decision to entrust the Loyalists' fate to what Kippis called "the wisdom and liberality of the American States" was deeply embarrassing to the British government, suggesting (cor-rectly) that Britain placed a higher value on ending the war with the United States than it did the welfare of thousands of its own subjects.[74] The British records of the 1780s and 1790s are full of stories like those of John and Mary Port Macklin, English tavern keepers from Charleston who operated a dockside eatery on a converted ship before the war. In 1778 the Macklins lost everything that they had and spent eight months in a Charleston jail because John refused to swear allegiance to the revo-lutionary government of South Carolina. Under a cartel with British au-thorities in East Florida, the Macklins were eventually allowed to go to St. Augustine, where John took command of a privateer and participated in the siege of Charleston. But Mary's health steadily declined. At the war's end, the two separated (perhaps by mutual agreement), with Mary becoming the servant of a planter in the Bahamas and John spending three years in London's Fleet Prison for debt. In 1787 the London-based American Claims Commission that the British government established to deal with such cases awarded John £30, enough to win his release from prison though far less than the £1,171 that he had requested. Nei-ther he nor Mary received anything from South Carolina. "The last time he came," wrote Mary of her husband's final leave-taking in Florida, "he told mee [that] he had not ben to see mee som deys for he was veri sik himself but as soon as he got a little more strength he would come agen to see mee. I never sen him no more."[75]

For the British public, such stories resonated in many of the same ways as the suffering of Continental soldiers on Britain's prison ships did for Americans, and they ensured that, in relations with the United States, the British government continued to regard Congress as something less than a fully competent, treaty-worthy sovereign. In the words of the Philadelphia Loyalist Joseph Galloway, Congress and the Continental army repeatedly showed during the war how little they felt bound by the obligations that governed relations between civilized nations in Europe. Speaking of the Loyalist soldiers taken as prisoners of war with Cornwallis's army at Yorktown in 1781, Galloway claimed that high-ranking officers were confined in the same quarters as slaves, that some had to pay their captors for daily water rations, and that many would have been put to death had there been "a law in Virginia, similar to what had been passed in other provinces, for punishing Loyalists as traitors." "From this plain unadorned narrative of facts," wrote Galloway, "the *perfidy* of Congress, the *inefficacy* of their *recommendations,* and the *rancorous blood-thirsty spirit* of the Rebel rulers in general" were all too clear.[76] "The case of the loyalists was undoubtedly a hard one," concurred South Carolina's David Ramsay in his 1790 history of the revolution, adding that the failure to compensate them after the war was attributable to "the complex constitution of the United States" and the difficulties that it posed for meeting the Union's treaty obligations.[77] As John Adams, who served as ambassador to Britain after the war, warned, Americans were hardly in a position to "complain of breaches of the treaty, when the British court [had] it in their power to prove upon us breaches of the same treaty, of greater importance." "What then is to be done?" asked Adams. "The States, it may be said, will not repeal their laws. If they do not, then let them give up all expectation from this Court and country, unless you can force them to do as you please by investing Congress with full power."[78]

For the delegates who attended the Constitutional Convention in Philadelphia during the summer of 1787, the need for better relations with nations in Europe supplied one of the main reasons for drafting a new charter to replace the Articles of Confederation.[79] As John Jay argued in the third *Federalist* essay—one of eighty-five that he wrote with Alexander Hamilton and James Madison in 1787 and 1788 to build support for ratifying the Constitution in New York—the most important task facing any government was to maintain peace, both among its own people and in its relations with other powers. On the assumption that a strong "national government" would be less likely than the individual states to commit unprovoked hostilities in the Union's own "neighborhood," whether against nonbelligerent Indians or against Europeans in the adjacent territories of Britain and Spain, Jay wrote that a *"united America"* stood a much better chance of fulfilling its international obligations than a *"disunited America."* Jay also maintained that a strong central government would be a more effective guarantor of the law of nations and the Republic's treaties with other powers.[80] Even the right to remain neutral—already the great desideratum of American foreign policy—would become easier to sustain. "[W]hatever may be our situation," wrote Jay,

certain it is that foreign nations will know and view it exactly as it is; and they will act towards us accordingly. If they see that our national government is efficient and well administered, our trade prudently regulated, our militia properly organized and disciplined, our resources and finances discreetly managed, our credit reestablished, our people free, contented, and united, they will be much more disposed to cultivate our friendship than provoke our resentment. If, on the other hand, they find us either destitute of an effectual government (each State doing right or wrong, as to its rulers may seem convenient), or split into three or four independent and probably discordant republics or confederacies, one inclining to Britain, another to France, and a third to Spain, and perhaps played off against each other by the three, what a poor, pitiful figure will America make in her eyes![81]

As these words suggest, the Constitution's supporters recognized that the Union was still part of Europe's treaty-based republic. They also knew that the only rights that they could hope to exercise under that regime were those that other governments were willing to grant them. "Spain thinks it convenient to shut the Mississippi against us on the one side," wrote Jay of the Republic's continued dependence on Europe's maritime powers, "and Britain excludes us from the St. Lawrence on the other."[82] In his own contributions to the *Federalist* essays, Hamilton said the same thing, noting that despite the world's division into four separate political and geographical parts, Europe had "extended her dominion over them all."[83] In such a threatening, European-dominated neighborhood, the only way for Americans to persuade Europe's "superior powers" to respect the Union's still-fragile unity and independence, added Madison, was to form a strong central government.[84] Furthermore, as all three *Federalist* authors recognized, only a government capable of regulating illegal acts of hostility on the part of Americans themselves could make the Republic worthy of Europe's recognition.[85] "The Union will undoubtedly be answerable to foreign powers for the conduct of its members," wrote Hamilton of what was bound to happen if the federal government remained powerless vis-à-vis states and individual citizens that violated European treaties or failed to uphold the law of nations. "The peace of the WHOLE ought not to be left at the disposal of a PART."[86]

Despite the ambivalence that many Americans felt toward the new Constitution, most of the document's anti-Federalist critics admitted that there was a pressing need to "organize the national government on different principles," as Richard Henry Lee wrote in his influential *Letters from a Federal Farmer* (1787–1788), and most believed that only a strong union could safeguard American interests with other nations. Speaking of the powers that could "be lodged nowhere else," Lee, for one, emphasized that the central government alone ought to be responsible for "external objects," including "commerce, imposts, all causes arising on the seas, peace and war, and Indian affairs."[87] Often, the Constitution's Federalist supporters carried matters further, hoping that the new government would rein in domestic malcontents such as the poverty-stricken farmers who joined Daniel Shays's rebellion in western Massachusetts and Vermont in 1786 and 1787, yet they too stressed the need for greater accountability in foreign affairs. "[T]he federal [government] must have the power to control the individual Governments of the States, in some points at least," insisted Stephen Higginson of Boston in February 1787.[88] In the words in a pamphlet sometimes attributed to Higginson's commercial partner Jonathan Jackson,

We have tried our separate sovereignties long enough to see, to feel, that they are puny governments only, while not cemented by one common interest—while not assisted by some higher authority, established equally by all, and common to all. We have passed the Rubicon, and in my mind, the question now is, whether we shall break up into separate disproportioned clans and hordes, each under petty captains and rulers, who will be as tyrannical as they dare to be, and will keep the whole continent in a constant state of turbulence . . . or whether we will all unite, or the great majority of us, in establishing a general and efficient government, which shall include the whole territory ceded to the *United States* by the treaty of *Paris* in 1783.[89]

Viewed from this perspective, the Constitution resembled nothing so much as a "peace pact" in the tradition of Westphalia and Utrecht, an agreement between states that would at last realize the pacific goals that Britain had proclaimed as its objective in the decade before the revolution.[90] "Though the world has never known anything like universal peace," wrote Jonathan Jackson in 1788, "a wise and well regulated government, ever peacefully disposed, might, in a territory like that of the *United States,* make such establishments and use such precautions as would perpetuate peace among themselves, and secure them against any attacks from without."[91] John Adams's three-volume *Defence of the Constitutions of Government of the United States* (1787–1788), written while Adams was in London, made the same claim. Noting that Congress was "a diplomatic assembly," not a "legislative" or "representative assembly," Adams wrote that as with all federal bodies, its members were "responsible to the states; their authority [was] clearly ascertained; and the states, in their separate capacities, [were] . . . able to form an effectual balance."[92] The Constitution transferred many of those powers to the central government, making it possible for "the United States . . . to unite their wills and forces as a single nation." Because his purpose was to answer critics of the new state constitutions, Adams was careful not to disparage either the states or the original union. Still, by curtailing the states' autonomy, the "new system" seemed "admirably calculated to unite their interests and affections" under a single government, and Adams hoped that it would lay the basis for a greater "uniformity of principles and sentiments." The result, he wrote, was "the greatest single effort of national deliberation that the world has ever seen."[93]

In many ways, Adams was justified in his optimism. Even before the inauguration of George Washington in April 1789, it was clear that Federalists who supported the Constitution during the ratification debates of 1787 and 1788 would have a substantial majority in both houses of the newly elected Congress, and Hamilton, in particular, played a leading role as Treasury secretary in creating a central government with the fiscal powers that Americans had refused to allow Parliament before 1776, notably the power to tax for revenue. Congress also established a federal judiciary with the authority to review the actions of state courts and legislatures; it gave the president and secretary of state broad—though by no means unlimited—control over foreign policy; and it authorized the Treasury to assume the states' war debts and to entrust the management to a new Bank of the United States, which was to be modeled on the Bank of England.[94] To Federalists of Stephen Higginson's ilk, there was no question that such measures were designed to "ensure permanent safety and happiness," but even those who had opposed the Constitution appeared reluctant to defy the new government openly.[95] During the celebrations that accompanied Washington's triumphal journey from Mount Vernon to New York in 1789, supporters of the new government took care to project an image of national unity, replete with reminders of Washington's virtues as "the father of his people," the breadth of the president's support among the general populace, and the high regard in which he was held by European governments. In its account of the inauguration ceremony on April 30, New York's *Daily Advertiser* made a point of noting that the French and Spanish ambassadors both illuminated their houses. The residence of Spain's Gardoqui was particularly beautiful, with a display that was reported to include several transparent paintings and "a great assemblage of beautiful figures, executed in the most masterly and striking manner."[96]

Despite gathering clouds from the French Revolution in Europe, Washington and his supporters largely succeeded in establishing a strong government along lines that the Constitution's authors had envisioned. Of the federal government's new powers, those pertaining to

Hamilton's Treasury were particularly intrusive and controversial, with the excise that Congress placed on distilled spirits in 1791 encountering widespread opposition. In Pennsylvania, North Carolina, Maryland, and Virginia, state legislatures responded with resolutions denouncing the tax. Over the next three years, the inhabitants of Pennsylvania's westernmost counties—Allegheny, Westmoreland, Fayette, and Washington—went further still, with acts of resistance that included tarring and feathering federal excise men, sabotaging the stills of local farmers suspected of complying with the new measure, burning the house of the local excise officer John Neville, fomenting riots as far east as Hagerstown, Maryland, and Carlisle, Pennsylvania, and forming Democratic Societies to correspond with disaffected settlers in western Virginia and Kentucky. On August 1, 1794, at the height of the unrest, six thousand militiamen mustered in a grand review at Braddock's Field near Pittsburgh, threatening civil war and secession.[97] According to George Hammond, Britain's ambassador, a delegation approached him at New York about placing the four western counties "under the protection of the British government." "Before he left," reported Hammond after meeting with one of their number, "he enquired the address of the Spanish Commissioners, and assured me that, if I would have listened to him, he had the *means* of *proving* that he did not speak [for] *himself alone*."[98]

Although the Whiskey Rebellion ended without bloodshed, the unrest in Pennsylvania supplied a dramatic indication of the magnitude of the changes that the Philadelphia Constitution had wrought, as well as the high cost of winning European recognition—which was a major part of what the American Revolution was ultimately about—and the continued vitality of the centrifugal forces that meeting those costs helped keep alive. No less important, though, the rebellion showed that the new government possessed the coercive powers that Congress had lacked under the Articles of Confederation and that it had the authority to use force against groups that openly defied its authority without losing the support of the general public. As the Western Army that Washington raised to quell the revolt marched west, some observers mocked the untrained militiamen in its ranks, calling them a "watermelon army" of clam diggers and oystermen whose knowledge of war came from "warring with crabs . . . about the capes of Delaware."[99] Nonetheless, it was widely noted that at nearly thirteen thousand effectives, the army's numbers exceeded the figure in the government's initial call for troops. "[T]he Presdt.," wrote one officer, "means to convince these people at once of the *moderation and the firmness* of the Gov[ernment]."[100] As news spread that Washington was leading the army in person, the insurgents began to lose heart. In the market town of Chambersburg, where rioters had erected a liberty pole bearing the words "Liberty and No Excise on Whiskey," local magistrates "sent for the men," forced them to "cut it down," and ordered them to remove it "with the Same wagon that brought it into town." "The Circumstance was mortifying," wrote Colonel James Chambers of the culprits' humiliation, "and they behaived very well."[101] In the words of a resolution by the Democratic Society of Baltimore, many of whom doubtless sympathized in private with the insurgents' cause, Washington's response to the insurrection was "wise, prudent, and constitutional."[102]

Mindful of the assistance that French envoys such as André Michaux and Edmond Genêt were demanding from the United States, Britain and Spain eventually acknowledged the Union's altered circumstances by commencing full diplomatic relations with the United States. In the Anglo-American Treaty of London (the so-called Jay Treaty), which narrowly passed the Senate at the end of June 1795, the American government agreed to entrust resolution of the most urgent American disputes with Britain to three bilateral commissions: one to adjudicate the pre-revolutionary claims of British creditors, another to compensate the American owners of ships and cargo seized in the Caribbean in 1793 and 1794, and a third to adjust the eastern boundary of Maine. Because it obligated Britain to do nothing that it had not already agreed to do in the Anglo-American treaty that ended the Revolutionary War, the Washington administration's critics—including both Madison and Jefferson—perceived in the Jay Treaty what a writer in the *Philadelphia Minerva* called a humiliating capitulation to an "insatiable despot," yet the agreement clearly signaled a willingness on Britain's part to give Americans the peace that it had been unwilling to make in 1783.[103] In exchange for the settlement of its merchants' prewar debts, Britain abandoned the posts that its forces still occupied in the Northwest Territory, and it made some small (though, to American minds, unacceptable) concessions to American shipping in the West Indies. By ignoring the question of Loyalist compensation, the treaty also implicitly endorsed the adequacy of the British awards to refugees such as John Macklin, and it signaled that London would not continue making an issue of the states' failure to make comparable gestures. Most important of all, Britain's willingness to treat induced Spain to open negotiations of its own. In 1795 Spain and the United States signed the Treaty of San Lorenzo, which opened New Orleans to American shipping and accepted American claims east of the Mississippi River and north of the Anglo-American treaty line of 1783.[104]

In all these areas, the Jay Treaty proved to be a watershed. Despite the United States' neutrality in the Anglo-French war being fought in Europe and America, it confirmed the Union's abandonment of the French alliance of 1778 in favor of an understanding with Britain, it speeded the emergence of a Democratic Republican opposition based, in part, on hostility to the Federalists' Anglophilia, and it underscored the extent of the government's diplomatic authority under the Constitution. Following the treaty's ratification, Democratic Republican clubs organized protests in several cities on July 4, 1795, hanging the American envoy John Jay in effigy on his own doorstep in New York and drawing explicit comparisons between the senators who voted to ratify and the "British thralldom" that threatened Americans in 1776. "Today," claimed a writer in the *Philadelphia Minerva,* "we have no reason to rejoice; our bells should rather be muffled, and drums beat the dead march."[105] From Nashville, Andrew Jackson wrote that President Washington and his Federalist allies in the Senate had brought the Union to the brink of "Civil war." Citing Vattel, among others, Jackson maintained that the Jay Treaty violated both the Constitution and the law of nations by "erecting Courts not heard of in the Constitution" (to enforce the treaty's terms), by forcing the House of Representatives to enact "bills for reaping a revenue" (to fund the three bilateral commissions), and by surrendering rights of which the president and Senate had no "reason to presume that the Nation itself would dispose."[106] On these grounds, Benjamin Bache's *Aurora* demanded that Washington be impeached. As the transplanted Englishman—and Federalist pamphleteer—William

Cobbett wryly noted, it was as if the treaty's opponents wished to re-create the diplomatic uncertainty that the Constitution had been drafted to forestall.[107]

In fact few Americans desired such a thing. Whatever people at the time said and thought, history has come to regard the Jay Treaty as a decisive moment in consolidating the independence that Congress had unilaterally declared nearly twenty years earlier. Significantly, in the political debates that gripped both Congress and the public during the summer of 1795, one of the agreement's defenders was an anonymous "gentleman" from Vermont, whose faction-ridden state had spent the previous decade vacillating between declaring outright independence from all foreign powers (including the United States) and rejoining the British colonies to the north.[108] "Look round you," wrote William Cobbett in an open appeal to readers of Bache's *Aurora,* "and observe well the spectacle that the United States present at this moment":

> If you have wished to enjoy, once more, the charms of change, and taste the sweets of war and anarchy (for I look upon them as insepa-rable in this country), then the President may merit an impeachment at your hands; but, if you have desired to live in peace and plenty, while the rest of the world has been ravaged and desolated, to accuse the President now, is to resemble the crew of ungrateful buccaniers, who, having safely arrived in port, cut the throat of their pilot.[109]

Although rough waters still lay ahead, Cobbett was sure that Americans had been given a chance to end the condition of perpetual warfare *(bellum eternum)* that had characterized their relations with Europe's colonial powers since the revolution. After almost twenty years of hostility, avowed as well as undeclared, the United States was at last free to embrace the "maxim[s]" that governed the foreign relations of every "other state in the world." These, Cobbett reminded his readers, were the same principles that Congress had avowed when it declared independence from Britain: "enemies in war—in peace friends."[110] On this basis alone could the United States hope to join Europe's diplomatic republic.

(4)

Britain's dramatic surrender of the western forts during the summer of 1796 suggested that Cobbett's hopes for peace were not unfounded. "Events strike more powerfully than systems," wrote William Vans Murray of Maryland on learning of the handover of the British stronghold at Detroit. "Could we . . . have but seen [General] W[ayne]'s Entre into Detroit! when he pranced over the Barbacon."[111] The Federalist *Columbian Centinel* struck an equally triumphal note, asking its readers: *"What think ye of the treaty now?"* The posts are taken, and not one drop of blood shed!"[112] To Americans who had endured years of British hostility and condescension, the decorous and orderly nature of the transfer seemed especially significant, suggesting an equality and mutual respect that had been conspicuous mainly by its absence. According to Captain Thomas Lewis, the U.S. attaché who handled preliminary arrangements at Quebec, the British governor Lord Dorchester showed him every courtesy during his mission, making particular inquiries after Washington's health and introducing him to his family. "The first toast was The King of Great Britain," reported Lewis, "the second, invariably, the President."[113] Despite fears that the departing British would wreck the fortifications, even the remote outpost on Mackinac Island was serviceable when it was surrendered, with stone walls intact and a garden full of vegetables.[114] Speaking of the transfer at Detroit, a correspondent in Baltimore's *Federal Gazette* wrote that "the works . . . were evacuated with much propriety and great harmony by both parties."[115] As a British observer noted after the final handover in September, the "mutual civility and attention" with which the two sides conducted themselves appeared "highly creditable" both to "His Majesty's Government of Canada and . . . [to] the United States."[116]

But just what sort of peace had Americans succeeded in making? To answer this question is, in many ways, to confront what was most radical and transformative about the American Revolution. At Detroit and the other forts that Britain evacuated, the ceremonies confirmed that the United States now had a government worthy of Europe's respect: a government at "peace on all [its] borders," as Secretary of State Timothy Pickering wrote Rufus King at the end of August, and blessed with "internal tranquility" at home.[117] Although the Union was not quite as devoid of conflict as Pickering's words suggested, Britain proved willing to accept this assessment. Shortly after taking command of the American post at Niagara, Captain James Bruff requested additional funds from the War Department so that he could "keep up such an intercourse with the officers of the British Garrison" on the opposite bank of the Niagara River "as may comport with the obligation of treaty—or *arise* out of *politeness* and *contiguity* of station."[118] Over the next decade, the American commandants at both Detroit and Niagara cooperated on an array of issues with their British counterparts, lending provisions, returning deserters, and coordinating relations with Indians. During the late 1790s, relations at Niagara grew so cordial that officers from Canada began visiting the American side "whenever the river is free of ice," often accompanied by "their ladies." "It is truly a pleasing circumstance," wrote the American commandant in 1799, "to see the friendly unreserved intercourse which subsists between the two Garrisons."[119]

Taken together, such encounters showed that, having overthrown what Vattel would have called the high sovereignty of the British Crown and Parliament, the United States now had a government capable of exercising the most important attributes of that sovereignty. Considered as a military-fiscal entity, the new U.S. government was, at best, a pale imitation of the British leviathan that some of its Federalist architects hoped to emulate and that Jeffersonian Republicans feared it would become. In his request for additional funds at Niagara, Captain Bruff, for one, was keenly aware of the comparison. Noting that British officers received an entertainment allowance that often exceeded their pay, he asked whether "our Government (founded in justice) would be the only one that requires officers to be polite, conciliatory and to *keep up an intercourse* with foreigners . . . at their private expense?" "Whoever reckons that these points can be effected without a table—and now and then a good glass of wine," wrote Bruff, "does it without his host."[120] If the new government did not always meet the refined standards of Western Europe, however, it was still a treaty-worthy sovereign, one that appeared to possess all the powers that Congress had claimed for the former colonies in 1776. Moreover, despite continued conflict in Indian country and at sea, the government of the United States was legally at peace, more so, certainly, than the warring rulers of Europe. In the words of a Thanksgiving sermon that Zephaniah Swift Moore preached to his congregation at Peterborough, New Hampshire, in 1796:

> [W]hile among the nations of Europe are exhibited the direful effects of war, America enjoys peace, with all its concomitant blessings. . . . Here there is none to molest or make afraid. While the first business of the youth of the different kingdoms of Europe is to acquire a knowledge of the military art, the first business of ours, is to acquire a knowledge of the arts of peace.

"As a neutral nation," Moore concluded, "we are reaping the spoils of Europe."[121]

As Americans would discover, of course, these last words were significant. Although Americans were at peace, the European world to which they belonged was still at war, and the peace that came from being a neutral nation in a time of global belligerence was not the same thing as peace in a time of universal tranquility. Over the next decade, Europe's colonial powers would repeatedly give Americans reason to remember that. In the case of France, the United States' oldest European ally responded to the Jay Treaty with a punishing war of depredation on American shipping, leading Congress to suspend the Franco-American Treaty of 1778 and to authorize the federal government to begin building a professional navy. Although President Adams stopped short of making a formal declaration of war, the Quasi-War, as the naval war that resulted between 1798 and 1800 came to be known, plunged Americans into the wars of the French Revolution in the Caribbean and briefly turned the United States into a de facto ally of Britain. Nor were relations with Spain any easier, especially in the lands that Congress had claimed in the Model Treaty. In 1798 Bourbon officials once again closed New Orleans to American ships and goods, creating a fresh round of conflict on the Gulf Coast and setting the stage for the Louisiana Purchase of 1803. The rapprochement with Britain also proved fragile. Deeply unpopular with Democratic Republicans and many Federalists, the Adams administration's handling of the war with France brought the American union to the brink of what some feared would be a civil war in the late 1790s and contributed to Adams's electoral defeat in 1801. While never the lackeys of Napoleon that their opponents feared, Thomas Jefferson and the Democratic Republicans who took the Federalists' place were much less forgiving of Britain. There was bound to be trouble.

Even so, the American union retained its character as a unified, legally effective sovereign, and it did so without becoming the colossus that Republicans had feared (and historians have occasionally implied).[122] Although recognized as a treaty-worthy nation in Europe, the United States remained, in many respects, a loose-knit union of states, whose citizens continued to freelance in many of the ways that they had as colonial subjects in order to advance their own interests, as merchants, settlers, and adventurers. As the French Creole and Kentucky separatist Michel Lacassagne observed in a letter to the governor of Spanish Louisiana in 1794, Congress's difficulty in levying taxes and raising soldiers occasionally led "foreigners" to the mistaken conclusion that "the United States are weak" but, Lacassagne cautioned, "they look weaker than they really are."[123] Instead, the Union was both strong and weak, with the high sovereignty of the United States shielding citizens from the consequences of actions that violated the Union's international agreements while, often, serving its interests. On learning in 1797 of a French-backed plot by Ethan Allen's brothers to invade Lower Canada from Vermont, Robert Liston, Britain's ambassador, was sure that American officials would take "every measure that the nature of Federal Government will permit" to thwart incursions from "within the Territory of the Union." As Liston recognized, however, Britain often had no choice but to turn a blind eye to actions by American citizens that the U.S. government lacked the authority to restrain.[124]

Over the next decade, Americans benefited in countless ways from these bifurcated relations with their neighbors. In the decade following the Jay Treaty, the United States became, with Britain's tacit consent, the most important neutral carrier in the Western Hemisphere, ushering in a "golden age of American shipping" during which U.S. merchants engrossed the carrying trade of France, Spain, and, eventually, Britain.[125] In 1790 the vessels in America's merchant marine displaced 355,000 tons; seventeen years later, the Republic's total capacity had risen to more than a million, representing a threefold increase. In 1800, some 95 percent of the trade between British West Indian and American ports traveled in American bottoms (compared with slightly less than 50 percent in 1790), and American vessels carried a significant share of the British Caribbean's exports to Europe.[126] As Jacob Crowninshield observed:

> We sail our vessels cheaper than most other nations; we make shorter voyages; we are more economical in our expenses. Our vessels stay but little time in port. The captains transact their own business, seldom going consigned. Here two commissions are saved, one on the sales and another on the purchase. English vessels from Europe go out half loaded and frequently with ballast. They frequently make but one voyage in a year, seldom more than two. Our northern vessels make three and four, southern vessels more, and go full loaded and do not depend on freights out or home.[127]

It seemed only a matter of time before the waters in the Union's vicinity became an American lake.

Nor were these commercial inroads an isolated phenomenon. In the Ohio and Mississippi valleys, the opening of New Orleans to American ships and goods triggered a similar expansion. In November 1795, within weeks of the signing of the Treaty of San Lorenzo with Spain, it was reported in the *Pittsburgh Gazette* that "immigration to this country this fall seems likely to surpass that of any other season." "We are informed," the writer noted, "that the banks of the Monongahela, from M'Kees Port to Redstone, are lined with people intending for the settlement[s] on the Ohio, and Kentucky."[128] As the restrictions on the Mississippi began to lift, this stream of people became a flood. By the late 1790s, settlers were moving into the Green River valley in western Kentucky and beyond, some as veterans claiming Revolutionary War bounties, others as beneficiaries of state and federal land acts, and still others as squatters.[129] Regardless of the legality of their claims, these immigrants often came into conflict with the rights of the region's other inhabitants—fellow settlers, Indians, Loyalists, and Spaniards—and growing numbers traveled with slaves. As had been true of colonial Anglo-America since the seventeenth century, citizens of the United States inhabited societies that differed in fundamental ways from the nations of Western Europe, but the Union to which they belonged now possessed all the international rights of a European sovereign. Although an empire of liberty, the American union was also a treaty-worthy nation. There were no limits, it seemed, to what its citizens could do.

CHAPTER 5

A Slaveholding Republic

As HE WATCHED the Royal Navy's sloop *Abrina* approach, Paul Cuffe must have known that there would be trouble. Although he had spent nearly a year in Britain and Africa, most recently as a guest of the London-based African Institution in Sierra Leone, Cuffe was master of the Westport, Massachusetts, brig *Traveller,* and Britain and the United States were about to become embroiled in the War of 1812. According to the account that Cuffe recorded in the ship's log, the British commander, Captain James Tidwell, followed the navy's standard procedure when stopping foreign ships. Convinced that Cuffe was engaged in "a clandestine trade," Tidwell dispatched a boarding party, who "overhaul[ed] our papers and people," demanded to see "the logbook, all account books, my two chests and two trunks," and "took the brig in tow," fastening its hawser to the British warship. Over the next two days, Tidwell and his men searched every inch of the vessel. While unable to prove that Cuffe was smuggling, they discovered two Africans—both British subjects—who had secretly joined the ship's crew before it set sail. Armed with this evidence, Tidwell took the men into custody and ordered Cuffe to return to Freetown. Although Cuffe reported that the British captain "used [him] kindly," Tidwell said that he could not let him go. "To Sierra Leone I must go, and to Sierra Leone he carried me."[1]

For Americans everywhere, this encounter would have sounded familiar, highlighting the maritime differences that would shortly lead Congress to declare war on Britain. Paul Cuffe, however, was anything but typical. In an age when American ship captains were almost exclusively white, Cuffe was black—quite possibly the wealthiest man of color in the United States—and he was a leading figure in the transatlantic movement to abolish the slave trade. For both reasons, his attitude toward Britain was less hostile than that of many Americans. Not only was Sierra Leone, which Britain established after the American Revolution, the only free black settlement under the "guardianship of a civilized power," as Cuffe wrote in 1812, but Parliament had joined Congress in 1807 in enacting legislation to suppress the African slave trade.[2] Although its colonies had some of the largest slave populations in the world, Britain was the leading antislavery power in the European Atlantic. On meeting the abolitionist member of Parliament William Roscoe, Cuffe did not object when Roscoe claimed that the only way to "make a complete work of the slave trade" would be for Britain's cruisers to seize the slave ships of other nations, including ships belonging to the United States. Nor, apparently, was he troubled by the prospect that the African Americans whom he hoped to settle in Sierra Leone would have "to place themselves under the British government."[3] On several occasions, Cuffe considered becoming a British subject himself, either by moving with his family to Sierra Leone or by sailing as a commercial agent or "supercargo" on a British ship. Upon his death in 1817, he was still living in Massachusetts, but, according to his friend and fellow black abolitionist Peter Williams, that was only because "as a member of the African family" he did not want to abandon "that part of it which was in America."[4]

That a man of Paul Cuffe's stature would hold such views is a reminder of the fissures that the American Revolution helped open in slavery's once-monolithic edifice, but it also underscores the success with which American slaveholders managed the change. Driven by the appearance of free-soil jurisdictions during the 1780s and 1790s, first in New England but eventually in Canada, Sierra Leone, and the French Caribbean, the terms used to legitimate the buying and selling of human beings narrowed considerably in the years following the revolution: from a practice that was assumed to be customary in every part of the world except Europe to one that required the sanction of positive law. As Cuffe's interview with William Roscoe made clear, one effect was to give Britain the right to stop foreign slave ships on the high seas. Another was to strengthen the case for limiting slavery's presence within the Union's own borders. Just as clearly, though, slavery itself remained legal, and nowhere more so than in the treaties that anchored the law of nations in Europe. Although it was not hard to find jurists who viewed both slavery and the laws that sanctioned it as "odious," as Lord Mansfield wrote when he freed James Somerset in 1772, any nation that wished to allow its citizens to continue owning slaves was free to do so. In this spirit, slavery appeared in all three of the Union's founding documents—the Declaration of Independence, the Anglo-American Treaty of 1783, and the Constitution of 1787—and each presented chattel servitude as a legitimate, if cruel and unfortunate, institution.[5] In the effort to turn the United States into a nation that other nations would accept as a treaty-worthy equal, no group had more to gain than the merchants and planters whose human property these texts protected, and no one had a greater stake in securing the national rights that Paul Cuffe viewed with such apparent indifference.

(1)

Slavery's changing legal geography was a direct consequence of the fact that, for most of the forty years between the start of the American Revolutionary War and Napoleon's defeat at Waterloo, Europe's colonial powers were at war. Although abolitionists often described ending slavery as a way to make peace, war was the only time when Europeans and Americans emancipated large numbers of slaves. When they did, they usually targeted the slaves of their enemies. Before its own colonial slave population began to grow during the 1760s, Spain had an unofficial policy of freeing British slaves who reached Florida and Puerto Rico, doing so with particular alacrity if the fugitives were Catholic or expressed a willingness to convert.[6] Following the outbreak of war with Britain in 1793, French Republicans in Saint-Domingue did the same, with offers of freedom not only to the slaves of Bourbon planters but to slaves in nearby Santo Domingo and Jamaica as well.[7] Not surprisingly, such tactics were controversial. Until the American and French Revolutions prompted significant numbers of slaves to take matters into their own hands, Britain and France both refrained from wartime acts of emancipation. During the 1740s and 1750s, and again during the American Revolutionary War, the fighting between the two rivals in the Caribbean was sometimes as decorous and rule-bound as the fighting in Europe (if not more so), and Britain's colonies had a history of forming cartels with neighboring colonies whereby they promised not to interfere with each other's property.[8] For the soldiers and sailors who defended them, a recurring complaint was that planters in America cared more about safeguarding their interest in human chattel than they did defeating their nation's enemies. Wherever slaveholders were in charge, it seemed, "making plantation colonies into battlefields was in nobody's interest."[9]

That, however, is exactly what Britain did during the American Revolution. Throughout the Revolutionary War, British officers made widespread use of black soldiers, extending offers of emancipation not only to white convicts and servants who joined the king's forces but to slaves "who thought they had a right to freedom as well as others."[10] To avoid antagonizing Loyalists, Britain limited such offers to the slaves of patriot masters, yet as many as twenty thousand men and women may have fled to British lines (and possibly more), inflaming white opinion up and down the Eastern Seaboard and helping make the revolution the largest slave insurrection in North America before the Civil War.[11] On learning of Lord Dunmore's plan to arm escaped slaves in Virginia, Janet Schaw, for one, could only surmise that the report was an "artifice" spread by patriots to show "the implacable cruelty of the king of Great Britain." "Every [white] man is in arms," wrote the loyal Scot of the response near her brother's estate in Wilmington, North Carolina, with "patroles going thro' all the town and searching every Negro's house."[12] In Norfolk, where nearly three hundred slaves joined Dunmore's Ethiopian Regiment, inhabitants implored the Virginia Convention to protect their families from the horrors of a "lawless, plundering Soldiery and the more Savage Slave."[13] When rumors of a similar plot reached Wilmington, Schaw wrote that the news led to denunciations of both the king and his government.[14] "Hell itself," claimed an observer in Philadelphia, "could not have vomited any thing more black than [this] design."[15]

In terms of the army's intentions, such fears were overblown. Despite the "Liberty to Slaves" emblazoned on the uniforms of Dunmore's Ethiopians, Britain envisioned freeing and arming slaves not as a first step toward ending slavery but as an instrument of war.[16] "Proclaim *Freedom* to their Negroes," wrote Sir William Draper upon returning from a tour of the colonies in 1774, "then how long would they be a people?"[17] For slaves who entered the king's service, the liberty on offer typically fell short of complete freedom, with recruits "changing one master for another," as John Cruden of South Carolina wrote in a proposal for a black regiment in 1782.[18] Furthermore, emancipation was only for slaves who left their masters voluntarily. When British and Loyalist units captured slaves on rebel plantations, they sometimes treated them as contraband to be plundered and sold in the same manner as "horses, cattle, and plate."[19] During the British invasion of Virginia in 1781, Thomas Jefferson claimed that Lord Cornwallis's army carried off nearly thirty thousand slaves on this basis, recruiting some into the army but sending many to the West Indies where they were exchanged for "rum, sugar, coffee, and fruit." Speaking of thirty slaves that the British took from his plantation at Elkhill, Jefferson told the Scottish historian William Gordon that had Cornwallis intended "to give them freedom, he would have done right: but it was to consign them to inevitable death from the small pox and putrid fever then raging in his camp. This I knew afterwards to be the fate of twenty-seven of them. I never had news of the remaining three, but presume they shared the same fate."[20]

If Britain did not fight the Revolutionary War as a struggle for black freedom, many African Americans came to see it that way. During the final campaigns in Virginia and the Carolinas, large numbers of fugitives crossed British lines, placing enormous burdens on the army's resources. In his account of General Augustin Prévost's brief incursion up the coast of South Carolina in 1779, David Ramsay wrote that the invading soldiers attracted hundreds of slaves "with hopes of freedom," so many, in fact, "that they could not be accommodated." Some managed to follow the king's forces when they retreated to Georgia, but a scarcity of boats forced Prévost to leave most behind. "They had been so thoroughly impressed by the British with the expectations of the severest treatment" from their masters, wrote Ramsay, that many attempted to hang onto the sides of the boats as the soldiers departed. "To prevent this dangerous practice, the fingers of some of them were chopped off, and soldiers were posted with cutlasses and bayonets to oblige them to keep at their proper distances." When the British captured Charleston in 1780, the response was the same. "The slaves a second time flocked to the British army," Ramsay observed,

> and . . . were visited by camp-fever. The small-pox, which had not been in the province for seventeen years, broke out among them, and spread very rapidly. From these two diseases, and the impossibility of their being provided with proper accommodations . . . in the British encampments, great numbers of them died, and were left unburied in the woods. A few instances occurred, in which infants were found in unfrequented retreats, drawing the breasts of their deceased parent some time after life was gone.[21]

Despite the army's inability or, at times, unwillingness to cope, the scale of this exodus eventually forced Britain to adopt a liberationist role. Nowhere were the effects more apparent than in negotiations over the fate of the Black Loyalists at the war's end. According to the preliminary treaty, which Britain and the United States concluded at Fontainebleau in November 1782, the British government agreed to withdraw its forces from the Union's territory, pledging, at the insistence of Henry Laurens of South Carolina, to do so without "carrying away any negroes or other property of the American inhabitants."[22] In places that were still in Britain's possession, African Americans responded with outrage, with many refusing, in the words of the Hessian officer Carl Leopold Baurmeister, "to be delivered in so unwarrantable a manner."[23] As Boston King, who had gained his freedom in South Carolina, recalled of the announcement of the preliminary articles at New York, the coming of peace "diffused universal joy." But for the men and women "who had escaped from slavery and taken refuge in the English army," rumors that "[we] were to be delivered up to [our] masters . . . filled us all with inexpressible anguish and terror."[24] At Charleston, where General Alexander Leslie put the number of voluntary fugitives at four thousand—in addition to nearly six thousand slaves sequestered from rebel estates—

the demand for freedom was so great that the British were forced to include many in the evacuation at the end of 1782, and thousands more left on their own.[25] When George Washington requested a conference in 1783 on former slaves in the British garrison at New York, the commander, Sir Guy Carleton, informed him that there was nothing he could do to prevent their departure. Should Britain refuse to let them leave, as the treaty required, "numbers . . . would very probably go off" by land, while many more would "clandestinely get on Board the Transports" that were taking white refugees to Nova Scotia.[26]

Faced with a movement that he was powerless to stop, Carleton opted for a kind of humanitarian *real politique*. To mollify the Americans, the British commander gestured in the direction of recognizing the rights of masters who had lost slaves. During the summer of 1782—while the preliminaries were being negotiated in France—Carleton authorized General Leslie at Charleston to return sequestered slaves who had been taken without promises of freedom, using his discretion as to whom to restore and whom to keep, and he eventually established a joint Anglo-American commission to adjudicate the claims of aggrieved slave owners at New York. At the same time, though, he ordered General Leslie to honor the Crown's obligations to all blacks who had received explicit promises of emancipation for leaving their masters and joining the British army.[27] As Carleton informed Washington when the two generals met in 1783, "violating" the government's "faith to the Negroes who [voluntarily] came into the British Lines" could not have been part of Britain's intention at the Paris peace talks; the army therefore had no choice but to allow the refugees to leave with the other Loyalists. As part of this decision, Carleton conceded that "sending off the Negroes [might] hereafter be declared in Infraction of the Treaty," in which case Britain would need to compensate their masters. Toward that end, he directed his subordinates to compile a register of "all the Negroes who were sent off, specifying the Name, Age and Occupation of the person, and the Names, and Place of Residence of his former Master." But Carleton also made clear that he had no intention of returning anyone whom the army had liberated. To take such a step would be nothing less than a "dishonorable violation of the public Faith" and a "flagrant injustice to the slaves that [Britain had] manumitted."[28]

In reaching this decision, Carleton used two contradictory definitions of what it meant to be a slave in wartime. Drawing on the customs that governed the disposition of property during military conflicts, Carleton argued that Britain had the same title to blacks in its possession, whether enslaved or liberated, as it did to "any other acquisition or article of prize."[29] From a juridical standpoint, slaves who gained their freedom by crossing British lines retained some of their character as movable property. With this, Carleton was clearly responding to Washington's insistence that the treaty prohibited the removal of any person who was still a slave according to the laws of the United States, including slaves whom the army had emancipated. While refusing to break faith with the Black Loyalists, Carleton acknowledged that Britain might eventually have to purchase their freedom by compensating their former owners. In addition, Carleton may have hoped to forestall disputes over captured bondsmen and women who, though initially taken by force, had later been promised freedom on the basis of their loyalty and service to the Crown.[30] Speaking of the difficulties that had arisen on this score during the 1782 evacuation of Charleston, General Leslie cautioned that many officers in the British garrison had formed attachments with sequestered slaves, whether as personal servants or, in some cases, as lovers and concubines. Because nearly every officer wished "to include his slave into the number to be brought off," wrote Leslie, "they pretend them spys, or guides, and of course obnoxious [to their former masters], or under promises of freedom from Gen[era]l Prevost, L[or]d Cornwallis, L[or]d Rawdon, or some other officer of rank, or free by proclamation."[31] If Congress chose to press the issue, who was to say who had a bona fide claim to freedom and who was still in bondage? Whether they were legally free or not, slavery remained part of the Black Loyalists' status.

Nonetheless, Carleton insisted that the former slaves' military service imposed a second and even more compelling set of "national obligations," with emancipation conferring rights that trumped Britain's obligations to Congress. Mindful that these rights might not meet with universal recognition, whether by former masters in the United States or by settlers and colonial officials elsewhere in the British Empire, Carleton ordered that every freedman and woman be given a certificate confirming that the recipient was protected by Britain's "Proclamation respecting the Negroes," and he made sure that his interpretation of the Anglo-American treaty had London's support.[32] Boston King, for one, had a keen sense of the significance of what Britain had done. "The English," wrote King, "had compassion on us in the day of our distress, and issued out a Proclamation, importing, that all slaves should be free, who had taken refuge in the British lines": "In consequence of this, each of us received a certificate . . . which dispelled all our fears, and filled us with joy and gratitude."[33] As the New York Loyalist Thomas Jones later recalled, the willingness of Britain's peace commissioners to sacrifice the fugitives who had sought the king's protection was shameful, suggesting that they viewed the army's promises to the "blackamoors" in its ranks as a "mere bagatelle," but Carleton refused to follow suit. "Sir Guy," wrote Jones,

> thought differently of national honour and public faith. He possessed the honour of a soldier, the religion of a Christian, and the virtues of humanity. He loved his country, he loved his King, and was determined to see neither disgraced. He shuddered at the article that gave up the blacks, and at once resolved to apply a substitute. He was lucky in the thought.[34]

The result was a significant shift in the legal status of both slaves and slavery in times of war. Although there were precedents for using slaves and freedmen as soldiers—at the siege of Savannah in 1779, for example, Henri Christophe, future king of Haiti, served with the French army in a black regiment from Saint-Domingue—the decision to place Britain's obligations to the Black Loyalists above its obligations to the United States heralded a new government-level commitment to emancipation.[35] During the Orangetown conference with Washington, Carleton reminded the American commander that by refusing to comply with his demands, he was merely acknowledging that he had "no right to deprive [the Black Loyalists] of that liberty that I found them possessed of."[36] Even so, the army's evacuation of New York, in particular, came to exemplify a new-found willingness on Britain's part to regulate its empire according to a "higher law of humanity," as William Pitt is alleged to have told John Adams while Adams was ambassador to Britain.[37] Whatever misgivings he may have had about former slaves whose claims to protection were ambiguous, Carleton himself ended up taking an expansive view of black rights, affirming, in what was by now a common misreading of the *Somerset* case, that all who came into British lines were free because "the British Constitution did not [allow] slavery."[38] Of the nearly three thousand names that appear in Carleton's "Book of Negroes," many belonged to men and women such as Thomas Peters, who had escaped bondage in Wilmington, North Carolina, to become a sergeant in the Black Pioneers; Judith Jackson, who before gaining her freedom as a laundress in Dunmore's Ethiopian Regiment had labored on a Tidewater plantation; and Joseph Clayton, "formerly the property of John Clayton in the Province of Virginia," whose certificate stated that he had "come within the British lines under the Sanction . . . of the Proclamation."[39] But a significant number of refugees—over eight hundred, in fact, or more than a quarter of the total that left New York in 1783—made no claim whatsoever to having been given promises of freedom.[40] They, too, received certificates and were allowed to board the departing transports.

In taking such a broad view of black liberty, emboldened, no doubt, by the embarrassment that he knew his actions would cause the Americans, Carleton helped launch Britain's career as the best friend that "the coloured people have upon the earth," as the African American abolitionist David Walker wrote in 1830.[41] He also opened the way for Britain to begin creating free-soil jurisdictions outside Europe, doing so first in Nova Scotia, where most of the former slaves initially went, but eventually in Africa as well. The most important of these was the settlement that British philanthropists established on the Sierra Leone River in 1787. By sponsoring the project—first as a self-governing Province of Freedom for Black Loyalists from London and white Englishwomen "of the lowest sort," then as a territory under the jurisdiction of a joint stock company in London, and finally, in 1808, as a colony administered directly by the British government—Britain signaled its determination to honor the Crown's obligations to the freedmen and women who had fought for the king in America. Initially, both the settlers and their British patrons hoped that the settlement would become a "free community . . . out of the bounds of Europe," as Carl Bernhard Wadström, a Swedenborgian abolitionist who was based in London, wrote in 1789.[42] At the very least, this meant a community where slavery was prohibited by law, but some hoped that the Province of Freedom would be politically independent as well, freeing the former slaves who settled there from ever again having to depend on the goodwill of a European power. According to the regulations that Granville Sharp drafted in 1786, effective authority was to be in the hands of the settlers, with a universal militia for defense, common ownership of unoccupied land, and the right to vote for all householders, male and female. Although the settlement was loosely subject to the British Crown, its ultimate goal was to become what another supporter, the West Indian Quaker William Thornton, called a "nation of Blacks," with minimal supervision on the part of the British government.[43] On making landfall in 1787, the settlers' first act was to hoist the Union Jack, but their next was to elect the Philadelphia-born freedman Richard Weaver as their "chief in command." Captain Thomas Thompson, the naval officer who accompanied the expedition, returned to England.[44]

While hopes for Sierra Leone's independence proved short-lived, the African Americans who moved there succeeded in establishing a free-soil outpost in one of the main centers of the African slave trade. In 1792 the London directors of the newly chartered Sierra Leone Company augmented the ranks of the original "black poor" settlers with nearly twelve hundred Black Loyalists who had left the United States for Nova Scotia in 1783. In 1800 the colony received another influx, this time of five hundred maroons—also by way of Nova Scotia—who left Jamaica after the Maroon War of 1795–1796.[45] Following the example of General Washington's former slave Harry Washington, who built a plantation that he called Mount Vernon near Freetown, some Nova Scotians, as the Loyalists came to be known, became farmers, while others worked as laborers and artisans, residing on streets named for the British generals under whom they had served in America: Tarleton, Rawdon, and Howe.[46] During the mid-1790s several also became innkeepers and retailers. Among these was Sophia Small, who built a large house on Charlotte Street with outbuildings that covered three lots. Mary Perth, another former slave from Virginia, managed the household of the company's British governor and ran a boardinghouse, at one point taking her only daughter to see a doctor in England.[47] At the time of Cuffe's visit in 1812, Freetown had a population of nearly two thousand men, women, and children, more than half of whom were Nova Scotians. Although the first settlers' ranks were beginning to thin, those still alive included James Reid, a Virginia-born freedman who had left New York with Carleton; Peter Francis, who owned several houses in Freetown, one of which he leased to Cuffe's nephew; and Charlotte Simpson, the last and most formidable of the colony's female merchants.[48]

Because of this free-soil legacy, Freetown eventually became a stronghold of the British effort to abolish the slave trade. From the outset, there were conflicts with merchants on the coast. "We live in Africa," wrote Zachary Macaulay, the settlement's company-appointed governor (and father of the English historian), after a Bristol privateer captured and sold a black crew from the settlement into slavery in 1793. "If we mean to live and do good, we must suppress our emotions."[49] While conceding that officials in Africa would need to show prudence in deciding how to handle such encounters, the founders of the Province of Freedom and the directors of the Sierra Leone Company each banned slavery within the settlement's confines, and the company instructed its officials not to return fugitive slaves to native and European traders "merely [for] being slaves."[50] On several occasions, merchants on nearby Bance Island responded by kidnapping free blacks from the settlement, leading Richard Weaver to complain that "Government did not . . . send us here to be made slaves of."[51] In 1793 tempers ran so high that Macaulay had to convene a special palaver with the settlers' elected representatives. Quoting Parliament and Blackstone, Macaulay managed to persuade the assembly that British merchants in their vicinity had a right to buy and hold slaves, even though slavery was illegal within the settlement itself.[52] The following summer, however, Macaulay himself got into trouble. Because the slave trade was illegal in Massachusetts—and, he appears to have mistakenly believed, the United States—he provided sanctuary to two slaves who had escaped from a slave ship belonging to Captain David Newell of Boston. When French privateers captured and sacked Freetown later that year, Newell played a leading role, driven, apparently, by a desire to avenge his loss.[53]

As the Province of Freedom's travails suggested, slavery was still legal in the extra-European Atlantic, but thanks to the changes that the American Revolution had helped set in motion, it was no longer universally the legal norm. Of course, 1794 turned out to be a pivotal moment in

Britain's relations with the Black Loyalists' former masters in America in
a number of other areas. At Quebec, Guy Carleton—now Lord Dorchester and governor-general of British North America—brought the two
governments to the brink of war with a speech encouraging Britain's Indian allies in the Northwest Territory in hostilities against the Union.
Meanwhile, as the navy clamped down on neutrals who traded with
revolutionary France, American seamen languished on British prison
brigs in the West Indies, and Britain's policies in the Mediterranean ex-
posed them in growing numbers to slave marts on the Barbary Coast. As
he guided the Bordeauxmen into the road at Freetown, Captain Newell
could have had such things in mind. Or maybe he thought no one would
notice, let alone care about, an attack on the free-soil outpost. If so, he
was mistaken. In both Britain and America, the raid became one more in
the litany of grievances against the United States. In early 1795, William
Wilberforce, leader of the antislavery cause in Parliament and a director
of the Sierra Leone Company, sent a report detailing a series of depredations by American slave traders against the settlement to John Jay, who
was in London to negotiate the treaty that bears his name.[54] Britain also
lodged a formal complaint with the Washington administration in Philadelphia, alleging that the raid, though carried out by French privateers,
had been the work of Newell and Peter William Mariner, a former British
naval lieutenant living in New York, and it demanded "exemplary punishment" for both culprits.[55] In matters involving slavery and the slave
trade, Britain, it was clear, had a potent weapon with which to chastise
the former colonies, and in so doing to complicate the Union's quest to
be accepted as a treaty-worthy nation in Europe.

(2)

Although Britain soon let the Freetown raid drop, the creation of free-
soil jurisdictions in Africa and America underscored the Union's weakness, both in terms of its ability to control freelancing citizens like David
Newell and in its relations with Britain, France, and Spain. Into the mid-
1790s Britain's refusal to compensate the Black Loyalists' masters remained a particularly bitter sticking point, and not just with slaveholders
in the South but with antislavery leaders as well, including Benjamin

Franklin, John Adams, and John Jay. Spain's policy of granting sanctuary to African Americans who escaped from Georgia to East Florida was another area of contention, as was the slave insurrection on Saint-Domingue, which so alarmed the Washington administration that it advanced over $700,000 between 1791 and 1793 to the colony's embattled planters, deducting the sum from the Union's Revolutionary War debt to France.[56] Conflict over the British campaign to suppress the African slave trade also seemed likely. As became clear during Parliament's debate over the first, unsuccessful antislave trade bill in 1789, Britain had no intention of allowing other nations to profit from a business that its own merchants were being forced to give up. In his speech introducing the measure on May 12, 1789, Wilberforce claimed that once Britain made the trade illegal, no other nation would want to "court the odium and disgrace of continuing it." Should such hopes prove misplaced, there was always the Royal Navy. With nations that failed to follow Parliament's lead, Britain would be free to "exert her means," as Charles James Fox said during the debate, and force them to do so.[57] For Americans who knew what it was like to be stopped by a British cruiser, there was no question what such words meant.

Faced with this threat to the Union's international standing, Americans responded in two different ways. First, they enshrined antislavery principles in their own laws and constitutions. By the end of the Revolutionary War, several states, including Virginia, had laws banning the African slave trade, and Pennsylvania and Massachusetts had taken steps to abolish the institution outright. Building on the prohibition on slavery in the Northwest Territory in 1787 and the federal government's authority to regulate international trade under the U.S. Constitution, Congress outlawed the shipment of slaves to foreign countries in 1794, and every state in the Union—including, for a time, South Carolina—banned the importation of slaves.[58] Often, the constraints in these measures were as striking as the freedoms that they endorsed. In the case of the American movement to withdraw from the African slave trade, the Constitution authorized Congress to enact legislation banning the importation of slaves; however, it postponed the event until 1808. Until then, the states were free to do as they pleased. So, too, in the Northwest Ordinance, Congress prohibited slavery north of the Ohio River; however, the law required magistrates in the new free-soil states to enforce the slave codes of other states by returning fugitives to their masters.[59] Still, the idea that all men are created equal, as James Forten, leader of Philadelphia's free black community, wrote in 1813, appeared, at last, to include everyone: "the Indian and the European, the Savage and the Saint, the Peruvian and the Laplander, the white Man and the African."[60]

In seeking to limit slavery's presence within the Union, Americans repeatedly mentioned abolition's growing support elsewhere, arguing that to do nothing would "appear to the world absurd and disgraceful," as Luther Martin of Maryland remarked in 1788.[61] Indeed, in some minds, abolishing slavery formed a necessary part of the Union's quest to be accepted as a treaty-worthy nation in Europe. "You, gentlemen," wrote New Jersey Quaker David Cooper in a 1783 address to Congress, have "*declared* to Europe, to the world, 'That all men are born *equal* . . . and are *equally* entitled to liberty.' We expect, mankind expects, you to demonstrate your *faith* by your *works*."[62] Slavery's opponents also appealed to Americans as Christians, economic rationalists, and patriots, noting the ways in which slaveholding was a sin, the inefficiencies that slavery placed on the economy, and the threat that disaffected slaves posed to the Republic's security.[63] Yet Americans were well aware of the strength of antislavery sentiment in Britain and Europe, and many saw that opinion as another reason to act. During the debate in Congress over the 1794 statute banning American participation in the slave trade to foreign nations, the bill's supporters drew much of their evidence from British sources, quoting, among other authorities, the Lords of Trade's report on the slave trade in 1789 and the parliamentary speeches of Wilberforce, Pitt, and Fox.[64] Speaking of the clause that authorized Congress to prohibit the importation of slaves in twenty years' time, James Wilson assured the Pennsylvania convention that ratified the Constitution in 1787 that there was no more "lovely part" of the new charter, nor one more likely to "expand the breast of a benevolent and philanthropic European."[65]

Bolstered by such perceptions, slaveholders in a number of states came to embrace at least parts of the abolitionist cause. In 1789, noting the support for abolition in "Europe and America," the Maryland Society for Promoting the Abolition of Slavery insisted that the present was an especially propitious moment to act.[66] During the 1780s Maryland and

Virginia passed legislation to make it easier for masters to manumit their slaves at their death, and both legislatures considered—and narrowly rejected—bills calling for gradually ending slavery entirely, often in terms that drew on the antislavery movement in Britain and Europe's other colonial powers.[67] Writing in support of one such proposal in Virginia in 1796, St. George Tucker, professor of law at the College of William and Mary, cited various British authorities, including Blackstone, Granville Sharp, and Francis Hargrave, the English attorney who represented James Somerset in 1772. In a passage that he attributed to Jefferson but that Jefferson had taken from David Hume, Tucker described the "commerce between master and slave" as an "exercise of the most boisterous passions." Although events on Saint-Domingue gave him pause, slavery's "unhappy influence on [our] manners," also taken from Hume by way of Jefferson, troubled him even more. Among the more worrying effects were the degrading conditions that the institution imposed on slaves themselves and the despotism that it encouraged in their masters. A law professor in Virginia probably knew more about such things than a man of letters in Edinburgh, but it was the Scot who supplied the words.[68] By 1800 Virginia had a growing free black population, and freedmen and women accounted for nearly a quarter of all African Americans in Maryland.

Despite the first stirring of proslavery opinion in both Congress and the southern states, antislavery continued to enjoy broad support in many parts of the Union. Significantly, most Americans, including most slaveholding Americans, eventually decided that it was in their interest to accept the cause's centerpiece, the movement to abolish the African slave trade. In each of the federal statutes restricting American involvement in the trade—those of 1794 and 1800 made it illegal to carry slaves to foreign destinations, while the act of 1807 banned the importation of slaves into the United States—southerners joined their northern compatriots in condemning what Thomas Jefferson, in his annual message to Congress in 1806, called the "violations of human rights" that had for too long been inflicted on the people of Africa.[69] As Speaker Nathaniel Macon of North Carolina assured the House of Representatives when it took up the bill abolishing importations, there was "but one opinion" on the subject.[70] To a surprising degree, this was even true of South Carolina. Although the legislature repealed its ban on the slave trade in 1803, none of South Carolina's eight-member delegation to Congress supported the trade's resumption nor, for that matter, did any of the state's slaveholding neighbors.[71] Speaking of the thirty-nine thousand Africans who were brought to Charleston between 1804 and 1807, the *Washington Expositor* asked how anyone who "prides himself upon the independence of his country" could fail to be embarrassed.[72] When Congress finally abolished the trade, a group of free blacks, meeting at the African School Room in New York, submitted a petition of thanks, expressing their gratitude to the United States for cooperating with the "friends of humanity."[73] As Jefferson said, the slave trade was an unacceptable blot on "the morality, the reputation, and the best interests of our country."[74] Its abolition was long overdue.

Even as antislavery in America drew strength from antislavery in Britain and Europe, however, slaveholders continued to insist that the United States protect the rights to which they were entitled under slavery's positive law. This was abundantly clear from the American government's repeated efforts to gain compensation for the masters of the Black Loyalists who left New York in 1783. During the 1780s and early 1790s Britain put the narrowest possible interpretation on the relevant section in the Anglo-American treaty, holding that it only applied to slaves who crossed British lines after the preliminary articles were signed in November 1782. Yet to many Americans, the issue was not so clear-cut. Not surprisingly, some of the most forceful objections came from Virginia, where Patrick Henry led a movement in the legislature to prevent British creditors from collecting nearly two million pounds in prewar debts until Britain paid in full for what Jefferson euphemistically called the "property" that the king's forces had carried off. In his 1784 letter to the *Leiden Gazette,* Jefferson put the value of the state's wartime losses—most of it in the form of escaped slaves—at £500,000. By the time of his exchange with Scottish historian William Gordon in 1788, the figure had risen to £3 million.[75] In South Carolina, the costs were equally high. Recalling the siege of Charleston in 1780, David Ramsay claimed that the British army "plundered by system," sending off "two thousand plundered negroes . . . at one embarkation." "It has been computed," claimed Ramsay, that "South-Carolina was deprived of negroes to the amount of twenty-five thousand."[76] If true, fugitive slaves alone accounted for losses of nearly £2.5 million.

Jefferson and Ramsay both had reason to exaggerate the number of slaves that fled to British lines, so their figures may have been inflated. Still, they carried weight with other Americans, including those with abolitionist sympathies.[77] During the peace negotiations at Fontainebleau in 1782, John Adams, for one, described the plunder of slaves in Virginia and South Carolina as an enormity comparable to the burning of North American ports, the confinement of Continental prisoners on British ships, and the theft of Benjamin Franklin's library. For his part, Franklin proposed language that would have required Britain to pay compensation for any slave taken from a plantation on American soil, placing the loss to their masters on a par with the goods that the army had taken from American merchants, the towns, villages, and farms that British forces had devastated in every part of the Union, and the "tobacco, rice, [and] indigo" that was seized during the final campaigns in Virginia and the Carolinas.[78] During his three years as minister to Britain, Adams repeatedly raised the question of compensation. As he told the provost of Glasgow when the two met in 1785, the slaves that General Carleton evacuated from New York would have been at work to pay off their masters' British debts, including those owed to Scotland's tobacco merchants, had they been returned as the treaty required, and he said the same thing to William Pitt and Britain's foreign secretary Lord Carmarthen.[79] While each politician listened patiently, none of them proved willing to do anything more.[80]

Given Britain's intransigence, the Washington administration eventually abandoned the effort to win compensation, though in ways that affirmed the Black Loyalists' status as property. To the fury of southern politicians, including Secretary of State Edmund Randolph, the Jay Treaty, which Americans hoped would clear up all outstanding differences with Britain, made no mention of the former slaves, leading to allegations that it was "grossly unequal and partial" and to suspicions that Jay had allowed his abolitionist views to influence the negotiations.[81] According to Randolph, who sent several letters on the subject to Jay while he was in London, the law of nations was on the side of the former slaves' masters. Although Britain was free to liberate slaves in its possession during the war, Congress was under no obligation to recognize the liberty so granted, nor did the treaty impose such an obligation once the war was over. Instead, the treaty's "use of the term '*negroes*'" rather than slaves suggested that the framers intended Britain to return every slave whom the army had taken, regardless of the condition of the men and women in question when the treaty was signed.[82] In a report to Congress in 1786, Jay took a slightly narrower view, but he, too, concluded that American slaveholders had rights that Britain could not ignore. While professing discomfort over using people as "booty," Jay said that the treaty offered no protection to the Black Loyalists because slaves, by definition, could not "extinguish the right or title of their Masters" simply by fleeing and because Britain could not destroy those rights by "receiving" them.[83] However satisfying Britain's position might be from a humanitarian standpoint, the liberty offered to slaves during the Revolutionary War was invalid according to the United States' understanding of the Anglo-American treaty, and their former owners had a strong case for compensation.

This of course was not far removed from the position that General Carleton had taken when he compiled his Book of Negroes, reasoning that a census of the Black Loyalists who left New York might be necessary if Britain ever had to pay for their freedom. When Jay raised the issue in London, however, the British Foreign Secretary Lord Grenville dismissed this construction of the treaty as "odious," pointing out that for Britain to accept the United States' claim would be to break faith with people who were now legally British subjects. In relating the conversation to Randolph, Jay admitted that this interpretation of the treaty "made an impression" on him.[84] But Randolph was quick to see the influence of British antislavery and, he claimed, hypocrisy. In a long letter to Jay, Randolph warned that the foreign secretary was using "moral reasoning" to shelter "himself from the true construction of . . . the treaty." "What is more customary," he asked, "than for [nations] to surrender, on peace, rights acquired purely and solely through a war?" Randolph also noted that Britain recognized the right of its own subjects to own slaves, writing that the United States' understanding of the treaty was

> not odious because the British Government hate slavery. No sir, they established it in the United States, while colonies; they continued the

> importation of slaves against the will of most of the States; it exists,
> by their authority in many of their foreign dominions.[85]

If there was any "odium" in the American position, it had to be in "depriving the slaves of the liberty" that Britain had given them, but on this question the law was clear. Blacks who joined the king's forces would have "reverted to the condition of slaves" had they been captured by Washington's army, and "what the war gave might, by a peace, be taken away." Given the lack of ambiguity on these points, the only explanation that Randolph could see for Jay's failure to press the issue was the doubt cast by the foreign secretary's "vague" use of moral language.[86]

If so, the Jay Treaty nonetheless affirmed the validity of treating the former slaves as property, and it did so both for Britain and for the treaty's Federalist supporters and Democratic Republican opponents. Even Jay said so. In remarks to Randolph, he admitted that Grenville's use of antislavery was unsettling, but that was not what thwarted his effort to gain compensation. Instead, it was the foreign secretary's contention that Britain had the same right to emancipated slaves as it did to livestock that "strayed from within American lines." Ultimately, the dispute was over who had the better title to the Black Loyalists in their capacity as chattel.[87] According to South Carolina's William Loughton Smith, who supported the treaty in Congress, Britain's "affected philanthropy" clearly placed Jay at a disadvantage—as it did some of the treaty's opponents in America—however, Smith insisted that the controversy was really over a "species of property" and had to be decided on that basis.[88] Significantly, during the summer of 1795, Federalists justified the administration's decision to drop the question of compensation not by denying the legitimacy of the slaveholders' claims but by reducing the number of slaves for which compensation was due, with the number of fugitives falling from five thousand (or more), which Brockholst Livingston of New York claimed would have yielded a compensatory sum equal to the prewar debt that Americans owed their British creditors, to one or two thousand.[89] To continue pressing the issue over such numbers would be to risk going to war for stakes of diminishing value, and the war that resulted would be for a principle that even slaveholders said was repugnant. "Shall we *persevere*," asked the *Providence Gazette*, "when more than half the people of the United States consider the number of slaves [that] we now have as a national calamity?"[90]

Although the answer to this question was no, the United States continued to look for ways to reconcile the widespread belief that slavery was repugnant to the Union's founding ideals with the right of its citizens to participate in the institution. When they could do so quickly and without fear of undue scrutiny, American officials acted forthrightly in slavery's defense, negotiating a treaty with the Creeks in 1783 that required the Indian nation to return or pay compensation for several hundred slaves who had fled to its territory during the Revolutionary War, and using Spain's embarrassment during the Nootka Sound crisis with Britain in 1790 to persuade Bourbon officials to close East Florida to fugitives from Georgia.[91] Often, though, the government maintained its support for antislavery, but in ways that protected the rights of slave owners. This was especially true of the growing pressure to allow the Royal Navy to stop suspected American slave ships, which became a major issue during the crackdown on neutral trade that followed Nelson's destruction of the French and Spanish navies at Trafalgar. In 1806—before either Congress or Parliament had enacted legislation ending the slave trade—James Monroe, the American minister in London, and William Pinkney negotiated a new commercial treaty with Britain, one provision of which gave each nation's warships the right to enforce the other's laws against the slave trade. Because the Constitution's twenty-year window upholding the right to bring slaves into the United States had yet to close, the two envoys wrote that the agreement's "sphere of operation would be a very restricted one" until 1808. Even then, Britain would be obligated to respect whatever rights Congress and the states chose to leave undisturbed, including the right of American ships to carry slaves from the United States to the British West Indies.[92] Jefferson decided not to send the treaty to the Senate, hoping, mistakenly, as events would show, that if the negotiation were allowed "to take a friendly nap" then the differences that it had been meant to resolve might subside, but he also did not challenge Britain's right to interfere with the American slave trade.[93]

Ironically, in view of the public outcry over Britain's treatment of American ships and sailors, James Madison, Jefferson's successor as president, eventually acknowledged Britain's right to seize American slave ships.[94] For abolitionists, of course, there were good reasons to do so. Because the U.S. Navy lacked the resources of its British counterpart, the state and federal laws banning American involvement in the slave trade looked good on paper but often had little impact.[95] In 1800, when an American warship brought a Charleston slave ship into Philadelphia and released the 118 captives at Lazaretto Station, Elizabeth Drinker was so moved by the news that she "set about making up a bundle . . . of good and sutable things for the poor naked creatures." "I look'd upon this as a call upon humanity," she wrote.[96] Yet the laws against the slave trade were difficult to enforce, especially in distant waters, as Turell Tufts, the American consul to British Guyana, lamented in 1800.[97] Indeed, American involvement in the foreign slave trade almost certainly increased after the trade became illegal in 1794, with the relative number of Africans being carried annually in U.S. vessels rising from 2 percent of all shipments to the Americas in the 1780s to 16 percent twenty years later.[98] As the New York ship captain and memoirist, George Coggeshall, recalled, large numbers of Americans were still smuggling slaves when Congress belatedly declared the trade to be a form of piracy in 1820, and "the most reckless" continued to do so.[99] Writing in 1808, as Congress's ban on slave importations to the United States was about to take effect, Governor Thomas Ludlam of Sierra Leone was under no illusions about the likely results. Americans, he wrote, had long supplied Spanish America with slaves despite "prohibitions" by their own governments. Unless Britain intervened, what was to prevent them from continuing to do so?[100]

Because the laws that made the slave trade illegal—within the Union no less than in Britain and Europe—still recognized the right to own slaves, however, even rigorous enforcement of the new measures posed less of a threat to American slaveholders than at first seemed to be the case. This was amply clear from the fate of captives whom American officials took from condemned slave ships. At the insistence of southerners in Congress, none of the federal statutes that outlawed the slave trade specified what was to be done with the ships' human cargo. When the problem first arose in 1800, Secretary of the Navy Benjamin Stoddert surmised that Congress had been silent because it expected that naval officers would sell slaves along with the vessels from which they had been taken in the West Indies, but for ships that were brought to North America and condemned in U.S. ports, the captives' fate depended on where their cases were tried.[101] In Philadelphia, where the navy brought in several "black birders" during the final year of the Quasi-War with France in 1800, the authorities freed the captives and bound them out as indentured servants, with local humanitarians—Elizabeth Drinker among them—supplying the captives with food and clothing until suitable accommodations could be found. On meeting two boys in 1806 who had been liberated at Philadelphia and indentured to a Quaker family, Robert Sutcliff, a Quaker traveller from Yorkshire, exulted in comparing their "orderly conduct and pleasing dispositions" with the barbarism of the trade from which they had been rescued.[102] On the other hand, had the ship from which they were taken been condemned at Charleston or Norfolk, the boys almost certainly would have been re-enslaved. Under the laws of Virginia, the only requirement governing the disposition of recaptured slaves was that their captors had to take them out of the state.[103]

Nor was this paradox limited to the United States. After Parliament abolished the slave trade in 1807, Britain established a vice-admiralty court at Freetown and authorized its warships to target both British ships and the ships of other nations, including Spain, France, Portugal, and the United States. Between 1807 and 1816, the court freed more than seven thousand African slaves, most from ships captured off Sierra Leone's coast.[104] As in the use of prize law to free the slaves of patriot masters during the Revolutionary War, people taken from illegal slave ships became the property of the Crown. While stipulating that the forfeiture's sole purpose was to extinguish "all other property, right, title, or interest," Parliament authorized British officials to provide for the redeemed captives' needs either by enlisting them into the king's armed forces or by indenturing them to local farmers and merchants.[105] In 1812, five years after the abolition of the slave trade, Thomas Coke, superintendent of Methodist missions in England, observed during a visit to Sierra Leone that "recaptured slaves" already made up a considerable portion of the colony's population. "There is scarcely a family, however poor," wrote Coke, "that has not one, or more of these apprentices, and some have so many as twenty."[106] While he was in Sierra Leone, Paul Cuffe made similar comments, noting the remains of several "hulks that had been condemned in [the] slave trade" and attending the trial of a Portuguese schooner accused of "trading contrary to the [law] of nations." On visiting the plantation of former governor Thomas Ludlam, he observed that the labor was done entirely by "captured natives" from such vessels.[107] As part of the African Institution's invitation to move to Sierra Leone in 1812, William Allen and Thomas Clarkson assured Cuffe that he and his fellow settlers would have no difficulty obtaining laborers from Africans who had been liberated from condemned slave ships.[108]

Then, as now, critics in both Britain and America were quick to note the shortcomings of the policies that made such offers possible, especially Britain's continued use of black servitude in its campaign against the slave trade. For warships on the Sierra Leone station, capturing slave ships could yield handsome profits, with the Crown offering bounties of £40 per man, £30 per woman, and £10 per child for each slave whom a captor seized. Although such figures paled when compared to the price that slaves typically commanded in the West Indies, the Treasury paid out nearly £200,000 on this basis between 1808 and 1815, inviting comparisons with the traffic that the king's ships were there to suppress.[109] Likewise, the distribution of recaptives once they made landfall at Freetown bore more than a passing resemblance to a slave mart, with recruiters from the British army getting first dibs—including, according to vice-admiralty judge Robert Thorpe, women and girls who were chosen "for the basest of purposes"—followed by the owners of large plantations, with the Black Loyalists and other "settlers obtain[ing] the refuse as apprentices for fourteen years." All too often, wrote Thorpe, the apprenticeship system allowed former slaves "to change their masters, not their condition."[110] Thomas Coke took a less jaundiced view, writing that as soon as "captured slave-ships arrive . . . the slaves have their chains knocked off by the command of the Governor," yet he, too, noted that recaptives tended to be "insensible of the services that have been done them."[111] Britain might be the leading antislavery power in Europe and the European Atlantic, but it still sanctioned coerced labor in all its forms.

Given the extent to which the laws abolishing the slave trade remained entangled with the right to own slaves, Federalists and Democratic Republicans alike found in the years before the War of 1812 that they could live with the effects of Britain's campaign. Significantly, though, the Madison administration based its acceptance, not on an international agreement like the aborted Monroe-Pinkney Treaty, but on the president's willingness to accept the maritime rights that Britain claimed under the rules of war. The key moment came with the landmark case of the South Carolina slave ship *Amedie,* which Sir William Grant, judge of the English Prize Court of Appeals, decided in the British captor's favor in 1810. In upholding the ruling of the vice-admiralty court in the British Virgin Islands, Grant wrote that in December 1807, when the *Amedie* was taken, Parliament had declared the trade to be "contrary to the principles of justice and humanity." As a result, the trade could no longer "be said to have a legitimate existence" in a British court. Noting that Parliament could not "legislate for other countries," Grant conceded that a foreign legislature, including Congress, if it so desired, might "dissent from this doctrine and give permission to its subjects to prosecute [the] trade." But in an echo of the *Somerset* principle that slavery, because it was morally repugnant, could only be sanctioned by positive law of a sort that England lacked, Grant maintained that Britain had the right to seize the slave ships of other nations, the only exception being ships whose masters could show that they were authorized by the "particular law[s] of [their] own country."[112] Slavery, which jurists in Britain had once viewed as an abuse that had been "happily banished from Europe," as Vattel wrote, while being customary in most other parts of the world, had become an anomaly that violated the natural order everywhere.[113] Because Congress had also outlawed the trade, British warships could take slave ships flying the stars and stripes.

In accepting Grant's ruling—via a letter from Secretary of State Robert Smith to William Pinkney, now American ambassador in London—Madison wrote that he was pleased that Britain shared the Union's determination to bring the slave trade to a speedy conclusion, and—without mentioning Britain—he included a call in his annual message to Congress in December 1810 for the U.S. government to redouble its own efforts against American slave ships. Mindful of the looming controversy over Britain's treatment of American ships and sailors, Madison made clear that the right that the administration was conceding only applied to the slave trade, but he directed Pinkney to "facilitate" the Royal

Navy's efforts to interdict American slavers "as far as the respect . . . due to national prerogative will permit."[114] In exchanges with Britain over the captivity of American seamen in North Africa, the U.S. government had occasionally mentioned the slave trade, hoping that Britain would protect Americans from Barbary corsairs in ways that anticipated the navy's efforts to thwart slave traders in Africa.[115] During the War of 1812, this convergence appeared sufficiently close for Jonathan Russell, American chargé d'affaires in London, to mention the consensus on the slave trade as an example of the agreement that the United States thought the two governments ought to be able to reach on the Royal Navy's impressment of American seamen.[116] As Henry Wheaton, who became the leading American expert on international law, noted in 1815, the *Amedie* decision had an "anomalous tendency" because of the powers that it gave British warships to seize neutral vessels. Yet, according to Wheaton, the ruling was "strictly conformable to principle," and he wrote that it flowed "with irresistible force from the three-fold operation of the law of nature, the act of Congress, and of Parliament."[117]

What the United States refused was to give Britain the right to police the American slave trade under the positive law of a European treaty. Although the Treaty of Ghent, which brought the war with Britain to a close in the waning days of 1814, included a joint Anglo-American statement declaring the slave trade to be illegal, efforts by U.S. diplomats to secure an agreement that would allow the Royal Navy to seize American slave ships encountered stiff opposition in the American press and repeatedly failed to win the support of Congress. Speaking of the slave trade clause in the Monroe-Pinkney Treaty, Charles Brockden Brown dismissed the idea of allowing Britain to help police American slave ships as "a fair flower of philosophy." "To abolish the slave trade," wrote Brown, "is good sound British policy" but offered no advantage to the United States. Why should Americans accept an agreement whose main beneficiary would be their former master?[118] Following the War of 1812, resentment over Britain's treatment of American seamen during the long struggle with Napoleon turned the anti-British sentiment in Brown's pamphlet into national policy. When Stratford Canning, Britain's ambassador to the United States, asked John Quincy Adams in 1822 if he could think of a worse evil than the slave trade, the secretary of state was quick to reply, "Yes: admitting the right of search by foreign officers of our vessels upon the seas in time of peace."[119] By the early 1820s even William Pinkney seemed to think better of the principles that had once led him to support the slave trade's joint suppression. It was not "humanity," he said, or "respect for the philanthropic principles of Mr. Wilberforce" that had prompted Parliament to abolish the slave trade in 1807 but "cold calculations of interest."[120] There were still plenty of Americans who cheered Britain's efforts to end the slave trade. But as citizens of a union with the same treaty-making rights and powers as the sovereign nations of Europe, Americans would decide for themselves whether to follow its example.

The result was to ensure that slavery remained legal, both in the Union's own courts and statutes and in the treaty law that the United States shared with Europe. As the Jay Treaty and the protracted negotiations over the suppression of the slave trade showed, neither Britain nor the United States questioned the international right to own slaves. Although every state in the Union had laws prohibiting the slave trade by the late 1790s and many took steps to abolish slavery itself, the decades following the revolution witnessed the codification of the right to own slaves on the state and federal levels, with Congress enacting the Fugitive Slave Law in 1793 and the federal government moving the capital from the free soil of Pennsylvania to the District of Columbia, where the slave of a southern politician could no longer escape to freedom, á la *Somerset,* by walking out of her master's front door. No less important, the laws that limited the rights of slaveholders in some areas invariably affirmed—and sometimes strengthened—the right to own slaves in others. According to the English abolitionist Edward Rushton, who wrote an *Expostulatory Letter* to George Washington in 1797 calling on the former president to emancipate his own slaves, the movement to abolish slavery seemed to have made almost no impression on southern slaveholders:

> [T]he men of Maryland, of Virginia, of the two Carolinas, of Georgia, and of Kentucky, they smile contemptuously at the idea of negro emancipation, and with the State Constitution in one hand, and the cow-skin in the other, exhibit to the world such a spectacle, as every real friend to liberty must from his soul abominate.[121]

As a characterization of southern attitudes, Rushton's portrait was over-drawn; as a description of federalism, it was not. The same union that upheld the slave trade's abolition was also, in unmistakable ways, one that sanctioned slavery.

By the time Paul Cuffe returned to Massachusetts from his travels, the struggle to safeguard slavery's place within the Union had largely been decided, and the components of a pro-slavery ideology, one that depicted chattel servitude as "indispensable to the peace and happiness" of blacks and whites, as John C. Calhoun of South Carolina would insist in 1837, were starting to fall into place.[122] So, too, for that matter was the sense that in internal conflicts over slavery the free states would have to yield. It is no wonder that Cuffe continued to entertain the possibility of emigrating. Still, in a sign of his stature as one of the Union's leading black abolitionists, President Madison agreed to meet with him during the spring of 1812. On the journey to Washington, Cuffe noticed that people "seemed to have [a] great knowledge of me," probably because of the attention that his travels had received in the American press. The only "objection" came from "a Southward man" somewhere between New York and Philadelphia, "who seemed to be [a] good deal tried" when he had to eat at the same table with a man of color. On the return trip, though, Cuffe endured one indignity after another. In Baltimore and New York, tavern keepers refused to take him in or to give him dinner with the other guests. On the stage from Washington, a "bustling powder-headed man" ordered him to give up his seat and treated him with contempt, though his behavior changed after a senator from Rhode Island accosted Cuffe at a tavern in Maryland. While Cuffe chose not to respond to most slights, he refused to hold his tongue when two Methodists in New York asked the Quaker ship captain if he could "understand English." In a reference to the Methodist Church's ambiguous stance on slavery, Cuffe responded that the only thing that he did not understand was how one Christian could make "merchandise of and [hold] in bondage" another. "This part I should be glad they would clear up [for] me."[123]

As is clear from Cuffe's writings and those of other African Americans, blacks in the United States had a keen understanding of the legal issues surrounding slavery and abolition, including the laws that relegated them to a position of inferiority in every state in the Union. In the speeches and parades that marked the abolition of the slave trade on January 1, 1808, black leaders noted the significance of the joint action by Britain and the United States, sometimes adding Denmark to the list of nations to whom thanks were due.[124] In northern seaports, New Year's Day eventually became an African American "National Jubilee," with speeches, parades, and collections for black charities.[125] Even as they celebrated what Jeremiah Gloucester, in a sermon at Philadelphia's Bethel Church in 1823, called an act of "genuine greatness and glory" by the United States, however, black orators noted how deeply entrenched the laws that sanctioned slavery still were and how far their reach extended, even in free-soil cities like Philadelphia, Boston, and New York. In an oblique reference to the Fugitive Slave Law and the threat that bounty hunters from the southern states posed to free people of color everywhere, Gloucester reminded his listeners that without the watchful vigilance of the Quakers and "a few others, you would not be able to let your children leave your sides. Nay, you would not be safe in your own house."[126] Although Gloucester had trained for the ministry at Princeton and belonged to one of Philadelphia's leading families, he was the son of a former slave from Tennessee.[127] He knew whereof he spoke.

(3)

Nothing demonstrated slavery's resilience more fully than the recognition that slaveholders obtained under the international regime that emerged with the end of the Napoleonic Wars in 1815. In many ways, this was a surprising outcome. In the various European peace conferences, including the Anglo-American Treaty of Ghent (1814) and the Congress of Vienna (1815), the former belligerents declared the slave trade to be "repugnant to principles of humanity and universal morality," and Britain seemed to be determined to use its maritime supremacy to enforce those principles on the high seas.[128] For slaveholders in the United States, this alone was cause for concern. Britain was by far the largest market for the cotton that was the slave states' principal export in the decades after 1815.[129] What was to prevent abolitionists in Parliament and the British press from using that fact to force Americans to end the peculiar institution altogether? By the time of Napoleon's defeat, however, it was clear that Britain's stance was less unyielding than at first appeared. In the Treaty of Ghent, Britain once again pledged not to carry away "any slaves or other private property" of the Americans, only this time the British paid more than a million dollars in compensation.[130] Britain's emissaries also allowed slavery to be restored in the West Indian islands that it returned to its European allies, and the government permitted France to resume the traffic in African slaves. "English bayonets," quipped London's *Examiner* in 1815, were to be congratulated on "the re-establishment of the Bourbons and of the Slave Trade."[131] In the words of the English jurist Sir William Scott, it seemed that "peace in *Europe*" was to be the occasion for continued "war in *Africa*."[132]

As the response to slavery's postwar revival suggests, one result of the wars of the American and French Revolutions was to give a slave's right to freedom an appearance of universality, whose implementation trumped all other considerations. With the return of peace, however, the right to decide whether and in what ways to abolish slavery (or not) reverted to the separate nations of Europe and America. According to William Grant's ruling in the *Amedie* case, Parliament's abolition of the slave trade meant that the trade could no longer be presumed to be legal for any nation, yet if other governments wished to enact laws permitting their citizens to continue the trade—or, it hardly needed to be said, if they wished to allow their citizens to own slaves within their own borders—neither Britain nor any other power could prevent them from doing so.[133] Although the *Amedie* decision limited those rights, it only did so in wartime. With Napoleon's defeat, Britain lost the legal authority to impose its laws on other nations, including nations that had abolished the slave trade. In the landmark case of the French slave ship *Louis,* which was condemned at Sierra Leone in 1816, Sir William Scott held that the slave trade, though "reprehensible" and, in the eyes of some people, piracy, carried the same rights and privileges as any other maritime traffic. Although Britain had the right to search and seize foreign slave ships as an act of war, to exercise that right in peacetime without the consent of the affected nation would be to pursue one great principle at the expense of another or, as Scott put it, "to force the way to the liberation of *Africa* by trampling on the independence of other States in *Europe.*"[134] Henceforth, the flag of any nation that refused to allow the Royal Navy to visit its ships would be an effective shield against the one maritime power capable of enforcing the trade's suppression.

Americans were well aware of these developments. Before the end of the Napoleonic Wars, American vessels routinely avoided British and U.S. laws against the slave trade by displaying the flags of Spain and Portugal—both had treaties with Britain exempting their ships from confiscation—and there was apprehension that slavers of all nations, including America, would do the same with the stars and stripes once peace was restored. Noting that the Anglo-American Treaty of Ghent (1814) had declared the trade illegal, Henry Wheaton, for one, hoped that the United States, which had taken "so distinguished a lead" in banning the trade in 1807, would enshrine its abolition in the "conventional law of nations" by negotiating a mutual right of search with Britain.[135] During the early 1820s there was also support for a joint Anglo-American convention that would allow the two navies to treat the slave trade as a form of piracy.[136] In a Massachusetts federal circuit court case involving the French slaver *Jeune Eugenie,* Justice Joseph Story sought on this basis to give U.S. warships a unilateral right to seize suspected slave ships. However, Washington repeatedly opposed any measure that threatened the Union's maritime independence, rebuffing Britain's overtures and pressing Story to restore the *Jeune Eugenie* to its French owners. Although Congress eventually did declare the slave trade to be piracy, the Supreme Court incorporated the *Louis* doctrine into U.S. law, ruling in the 1825 case of the *Antelope,* a Spanish slaver captured off Florida, that Americans could not seize the ships of foreign nationals without their government's consent.[137] In 1829, a year when the U.S. Navy seized no slave ships at all, more Africans crossed the Atlantic than in any other year of the slave trade's 350-year history, with an indeterminate number traveling in American holds.[138] As he surveyed the situation in 1830, David Walker concluded that the international effort to suppress the slave trade had been for naught, even though the "combined powers of Europe" agreed that the trade was illegal.[139]

During the early nineteenth century, opponents of the African slave trade thus found themselves in the same position as abolitionists in the

United States, with the sovereignty that nations enjoyed on the high seas supplying an obstacle to the trade's complete suppression that was as insurmountable as the sovereign rights of slave states within the American union. Because the illegal slave trade was such an entangled business, it was often difficult to blame its perpetuation on any one particular nation. On encountering a Puerto Rico-bound slaver near the Virgin Islands, the New York traveler James Smith's initial response was that the menacing, nondescript brig must be a pirate.[140] As George Coggeshall observed during a visit to Saint Thomas in 1831, the Danish island—notwithstanding Denmark's prohibition of the trade forty years earlier—was a notorious center of the illegal trade to Puerto Rico and Cuba, which slavers of every nation, including the United States, used to disguise their cargo's African origins. People rarely knew who owned the ships themselves, let alone where they were from. Based on the enormous sums involved, Coggeshall could only surmise that the real movers were "capitalists" who, he assumed, lived "sumptuously in England, France, [and] the United States."[141] Often, American firms collaborated with others to keep their identity secret. In the case of the slave ship *Venus*, the ruse entailed sailing the Baltimore-built clipper to Mozambique under the stars and stripes, using Portuguese colors on the second leg to land "860 negroes near Havana," and, finally, selling the vessel and renaming it the *Duquesa di Braganza*.[142] Americans also participated in the slave trade as seamen on board foreign-owned ships, as sellers of provisions, as owners of plantations in the West Indies, and as intermediaries of various sorts. Whatever the circumstances, their involvement was undeniable.

Given the impunity with which Americans continued to traffic African slaves, it is little wonder that southern slaveholders became such a confident, self-assured group in the decades after 1815. As Britain's refusal to recognize the Confederacy during the American Civil War would show, slavery was not quite as secure under this liberal international order as its defenders in the United States thought, nor was it always apparent to others that the right to own slaves was a "positive good" and a source of "peace and happiness" for blacks and whites, as Senator Calhoun would claim in 1837.[143] With the abolition of slavery in its own colonies during the mid-1830s, Britain showed a growing willingness to use the considerable informal powers at its disposal to force weaker powers, especially

Portugal and Brazil, to conform to the humanitarian norms enshrined in its own laws, and there was every reason to think that, should circumstances permit, it would do the same with the United States.[144] At the time of Paul Cuffe's death in 1817, however, this was all well in the future. With its fiftieth birthday less than a decade away, the United States enjoyed all the rights of a treaty-worthy nation, and those rights worked almost entirely to the advantage of the Union's slaveholding citizens. If history would eventually change course and come down on the side of Americans of color, Paul Cuffe died without knowing it.

CHAPTER 6

The New World and the Old

W HEN DID THE COLONIAL ERA in American history end? The answer depends on where one stands. In some places—eastern Georgia, for example—it makes sense to think of 1776 as marking the beginning of the United States' history as an independent nation. For the Indians of Apalachee Bay, however, Florida was still part of Spain's empire when Milly Francis saved the life of Duncan McKrimmon, a Georgia militiaman whom warriors from her town captured during Andrew Jackson's invasion in 1818. By all accounts, Milly, who was probably fifteen, possessed uncommon grace, beauty, and intelligence. Because her father was the métis prophet Hillis Hadjo (Josiah Francis) and a Red Stick Creek leader, she was also influential, more so, in all likelihood, than she would have been had she been the daughter of a white settler or a civilized Indian. For the hapless captive, this was enough to save his life. Although we do not know why she intervened—Duncan, who had been stripped naked and was about to be shot, may have looked like a potential husband—Milly was aware of the intermediary role that Muscogulge women had often played at such moments. Following a pacification ritual that Duncan may or may not have understood, she brokered a deal whereby the warriors agreed to spare the soldier's life if he would have his head shaved and "live with the Indians."[1] Under different circumstances, Duncan might have ended his days as Milly Francis's husband and, possibly, an adopted member of the Creek Nation.[2]

Instead, Jackson's campaign turned Milly's world upside down. In early April, Milly's father, who wore the red coat of a British officer during Duncan's ordeal, was hanged on Jackson's orders from the yardarm of an American gunboat that had tricked him into coming onboard by flying the Union Jack. At the time of his capture, Hillis Hadjo was carrying an English rifle, a brigadier's commission in the British army, and a snuff box that had been a present from the prince regent. Intent on curtailing Britain's influence in the region, Jackson also executed two British subjects, Alexander Arbuthnot and Robert Christie Ambrister, on charges that they had encouraged the anti-American hostilities of the Red Sticks and Seminoles, as Muscogulges who lived on the Spanish side of the border were known. And in the most daring stroke of all, the hero of New Orleans pledged to hold Florida until Spain acquired "the power or will" to keep the peace there on its own.[3] During the crisis that ensued—Britain, France, and Spain all viewed the invasion as an act of war—Washington agreed to restore San Marcos (St. Marks) and Pensacola, the two Spanish posts that Jackson had seized, but the way was clear for the United States to annex the contested borderland.[4] When Milly Francis and what was left of her family surrendered to American forces in August, they were on the verge of starvation. On learning of Milly's plight, Duncan, whose regiment had been sent home, returned to Florida and offered "to make her his wife." This time, though, he was the one who set the terms, the most important of which was that Milly agree to live with him in "the settled parts of Georgia." Milly politely declined.[5]

As the saga of Milly Francis suggests, the First Seminole War underscored the United States' emergence as a regional power, one that was not only a treaty-worthy nation in its own right but was increasingly able to impose its views on others. In the war's aftermath, Britain and Spain both withdrew from East Florida and what was left of West Florida, forcing Indians on the Gulf Coast to accept a position as "dependent nations" and preparing the way for their eventual removal to the west.[6] Because it coincided with the final crisis of Spain's American empire, the war also affected the United States' relations in Europe. Between 1819 and 1823, Secretary of State John Quincy Adams compelled Madrid to accept a North American border that stretched from the Gulf of Mexico to the Pacific, Washington stunned reactionaries everywhere by recognizing the new Latin American republics, and President James Monroe declared North and South America to be off-limits to future European colonization.[7] In a sense, by seizing Florida, the man whom the Creeks called Sharp Knife helped place the United States at the head of a new hemispheric community of nations, replacing what the French abbé de Pradt described as Europe's "irregular and distant" authority with a system of "regular and local governments."[8] For the United States, if not for other people in its neighborhood, the result was a regime of security and, people hoped, enduring peace. Although we have no way of knowing how much of this entered the thoughts of Milly Francis, her efforts on Duncan's behalf eventually made her famous. In 1844, following a chance meeting with a sympathetic army officer in Oklahoma, Congress awarded her a pension and a medal, making her the first woman of any race in U.S. history to be so honored. Having declined to become Duncan's wife, Milly ended her days as the "Florida Pocahontas"—a reminder of the status that had once been hers, as well as a symbol of the "gratitude and bounty" that Americans felt toward a people over whom they claimed undisputed dominion.[9]

(1)

In 1818 the United States' growing sense of entitlement, so evident during Jackson's invasion of Florida, came from two sources: for the first time in the Union's brief history, Europe was at peace and, as a result, Americans were free to claim all the rights of a great treaty-worthy nation, including the right to make whatever peace they chose with neighbors who lacked that status. To Jackson's critics, of course, the First Seminole War suggested anything but a desire for peace. In Spain the brief war earned the Tennessee general a reputation as "the Napoleon of the woods," while the execution of Arbuthnot and Ambrister so inflamed British opinion that Lord Castlereagh claimed he could have gotten Parliament to declare war "by holding up a finger."[10] Because Jackson acted without authorization from either Congress or the president, the outcry in Washington was equally intense, prompting Speaker of the

House Henry Clay to undertake an investigation into what he depicted as Jackson's "open, undisguised, and unauthorized hostility." According to Clay, who had spent 1814 and 1815 as an envoy to Britain, there were two charges that Europeans invariably made "against our country." One involved the Republic's "inordinate spirit of aggrandizement" against its neighbors; the other, "the treatment which we extend to the Indians." By invading Florida, Jackson had given America's critics ample proof of both. "Behold . . . those who are constantly reproaching Kings," Clay imagined conservatives in Europe saying. "When the minions of despotism in Europe heard of the seizure of Pensacola, how did they chuckle and chide the admirers of our institutions."[11]

Whatever people thought of his methods, Jackson's goal was to force Britain and Spain to fulfill their treaty obligations to the United States. As Americans were well aware, the war occurred at a moment when the United States seemed to be reaching a position of equality with Europe's most powerful nations—"a proud and lofty station among the first nations of the world," as Clay boasted in the House of Representatives.[12] The inconclusive War of 1812 was the signal event in this rise, ending as it did with Jackson's drubbing of the British at New Orleans. In the words of the French émigré Arsène Lacarrière Latour, Americans had showed that they "were not to be intimidated by . . . the heroes of Wellington."[13] In Massachusetts, where the war aroused intense opposition, the Republican caucus claimed that Jackson had stirred sensations at New Orleans not unlike what an adventurer might feel upon beholding the "*chief of the Andes,* rising in majesty above the surrounding mountains."[14] Because the Madison administration failed to achieve its central objectives—seizing Canada and ending British impressment of American seamen—Britons scoffed at the idea that the war had been an American triumph, let alone a British defeat, but the prevailing view in the United States was that Americans had proved that they were Britain's equals at sea, that they could beat the British army on land, and that they were united enough to withstand the forces that once threatened to undo the Union. Unlike the Revolutionary War, when they got help from France and Spain, Americans were especially proud that they had fought Britain "single-handed," as Thomas Jefferson boasted, triumphing without allies in Europe. "The British war has left us in debt," wrote the former president, with evident satisfaction, in 1815, "but that is a cheap price for the good it has done us."[15]

Given how widespread such attitudes were, it is perhaps not surprising that Jackson proved willing to confront the British in Florida. For Native Americans, of course, there was nothing novel about how Jackson's soldiers treated the Creeks and Seminoles. Although the execution of Josiah Francis and Homathle Mico, another Red Stick leader, attracted criticism in Congress, Europeans had been using scorched-earth tactics against the continent's indigenous peoples since the seventeenth century. In his dispatches from Florida, Jackson, for one, made no apology for his methods. Speaking of the destruction of the Seminole and maroon villages at Miccosukee (near Tallahassee), Jackson reported that everything "was executed to my satisfaction: nearly three hundred houses were consumed [by fire], and the greatest abundance of corn, cattle, &c., [was] brought in."[16] In the words of the defense that John Quincy Adams penned in his public letter of November 28, 1818, to George Erving, U.S. ambassador to Spain, "war in its mildest forms" was cruel, but it was "doubly cruel when waged with savages"; on this point, the "dictate[s] of common sense," the "soundest authorities of national law," and Vattel all agreed.[17] Even Henry Clay, who denounced the hanging of Josiah Francis in stark and unyielding terms, viewed the burning of Indian crops and towns as an acceptable "deviation from the code which regulated the warfare between civilized communities."[18] As Walter Bromley, head of the Royal Acadian School in Halifax, Nova Scotia, lamented in a pamphlet on the war, the Indians' fate appeared to be "inevitably fixed." In the three centuries since the first European set foot on American soil, "every day, every hour, and every moment [had] been marked with some act of cruelty and oppression." Jackson's rampage through Florida was simply the latest installment.[19]

If the rules of war authorized the devastation of Indian country, Jackson's refusal to spare Britain's own subjects was another matter. Because Alexander Arbuthnot and Robert Ambrister were in Florida at the behest of the Indians and because the territory where they were captured was under the jurisdiction of Spain, their execution did not directly affect Washington's relations with Britain, yet there was no question that Jackson meant to disrupt the influence that British merchants and adventurers had long enjoyed with Indians in American territory.[20] In words that evoked memories of George III's use of native auxiliaries during the Revolutionary War, the assistance that British officials in Upper Canada had given to Indians in the Northwest Territory during the 1790s and the War of 1812, and the Indian trade that British firms still controlled from Lake Superior to the Gulf of Mexico, Jackson made clear that he intended the trial to serve as an "awful example to the world" and, in particular, to the British government and people.[21] According to a letter in the New York *National Advocate,* Jackson was to be congratulated on "having beaten the English at New Orleans, and baffled their intrigues in Florida."[22] In Britain, where the incident led to demands to suspend relations until "the dignity of the nation [had] been satisfied," the press took a different view, lambasting the presumption of what the *Caledonian Mercury* called "an obscure Court-Martial of American officers, holding their sittings in the back woods of their half cultivated country." "Who," the paper continued, "empowered *them* to constitute this new and capital offence in the law of nations?"[23] Still, no one questioned the momentousness of what Jackson had done, nor did anyone doubt that it carried potentially far-reaching implications. "Always disavowed, yet always felt," wrote John Quincy Adams of Britain's history of making trouble in Indian country, adding, somewhat ominously, that adventurers like Arbuthnot and Ambrister had "more than once [been] detected, but never before punished."[24]

From the standpoint of Americans, the conflict that produced this outcry had its origins in Britain's refusal to sever ties to the king's native allies in the territory that it ceded to Spain and the United States in 1783. Despite the failure of Britain's treaties with either power to mention the Indians—an omission that encouraged Americans, in particular, to view native people as "conquered subjects"—Britain maintained what, to many people, looked like an informal Native American empire in the territory of both cessions.[25] Because this presence was not sanctioned by the treaties of 1783, it depended, first and foremost, on the Indians themselves. Sometimes, following the example of the Scottish-Creek leader Alexander McGillivray, Indians balanced their commitments to Britain with overtures to Spain and the United States. In other instances, they chose one side or another. Among the Lower Creeks who lived on the Chattahoochee

River in western Georgia, most chiefs eventually accepted the "plan of civilization" that the Washington administration began advocating during the mid-1790s, but as late as the War of 1812, Britain retained ties to the Upper Creeks in Alabama and to the Creeks' Seminole cousins in Florida. After a party of Seminoles mistook him for an American at St. Augustine in 1818, Freeman Rattenbury, a British soldier of fortune, pointedly compared the "natural antipathy" of Native Americans toward the United States with the "courtesy [that] they always feel towards an Englishman."[26] Writing in the 1840s, the métis Creek George Stiggins recalled that his people had an almost "magnetic predilection for the British." "It is notorious," wrote the pro-American leader,

> that all such Creek Indians as have had any intercourse or transactions of any kind or magnitude with the British or their emissaries, whether of importance or not, were ever partial to them and favorable to their interest. . . . [M]any old men of the present day . . . expiate on the candid, honest, and liberal disinterestedness of the British as friends to the Indians . . . [and] remark with wrath the contrast between the latter and the Americans.[27]

Sometimes, the British merchants and agents who maintained these ties worked within formal channels, doing so with the consent of Spain and the United States. In the Floridas, where Britain's presence depended heavily on the Scottish house of Panton, Leslie, a Spanish license from 1784 enabled the firm's merchants to conduct a brisk trade in deerskins, which Indians as far north as Kentucky and Tennessee exchanged for manufactured goods, guns, and alcohol. Until Jefferson's embargo intervened in 1808, the Montreal-based companies that dominated the fur trade south of the Great Lakes were likewise beneficiaries of a clause in the Jay Treaty that permitted free trade in the North American interior. Britain's Indian Department in Upper Canada was another authorized point of contact, maintaining ties with Native Americans in the United States through agents at posts opposite Detroit, Niagara, and Mackinac. In the memoirs of her childhood on Mackinac Island in Lake Huron, Elizabeth Thèrése Baird, whose maternal grandmother was a métis French-Ottawa fur trader, recalled annual Native American pilgrimages past her family's house well into the 1820s, as Indians traveled from villages in Michigan, Wisconsin, and Illinois to collect the yearly "annuity"—broadcloth, hats, and silver ornaments—that Canadian officials distributed to warriors who had fought for Britain during the War of 1812.[28] According to Morrell Marston, commander of Fort Armstrong in the Illinois Territory, nearly all of the goods being traded in his district in 1820 were British, and the Fox and Sauk Indians all displayed British flags and medals. The reason, Marston claimed, was that Britain's flags were made of silk (instead of worsted) and were "considerably larger than the American Army's [own] standards." Until that changed, the Indians would do business with whichever nation offered the better terms.[29]

If Britain's presence was sanctioned by the positive law of treaties, commercial licenses, and charters, however, it also depended on localized systems and networks that were ostensibly beyond any government's control. Because the British adventurers upon whom these networks depended tended to be liminal figures—many were Loyalists with their own history of abandonment and exile—British, Spanish, and American officials often described them as freelancers and renegades, lacking even the status of the Indians with whom they associated.[30] Speaking in 1790 of Britons who remained in East Florida after the province was returned to Spain, the governor, Vicente Manuel de Zéspedes, had nothing but disdain, writing that most were "a species of white renegade" that the locals referred to as "crackers." These, Zéspedes explained, were "nomadic like Arabs and . . . distinguished from savages only in their color, language, and the superiority of their depraved cunning and untrustworthiness."[31] During the Indian wars that beset the Northwest Territory in the 1780s and early 1790s, Americans frequently described traders who operated from British posts in similar terms. As Oliver M. Spencer, head of the American Bible Society in Cincinnati during the 1830s, recalled of his boyhood captivity by Wyandot Indians, the Indians and the officers in the British garrisons at Niagara and Detroit—especially those who were British natives—treated him with kindness, but he never forgot the callous behavior of James Girty and Matthew Elliott, Scots-Irish traders from Pennsylvania who had fought for the Crown during the Revolutionary War and who had Shawnee wives and lived with the Indians. On learning how Elliott, in particular, had treated

Spencer, Governor John Simcoe of Upper Canada observed that "such behavior in a British officer would have subjected him to trial before a court martial." With backwoods merchants like Elliott, however, the governor "was obliged to overlook many improprieties" because they had "such influence with the Indians and were so necessary to His Majesty in his intercourse with them."[32]

While sharing Simcoe's view of Indian traders, Americans frequently suspected military and civil officials in Canada and the Bahamas of abetting their activities. Not surprisingly, these suspicions loomed large in the Anglo-American differences that flared with such rancor from 1807 onward, culminating in the War of 1812. Although the American drive to war was chiefly in response to Britain's actions on the high seas, many westerners viewed the breach as a chance to avenge what a Lexington, Kentucky, newspaper called "the tomahawk and the scalping knife, which . . . the inhuman blood-thirsty cabinet of St. James had incessantly endeavored to bring on the *women* and *children* of our western frontiers."[33] During an American incursion across the Detroit River in 1812, General William Hull, commander of the U.S. forces, offered the usual assurances to the inhabitants of Upper Canada, many of whom, as he noted, were "children . . . of the same family as us," but he promised "instant destruction" to any white man who was "found fighting by the side of an Indian."[34] Of particular concern were Britain's ties to nativist Indians like the Shawnee Prophet Tenskwatawa and his brother Tecumseh and, south of the Ohio, to Hillis Hadjo and the Red Stick Creeks.[35] Although Britain played no role in William Henry Harrison's victory over Tecumseh's pan-Indian league at Tippecanoe in 1811 or Jackson's slaughter of the Red Sticks at Horseshoe Bend in 1814, British forces repeatedly made common cause with nativist Indians during the War of 1812, fighting alongside Tecumseh in Michigan and Upper Canada, recruiting Creek and Seminole warriors for the assault on New Orleans, and building the so-called Negro Fort on the Apalachicola River in Spanish Florida. For a brief period in 1814 and 1815, a detachment under Colonel Edward Nicholls of the Royal Marines turned Spanish West Florida from Pensacola to the Apalachicola River into an Anglo-Creek enclave, backed by what John Quincy Adams later called a "motley tribe of black, white, and red combatants."[36]

While assisting hostile Indians could be justified as an act of war, continuing to do so was legitimate ground for complaint (or worse) once hostilities ended. Under the treaty that Britain and the United States concluded at Ghent in December 1814, both parties agreed to return all Indian land taken during the war. Toward that end, Colonel Nicholls, who was still in Florida, spent the spring of 1815 urging the Americans to restore twenty million acres of land—roughly half the Creek homeland—that the Creeks had ceded in Georgia and Alabama. However, Nicholls disregarded the treaty's requirement that the Indians suspend hostilities. Until American gunboats destroyed it in 1816, the Negro Fort was an especially visible sign of Britain's continued involvement, flying the "English Jack" from its ramparts and providing a stronghold from which Indians and escaped slaves could mount their own cross-border demands for justice. At the time of its destruction, the fort contained an enormous cache of weapons, including swords, firearms, and several hundred casks of powder (cannon as well as rifle), all supplied by the king's forces.[37] Although Nicholls returned to England in June 1815, taking Hillis Hadjo and several other Creeks with him, two of his former officers, George Woodbine and Robert Ambrister, remained in Florida, as did Alexander Arbuthnot. By all accounts, Arbuthnot hoped to assume the mantle that had belonged to Panton, Leslie, controlling Britain's trade with the Creeks and Seminoles and managing the Indians' relations with Spain and the United States, but Woodbine and Ambrister had grander plans. Outspoken abolitionists and friends of the Indians, they may have aspired to confederate Florida as an independent republic with Simón Bolívar's patriots in Venezuela and Gran Colombia. Barring that, they hoped for the creation of a British protectorate. If the witnesses at his trial are to be believed, Ambrister's first act on learning that Jackson's army was approaching was to appear, with his sword and uniform, in the Indian village where he was living. He also attempted to raise a force of black soldiers with which to seize the Spanish fort before it fell to the Americans.[38]

For Americans, such activities fit a familiar pattern, one shaped by the rivalries of Europe's colonial powers before the revolution and the long-standing European habit of treating North America as a place that was only partly subject to European treaties and customs. This time, though, there were two differences: Britain and the United States were no longer in a state of belligerence, as they had intermittently been since 1776, and Europe's Atlantic powers were at peace.[39] By executing the two prisoners, Jackson gambled—correctly, as it turned out—that Britain would place a higher value on peaceful relations with the United States than it did the welfare of its own subjects, let alone its obligations to the Indians. Because he was seventy when he went to the gallows, much of the postmortem controversy focused on whether Arbuthnot, in particular, deserved such a grisly fate. In a number of accounts, the Scot emerged as a gentle and benevolent figure, with some observers casting him as a humanitarian martyr to the Americans' "inventive malice" and greed for Indian land.[40] He was also dismayed by Britain's refusal to come to the Indians' assistance. In a widely reprinted letter to an unnamed "officer of rank in England," written as Jackson was preparing to invade, Arbuthnot pleaded that Britain "really . . . should do something for these people."[41] Elsewhere, he cast aspersions on adventurers from both Britain and the United States, describing Americans who encroached on Indian land as murderers and thieves, while castigating Woodbine and Ambrister, in particular, for their repeated, empty promises of British assistance.[42] According to London's *Morning Chronicle,* Arbuthnot was a "man of virtue and humanity," who took a "deep interest" in the Indians' well-being. "There is evidence that he wished to preserve the Indians from destruction," the writer claimed, "but not the smallest that he instigated them to active hostilities against the Americans."[43]

If so, the one thing that both he and Ambrister lacked was a commission or formal authorization from the British government. Despite their sympathetic qualities—as a former lieutenant in the Royal Marines, Ambrister, in particular, seems to have cut an appealing figure with some of Jackson's officers—the court-martial that Jackson convened at San Marcos declared the two Britons to be freebooters who were beyond the protection of the United States' treaties with Britain and the customs that sovereign nations in Europe and America observed in relations with each other. In an act that the British press viewed as especially insulting, Ambrister, who, as Jackson may have known, was the son of a South Carolina Tory, received a reduced sentence, but the general overruled the tribunal, insisting that the prisoner had acted the part of an "outlaw and pirate," a description that he later also applied to Arbuthnot.[44] In a memorial justifying his conduct to the Senate, Jackson explained that while the "laws of civilized warfare" required combatants to treat each other's prisoners with humanity, such strictures only applied to the citizens of civilized nations. By acting as agents, paymasters, and military leaders for a band of Indians and fugitive slaves, both men had forfeited their rights as British nationals. Indeed, Jackson claimed, because they "had exiled themselves from their native land," their crimes were worse than those of the Indians and banditti in whose company they had been captured.[45] In the concurring words of Congressman John Rhea of Tennessee, who took the lead in defending Jackson's conduct in the House of Representatives, the British prisoners had withdrawn from "the customs and laws of civil life, and associated and identified themselves with savages at war with the United States." In short, they had *"denationalized themselves."*[46]

This was a position that no one in Britain was eager to endorse, yet Jackson gave the government little choice. Under the British constitution, it was impossible for an Englishman to "relieve himself from the natural allegiance due to the institutions of his country," as the British adventurer Freeman Rattenbury, who was in Florida at the time, noted in a pointed response to John Quincy Adams's letter to George Erving. For this reason, Arbuthnot and Ambrister deserved to be treated with the humanity that the law of nations prescribed for the subjects of civilized nations, and some Britons went further, noting that the Indian rights for which the two prisoners had been contending had the sanction of a European treaty.[47] As even Jackson's British critics conceded, though, individuals who engaged in hostilities against a power with which their own government was at peace did so at their own risk. If the other government chose to treat them harshly, the neutral power had no right to object. By executing the two prisoners, Jackson forced Britain to choose between abandoning its neutrality with a formal demand for reparations and appearing to accept that what he had done was legal. Convinced that an official complaint would be greeted in Washington as an act of hostility (if not war) and mindful, perhaps, of what had happened at New Orleans to the last British expedition to the Gulf Coast, Britain opted for the latter course. While denying that the case deserved to be "a precedent and adopted into the law of nations," the government ended up endorsing Jackson's own view. As Lord Bathurst reminded the House of Lords during the final debate on the matter, all the evidence suggested that the two Britons were "in the service of the Indians." Under such circumstances, Jackson had the right to administer whatever punishment he and the American government saw fit.[48]

(2)

Although the furor over Jackson's capture of the Spanish forts at San Marcos and Pensacola differed in important respects from Britain's response to the execution of Ambrister and Arbuthnot, the American government followed a similar strategy, using allegations of lawlessness and piracy to justify actions that, to the rest of the world, looked like brazen violations of Spanish sovereignty. In many ways, Spain's case was stronger than Britain's. Whereas the two Britons were, by their own government's admission, freelance adventurers, Florida was legally Spanish territory during the Seminole War, and the strongholds that Jackson seized were garrisoned by the soldiers of a ruler with whom the United States was at peace and whose dominion it had recognized in international treaties. Because Spain's American empire was on the brink of dissolution, moreover, the question of whether—or how—to preserve that dominion was a matter of considerable interest in Europe. Mindful of this, Spain's ambassador, Luis de Onís, suggested at one point that the Spanish and Americans refer their differences to the European congress that was meeting in 1818 at Aix-la-Chapelle, while Americans worried that the incident could lead to war with one of Spain's European champions.[49] Nonetheless, at the urging of Secretary of State Adams, President Monroe chose to sanction Jackson's actions, rebuffing demands that the Tennessean be punished for what Onís called "outrages [that] will scarcely find a parallel in history."[50] If anyone deserved punishment, wrote Adams, it was the Spanish officials who had failed to stop Florida's Indians from committing "hostilities against the United States, which it was their official duty to restrain." As with Arbuthnot and Ambrister, Adams claimed that Americans were chastising the agents of a European power, from whom they had a right, as citizens of a nation with which Spain was at peace, to expect better treatment.[51]

Once again, the roots of these differences lay in ambiguities in the peace settlement that ended the American Revolutionary War in 1783, albeit in ways that the subsequent course of events greatly exacerbated. In the Model Treaty, Congress named the two Floridas among the British possessions that no power allied with the United States might acquire.[52] Nonetheless, both provinces went to Spain, and Spanish officials continued to use them as a base from which to thwart the expansionist ambitions of settlers on the American side of the border. When Napoleon sold Louisiana to the United States in 1803, his emissaries suggested that the sale was to be of the original French colony, which until 1763 included the West Florida garrison towns of Baton Rouge and Mobile. Spain, however, still had possession of both West Florida and Louisiana, which it had only recently ceded to France, and it refused to recognize the emperor's right to sell either to the Americans.[53] Although Madrid reluctantly (and provisionally) acknowledged the cession of New Orleans and Saint Louis in 1804, it disputed the Union's claim to the vast, ill-defined domain to the west of the Mississippi River—according to Jefferson, the Louisiana Purchase included a substantial portion of what is today Texas—and the white flag with the burgundy cross continued to fly defiantly over all of West Florida. When Congress attempted to force the issue by authorizing a customs house at Spanish-held Mobile, Spain's ambassador, Carlos Martínez de Yrujo, denounced the act as an "atrocious libel." How, Yrujo wondered, could the American government, "which is so zealous in the preservation and defense of its own rights," have so little regard for the rights of its neighbors?[54]

According to many Americans, the answer to Yrujo's question was that Spain's empire in the Floridas was an empire in name only. Despite the Spanish conquest of British West Florida during the Revolutionary War and the resumption of Bourbon rule at St. Augustine, the only places east of New Orleans where Spain enjoyed undisputed authority after 1783 were at Mobile, Pensacola, and San Marcos and along a narrow strip of Atlantic coastline that ran from the Saint Marys River, marking East Florida's northeastern border with Georgia, to St. Augustine and New Smyrna, ninety miles to the south. On the other hand, in the fertile West Florida districts between the Mississippi River and Mobile Bay, power was increasingly in the hands of Anglo-Americans, who had become naturalized Spaniards, while the rest of the Floridas belonged to Creeks and Seminoles, including, in the Indian towns just below the Georgia line, black Muscogulges who were fugitives or the offspring of fugitives from the plantations to the north. For these reasons, even the Spanish viewed the two colonies as a natural haven for brigands and adventurers of every description. As Vicente de Zéspedes warned his superiors in 1790, Spain's only chance of retaining possession over such a far-flung, ungovernable region was to encourage respectable settlers— Loyalist planters from the Bahamas, for example, or Irish and Anglo-American Catholics—who could form a "living wall of industrious citizens" against interlopers from the United States. But most people who came to the Floridas were renegades and crackers. During the Revolutionary War, some had sided with Britain, while others claimed to be loyal to the United States. For the most part, their real allegiance was to themselves.[55]

With Napoleon's invasion of Spain in 1808 and the arrest and forced abdication of Ferdinand VII, Spain lost most of its remaining authority on the Gulf Coast. Following the lead of patriots elsewhere in Spanish America, Spain's northernmost subjects in Texas and the Floridas filled the vacuum by forming juntas and popularly elected governments, doing so ostensibly in the name of the deposed Bourbon king, though often, it was suspected, with the goal of making themselves "independent of the world."[56] In West Florida, where the crisis first broke during the summer of 1810, Anglo-Americans in the province's four westernmost districts responded to the turmoil in Spain by summoning a convention, drafting a constitution, and taking control of the courts and the militia, all with the apparent consent of the Spanish commandant at Baton Rouge. Even as they insisted that they intended to govern on behalf of Ferdinand "if he should again be restored to the throne of old Spain," however, several delegates hedged their bets by opening negotiations with the Madison administration.[57] On the night of September 23, after learning that authorities in Cuba had discovered their plot, the insurgents seized Baton Rouge amid cries of what, to one Spaniard, sounded like "Uurra! Waschintown!"[58] Three days later, the members of the West Florida Convention gathered under a blue flag with a single white star at the town's dilapidated citadel and proclaimed the districts that they represented to be "a free and independent state." Casting an eye to the north, the delegates called upon foreign nations—meaning, above all, the United States but also, should Washington hesitate, Britain—to acknowledge the "lone star" republic's pretensions and to give them "such aid as may be consistent with the laws and usages of nations."[59]

Invoking the Louisiana treaty with Napoleon, officials in Washington responded by casting the United States as the rightful successor to the North American empire that Spain seemed about to vacate, and they sought to discredit all other rivals, including the self-styled Republic of West Florida. To establish the Union's dominion, however, and to do so without giving umbrage to Ferdinand's European allies—especially Britain but also, after 1815, Russia, Austria, and France—Americans needed Spain to accept a treaty that would transfer the rights that it still possessed in law, if not in fact. During each of the United States' incursions into Spanish territory, starting with the occupation of Baton Rouge in December 1810, Washington insisted that it had no desire to settle its differences by force of arms. Despite Ferdinand's uncertain prospects in Europe, the American government maintained that its ultimate goal was to validate its claims through what President Madison, in his proclamation of October 27, 1810, called "amicable negotiation with a just and friendly power." This was even true in West Florida, where the four western districts joined the Union with Louisiana in 1812, forming what are known to this day as the "Florida parishes." Mindful that Spain controlled Mobile and that it had yet to acknowledge American claims elsewhere—and conscious, perhaps, of critics in Europe who viewed the entire Louisiana Purchase as the sale of stolen goods, as William Cobbett would write—Madison claimed that the Union was willing to submit all its Spanish differences, including places already under the American government's jurisdiction, to a "fair and friendly negotiation and adjustment."[60] In the Seminole War's aftermath, while reserving the right to seize Florida unilaterally, John Quincy Adams employed the same strategy in his letter to George Erving, emphasizing the speed with which Washington had restored San Marcos and Pensacola and using the handover as evidence that American forces had not invaded "with any view of wresting the province from the possession of Spain, nor in any spirit of hostility to the Spanish government."[61] Although Spain's hold was tenuous,

Americans wanted to take its place with Ferdinand's consent, and they acknowledged that, from the standpoint of European treaty law, Spain still had the best claim.

Because of the unsettled nature of Spain's dominion, though, the United States could not trust to diplomacy alone, or so Americans claimed. As long as the Spanish king was incapable of governing his possessions on the Gulf Coast—between 1808 and 1814, Ferdinand's authority in Spain depended on Wellington's army and a liberal constitution that he eventually repudiated—there was a danger that the region would become what Adams called an autonomous "receptacle" for "every enemy, civilized or savage, of the United States," including Indians, British adventurers, and, it was feared, disaffected Anglo-Americans.[62] In 1810, during the United States' occupation of the districts controlled by the West Florida Convention, the expedition's commander, Governor William Claiborne, of the Orleans Territory, was under strict orders to negotiate only with legal representatives of the Spanish government and to take "no notice . . . of the Revolutionary Government there."[63] By the time Claiborne reached Baton Rouge, the insurgents had elected a Congress and president, raising the prospect that a foreign government, especially Britain, might recognize the self-styled republic as Spain's rightful successor. Given the number of Britons and Loyalists in West Florida— four of the convention's original fourteen delegates came from such a background—there was a particular danger that the new government would league with a British-backed junta in Cuba or South America.[64] Although the republic's president, Fulwar Skipwith, a diplomat from Virginia who had helped negotiate the Louisiana Purchase, claimed to be motivated by the same principles as George Washington in 1776, who knew what those principles really meant?[65] In the event, fears that the Union would lose West Florida came to naught, but that did not mean they were groundless. In December, shortly before Claiborne occupied Baton Rouge, authorities in West Florida jailed one of his officers for reading Madison's proclamation claiming the territory for the United States. On the way to the dungeon, the commandant pointed to the republic's "Independent Colors flying on the flagstaff, and told him [that] it would take a good deal of blood to pull them down."[66] "Let the Florida Convention cast a retrospective eye over the miseries of Spain," warned a writer in the Natchez *Weekly Chronicle*. History showed where such confrontations inevitably led.[67]

Nor were Americans alone in worrying about what might emerge from the detritus of Spain's collapsing empire or how the conflict might affect other powers. Despite Ferdinand's restoration in 1814, the end of the Napoleonic Wars in Europe only intensified the unrest in America, as thousands of British, French, and Spanish veterans crossed the Atlantic, creating a veritable *"demimonde* of spies, mercenaries, and privateers" in Spain's wayward colonies. Some came to make common cause with Spanish American patriots and others to assist the Bourbon monarchy, but most intended to enrich themselves.[68] Of particular concern were the activities of British freelancers in East Florida and the patriot-flagged corsairs that sailed from bases throughout Spanish America, as well as New Orleans and ports on the United States' Eastern Seaboard. During the summer of 1817, Gregor MacGregor, a Scottish adventurer who had been an officer in the Venezuelan armies of Francisco Miranda and Bolívar, seized Amelia Island on East Florida's border with Georgia, ostensibly as a prelude to selling the Spanish province to the United States but in actuality to establish a base for smuggling and privateering. When Freeman Rattenbury arrived in October to offer his services to the self-styled republic, MacGregor had just left for the Bahamas to recruit Charles Woodbine and Robert Ambrister, among others, for an expedition to Tampa Bay. In his place was a "government" consisting of a former Congressman from Vermont and two patriot-flagged privateers. One, commanded by the French naval veteran Louis Aury, displayed the united colors of Venezuela and Mexico; the other displayed the flag of Buenos Aires.[69] By the time that U.S. forces seized the island in December, Aury's crew of Haitians, free blacks, and mulattoes had smuggled goods across the Georgia line that Lloyd's of London subsequently valued at $500,000. In a clear violation of American law, most of the property consisted of Africans taken from captured Spanish slave ships.[70]

The result was a strong argument under international law for the United States to assume the responsibility for governing the two Floridas that Spain seemed unable to fulfill. Although neither the Congress of Vienna nor the European congresses that followed took a formal stance on the collapse of Spain's American empire, the outcome was deeply interesting to Europe's great powers, all of whom were committed, at least in principle, to upholding the Spanish dominion that the crisis threatened to subvert.[71] During the fall of 1817, at the same moment preparations were under way in America to occupy Amelia Island and chastise the Creeks and Seminoles, Alexander I, Russia's mercurial and autocratic czar, attracted widespread attention with a proposal for the European powers to come to Ferdinand's assistance by jointly declaring insurgents who sailed under Spanish American colors to be pirates.[72] "No flag is secure from their depredations," wrote an observer in Madrid. "Is not the whole of Europe interested in putting an end to the excesses of these pirates?"[73] Jackson, for one, worried that allowing the unrest in the Floridas to continue could easily lead to European intervention and to "war with Great Britain, or some of the Continental Powers combined with Spain." To forestall such an eventuality, he recommended crossing the Florida line on his own authority, placing his soldiers in the same position as MacGregor's filibusters and "Woodbine's British Partizens," or perhaps in an analogous situation to that of the American insurgents in the West Florida Convention in 1810.[74] Still, neither he nor Adams doubted that if Spain proved unable to prevent brigands in Florida from waging war on their neighbors, Washington was entitled to intervene forthrightly and unilaterally. In his letter to George Erving, which was meant to be read in chancelleries across Europe, Adams maintained that Florida had become a "nominal possession" of the Spanish crown and a "derelict," one that was "open to the occupancy of every enemy, civilized or savage, of the United States."[75] If they decided it was in their best interest, Americans had every right "to rely for the protection of their borders upon themselves alone."[76]

Unlike the execution of Arbuthnot and Ambrister, however, the United States eventually pulled back, though only just, from seizing Spanish East Florida and what remained of Spanish West Florida unilaterally. Despite the filibustering character of Jackson's intervention and the defiant tone of Adams's pronouncement, the Monroe administration preferred to take Florida by treaty, not by force of arms—or at least not by force of arms alone. This was true even though the territory was in the hands of a European ruler who had vacated nearly every part of his dominion, every part, that is, except his right to the territory's dominion as recognized by Europe's other rulers. During the fifteen years that Americans spent wresting the Floridas from Spain, from Congress's failed attempt to take control of Mobile by authorizing a customhouse in 1804 to the diplomatic aftermath of the First Seminole War, officials in Washington repeatedly benefited from (and sometimes quietly encouraged) groups like the insurgents who seized control of West Florida in 1810. Ultimately, though, the dominion that Americans sought was the one that only a European government (and treaty) could bestow. By punishing the renegades, smugglers, and pirates whose depredations Adams named as the cause of the Seminole War in 1818, Americans were doing nothing that Europe's colonial powers had not done many times before. In the name of achieving lasting peace, they were curtailing the ability of such groups to wage war on their own, and they were doing so in ways that identified the Union's expansion with the need to uphold the treaty law upon which the peace of Europe and America ultimately depended. As long as governments in Europe concurred, it was a way of making peace in which even the Napoleon of the woods had a role to play.

(3)

Hovering over the United States' treaty relations with Britain and Spain, of course, was the question of the Union's relations with the Creeks and Seminoles. In 1818 the American regulars and militia who accompanied Jackson across the Florida line were not the only soldiers fighting for their nation's rights. Also present were approximately two thousand Creek warriors, or nearly two-fifths of the force under Jackson's command. For the Indians' leader, the métis Creek chief William McIntosh, the First Seminole War was an opportunity to reunite the Muscogulge nation on both sides of the border, Seminole as well as Creek, under the authority of the indigenous governing body known as the Creek National Council.[77] With personal holdings that included a tavern at Indian Springs, Georgia, plantations on the Chattahoochee and Tallapoosa Rivers, three wives, twelve children, scores of slaves, and hundreds of cattle, McIntosh was among the wealthiest men in Georgia. George Troup, the state's governor, was his first cousin; David Mitchell, head of the Creek Agency and another former Georgia governor, was a friend and business partner. If the United States annexed Florida, McIntosh and his allies on the Creek National Council stood to profit from the sale of Seminole land in the former Bourbon colony. No less important, by extending the Indian nation's jurisdiction to include what in 1818 was still Spanish territory, McIntosh planned to circumvent the American laws against the foreign slave trade and transport captured Black Seminoles across the Georgia line to sell to American planters.[78] Although they served different masters, Generals McIntosh and Jackson had quite a lot in common.

Ironically, this was a point on which practically everyone agreed. In his speech condemning Jackson's conduct in the House of Representatives, Henry Clay, for one, made clear that Indian nations, though not "civilized," were fully "capable of maintaining the relations of peace and war." On that basis, Milly Francis's father, Hillis Hadjo, and Homathle Mico, the two Indians whom Jackson hanged, and the British agents who had been helping them ought to have been given the same protection under the law of nations as citizens of the United States.[79] While taking a different view of the rights to which the Creek and British prisoners were entitled, Jackson's defenders also accepted that Indian nations, though not civilized, were independent sovereigns. Significantly, in his letter to George Erving, John Quincy Adams argued that the Red Stick Creeks and Seminoles deserved to be treated as outlaws, not because they refused to acknowledge the authority of Spain or the United States, but because they had violated the laws and treaties of the Creek National Council. By criticizing Jackson for denying them the status of lawful combatants, the general's critics appeared to believe that "half a dozen outlawed fugitives from the Creeks" had a legitimate claim to be "the Creek nation."[80] In 1819, when William McIntosh went to Washington with a Creek delegation to press his claims on Seminole land in Florida, he was told in no uncertain terms that he and his warriors had fought on the Union's behalf, not the Creek National Council's. "[T]hey are our enemy," explained Secretary of War John C. Calhoun. "We have a right to dictate the terms on which we will give them peace."[81] But no one disputed the Creeks' right to make the request, nor was it out of the question that as a government allied with the United States the National Council might receive some of the spoils of war.

What was unclear was what sort of sovereignty Indian nations possessed, especially in contested borderlands like the Floridas. Despite
abandoning the Indians in its treaties with Spain and the United States in
1783, Britain continued to treat its former allies in ways that suggested they
were not the "conquered people" that Americans, in particular, claimed.
In this sprit, Governor John Simcoe of Upper Canada offered in 1793 to
mediate an Indian peace treaty with the American government at Buffalo
Creek near the British-occupied fort at Niagara, prompting Secretary of
State Thomas Jefferson to object that Britain seemed determined to grant
Indians in the territory of the United States the sort of "independent sovereignty [that] would entitle them to a claim on the intervention of a third
power." Such a precedent, insisted Jefferson, would be a constant "source
of disquietude to both governments."[82] Twenty years later, Britain's envoys at the Ghent peace talks that ended the War of 1812 spent weeks attempting to persuade the Union's commissioners to accept a clause that
would have guaranteed Indians in Ohio and Indiana the territorial rights
that General Anthony Wayne had recognized in the Treaty of Greenville
in 1795.[83] When news of the ploy reached the United States, Americans
responded with outrage. "I ask Great Britain," thundered the *New York
Evening Post,* "if it has ever been heard of, that the Indians are considered
as independent nations?"[84] If implemented, wrote Treasury Secretary
Alexander James Dallas, Britain's proposal would require the American
government to recognize the rights of a "few thousand" Indians to "nearly
one third of the territorial dominion of the United States."[85]

In terms of the British government's intentions, there were good reasons to question how sincere such efforts were. Although Lord Bathurst,
British secretary for war and the colonies, instructed the Crown's civil
and military officers in North America to treat Britain's Indian allies as
independent "nations" during the War of 1812, many Britons seem to
have regarded the policy as, at most, a wartime expedient.[86] Speaking of
an embassy that he made with Colonel Nicholls to a Choctaw village
near the Negro Fort in December 1814, George Robert Gleig, a British
officer in the force that attacked New Orleans, wrote that the chiefs
dressed "in the most extraordinary manner," wearing scarlet jackets,
cocked hats, and shoes, but no trousers.[87] On the battle's eve, Captain
Edward Codrington of the Royal Navy was equally contemptuous,

remarking in a letter to his wife that a proclamation that addressed the Indians as sovereign allies would make her "laugh as it did me, whilst I was drawing it up." When a group of Creek warriors, Hillis Hadjo among them, boarded his vessel to watch the battle, Captain Codrington wrote that "we had the honour of these *Majestic Beasts* dining with us two days in the 'Tonnant,' and we are to be disgusted with a similar honour here to-day." "Some of them," he continued, were dressed in native garb, which he viewed with approval, but the entire party eventually donned "hats (some cocked gold-laced ones), and . . . jackets such as are worn by sergeants in the Guards." In the captain's unbiased opinion, "they have now the appearance of dressed up apes."[88]

If a British officer who was supposed to be cultivating the Indians' goodwill thought this way, it is hardly surprising that Britain did so little to insist that the United States respect its allies' rights once the war was over, as the Britons who remained in Florida hoped would happen. In an exchange that John Quincy Adams included in his letter to George Erving, Lord Castlereagh, the British foreign secretary, made clear during an interview in 1815 that Britain did not sanction Colonel Nicholls's activities at the Negro Fort, and he disavowed any intention to recognize a "treaty" that Hillis Hadjo and his fellow chiefs brought to London ratifying the clauses in the Anglo-American peace that guaranteed Indian rights. When Adams, who was the American envoy in London during the Indians' visit, raised the matter with Lord Bathurst, the colonial secretary dismissed Nicholls as a "very wild fellow," while Castlereagh said "with a smile that he had a good many treaties to lay before parliament," none of which resembled the one that Nicholls and the Indians had brought with them.[89] According to Walter Bromley of the Royal Acadian School in Halifax, the British were as guilty as the Americans of treating Indians as though they were brutes devoid of moral feeling. "[W]e are told," he wrote, "of the scalping-knife and the tomahawk; of our slaughtered women and children. We speak of these things as if women and children were unknown to the Indians—as if they have no such beings amongst them—no such near and dear relations; as if they belong only to us."[90] Given the role of moral sentiment in sustaining the reciprocity upon which Europe's treaty law depended, such perceptions practically guaranteed the Indians' exclusion from its benefits.

Nonetheless, even Britain's limited recognition of native rights had two far-reaching consequences. The first involved Indians themselves, who were quick to seize on the possibilities that Britain's patronage held out for independence from the United States. In the lead-up to the War of 1812, the Shawnee Prophet Tenskwatawa and his brother Tecumseh famously instructed their followers "not to know Americans on any account" and to consider the British as their "fathers and friends."[91] While taking their name from the Creek symbol for war and justice, the nativist Red Sticks did the same thing, dramatizing their defiance of the Americans through the conspicuous display of British emblems: peace medals from George III and the prince regent, drums embossed with the royal coat of arms, and red coats like the one that Hillis Hadjo was wearing when Milly Francis saved Duncan McKrimmon's life.[92] On the Gulf Coast and in the Lower Mississippi River valley, Indians also responded to the peace of 1783 by declaring independence from the Spanish and Americans, sometimes in ways that voiced anger over their betrayal by George III's emissaries in Paris but often with an eye to creating an opening for the British to return. In the words of a petition that the Loyalist adventurer William Augustus Bowles carried to London with a Creek and Cherokee delegation in 1791, Indians who were present when the British announced the terms of peace at St. Augustine in 1783 "hung their heads in despondency," and they were shocked to learn that the Americans and the Spanish viewed them as "their subjects." But they knew that the king had always treated them as "a nation independent of and allied with [him] upon terms that implied no sovereignty over us." On the strength of that history, they would continue to serve Britain's interests.[93]

The most flamboyant example of this sort of British-sponsored independence was the State of Muskogee, which Bowles founded in East Florida in 1799. Born to English parents in Frederick, Maryland, Bowles's career had taken him from Pennsylvania to Florida, the West Indies, Canada, England, Sierra Leone, and the Philippines. After serving as a Loyalist soldier during the Revolutionary War at Pensacola and as a protégé of Lord Dunmore, Virginia's last royal governor and governor of the Bahamas from 1786 to 1796, Bowles became an adopted Creek and had a wife and family.[94] In that capacity, he led a faction opposed to the Creek chief Alexander McGillivray's alliances with Spain and the United

States, but what propelled him to fame was the founding of Muskogee. Until his arrest by the Americans in 1803, Bowles made his capital at the Seminole town of Miccosukee (later destroyed by Jackson's forces), commissioned a "navy" of Bahamian privateers with which to prey on Spanish shipping, and raised an army of Muscogulge warriors, black as well as Indian. Backed by a group of Nassau merchants and proceeds from the sale of captured vessels, Bowles stunned his opponents during the spring of 1800 by capturing the dilapidated Spanish fort at San Marcos. As John Kelsall, British vice-admiralty judge for the Bahamas, noted in a case involving a Spanish fishing vessel that had been condemned by one of Bowles's magistrates, the entire project had a style "foreign [to] the known habits of Indian Savages."[95] But Muskogee also seized the attention of people in Europe and America, and it made a lasting impression on Florida's Indians.[96] When news of the San Marcos surrender reached London, *Lloyd's Evening Post* lost no time declaring (prematurely) that the Anglo-Creek leader had single-handedly "put a stop to the gradual extermination of the Natives" of the New World.[97]

The other consequence of Britain's involvement was to force Americans to come to terms with the reality of native sovereignty. When it suited their purposes, Americans had no objection to making common cause with both Indian and African American nations, including one as frightening to slaveholders as Haiti. During the Quasi-War with France, between 1798 and 1800, the Adams administration aided Toussaint Louverture's army of former slaves on Saint-Domingue in their efforts to turn the French colony into an "independent power."[98] Following an entente with Britain in 1798, whereby Louverture made peace with France's main European rival and opened the colony to British ships, Americans negotiated a similar arrangement. Over the next five years, British and American merchants engrossed most of Saint-Domingue's trade with the outside world, while the fledgling U.S. Navy established its first overseas station at Cap Français on the colony's northern coast.[99] According to Edward Stevens, who served as the American envoy from 1798 to 1800, Louverture continued to govern "*apparently* under the sanction of the French Republic."[100] But there was no question who had the real power. Speaking of the effect in nearby Jamaica, Lady Maria Nugent, Loyalist wife of the colonial governor, wrote that the "splendour of the black chiefs of

St. Domingo, their superior strength, [and] their firmness of character . . . are the common topics at dinner; and the blackies in attendance seem so much interested, that they hardly change a plate, or do anything but listen."[101] Possibly anticipating the Haitian Republic, whose independence Louverture's successors proclaimed on January 1, 1804, Charles Chalmers, another Loyalist, who had served with Maitland's forces during the British invasion and was a vocal critic of the "covenant" with Louverture, echoed these sentiments, predicting that Britain and the United States would find "the dangerous precedent of a Black empire" to be as threatening as it was to France.[102] But that precedent could also serve their interests.

In fact, the idea of Indian nationhood—what Chief Justice John Marshall would famously call a "domestic dependent nation" in the landmark case of *Cherokee Nation v. Georgia* (1831)—became a mainstay of the Americans who absorbed and established their dominion over the borderlands on the Gulf Coast.[103] With the Creek National Council, the attributes of dependent nationhood included a written code of laws, a clearly defined system of private property, and a representative council with full police powers. Under the watchful eye of the American agent for Indian affairs—between 1796 and his death in 1816, the Creek Agency was in the hands of Benjamin Hawkins, a North Carolina native who had been an officer on Washington's wartime staff before serving a term in the Senate—the council's speaker was always an Indian, with the office rotating between the Creeks' upper and lower branches. When the legislative body met at Coweta, the Lower Creeks had the right to choose the speaker; when the meeting was at Tuckabatchee (in modern Alabama), the choice fell to the Upper Creeks. "The government of the Creeks is not an ephemeral one," wrote Hawkins in 1815, noting that its duties included keeping the peace within its own borders and enforcing the Creeks' "treaty stipulations . . . with their white neighbors."[104] Thirty years later, the civilized Creek George Stiggins said much the same thing, likening the National Council to a "tyrannical oligarchy." For Indians who defied the council's wishes, especially in matters involving the United States, the chiefs had the authority to mete out a variety of punishments, including "beating[s], confiscation of their property, or even death."[105] There was no question whose interests the arrangement was meant to serve.

In the lead-up to the Seminole War, one of the clearest signs of the importance that Americans attached to Indian nationhood was the rhetoric of brigandage and piracy that it allowed the government to bring against renegade Indians like the Red Stick Creeks. Before its destruction in 1816, the Negro Fort served as a particularly vivid sign of the Red Sticks' buccaneering ways.[106] According to John Quincy Adams, the fort's sole purpose was to supply a haven for "all the runaway slaves, all the savage Indians, all the pirates, and all the traitors" who wished to carry on an "exterminating war" against the United States.[107] James Innerarity, a Scottish merchant with Forbes and Company (successor to Panton, Leslie) at Mobile, claimed that blacks and Indians in the garrison had all been "trained . . . to military discipline," which Innerarity blamed on Colonel Nicholls and his gang of "commissioned robbers."[108] Observers also noted that along with the Union Jack, the defenders displayed the "red or bloody flag"—the universal symbol of piracy and war without mercy.[109] In 1817, during General MacGregor's filibustering expedition, similar allegations greeted the multiethnic force with which the Scottish Venezuelan mercenary occupied Amelia Island. Though hardly an impartial observer, John Houston McIntosh, an Anglo-American planter in East Florida, claimed that the freelance republic depended on two factions: one an "American party" of American, English, and Irish sailors, and the other "about one hundred and thirty brigand negroes" from Haiti. Although the American party was more numerous, Commodore Aury and his "set of desperate bloody dogs" were clearly in control, making the "neighborhood extremely dangerous to a population like ours." "They have declared," wrote McIntosh, "that if they are in danger of being overpowered, they will call to their aid every negro within their reach."[110]

For Andrew Jackson, the need to check such activities gave him a compelling rationale for crossing the Florida line in 1818. Despite his well-known support for Indian removal, Jackson made clear that his objective was not to exterminate the Red Stick Creeks and their Seminole allies but to force them to heed their obligations both to the Creek National Council and, indirectly, to the United States.[111] Because the underlying dispute involved the vast acreage that the Creek Nation had ceded in Georgia and Alabama to the United States in 1814, this meant upholding the council's right to act as the sole "executive government" for all Creeks, no matter where they lived.[112] Toward that end, Jackson insisted that the Red Sticks, in particular, deserved to be treated as "outlaws" from their native country in the same manner as the British renegades to whom they looked for protection. In addition, Jackson intended to show Indians throughout the region that they could not "possibly . . . maintain a war with even partial success against the United States" on their own, that Spain was no longer able to come to their assistance, and that Britain would not do so.[113] As Benjamin Hawkins reminded Colonel Nicholls shortly before the British marine left Florida in 1815, the recent peace settlement—between Britain and the United States, as well as among the rulers of Europe—left the Indians on the Gulf Coast with no choice. Given the British king's "love of justice in time of peace, his systematic perseverance in support of legitimate sovereigns [in Europe], almost to the impoverishing of his own nation," it was unthinkable that he would "suffer any of his officers to go into a neutral country [in North America] to disturb its peace," especially when the beneficiaries were renegades like the Red Sticks. Henceforth, Europe's colonial powers would have to accept that the "laws of the United States provide completely for the protection of the Indian[s'] rights." Indians who believed otherwise risked the same fate as outlaws and vagabonds of European extraction.[114]

The result was an unconditional affirmation of the Union's dominion over the lands and people in its neighborhood. In the aftermath, Jackson's opponents were quick to seize on anything that could be used to discredit a man who, according to his enemies, aspired to become another Napoleon, yet few Americans questioned the legitimacy of what Edmund Doyle, a pro-American merchant at Prospect Bluff, described as Jackson's policy of "scourg[ing]" the Indians "into obedience."[115] Henry Clay, for one, denounced both the treaty with which Jackson had forced the Creeks to cede half their ancestral homeland in Georgia and Alabama in 1814 and the execution of Josiah Francis and Homathle Mico as evincing a "spirit of domination" that would have made even the Romans wince. Yet as one of the commissioners who had parried Britain's proposal to guarantee the Indians' territorial rights in Ohio and Indiana in the peace of Ghent, Clay approvingly noted that the Indians possessed "a qualified sovereignty only" and that "supreme sovereignty" belonged to the United States.[116] As Chief Justice Marshall, destined to become another of Jackson's critics during the Indian removal of the 1830s, wrote in the case of *Johnson v. McIntosh* (1823), Indians possessed some of the qualities of a "distinct people," but they lacked the standing both of European nations and of colonial people in other parts of the world, including native states under the British Empire's jurisdiction in Asia. "The words 'princes or governments,'" explained Marshall, "are usually [only] applied to the East Indians"; in America, on the other hand, "[w]e speak of [the Indians'] sachems, their warriors, their chiefmen, [and] their nations or tribes." Under such circumstances, the colonial powers of Europe and America—including, after 1783, the United States—were the only sovereigns in North America that could legitimately claim "ultimate dominion."[117]

(4)

For all these reasons, the First Seminole War proved to be a watershed. In terms of relations with Britain, the war formed part of a general clarification and hardening of the borders that were first articulated in the Anglo-American treaty of 1783 and had subsequently been affirmed in the Jay Treaty.[118] With Spain, the implications were more complex, as the administrations of James Madison and James Monroe sought to balance, on one hand, the sympathy that many Americans felt for Spanish American patriots who were fighting Metternich's Europe for liberty and independence against the need, on the other, to preserve Ferdinand's North American dominion so that he could cede it to the United States. In some parts of the Union there were also concerns over what it would mean for Americans to accept as equals new republics whose commitment to multiracial citizenship seemed to eclipse even that of the brigands whom Jackson had chastised in Florida. According to South Carolina's William Smith, slaveholders, in particular, had reason to think carefully before forming an "intimate connection" with any government in which "blacks and mulattoes are so numerous and . . . influential." Mexico alone contained more than eight million people, "four-fifths of [whom] are Negroes, Indians, Mestizos, Mulattoes, and Zambos"—and all were citizens. Casting an eye in the direction of Haiti, Smith wondered what was to prevent Congress "next year from recognizing our neighbors of the Islands?"[119] Ultimately, though, the desire to rid the Union's neighborhood of Spain was even greater. By the time the last of Jackson's soldiers left Florida, that day seemed to be fast approaching.

Not surprisingly, the hardening of the Union's presence on the Gulf Coast had dire consequences for enslaved Africans and African Americans. In the face that they showed Europe and the rest of the world, Americans tried, wherever possible, to honor the antislavery convictions that Congress and the states had first shown by banning the African slave trade. In his pronouncements on the military operations against Amelia Island and the Seminoles, President Monroe made a great deal of Florida's role in facilitating the smuggling of slaves into the United States, and he continued to press for an agreement with Britain that would allow the Royal Navy to search and seize illegal American slave ships. Just as clearly, though, the destruction of free black enclaves like the Negro Fort and the expulsion of Britain and Spain from the Gulf Coast reduced the possibilities for African Americans to liberate themselves, whether by escaping to freedom on the Spanish side of the border or by fighting with British soldiers against their former masters. Following the British evacuation of Mobile in 1815, James Innerarity could barely disguise his anger, denouncing the "*shewy* humanity of the African association, Abolition Society and others of a like stamp" in Britain, whose ideals the British had used as an excuse to raid plantations during the war, but the Aberdeen native also saw reasons for optimism. Predicting a "hundred fold" increase in profits from the cotton boom already underway in the port's hinterland, he wrote that Mobile, though at present a "dull" and quiet place, far removed from the commercial centers of Liverpool and Glasgow, would not "long continue so."[120] Emboldened by success and a new sense of security, Southerners would soon begin to reframe the debate over slavery, describing the peculiar institution as a form of "exalted benevolence"—as Virginia's Thomas Roderick Dew wrote in 1832—which turned the slave of a "good master [into] . . . his warmest, most constant, and most devoted friend."[121] No doubt, Dew assumed, slaves who felt that way had no other choice.

For Indians, the descent into unqualified dependency carried equally far-reaching implications. Among what became known as the five

"civilized nations" of the Southeast—the Cherokees, Choctaws, Chickasaws, Creeks, and Seminoles—the Seminole War strengthened the
hands of Indian "progressives" who favored the wholesale adoption of
white culture. By the mid-1820s, the wealthiest Indians had adopted
European-style agriculture, using slaves to grow cotton and other crops
for export, many communities had established English-speaking schools,
and the Cherokee had their own weekly newspaper, *The Cherokee Phoe-
nix,* which published its first edition in Cherokee and English in 1828.[122]
If anything, the changes were even more dramatic for Indians who were
unable to take advantage of the new regime, with many succumbing to
lives of poverty and dissolution. On Mackinac Island, where Elizabeth
Thèrése Baird spent her childhood, the consolidation of the U.S. government's authority during the 1820s meant that métis French and Indian traders like her grandmother faced a stark choice: either conform to
American laws and customs, especially in matters relating to marriage
and religion, or endure American ostracism and loss of influence. Baird's
grandmother and great-aunt, Thèrése Marcot Schindler and Magde-
laine Marcot La Framboise, respectively, both of whom had married
French traders in "the manner of the country," were able to maintain
their privileged position by validating their marriages in the local Catholic church and, eventually, becoming independent American women under
U.S. law. But for Indians who refused or were unable to follow their example, a very different fate awaited, one marked by dependency, penury,
and, often, dispossession.[123]

By methods such as these, peace finally came to Indian country—or,
rather, peace as the concept was understood by Americans. Although
Indians in the United States would continue to wage war and make peace
on their own terms well into the nineteenth century, control of both was
increasingly in American hands. According to Americans, who were all
too willing to put even "law-abiding" Indians in a legal station only mar-
ginally higher than pirates and outlaws, this was all for the best. Writing
from Saint Louis in 1827, Thomas Forsyth, U.S. agent for the Sauk and
Fox Indians, claimed that Indian wars were, by definition, wars without
limits, and they "always led to the final extermination of one [party] or
the other." "I never heard of any peace [being] made," wrote Forsyth,
"except when the government of the United States interfered."[124] In his

1843 memoir, the pro-American Creek George Stiggins essentially said the same thing, crediting the Indians' "great father," George Washington, with first instructing them in "the ways of peace and amity."[125] For Milly Francis, such claims would have made little sense, discounting as they did Creek pacification rituals such as the one that she used to save Duncan McKrimmon's life. As long as the United States was not the only European power vying for dominion in North America, Indians continued to make peace on their own terms by playing one set of rulers against another. Thanks to men like Andrew Jackson, that world was increasingly a thing of the past.

Epilogue

Mr. Monroe's Peace

I n many ways James Monroe, fifth president of the United States, would seem to be an unlikely symbol of national unity. Although he was the last president to play a leading role in the revolution—in Emanuel Leutze's epic tableau, *Washington Crossing the Delaware* (1851), Monroe is the standard-bearer in Washington's boat—the former senator, diplomat, and two-time Virginia governor was, by all accounts, a man of ordinary talents, "the third of the Virginia Dynasty," as George Dangerfield once wrote, "in the order of intelligence no less than in that of succession."[1] Yet Monroe had the good fortune to preside over a nation where the tumult and conflict of the Republic's early years seemed, for a brief moment, to be fading from view. During the summer of 1817, the president responded with the first of three processions through the Union, becoming the first head of state since Washington to travel beyond his home region. For newspapers, in particular, all three tours—which took Monroe from New England, where the Hartford Convention had flirted three years earlier with secession, to Detroit and the Alabama Territory—supplied an opportunity to note the flourishing state of the nation's agriculture, improvements such as the steamboats that carried the president along the Atlantic Seaboard, and the patriotism of Americans everywhere. More than anything else, though, Monroe underscored the fact that, for the first time in their history as an independent people, Americans were living in what his hosts in Boston called a "season of profound peace."[2]

In this, Americans owed a substantial debt to Europe, where the desire for peace was, if anything, even greater. Within months of the First Seminole War's end, which cut short Monroe's second tour in 1818, Luis de Onís, Spain's ambassador in Washington, agreed to sell Florida to the United States. Under the Adams-Onís, or Transcontinental Treaty, as the landmark agreement came to be known, Americans had to relinquish claims to Texas, already home to a growing and restless population of American settlers. But they gained an internationally recognized boundary that stretched from the Sabine River, separating Texas and Louisiana, to the present southern border of Oregon. No less important, Britain offered similar terms to the north, agreeing to limit naval armaments on the Great Lakes and clarifying the frontier with Canada as far as the Rocky Mountains. Mindful of Spain's waning power, Americans also began to make peace in Spanish America, which Monroe finalized early in his second term by recognizing the largest of Madrid's former provinces as independent republics.[3] After France invaded Spain in 1823—this time to support Ferdinand VII against a revolution by his own people—the president went further, warning in a speech to Congress that the United States would regard any attempt to recolonize the Americas as a hostile act. Because Britain and France, the only nations in Europe with the capacity to mount such a project, had already agreed not to intervene, Monroe's words served as a bold statement of American ambition, and little else.[4] Even so, the speech carried an unmistakable air of history-in-the-making. In his account of Monroe's first tour, published in 1818, the Hartford, Connecticut, biographer Samuel Putnam Waldo cautioned that the "Allied Sovereigns" of Europe—"that tremendous association of earthly potentates," as Waldo imagined them—threatened the rights of free men and women everywhere, including America.[5] By the end of Monroe's second term, such fears had lost much of their urgency.

Over the next century, the Monroe Doctrine would come to occupy an iconic place in the national imagination, both as a template for relations with Europe and, in the minds of many Americans, as a license for expansion within their own neighborhood. To Monroe's contemporaries, though, the main effect was to serve notice that the age of European co-lonialism in the Western Hemisphere was over and that the Republic's citizens could enjoy the fruits of peace.[6] In proclaiming the significance of this moment, Americans scarcely needed to be reminded that the first half century of their nation's existence had been a time of recurring hos-tility with Europe's colonial powers. Although Americans were only rarely formal belligerents after 1783, war, whether as a looming threat or a lived reality, had been a constant presence, shaping the Union's federal structure, dictating—and, often, inflaming—relations between Federal-ists and Republicans, influencing the attitudes of black and white Amer-icans toward chattel servitude, determining what rights Indians could claim and what rights they could not, and setting the tempo for industrial and commercial development everywhere. Those days seemed to be over. Americans, claimed a writer in Britain's *Monthly Magazine* in 1825, appeared to have a bright future:

> They have no popular discords, no insurrections, no civil wars. Their security is equivalent to their freedom. And what is the re-sult? At the commencement of the [present century], the population amounted to four or five millions; it is now eleven. Their towns were small and poor; they now rival in grandeur, population and beauty, the capitals of Europe. . . . Their commerce, their industry, even their agriculture, [are] . . . sufficient for an extent of enterprise, which spreads their commerce over Europe and the Indies, and car-ries the overflow of arts southward, over what was once Spanish America.[7]

The author, in his or her enthusiasm, passed a bit too easily over pros-perity's darker side: the social and environmental costs of industrializa-tion, the dislocation caused by the spread of commercial agriculture, and the boom-and-bust cycles that were suddenly an ordinary part of life.[8] And the writer exaggerated. How many American towns rivaled European capitals? War, however, was apparently something that Amer-icans no longer needed to worry about.

But what, exactly, did being at peace mean? As always, it meant, first and foremost, maintaining peaceful treaty relations with Europe's great powers. To be sure, Americans had little affection for the conservatives who dominated European politics following Napoleon's defeat, nor did they wish to be entangled in their affairs. According to an article in the *North American Review,* written on the eve of Monroe's speech to Congress in 1823, the United States' "very existence is an attack upon the monarchies of Europe; its economy is a reproach upon their wild extravagance; and its policy condemns their ambition, their unnecessary wars, and their whole political system."[9] Given the differences between their union for liberty and Europe's reactionary "union of 'Legitimate Sovereigns,'" Americans could be forgiven for thinking that the less they had to do with the Old World, the better.[10] Yet this did not mean they repudiated "the great society of nations," as Henry Wheaton wrote in the 1830s, or the public law of its members.[11] Monroe, for one, went out of his way to emphasize this point, mentioning in his first inaugural address the Union's history of expanding "by fair and honorable treaty" and insisting that the United States always observed "just principles" with foreign governments.[12] Commerce, in particular, was an area where the appearance of isolation from Europe obscured a deeper reality of convergence and integration. As evidenced by the cotton trade's spectacular growth, Americans were more fully integrated into the Atlantic (and global) economy at the time of Monroe's inauguration than they had ever been, with especially close ties to Britain.[13] Even the push for national improvement—evident in the rechartering of the Bank of the United States in 1816, the construction of roads and canals, and the strengthening of the Union's land and sea defenses—bespoke a continued awareness of connectedness to the world beyond the Union's borders. Wherever the strands of this web extended, Americans accepted the legal order of which Europe was still the center.[14]

The second meaning of peace was more problematic. From the standpoint of the Union's treaty relations with Europe's governments, the United States had broad, nearly unlimited rights over the lands and peoples under its dominion. This included both American citizens and people who were not citizens: Indians, African Americans, and other settlers. As Americans had learned, this dominion was less absolute in times of war than in times of peace. During the wars of the American and French Revolutions, Britain, in particular, used the rules of war to emancipate slaves, to support the independence of Indian nations, to encourage settlers' secessionist tendencies, and to interdict American slave ships, all without having to obtain their former colonies' consent, and Americans had often found it hard, if not impossible, to resist. In the treaties that ended the Napoleonic Wars—including the Anglo-American Treaty of Ghent (1814)—Britain sought to make the most important of these innovations permanent, inserting language that affirmed the slave trade's illegality and that obligated the United States to respect the rights of the Crown's Indian allies. Under peacetime conditions, however, the British government lost the right to compel other nations to respect these guarantees. To do so, even in a humanitarian cause, would be to violate what Henry Wheaton called the "reciprocal stipulation of perpetual peace and amity" that independent nations ordinarily observed in dealings with each other.[15] For Americans, the implications were clear. As long as the United States was at peace, only the federal government and the states had the right to decide whether the people under their dominion would enjoy the full benefits of peace for themselves.

For this reason, Indians and African Americans, in particular, had reason to view the United States' increasingly amicable relations with Europe after 1815 as a mixed blessing. Thanks partly to the annexation of Florida, where Amelia Island had long been an entrepôt for the illegal slave trade, and the suppression of piracy on the Texas-Louisiana border, Monroe's presidency marked the moment when the federal prohibition on slave imports, first sanctioned for the entire Union by Congress in 1807, came to look like something more than a well-meaning but hollow gesture. By the mid-1820s, the number of slaves being smuggled into the United States was no more than a few hundred per year, and the figure eventually fell to near zero.[16] The foreign slave trade, however, was another matter. Although Monroe supported a British agreement in 1823 that would have allowed the Royal Navy to stop suspected American slave ships, most Americans—including Secretary of State John Quincy Adams and a majority of senators—opposed anything that could be used to legitimate the rights that Britain had claimed over American ships and sailors before the War of 1812.[17] From the mid-1820s onward, as Britain compelled other nations in Europe and Latin America to abandon the slave trade, the stars and stripes became an increasingly popular flag of convenience for ships conveying African captives to Cuba and Brazil. From stations in the Caribbean and the South Atlantic, the U.S. Navy occasionally captured American slavers, yet this was a minor impediment, and nothing compared to what Britain, the one power with the naval capacity to bring the illicit slave trade to a full conclusion, might have achieved had the peacetime law of nations not prevented its cruisers from intervening.

No less troubling, the prosperity that came with peace helped entrench slavery in those parts of the American union where chattel servitude remained legal, and it created a powerful incentive for extending slave-based agriculture to places where the institution had yet to be established, often by dispossessing the territory's Indian proprietors. As Chief Justice Lemuel Shaw of Massachusetts observed in *Commonwealth v. Aves* (1836), the result was to accentuate the Constitution's dual character as "a treaty and . . . a form of government." In its foreign relations (including with Indians), the United States comprised "one community," enabling Americans to safeguard their rights and fulfill their obligations to other European and American nations. In matters of domestic governance, on the other hand, the Union resembled a compact between sovereign polities, with each state retaining broad authority over its own affairs.[18] As was clear from the Missouri crisis of 1819 and 1820, which pitted the House of Representatives' right to prohibit slavery in prospective states against the states' right to decide for themselves whether their citizens could own slaves, the Union's federal structure ensured that Congress and the president would have limited sway over the peculiar institution. Indeed, until the Union split over slavery in 1861, the U.S. Constitution continued to be one of the principal bulwarks of the right to own human property, with the treaty law of Europe and America being another.[19]

The third and final consequence of peace was to enable the United States to assume the role of a great nation in the lands and waters in its immediate vicinity.[20] In terms of raw power politics, it can be tempting to dismiss the nationalist pretensions that swept American society during Monroe's presidency. In 1818, while Andrew Jackson was chastising Florida's Indians with an army of five thousand, most of them Creek and American irregulars, France was under military occupation by a force that, in the immediate aftermath of Napoleon's defeat at Waterloo, had consisted of 1.2 million British, Russian, and German regulars.[21] Compared to Europe's great powers, the American union was a lightweight. It was, however, a lightweight that no longer felt threatened by European governments in its neighborhood. As was clear from the response to the final collapse of Spain's American empire during the early 1820s, even Britain had little inclination to project the full weight of its military and naval power in the Western Atlantic. Conscious of London's disenchantment with Europe's conservative Holy Alliance, some Americans, including, briefly, Thomas Jefferson, thought they detected in these developments the makings of a British-American condominium, with the two English-speaking empires "acting in concert . . . [to] protect the whole of the new world against all the force and machinations and despotism of the old," as a writer in Boston's *Christian Advocate* contended in 1824.[22] Others, following Monroe's lead, preferred to hew to an independent course and steer clear of European alliances. Either way, the dangers that had beset the Union in its early years were clearly receding. Whether the issue was the United States' limited success in suppressing the slave trade or Monroe's speech closing the Americas to future European colonization, the desire for peace in Europe left Americans free to make whatever peace they wished in their own neighborhood.

And this was by no means the whole story. Although Americans were beneficiaries of circumstances beyond their control, they also owed their growing regional stature to what, in many ways, was the most lasting and profound of the revolution's consequences. As the liberal abbé de Pradt remarked in 1821, the European Atlantic empires to which Americans themselves had once belonged were, by their very nature, "irregular and distant" polities, which made relatively few demands on their colonial subjects.[23] By turning the former British colonies into what Monroe called "a great nation, composed of many confederated republics," and by endowing that nation with the unlimited sovereignty of the people, Americans created a government whose leaders were far more effective than their colonial predecessors had ever been in terms of the taxes and soldiers that they could raise, the internal improvements that they could sponsor, and the popular allegiance that they could command. Although the price was nothing compared to what governments demanded of ordinary men and women in Britain and Europe, the military and fiscal burdens that the American union placed on its citizens easily eclipsed what George III's subjects in Canada had to bear at the time of Monroe's tour, and they were far greater than the parliamentary taxes that had started the American Revolution half a century earlier.[24] As the president reminded the people of Athens, Georgia, when he visited in 1819, the United States had been "founded on the equal rights of the people." On that basis, its government had both the right and the authority to muster whatever resources seemed necessary "to accomplish all the great objects for which it was initiated." As Jefferson had said, the United States was an empire of liberty, but it was also an empire.[25]

In time, events would show that the Union that Congress founded in 1776 was capable of transcending the limitations of its early history. For whites on the margins of American society, notably the Loyalists, but before them the Acadians, the opportunities for wealth and status could be great indeed. When Charles White arrived in Pennsylvania during the mid-1750s, he was Charles Leblanc, a nine-year-old who had been orphaned by his family's expulsion from a neutral French village near Minas Basin. By the time of his death in 1816, he was a successful merchant, ship owner, and shopkeeper, with real estate in Philadelphia that was worth more than thirty-five thousand dollars. When his estate was settled, White's beneficiaries included more than a hundred relatives in Pennsylvania, Louisiana, and Maryland.[26] Nor were such outcomes limited to Americans of European ancestry. As was clear from the experiences of the black ship captain Paul Cuffe and the métis Creek soldier and planter Thomas Woodward, who served with Jackson's forces during the First Seminole War, the American union was potentially a place of opportunity for people of color as well, especially if they found ways to parry what Woodward, speaking of his white neighbors in Alabama, called "indignities or insults . . . that under other circumstances I should have slapped a rod."[27] In history, as in music, it can be hard to distinguish a work written in a major key from one in a minor key, especially when the modulation is between relative scales with the same key signature. For Charles White and—in very different ways—for Paul Cuffe and Thomas Woodward, change had often come suddenly and unexpectedly, and the effects had typically cut several ways. Whatever they made of the nation's shortcomings, perhaps even they would have hesitated to say how, or in what key, their own stories should be rendered.[28]

For that reason alone, the United States' emergence during the 1820s as a great nation at peace needs to be seen as a moment with a complicated legacy. As President Monroe's speech warning Europe's colonial powers out of the Americas showed, the Union's history remained entangled in deep and profound ways with the history of Europe, including, especially, Britain, and the same was true of the nations and peoples in the Union's immediate vicinity. Both for the holder of the nation's highest office and for the nation as a whole, Americans could only make the history that others allowed them to. Nonetheless, during the century-long era of European peace that began in 1815, the ability of Americans to turn the legal rights of peace to their advantage repeatedly served as a check on the ability of Britain and Europe's other powers to intervene in the Union's affairs. It did so, moreover, whether the issues involved the treaty rights of Indian nations in the Union's territory or the increasingly bitter controversy over slavery and the right of Americans to end the peculiar institution without having to worry overly about the international consequences. Ironically, on this last point, the creation of a great treaty-worthy nation in North America, one whose founding documents sanctioned the right of Americans to own human property in clear and unyielding terms, was ultimately also a vital part of what enabled Americans to take that right away. In 1861, when the great crisis over slavery finally came, Americans had far more liberty—if not complete freedom—to decide for themselves exactly what the shape of their more perfect Union would be. Though at war with each other, they were at peace with the world.

Notes

Acknowledgments

Index

Notes

The following abbreviations are used in the notes.

Annals of Congress	*The Debates and Proceedings in the Congress of the United States*, compiled by Joseph Gales and William Winston Seaton, 42 vols. (Washington, 1834–1856)
ASP	*American State Papers*, ed. Walter Lowrie, et al., 38 vols. (Washington, 1832–1861)
BNA	British National Archives (formerly Public Record Office), London
	CO Colonial Office Papers
	FO Foreign Office Papers
	HCA High Court of Admirality
	HO Home Office Papers
	PRO Public Record Office, Domestic
	T Treasury
Evans	*Early American imprints. Series I, Evans (1639–1800)* [electronic resource]
H.R. Doc.	*United States Congressional Serial Set*, House of Representatives report or document
LO	Loudoun Papers, Huntington Library, San Marino, Calif.
U.S. Statutes at Large	*Statutes at Large of the United States of America, 1789–1873*, ed. Richard Peters, et al., 17 vols. (Boston, 1845–1873)

Unless otherwise indicated, italicized words are reproduced as they appear in the original quotation.

INTRODUCTION: A NATION AMONG NATIONS

1. This is the part of the Model Treaty that historians have often emphasized, seeing in its emphasis on peaceful relations a "radical departure from contemporary norms" or, even, an attempt "to create a . . . system that would reduce international conflicts": Bradford Perkins, *The Creation of a Republican Empire, 1776–1865*, vol. 1 of *The Cambridge History of American Foreign Relations*, ed. Warren I. Cohen (Cambridge, 1993; reprint, 1995), 24–25. Probably the most influential statement is Felix Gilbert, *To the Farewell Address: Ideas of Early American Foreign Policy* (Princeton, N.J., 1961); see also Gordon S. Wood, *Empire of Liberty: A History of the Early Republic, 1789–1815* (Oxford, 2009), 191, who quotes Adams as saying that if its principles were "established and honestly observed," the Model Treaty might "put an end forever to all maritime war." Although the treaty broke with prevailing trends in British maritime policy, James H. Hutson's "Early American Diplomacy: A Reappraisal," in *The American Revolution and "a Candid World,"* ed. Lawrence S. Kaplan (Kent, Ohio, 1977), 40–68, takes issue with Gilbert's emphasis on the economic thought of the French enlightenment and situates the Model Treaty in conventional ideas about European power politics; for a similar reading, see Walter A. McDougall, *Promised Land, Crusader State: The American Encounter with the World since 1776* (Boston, 1997), 24–25. The importance of European antecedents in Adams's thinking is evident in the use that he made of two English collections of European treaties from the first decade of the eighteenth century to help with the drafting of the articles that deal with commerce: see editorial note on the plan of treaties in Robert J. Taylor et al., eds, *Papers of John Adams, The Adams Papers, Series III: General Correspondence and Other Papers of the Adams Statesmen*, vol. 4, *February–August 1776* (Cambridge, Mass., 1979), 262.

2. "Plan of Treaties as Adopted [by Congress] (with Instructions)" [September 17, 1776], in *Papers of John Adams*, vol. 4, 292. On the territorial claims in the Model Treaty and the problems that they posed for the United States' relations with Spain, see J. C. A. Stagg, *Borderlines in Borderlands: James Madison and the Spanish-American Frontier, 1776–1821* (New Haven, Conn., 2009), 14–17.

3. On the "colonial" character of the United States, see Jack P. Greene, "Colonial History and National History: Reflections on a Continuing Problem," *William and Mary Quarterly*, 3rd ser., 64 (2007): 235–250; see also Peter Hulme, "Postcolonial Theory and Early America: An Approach from the Caribbean," and Michael Warner, "What's Colonial about Colonial America?" in *Possible Pasts: Becoming Colonial in Early America*, ed. Robert Blair St. George (Ithaca, N.Y., 2000), 33–48, 49–70.

4. Often, Europe's colonial powers only *appeared* to be in control. For a bracing and salutary reminder of the extent to which North and South America remained Indian country throughout the European colonial era, see Amy Turner Bushnell, "Indigenous America and the Limits of the Atlantic World, 1493–1825," in *Atlantic History: A Critical Appraisal*, ed. Jack P. Greene and Philip D. Morgan (Oxford, 2009), 191–221.

5. For the United States as a nation among nations, see Thomas Bender, *A Nation among Nations: America's Place in World History* (New York, 2006).

6. On both points, see, especially, Peter S. Onuf, "A Declaration of Independence for Diplomatic Historians," *Diplomatic History* 22 (1998): 71–83. For the British response to the American Revolution as a European crisis, see Eliga H. Gould, "American Independence and Britain's Counter-Revolution," *Past & Present* 154 (1997): 107–141. For the response in Europe, see R. R. Palmer, *The Challenge,* vol. 1 of *The Age of the Democratic Revolution: A Political History of Europe and America, 1760–1800* (Princeton, N.J., 1959); Franco Venturi, *The Great States of the West,* vol. 1 of *The End of the Old Regime in Europe, 1776–1789,* trans. R. Burr Litchfield (Princeton, N.J., 1977), chap. 1, 2. As historians have often noted, Congress wrote the Declaration as an address to "the [European] powers of the earth": see, especially, David Armitage, *The Declaration of Independence: A Global History* (Cambridge, Mass., 2007), 10; Thomas M. Franck, "The Emerging Right to Democratic Governance," *American Journal of International Law* 86 (1992): 46; however, the one-sided nature of the statement can also be read as laying the groundwork for the unilateralist tradition in American foreign policy. See, for example, Robert Reiss, "Toward a Declaration of Interdependence for 1976," *Journal of Aesthetic Education* 6 (1972): 109–110; and, from a less critical standpoint, McDougall, *Promised Land,* 55–56, 76–77.

7. Cooper, "A Sermon Preached . . . [on] October 25, 1780. Being the Day of the Commencement of the Constitution and Inauguration of the New Government," in *Political Sermons of the American Founding Era, 1730–1805,* ed. Ellis Sandoz (Indianapolis, 1991), 653.

8. Adams to John Winthrop, Philadelphia, June 23, 1776, in *Papers of John Adams,* vol. 4, 332.

9. Cooper, "Sermon," in Sandoz, *Political Sermons,* 655.

10. The literature on Indian relations in colonial and revolutionary America is vast, and continues to grow. For relations during the mid-century Anglo-French wars, see Peter Silver, *Our Savage Neighbors: How Indian War Transformed Early America* (New York, 2008); see also, Daniel K. Richter, *Facing East from Indian Country: A Native History of Early America* (Cambridge, Mass., 2001) and, for the seventeenth century, Cynthia Jean Van Zandt, *Brothers among Nations: The Pursuit of Intercultural Alliances in Early America, 1580–1660* (Oxford, 2008).

11. Christopher L. Tomlins and Bruce H. Mann, eds., *The Many Legalities of Early America* (Chapel Hill, N.C., 2001). See also Eliga H. Gould, "Zones of Law, Zones of Violence: The Legal Geography of the British Atlantic, Circa 1772," *William and Mary Quarterly,* 3rd ser., 60 (2003): 471–510; Lauren A. Benton, *Law and Colonial Cultures: Legal Regimes in World History, 1400–1900* (Cambridge, 2002).

12. See James Muldoon, "Discovery, Grant, Charter, Conquest, or Purchase: John Adams on the Legal Basis for English Possession of North America," in *The Many Legalities of Early America,* ed. Tomlins and Mann, 25–46. As the discussion here suggests, dominion, or *dominium,* was related to sovereignty but not the same thing; it was possible for European rulers (and, after 1776, Congress) to claim do-

minion over a territory while recognizing that the actual sovereignty and right of government were in the hands of the land's indigenous inhabitants. Also, dominion and sovereignty were different from property, hence the need to negotiate treaties with Indians in order to acquire land over which Europeans already claimed dominion. For the difference between sovereignty (in all its variations) and property as it related to American-Indian relations, see Stuart Banner, *How the Indians Lost Their Land: Law and Power on the Frontier* (Cambridge, Mass., 2005), 6–9; on the different forms of sovereignty and dominion, see Lauren A. Benton, *A Search for Sovereignty: Law and Geography in European Empires, 1400–1900* (Cambridge, 2010), esp. 4–5; see also Leonard J. Sadosky, *Revolutionary Negotiations: Indians, Empires, and Diplomats in the Founding of America* (Charlottesville, Va., 2009).

13. William Blackstone, *Of Public Wrongs,* vol. 4 of *Commentaries on the Laws of England,* ed. Stanley N. Katz (Chicago, 1979 [orig. publ., 1765–1769]), 66. There is a large and expanding literature on the law of nations in early modern Europe and the extra-European world; see, esp., Peter S. Onuf and Nicholas Greenwood Onuf, *Federal Union, Modern World: The Law of Nations in an Age of Revolutions, 1776– 1814* (Madison, Wisc., 1993); Richard Tuck, *The Rights of War and Peace: Political Thought and the International Order from Grotius to Kant* (Oxford, 1999); David Armitage, "The Declaration of Independence and International Law," *William and Mary Quarterly,* 3rd ser., 59 (2002): 39–64; Gould, "Zones of Law," 471–510; Benton, *A Search for Sovereignty.* For Blackstone's influence in the United States, see Ellen Holmes Pearson, "Revising Custom, Embracing Choice: Early American Legal Scholars and the Republicanization of the Common Law," in *Empire and Nation: The American Revolution in the Atlantic World,* ed. Eliga H. Gould and Peter S. Onuf (Baltimore, 2005), 93–111; for the general problem of adapting English common law to the American republic, see Mary Sarah Bilder, *The Transatlantic Constitution: Colonial Legal Culture and the Empire* (Cambridge, Mass., 2004), 186–196; Daniel J. Hulsebosch, *Constituting Empire: New York and the Transformation of Constitutionalism in the Atlantic World, 1664–1830* (Chapel Hill, N.C., 2005).

14. This paragraph draws on Max Savelle, *The Origins of American Diplomacy: The International History of Angloamerica, 1492–1763* (New York, 1967), and Elizabeth Mancke, "Negotiating an Empire," in *Negotiated Empires: Centers and Peripheries in the Americas, 1500–1820,* ed. Christine Daniels and Michael V. Kennedy (New York, 2002), 235–266. For a skeptical discussion of the diplomatic significance of the lines of amity in early modern Europe, see Garrett Mattingly, "No Peace Beyond What Line?" *Transactions of the Royal Historical Society* 13 (1963): 145–162; however, the idea of a distinction between how Europe's rulers interacted with each other in Europe and how they interacted in the wider world is well established in the scholarly literature: see, for example, Tuck, *Rights of War and Peace,* 14–15, who sees the tension between "liberal politics at home and the 'expansion of Europe' overseas" as being central to the modern law of nations; see also Geoffrey Best, " 'One World or Several?' Reflections on the Modern History of International Law and Human Rights," *Historical Research* 61, no. 145 (1988): 212–226, and Sadosky, *Revolutionary Negotiations,* 6–8, on North America as a "diplomatic borderland" of

the Westphalian system. For Britain's preoccupation with Europe during the wars of the mid-eighteenth century, often to the exclusion of America and the empire, see Stephen Conway, "Continental Connections: Britain and Europe in the Eighteenth Century," *History* 90 (2005): 352–374.

15. Although Britons and Americans frequently used "neighborhood" as a term to describe North America during the revolutionary era, there is, as far as I am aware, no scholarly study of the term's Anglo-American usage. For the Americas as a neighborhood in the United States' relations with Spanish America, see James E. Lewis, *The American Union and the Problem of Neighborhood: The United States and the Collapse of the Spanish Empire, 1783–1829* (Chapel Hill, N.C., 1998).

16. The best book-length study of the territorial dimensions of Britain's peacemaking efforts is Colin G. Calloway, *The Scratch of a Pen: 1763 and the Transformation of North America* (Oxford, 2006); see also Fred Anderson, *Crucible of War: The Seven Years' War and the Fate of Empire in British North America, 1754–1766* (New York, 2000). For the maritime effort to make peace, one must rely on a much older literature: see, for example, the discussion in Savelle, *Origins*, 436–510, as well as the sections dealing with the Peace of Paris (1763) in Richard Pares, *War and Trade in the West Indies, 1739–1763* (Oxford, 1936; reprint, 1963). The impact on American seamen is better documented: see Jesse Lemisch, "Jack Tar in the Streets: Merchant Seamen in the Politics of Revolutionary America," *William and Mary Quarterly,* 3rd ser., 25 (1968): 371–407; Peter Linebaugh and Marcus Buford Rediker, *The Many-Headed Hydra: Sailors, Slaves, Commoners, and the Hidden History of the Revolutionary Atlantic* (Boston, 2000), chap. 7; Paul A. Gilje, *Liberty on the Waterfront: American Maritime Culture in the Age of Revolution* (Philadelphia, 2004).

17. Henry Wheaton, *History of the Law of Nations in Europe and America* (New York, 1845). For Wheaton's role as the leading American writer on international law in the United States, see Nicholas Greenwood Onuf and Peter S. Onuf, *Nations, Markets, and War: Modern History and the American Civil War* (Charlottesville, Va., 2006), 58–69.

18. Alan Taylor, "The Late Loyalists: Northern Reflections of the Early American Republic," *Journal of the Early Republic* 27 (2007): 1–34. For the problem of high taxation generally, which the Constitution of 1787 partly relieved, see Max M. Edling, *A Revolution in Favor of Government: Origins of the U.S. Constitution and the Making of the American State* (Oxford, 2003).

19. For the strategic importance of Canada, see J. C. A. Stagg, *Mr. Madison's War: Politics, Diplomacy, and Warfare in the Early American Republic, 1783–1830* (Princeton, N.J., 1983); see also Alan Taylor, *The Civil War of 1812: American Citizens, British Subjects, Irish Rebels, and Indian Allies* (New York, 2010), which emphasizes the shared history that entangled people on either side of the border; and Elizabeth Mancke, *The Fault Lines of Empire: Political Differentiation in Massachusetts and Nova Scotia, ca. 1760–1830* (New York, 2005). The Ohio valley and Great Lakes have been especially important in Indian history: see Richard White, *The Middle Ground: Indians, Empires, and Republics in the Great Lakes Region, 1650–1815* (Cambridge, 1991); Eric Hinderaker, *Elusive Empires: Constructing Colo-*

nialism in the Ohio Valley, 1673–1800 (Cambridge, 1997); and Richter, *Facing East*, though Richter's book also covers Indian country south of the Ohio.

20. See, esp., David J. Weber, *The Spanish Frontier in North America* (New Haven, Conn., 1992); see also Claudio Saunt, *A New Order of Things: Property, Power, and the Transformation of the Creek Indians, 1733–1816* (Cambridge, 1999); Lewis, *American Union,* Stagg, *Borderlines,* Jane Landers, *Black Society in Spanish Florida* (Urbana, Ill., 1999); see, also, J. Leitch Wright, *Britain and the American Frontier, 1783–1815* (Athens, Ga., 1975).

21. East Florida was home to a community of Anglo-American planters along the northeastern coastal strip bounded by the Saint Johns and Saint Marys Rivers. On the Floridas as maritime territory, see Amy Turner Bushnell, "Borderland or Border-Sea? Placing Early Florida," *William and Mary Quarterly,* 3rd ser., 60 (2003): 643–653; Michael Jarvis, *In the Eye of All Trade: Bermuda, Bermudians, and the Maritime Atlantic World, 1680–1783* (Chapel Hill, N.C., 2010), shows why Congress included Bermuda in the British possessions that the Model Treaty claimed; for Newfoundland in the age of the American Revolution, see Jerry Bannister, *The Rule of the Admirals: Law, Custom, and Naval Government in Newfoundland, 1699–1832* (Toronto, 2003). See Andrew Jackson O'Shaughnessy, *An Empire Divided: The American Revolution and the British Caribbean* (Philadelphia, 2000), for the West Indies. On maritime borders and frontiers generally, see John R. Gillis, *Islands of the Mind: How the Human Imagination Created the Atlantic World* (New York, 2002).

22. See Onuf and Onuf, *Federal Union,* for Britain's maritime dominion; see Rafe Blaufarb, "The Western Question: The Geopolitics of Latin American Independence," *American Historical Review* 112 (2007): 742–763, for smuggling and privateering.

23. John Thornton, *Africa and Africans in the Making of the Atlantic World, 1400–1800* (Cambridge, 1992).

24. Calhoun, "Speech on the Reception of Abolition Petitions" (1837), in *Speeches . . . Delivered in the House of Representatives and in the Senate of the United States,* vol. 2 of *The Works of John C. Calhoun,* ed. Richard K. Crallé (New York, 1864), 626.

25. For similar usages of "nation," see David Waldstreicher, *In the Midst of Perpetual Fetes: The Making of American Nationalism, 1776–1820* (Chapel Hill, N.C., 1997); Peter S. Onuf, *Jefferson's Empire: The Language of American Nationhood* (Charlottesville, Va., 2000).

26. See Daniel H. Deudney, "The Philadelphian System: Sovereignty, Arms Control, and Balance of Power in the American States-Union, Circa 1787–1861," *International Organization* 49 (1995): 191–228. For a lucid discussion of the secondary literature on federalism and the nation, see the bibliographic essay at the end of David C. Hendrickson, *Peace Pact: The Lost World of the American Founding* (Lawrence, Kans., 2003), 281–297; see also Alison L. LaCroix, *The Ideological Origins of American Federalism* (Cambridge, Mass., 2010).

27. The argument here builds on Eliga H. Gould, "Entangled Histories, Entangled Worlds: The English-Speaking Atlantic as a Spanish Periphery," *American Historical Review* 112 (2007): 764–786.

28. Perkins, *Creation,* 29–31.

29. For the international dimensions of the making of the Constitution, see David M. Golove and Daniel J. Hulsebosch, "A Civilized Nation: The Early American Constitution, the Law of Nations, and the Pursuit of International Recognition," *New York University Law Review* 85 (2010): 932–1066; see also Don Higginbotham, "War and State Formation in Revolutionary America," in Gould and Onuf, *Empire and Nation,* 54–71.

30. Articles of Confederation, article IV, in Jack P. Greene, ed., *Colonies to Nation: A Documentary History of the American Revolution* (New York, 1975), 429.

31. For the general problem of statelessness in American history, see, esp., Linda K. Kerber, "The Stateless as the Citizen's Other: A View from the United States," *American Historical Review* 112 (2007): 1–34; see also Linda K. Kerber, "Toward a History of Statelessness in America," *American Quarterly* 57 (2005): 727–749.

32. "First Annual Message" (December 8, 1801), in *Thomas Jefferson, Writings,* ed. Merrill D. Peterson, vol. 15 of *The Library of America* (New York, 1984), 501–502.

33. Tuck, *Rights of War and Peace;* see also James Muldoon, *The Americas in the Spanish World Order: The Justification for Conquest in the Seventeenth Century* (Philadelphia, 1994), for notions of difference based on Christianity; and Marilyn Lake, *Drawing the Global Colour Line: White Men's Countries and the International Challenge of Racial Equality* (Cambridge, 2008), for race and international relations.

1. ON THE MARGINS OF EUROPE

1. For modern accounts of the Acadian removal, see Geoffrey Plank, *An Unsettled Conquest: The British Campaign against the Peoples of Acadia* (Philadelphia, 2001); John Mack Faragher, *A Great and Noble Scheme: The Tragic Story of the Expulsion of the French Acadians from Their American Homeland* (New York, 2005).

2. Guy Frégault, *Canada: The War of the Conquest,* trans. Margaret M. Cameron (Toronto, 1969), 185; for Winslow's military service and reputation, see Fred Anderson, *A People's Army: Massachusetts Soldiers and Society in the Seven Years' War* (Chapel Hill, N.C., 1984), 9, 169.

3. Plank, *Unsettled Conquest,* chap. 7, esp. 147.

4. Frégault, *Canada,* 186.

5. Peter Oliver, *Origin and Progress of the American Rebellion: A Tory View,* ed. Douglass Adair and John A. Schutz (San Marino, Calif., 1961), 34; Richard G. Lowe, "Massachusetts and the Acadians," *William and Mary Quarterly,* 3rd ser., 25 (1968): 214.

6. Faragher, *Great and Noble Scheme,* 424–425.

7. [Arthur Young], *Reflections on the Present State of Affairs at Home and Abroad* (London, 1759), 39, 38–42. For the British government's expanding military and political presence in the colonies during the Seven Years' War, see Eliga H. Gould, *The Persistence of Empire: British Political Culture in the Age of the American Revolution* (Chapel Hill, N.C., 2000); see also Fred Anderson, *Crucible of War: The*

Seven Years' War and the Fate of Empire in British North America, 1754–1766 (New York, 2000); Don Higginbotham, "The Early American Way of War: Reconnaissance and Appraisal," *William and Mary Quarterly,* 3rd ser., 44 (1987): 230–273.

8. Plank, *Unsettled Conquest,* 115–116.

9. To be without a nation was similar to being stateless, for which see Linda K. Kerber, "Toward a History of Statelessness in America," *American Quarterly* 57 (2005): 727–749.

10. J[ohn] Wright, *A Compleat History of the Late War, or Annual Register of Its Rise, Progress, and Events, in Europe, Asia, Africa, and America,* 4th ed. (Dublin, 1766), 2. Although Wright compiled the history and is therefore often listed as the author, most of the history consists of passages taken from the *Annual Register.* Burke founded the journal and, during its early years, wrote many of the entries.

11. Emer de Vattel, *The Law of Nations, or, Principles of the Law of Nature, Applied to the Conduct and Affairs of Nations and Sovereigns,* ed. Bela Kapossy and Richard Whatmore (Indianapolis, 2008 [orig. publ. London, 1797]), book iii, § 47 (p. 496). Although the Nugent translation is the one used here, the first English version was translated anonymously and appeared in 1760: see "A Note on the Texts," in ibid., xxi.

12. *Observations on the Conduct of Great-Britain, in Respect to Foreign Affairs,* 2d ed. (London, 1743), 7; on British xenophobia, see, esp., Linda Colley, *Britons: Forging the Nation, 1707–1837* (New Haven, Conn., 1992).

13. East Apthorp, *A Sermon on the General Fast, Friday, December 13, 1776 . . .* (London, 1776), 8. See also Eliga H. Gould, "American Independence and Britain's Counter-Revolution," *Past and Present* 107 (February 1997): 107–141.

14. For the European law of nations in the eighteenth century, see Geoffrey Best, *Humanity in Warfare: The Modern History of the International Law of Armed Conflicts,* rev. ed. (London, 1983); Peter S. Onuf and Nicholas G. Onuf, *Federal Union, Modern World: The Law of Nations in an Age of Revolutions, 1776–1814* (Madison, Wisc., 1993); Richard Tuck, *The Rights of War and Peace: Political Thought and the International Order from Grotius to Kant* (Oxford, 1999); David Armitage, "The Declaration of Independence and International Law," *William and Mary Quarterly,* 3rd ser., 59 (2002): 39–64. On the general idea of Europe as a republic with its own treaty-based public law, see J. G. A. Pocock, *The Enlightenments of Edward Gibbon, 1737–1764,* vol. 1 of *Barbarism and Religion* (Cambridge, 1991), 109–114.

15. David Hume, "Of Refinement in the Arts" [orig. publ. as "Of Luxury" (1752)], in *Essays: Moral, Political, and Literary,* ed. Eugene F. Miller (Indianapolis, 1985), 274.

16. Geoffrey Plank, *Rebellion and Savagery: The Jacobite Rising of 1745 and the British Empire* (Philadelphia, 2006), chap. 1.

17. [Sir Charles Hotham], *The Operations of the Allied Army under the Command of His Serene Highness Prince Ferdinand* (London, 1764), 9.

18. Peter K. Taylor, "Military System and Rural Social Change in Eighteenth-Century Hesse-Cassel," *Journal of Social History* 25 (1992): 485; Uriel Dann, *Hanover and Great Britain, 1740–1760: Diplomacy and Survival* (Leicester, 1991), 119.

19. *A Letter to the Right Honourable, P——p, E—l of Ch———d, &c. Containing, A Defence of the Conduct and the Character of the present King of France,* 2d ed. (London, 1747), 17.

20. Hotham singled out the duc de Randan, who was the French governor of Hanover in 1757 and 1758, for particular praise: [Hotham], *Operations,* 27.

21. [Samuel Bever,] *The Cadet. A Military Treatise* (London, 1756), 182.

22. Myron P. Gutmann, *War and Rural Life in the Early Modern Low Countries* (Princeton, N.J., 1980), 62–66.

23. "Letter from Oliver de Kermelle Penholt," in *Memoirs of the Most Christian-Brute; or, The History of the Late Exploits of a Certain Great K—g* (London, 1747), 56.

24. Gutmann, *War,* 66.

25. Adam Smith, *Lectures on Jurisprudence,* ed. R. L. Meek et al. (Indianapolis, 1982), 549.

26. During the Seven Years' War, Parliament included the English militia in the articles of war that governed military law in the regular army, though units were exempt from some of the harsher penalties: see Eliga H. Gould, "To Strengthen the King's Hands: Dynastic Legitimacy, Militia Reform and Ideas of National Unity in England 1745–1760," *Historical Journal* 34 (1991): 329–348.

27. James St. Clair, "Rule and Ordinances" (Plymouth Sound, September 14, 1746), LO 84, Huntington Library, San Marino, CA. The phrase "without orders" in the injunction against plundering was significant. On October 3, during the actual siege, Sinclair offered L'Orient terms that included permission to pillage the city "for the Space of four Hours." The garrison refused and, four days later, forced the British to abandon their attack: *"French Account of the Late Descent on the Coast of Britany," London Magazine* 15 (1746): 580–581.

28. *A Soldier's Journal, containing a Particular Description of the several Descents on the Coast of France last War* (London, 1770), 27.

29. Although some Scots perceived in Parliament's abolition of heritable jurisdictions a violation of the Treaty of Union, Lord Chancellor Hardwicke argued that the measure was consistent with the treaty and in fact was essential to strengthening it: Philip Yorke Earl of Hardwicke, *Two Speeches in the House of Lords: I. On the Bill, for Abolishing the Heretable Jurisdictions in Scotland. II. On the Militia-Bill* ([London], 1758), 6–15; see also Plank, *Rebellion,* 106–113.

30. Johnson, "Tour of the Hebrides," quoted in T. C. Smout, *A History of the Scottish People, 1560–1830* (Glasgow, 1969), 320–321.

31. Vattel, *Law of Nations,* book iii, chap. viii, § 150 (p. 553).

32. "The History of Europe," *Annual Register* 25 (1782): 219–220. See also Sarah Knott, "Sensibility and the War of American Independence," *American Historical Review* 109 (2004): 12–40.

33. [Richard Walter], *The History of Commodore Anson's Voyage Round the World* (London, 1764 [orig. publ., 1748]), 105–108. See also William Biggs, *The Military History of Europe, &c., since the Commencement of the War with Spain* (Limerick, 1749), 322–323.

34. *Letter to the Right Honourable, P——p, E—l of Ch——f——d, &c.,* 6.

35. [Henry Dell,] *Minorca. A Tragedy*, 2d ed. (London, 1756), 8, 10, 34. The play, which was printed shortly after Minorca's capture, was never staged. According to the *New Theatrical Dictionary*, the lack of success was largely because of its untimely nature (Michael T. Davis, "Dell, Henry [*b*. in or before 1733]," in *Oxford Dictionary of National Biography*, ed. H. C. G. Matthew and Brian Harrison [Oxford, 2004]; online ed., ed. Lawrence Goldman, January 2008, http://www.oxforddnb.com/view/article/7459 [accessed September 8, 2011]).

36. William Paley, *The Principles of Moral and Political Philosophy* (London, 1785), 641.

37. On the seas, see Richard Pares, *Colonial Blockade and Neutral Rights, 1739–1763* (Oxford, 1938); N. A. M. Rodger, "Sea-Power and Empire, 1688–1793," in *The Eighteenth Century*, vol. 2 of *The Oxford History of the British Empire*, ed. P. J. Marshall (Oxford, 1998), 175–178. On treaty rights within the empire, see [William Knox], *The Justice and Policy of the Late Act of Parliament, for Making More Effectual Provision for the Government of the Province of Québec, Asserted and Proved* (London, 1774), 10, 29; C. H. Alexandrowicz, *An Introduction to the History of the Law of Nations in the East Indies* (Oxford, 1967).

38. William Blackstone, *Of Public Wrongs*, vol. 4 of *Commentaries on the Laws of England*, ed. Stanley N. Katz et al. (Chicago, 1979 [orig. publ., 1765–1769]), 67.

39. "Abridgement of the Placart published by his Excellency General James Wolfe . . . on his Arrival in the River St. Lawrence, 1759," *London Magazine* 28 (1759): 568. In his ultimatum to the marquis de Vaudreuil, French governor of Quebec, Wolfe made similar promises, insisting that he was under explicit orders "to carry on the war with the utmost lenity," which he hoped would lead the governor to issue "like orders to all the people under his command" ("An impartial and succinct History of the Origins and Progress of the Present War," *London Magazine* 32 (1763): 20). The British eventually honored the second of these guarantees, permitting Quebec's garrison to surrender with full military honors. Under the terms of the capitulation, the town's Canadian inhabitants were guaranteed "the possession of their houses, goods, effects, and privileges"; the members of the militia received assurances that they would "not be molested on account of their having born arms for the defence of the town"; and the British promised not to interfere with "the exercise of the catholick and Roman religion": "Articles of Capitulation," *London Magazine* 27 (1759): 565.

40. Willson Beckles, *The Life and Letters of James Wolfe* (London, 1909), 482–487.

41. Remarks of Gen. George Tonwshend, quoted in C. P. Stacey, *Quebec, 1759: The Siege and the Battle* (Toronto, 1959), 93; *A Journal of the Expedition up the River St. Lawrence* (Boston, 1759), 24. See also Anderson, *Crucible*, 344.

42. *Journal of the Expedition*, 9.

43. Quoted in Frégault, *Canada*, 251.

44. *Annual Register* 3 (1760): 216.

45. The source for this paragraph is Max Savelle, *The Origins of American Diplomacy: The International History of Angloamerica, 1492–1763* (New York, 1967), esp. 233–250.

46. Trelawny to duke of Newcastle, Jamaica, December 4, 1738, *Calendar of State Papers, Colonial Series* 44, no. 529 (pp. 256–257); see also Stephen Brumwell,

Redcoats: The British Soldier and War in the Americas, 1755–1763 (Cambridge, 2002), 196.

47. Christopher L. Tomlins and Bruce H. Mann, eds., *The Many Legalities of Early America* (Chapel Hill, N.C., 2001).

48. See, for example, Nicholas P. Canny, "The Ideology of English Colonization: From Ireland to America," *William and Mary Quarterly,* 3rd ser., 30 (1973): 575–598; see also Arthur H. Williamson, "Scots, Indians and Empire: The Scottish Politics of Civilization, 1519–1609," *Past and Present* 150 (1996): 46–83.

49. The analysis in this paragraph, and in the ones that follow, draws on Eliga H. Gould, "Zones of Law, Zones of Violence: The Legal Geography of the British Atlantic, *circa* 1772," *William and Mary Quarterly,* 3rd ser., 40 (2003): 471–510.

50. Peter Silver, *Our Savage Neighbors: How Indian War Transformed Early America* (New York, 2008), 17.

51. Quoted in Brumwell, *Redcoats,* 198. The argument here about the distinctiveness of Indian warfare versus warfare in Europe draws heavily on Brumwell's analysis.

52. [William Currie], *A Sermon Preached in Radnor Church, on . . . the 7th of January, 1747 [o.s.]* (Philadelphia, 1748), 17.

53. Anderson, *Crucible,* 55.

54. [Dell], *Minorca,* 25–26.

55. *The Military History of Great Britain, for 1756, 1757* (London, 1757), 42.

56. Quoted in Ian K. Steele, *Betrayals: Fort William Henry and the "Massacre"* (Oxford, 1990), 150–151.

57. "Representation of President William Bull to Council of Trade and Plantations," *Calendar of State Papers,* 44, no. 243 (p. 100). See also Richard White, *The Middle Ground: Indians, Empires, and Republics in the Great Lakes Region, 1650–1815* (Cambridge, 1991). For the seventeenth-century roots of Indian diplomacy, see Cynthia Jean Van Zandt, *Brothers among Nations: The Pursuit of Intercultural Alliances in Early America, 1580–1660* (Oxford, 2008).

58. John Gyles, *Memoirs of Odd Adventures, Strange Deliverances, etc.* (Boston, 1736), in *Puritans among the Indians: Accounts of Captivity and Redemption, 1676–1724,* ed. Alden T. Vaughan and Edward W. Clark (Cambridge, Mass., 1981), 103, 105, 125. The secondary literature on Indian captivity narratives is large; see John Demos, *The Unredeemed Captive: A Family Story from Early America* (New York, 1994); Linda Colley, *Captives* (New York, 2002).

59. Gyles, *Memoirs,* in Vaughan and Clark, *Puritans,* 100. For Duston, whose last name is sometimes spelled Dustan, see also Laurel Ulrich, *Good Wives: Image and Reality in the Lives of Women in Northern New England, 1650–1750* (New York, 1982), 167–172.

60. Quoted in Steele, *Betrayals,* 117–118.

61. Cotton Mather, "A Narrative of Hannah Dustan's Notable Deliverance from Captivity" (from *Magnalia Christi Americana* [London, 1702]), in Vaughan and Clark, *Puritans,* 164.

62. Vattel, *Law of Nations,* book i, chap. vii, § 81, chap. xviii, § 209 (pp. 130, 216). In the sections from which the quotes are taken, Vattel's main emphasis was on the relationship between agriculture and populousness; however, he regarded the habits bred

by commerce and agriculture as necessary components of the higher virtues, contrasting the propensity of nomadic peoples (such as the ancient Germans and modern Tartars) to "live by plunder" with the "industrious" manners of the modern nations of Europe (§ 81 [pp. 129–130]). Elsewhere in the same section, Vattel made clear that he thought the Incas and Aztecs belonged in the former groups and the woodland Indians in the latter: "The people of those extensive tracts [i.e., North America] rather ranged through than inhabited them."

63. William Douglass, *A Summary, Historical and Political, of the First Planting, Progressive Improvements, and Present State of the British Settlements in North America*, rev. ed. (London, 1755 [orig. publ., Boston, 1749]), 1:152n, 153.

64. Cadwallader Colden, *The History of the Five Indian Nations Depending on the Province of New-York in America* (Ithaca, N.Y, 1964 [orig. publ. in two parts, 1727 and 1747]), x, xxi.

65. [Currie], *Sermon,* 17.

66. [Benjamin Franklin], *Plain Truth: Or, Serious Considerations on the Present State of the City of Philadelphia, and the Province of Pennsylvania* (Philadelphia, 1747), 13–14.

67. For piracy and privateering—and the porous boundary between the two—see Robert C. Ritchie, *Captain Kidd and the War against the Pirates* (Cambridge, Mass., 1986); Marcus Rediker, *Between the Devil and the Deep Blue Sea: Merchant Seamen, Pirates, and the Anglo-American Maritime World, 1700–1750* (Cambridge, 1987); Carl E. Swanson, *Predators and Prizes: American Privateering and Imperial Warfare, 1739–1748* (Columbia, S.C., 1991). In the West Indies, in particular, it remained difficult to distinguish piracy from privateering well into the eighteenth century.

68. [Cotton Mather], *Instructions to the Living, from the Condition of the Dead* (Boston, 1717), 23. In what may have been revenge for Brown's execution, Charles Johnson reported that Stede Bonnet plundered and burned the *Protestant Cesar* in Honduras Bay in 1718, "because she belonged to *Boston,* where some Men had been hanged for Pyracy": *A General History of the Robberies and Murders of the Most Notorious Pyrates* (London, 1724), 70.

69. John Barnard, *Ashton's Memorial. An History of the Strange Adventures, and Signal Deliverances, of Mr. Philip Ashton* (Boston, 1725), 6. Like the rest of Ashton's narrative, the words in the quoted passage were written by Barnard; however, Barnard claimed that he had "taken the Minutes" of Ashton's story "from his own Mouth" and that, after writing the first draft, he had "read it over directly to him, that he might Correct [any] Errors" (unpaginated preface).

70. *An Account of the Behaviour and last Dying Speeches of the Six Pirates, that were Executed . . . on Friday June 30th, 1704* (Boston, 1704), [2].

71. Benjamin Colman, *It is a Fearful Thing. . . . A Sermon Preached to some Miserable Pirates, July 10, 1726* (Boston, 1726), 29, 37.

72. Jack P. Greene, "Negotiated Authorities: The Problem of Governance in the Extended Polities of the Early Modern Atlantic World," in *Negotiated Authorities: Essays in Colonial Political and Constitutional History* (Charlottesville, 1994), 1–24.

73. [Cotton Mather], *Faithful Warnings to Prevent Fearful Judgments* (Boston, 1704), 37.

74. Vernon to the duke of Newcastle and Sir Charles Wager, August 30, 1740, *The Vernon Papers* (London, 1958), 125–126, quoted in Swanson, *Predators*, 67.

75. Thomas to Holdernesse, November 7, 1757, CO 152/46, 158, BNA.

76. Thomas to Pitt, January 13, 1758, CO 152/46, 160, BNA.

77. [Mather], *Instructions,* 4. Mather's reference was to the ascendancy that pirates gained in the ancient Mediterranean before being suppressed by the Roman leader Pompey. Although he thought the same could happen "on the *Atlantick,*" he trusted that the intervention of "the *British* Crown" would check their influence (4–5).

78. *American Weekly Mercury* (September 30–October 7, 1731), 2.

79. "Notes of correspondence between the Lords and [Rear Admiral] Stewart as to Spanish depredations, the orders for reprisals, and the difficulties they will raise," May 15, 1731, in R.G. Marsden, ed., *1649–1767,* vol. 2 of *Documents Relating to the Law and Custom of the Sea* (London, 1999 [orig. publ., 1915]), 278.

80. James Marriott, "Case of the Settlers in the Bay of Honduras" [letter to John Pownall, secretary to the Lords of Trade], April 21, 1766, CO 123/1, 123, 125, BNA. For the British settlements on the Central American coast, see Jennifer L. Anderson, "Nature's Currency: The Atlantic Mahogany Trade and the Commodification of Nature in the Eighteenth Century," *Early American Studies* 2 (2004): 47–80.

81. Marriott, "Case," CO 123/1, 123, BNA.

82. Governor Edward Trelawny to the duke of Bedford, July 17, 1751, CO 137/57/2, 231, BNA. In his report on the Mosquito Shore, the British superintendent Robert Hodgson wrote that the settlers "live much after the European manner in every thing," but they were "without Laws": "The first Account of the State of that Part of America called The Mosquito Shore" (1757), CO 123/1, 61, BNA.

83. Douglass, *Summary,* vol. 1, 89.

84. Barnard, *Ashton's Memorial,* 32.

85. Trelawny to duke of Bedford, Jamaica, April 8, 1749, CO 137/57/2, 201, BNA.

86. Tobias Smollett, *Continuation of the Complete History of England* (London, 1765), 5:365.

87. [James] Lawrie, "Answer to the Logwood-Cutters Memorial," and "A candid narrative of what has been transacted since the conclusion of hostilities," in *The General Magazine of Arts and Sciences* 14 (1764): 395–397.

88. Governor Philipps to Allured Popple, secretary of the Board of Trade, November 26, 1730 (oath); Lt. Governor Armstrong to Board of Trade, October 5, 1730 ("ungovernable" and payment of quit rents); Armstrong to Board of Trade, June 10, 1732 ("Laws of Paris"); and Governor Macarene, as quoted in Beamish Murdoch, *A History of Nova Scotia* (1865), all in *The Classical Period of the First British Empire, 1689–1783,* vol. 2 of *Select Documents on the Constitutional History of the British Empire and Commonwealth,* ed. Frederick Madden with David Fieldhouse (London, 1985), 173, 175–177.

89. [William Shirley], *Memoirs of the Principal Transactions of the Last War between the English and French in North-America,* 3rd ed. (Boston, 1758), 18.

90. *French Policy Defeated. Being, an Account of all the hostile Proceedings of the French, against the Inhabitants of the British Colonies in North America* (London, 1755), 36.

91. Quoted in Faragher, *Great and Noble Scheme,* 220.

92. Gyles, *Memoirs,* in Vaughan and Clark, *Puritans among the Indians,* 126, 128, 130. According to Gyles, the English commander, Col. John Hathorne, was sufficiently "honorable" that he spared "their cattle [and] other creatures . . . except one or two and the poultry for their use" (129).

93. [Samuel Johnson], "Introduction to the Political State of Great-Britain," *Literary Magazine* (1756), in *Political Writings,* vol. 10 of *The Yale Edition of the Works of Samuel Johnson,* ed. Donald Greene (Indianapolis, 2000 [orig. publ., New Haven, Conn., 1977]), 149. Although Johnson did not mention the Acadians by name, editor Donald Greene thinks they are "probably" whom he had in mind, an assessment with which I agree.

94. Memorandum of Jonathan Belcher, Chief Justice of Nova Scotia, July 28, 1755, in *Acadian Genealogy and Notes Concerning the Expulsion,* ed. Placide Gaudet (Pawtucket, R.I., 1996 [reprint]), 63–64; for the metaphor of Indian warfare, see Brumwell, *Redcoats,* 202–203.

95. Memorial of Sir W. Van Alzenheim (translation), Frankfort, March 16, 1751, CO 217/11, 51, BNA.

96. William D. Hoyt Jr., "A Contemporary View of the Acadian Arrival in Maryland, 1755," *William and Mary Quarterly,* 3rd ser., 5 (1948), 573–574.

97. [Jacob Nicolas Moreau], *A Memorial containing a Summary View of the Facts, with their Authorities. In Answer to The Observations Sent by the English Ministry to the Courts of Europe.* Trans. from the French (New York, 1757), 16.

98. *George II, His Majesty's Declaration of War against the French King* (London, 1756).

99. [Moreau,] *Memorial,* 16, 25, 190.

100. Anderson, *Crucible,* 54–58.

101. [Jacob Nicolas Moreau], *The Conduct of the Late Ministry, or, A Memorial; containing a Summary of Facts . . . In Answer to The Observations Sent by the English Ministry to the Courts of Europe* (1757), 20. See David A. Bell, "Jumonville's Death: War Propaganda and National Identity in Eighteenth-Century France," in *The Age of Cultural Revolutions: Britain and France, 1750–1820,* ed. Colin Jones and Dror Wahrman (Berkeley, Calif., 2002), 33–61; Bell, *The Cult of the Nation in France: Inventing Nationalism, 1680–1800* (Cambridge, Mass., 2001).

102. [Robert Martin Lesuire], *The Savages of Europe* (London, 1764), 63; trans. of *Les Sauvages de l'Europe* (1760).

103. *French Policy Defeated,* 66, 69.

104. See Gould, *Persistence,* chap. 4.

105. Colin G. Calloway, *The American Revolution in Indian Country: Crisis and Diversity in Native Americans Communities* (Cambridge, 1995); see also Daniel K. Richter, *Facing East from Indian Country: A Native History of Early America* (Cambridge, Mass., 2001), 191–193, 208–221.

106. *Knox's Journal,* vol. 1, 34, 297, 410n, 438.

107. Robert Rogers, *Journals of Major Robert Rogers* (London, 1765), 145.

108. *The Memoirs and Adventures of Robert Kirk, Late of the Royal Highland Regiment, Written by Himself* (Limerick, 1770), 44–45.

109. The classic statement is Higginbotham, "The Early American Way of War," 230–273.
110. Quoted in Brumwell, *Redcoats*, 188.
111. The articles of capitulation are in John Knox, *An Historical Journal of the Campaigns in North America for the Years 1757, 1758, 1759, and 1760* (1769), vol. 2, Publications of the Champlain Society, vols. 8 to 10, ed. Arthur G. Doughty (Toronto, 1914), 582.
112. Ibid., vol. 1, 410n.
113. Ibid., 438.
114. On the often porous boundaries between Indians and white "renegades," see Colin G. Calloway, "Neither White nor Red: White Renegades on the American Indian Frontier," *Western Historical Quarterly* 17 (1986): 43–66.
115. Knox, *Journal*, vol. 1, 428–429.
116. Ibid., vol. 2, 45. "The parish of Richelet, with the stately house lately occupied by the indiscreet priest, called Château Richelet," Knox wrote in his journal, "are now in flames."
117. Frégault, *Canada*, 179.
118. John [sic] Baptiste Galerm, *A RELATION of the Misfortunes of the FRENCH NEUTRALS, as Laid before the Assembly of the Province of Pennsylvania* (Philadelphia, 1756).
119. Faragher, *Great and Noble Scheme*, 448–449.
120. *Evangeline* (1847), in *The Poems of Henry Wadsworth Longfellow*, ed. Nathan Haskell Dole (New York, 1901), 166, 171–172, 175. According to Britons like the Halifax antiquarian Beamish Murdoch, author of the three-volume *History of Nova-Scotia* (1865), the chief responsibility for the expulsion lay not with "the British government and people" but with New England. "[I]f the expulsion be a stain on the annals of Nova Scotia," concurred Sir Archibald Adams George in the 1880s, "it is a stain from which Massachusetts, the country and home of the poet [Longfellow], cannot claim to be free": Faragher, *Great and Noble Scheme*, 461–462.
121. Gaudet, *Acadian*, 12.
122. Ibid., 20, 23.

2. THE LAW OF SLAVERY

1. Evangeline Walker Andrews, ed., in collaboration with Charles McLean Andrews, *Journal of a Lady of Quality: Being the Narrative of a Journey from Scotland to the West Indies, North Carolina, and Portugal, in the Years 1774 to 1776*, 2nd ed. (New Haven, Conn., 1934), 122–124.
2. Ibid., 108–109, 112, 127.
3. The literature on British antislavery is vast, but see David Brion Davis, *The Problem of Slavery in the Age of Revolution, 1770–1823* (Ithaca, N.Y., 1975); Seymour Drescher, *Capitalism and Antislavery: British Mobilization in Comparative Perspective* (Oxford, 1987); Robin Blackburn, *The Overthrow of Colonial Slavery, 1776–1848*

(London, 1988); David Eltis, "Europeans and the Rise and Fall of African Slavery in the Americas: An Interpretation," *American Historical Review* 98 (1993): 1399–1423; Christopher Leslie Brown, *Moral Capital: Foundations of British Abolitionism* (Chapel Hill, N.C., 2006). For the complex ways in which these currents played themselves out in British America, see J. William Harris, *The Hanging of Thomas Jeremiah: A Free Black Man's Encounter with Liberty* (New Haven, Conn., 2009).

4. William Blackstone, *Of the Rights of Persons,* vol. 1 of *Commentaries on the Laws of England,* ed. Stanley N. Katz, (Chicago, 1979 [orig. pub., 1765–1769]), 412. Despite the apparent lack of ambiguity in this statement, Blackstone qualified it by insisting that the master who brought a slave to England retained the same "right . . . to [his] perpetual service . . . as before" (412–413). On these grounds, Blackstone refused to assist Somerset in his suit; he also clarified his position somewhat in subsequent editions: see Davis, *Problem of Slavery,* 485–486.

5. Quoted in Gretchen Gerzina, *Black London: Life before Emancipation* (New Brunswick, N.J., 1995), 133.

6. Colin A. Palmer, *Human Cargoes: The British Slave Trade to Spanish America, 1700–1739* (Urbana, Ill., 1981), table 20 (p. 110); see also Adrian Finucane, "The South Sea Company and Anglo-Spanish Connections, 1713–1739" (Ph.D. diss., Harvard University, 2010).

7. On this point, see Daniel J. Hulsebosch, "The Ancient Constitution and the Expanding Empire: Sir Edward Coke's British Jurisprudence," *Law and History Review* 21 (2003): 439–482; Mary Sarah Bilder, *The Transatlantic Constitution: Colonial Legal Culture and the Empire* (Cambridge, Mass., 2004).

8. Edward Long, *The History of Jamaica. Or, General Survey of the Antient and Modern State of That Island* (London, 1774), 1:9–11.

9. Richard Bland, *An Enquiry into the Rights of the British Colonies* (London, 1769 [orig. pub., 1766]), in *Colonies to Nation, 1763–1789: A Documentary History of the American Revolution,* ed. Jack P. Greene (New York, 1975 [orig. pub., 1967]), 92.

10. Governor David Parry to Viscount Sydney, December 18, 1787, in *Imperial Reconstruction, 1763–1840,* vol. 3 of *Select Documents on the Constitutional History of the British Empire and Commonwealth,* ed. A. F. Madden and D. K. Fieldhouse (Westport, Conn., 1987), 331.

11. [John Randolph], *Considerations on the Present State of Virginia* (1774), in *Forming Thunderclouds and the First Convention, 1763–1774,* vol. 1 of *Revolutionary Virginia: The Road to Independence,* ed. Robert L. Scribner (Charlottesville, Va., 1973), 210.

12. Andrews, *Journal of a Lady of Quality,* 153–154.

13. William Tuckett to Gov. Robert Thomas, December 5, 1765, CO 152/47, 118, BNA.

14. Thomas to Henry Seymour Conway, December 21, 1765, CO 152/47, 116, BNA.

15. Long, *History of Jamaica,* vol. 1, 5.

16. Samuel Johnson, *Taxation, No Tyranny; an Answer to the Resolutions and Address of the American Congress* (1775), in *Political Writings,* vol. 10 of *The Yale Edition of the Works of Samuel Johnson,* ed. Donald Greene (Indianapolis, 2000 [orig. publ., New Haven, Conn., 1977]), 454.

17. G. B. to Benjamin Franklin, November 14, 1775, CO 5/40/1, 69–70, BNA.

18. Henry Laurens to John Lewis Gervais, February 5, 1774, in *Apr.19, 1773–Dec. 12, 1774,* vol. 9 of *The Papers of Henry Laurens,* ed. Philip M. Hamer (Columbia, S.C., 1981), 264.

19. Long, *History of Jamaica,* vol. 1, 5.

20. [Benjamin Rush], *An Address to the Inhabitants of the British Settlements, on the Slavery of the Negroes in America. To Which Is Added, a Vindication of the Address, in Answer to a Pamphlet Entitled, "Slavery Not Forbidden in Scripture; or, a Defence of the West India Planters,"* 2nd ed. (Philadelphia, 1773 [orig. pub., 1772]), 5–6. Poivre's *Voyages d'un Philosphe* (1768) appeared in four separate English editions between 1769 and 1770, two in London (by different translators) and one each in Glasgow and Dublin; see, for example, Pierre Poivre, *Travels of a Philosopher; or, Observations on the Manners and Arts of Various Nations in Africa and Asia* (London, 1769), published by T. Beckett and Co. and probably the version reprinted at Glasgow and Dublin. Rush could also have had access to the original: Pierre Poivre, *Voyages d'un Philosophe, ou, Observations Sur Les Moeurs & Les Arts Des Peuples de l'Afrique, de l'Asie et de l'Amerique* (Yverdon, Switzerland, 1768; reprint, 1769, [Lyons]). For Poivre's influence generally, see Richard Grove, "Conserving Eden: The (European) East India Companies and Their Environmental Policies on St. Helena, Mauritius and in Western India, 1660 to 1854," *Comparative Studies in Society and History* 35 (April 1993): 332–338.

21. Johnson, *Taxation,* in Greene, *Political Writings,* 429, 431.

22. *Speech of Edmund Burke, Esq., on Moving his Resolution for Conciliation with the Colonies, March 22, 1775* (1775), in *Thoughts on the Cause of the Present Discontents and The Two Speeches on America,* vol. 1 of *Select Works of Edmund Burke: A New Imprint of the Payne Edition,* ed. Francis Canavan and E. J. Payne (Indianapolis, 1999 [orig. pub., 1874–1878]), 241.

23. Josiah Tucker, *A Treatise Concerning Civil Government, in Three Parts* (London, 1781), 169.

24. Ibid., 167–168.

25. Somerset v. Stewart, Easter 1772, in Capel Lofft, *Reports of Cases Adjudged in the Court of King's Bench from Easter Term 12 Geo. 3. To Michaelmas 14 Geo. 3. [1772–1774]* (London, 1776), 18–19.

26. Francis Hargrave, *An Argument in the Case of James Sommersett a Negro. Wherein It Is Attempted to Demonstrate the Present Unlawfulness of Domestic Slavery in England* (London, 1775 [orig. pub., 1772]), 21, 24.

27. [Edward Long], *Candid Reflections upon the Judgement Lately Awarded by the Court of King's Bench, in Westminster-Hall* (London, 1772), 31, 43.

28. Eliga H. Gould, "Zones of Law, Zones of Violence: The Legal Geography of the British Atlantic, circa 1772," *William and Mary Quarterly,* 3rd ser., 60 (2003): 471–510.

29. Blackstone, *Commentaries,* vol. 1, 411.

30. Smith v. Brown and Cooper, in William Salkeld, *Reports of Cases Adjudged in the Court of King's Bench . . . From the First Year of King William and Mary, to the Tenth Year of Queen Anne,* 6th ed. (London, 1795), 2:666.

31. Sir John Fielding, *Extracts from Such of the Penal Laws, as Particularly Relate to the Peace and Good Order of This Metropolis,* new rev. ed. (London, 1768), 145. See also Drescher, *Capitalism and Antislavery,* 27–34.

32. Ruth Paley, "After *Somerset*: Mansfield, Slavery and the Law in England, 1772–1830," in *Law, Crime, and English Society, 1660–1830,* ed. Norma Landau (Cambridge, 2002), 180.

33. John Riddell to Charles Stewart, July 10, 1772, quoted in Oldham, "New Light on Mansfield and Slavery," *Journal of British Studies* 27 (1988): 66

34. Tucker, "On the State of Slavery" (1796), in St. George Tucker, *View of the Constitution of the United States, with Selected Writings,* ed. Clyde Norman Wilson (Indianapolis, 1999), 405. Tucker gave 1620 as the arrival date for the first African slaves in Virginia, though it was actually 1619.

35. Jefferson, *A Summary View of the Rights of British America* (1774), in *Thomas Jefferson, Writings,* vol. 15 of *The Library of America,* ed. Merrill D. Peterson (New York, 1984), 107, 115–116.

36. For more on this point, see George van Cleve, "'Somerset's Case' and Its Antecedents in Imperial Perspective," *Law and History Review* 24 (2006): 642–645.

37. "Report of His Majesty's Advocate, Attorney & Solicitor Generals respecting the Establishment of a form of Government and Police in Honduras," December 9, 1790, HO 48/1B/575–576, BNA. For British humanitarianism and imperial policy generally, see P. J. Marshall, "Empire and Authority in the Later Eighteenth Century," *Journal of Imperial and Commonwealth History* 15 (1987): 105–122. Andrew Jackson O'Shaughnessy, *An Empire Divided: The American Revolution and the British Caribbean* (Philadelphia, 2000), 238–248, gives a good overview of implications for West Indian planters.

38. Thomas Day, *Fragment of an Original Letter on the Slavery of the Negroes Written in the Year 1776* (London, 1784), 13.

39. Quoted in Elsa Goveia, "The West Indian Slave Laws of the Eighteenth Century," *Chapters in Caribbean History* 2 (1970): 35.

40. Andrews, *Journal of a Lady of Quality,* 108–109.

41. Ottobah Cugoano, *Thoughts and Sentiments on the Evil and Wicked Traffic of the Slavery and Commerce of the Human Species, Humbly Submitted to the Inhabitants of Great-Britain* (London, 1787), in *Pioneers of the Black Atlantic: Five Slave Narratives from the Enlightenment, 1772–1815,* ed. Henry Louis Gates and William L. Andrews (Washington, D.C., 1998), 99.

42. Blackstone, *Commentaries,* vol. 1, 412.

43. For the text of the *asiento,* see Philip V, king of Spain, "The Assiento, Adjusted between Their Brittanick and Catholick Majesties" (1713), in [Casimir Freschot], *The Compleat History of the Treaty of Utrecht [Histoire Du Congres Et De La Paix D'utrecht]* (London, 1715), vol. 1, part 2, 155–182; see also Palmer, *Human Cargoes,* for the *asiento*'s operation between 1714 and 1739 and the agreement's final termination in 1750.

44. Don E. Fehrenbacher, *The Slaveholding Republic: An Account of the United States Government's Relations to Slavery* (Oxford, 2001), 91–96; Hugh Thomas, *The Slave*

Trade: The Story of the Atlantic Slave Trade, 1440–1870 (New York, 1997), 583–584, 587, 591, 595, 598.

45. Emer de Vattel, *The Law of Nations, or, Principles of the Law of Nature, Applied to the Conduct and Affairs of Nations and Sovereigns,* ed. Bela Kapossy and Richard Whatmore (Indianapolis, 2008 [orig. publ., London, 1797]), book iii, § 152 (p. 556).

46. Somerset v. Stewart, in Lofft, *Reports,* 7.

47. Anna Maria Falconbridge, *Two Voyages to Sierra Leone* (1794), in *Maiden Voyages and Infant Colonies: Two Women's Travel Narratives of the 1790s,* ed. Deirdre Coleman (London, 1999), 135.

48. Cugoano, *Thoughts and Sentiments,* in Gates and Andrews, *Pioneers,* 95, 142.

49. *Report of the Lords of Trade on the Slave Trade* (1789), in *George III: Report of the Lords on the Slave Trade 1789, Part 1,* vol. 69 of *House of Commons Sessional Papers of the Eighteenth Century,* ed. Sheila Lambert (Wilmington, Del., 1975), 26, 36.

50. James Swan, *A Dissuasion to Great-Britain and the Colonies, from the Slave-Trade to Africa,* 2nd rev. and abridged ed. (Boston, 1773), 12–13. For Swan's background and involvement in the antislavery movement in New England, see Howard C. Rice, "James Swan: Agent of the French Republic 1794–1796," *New England Quarterly* 10 (September 1937): 464–465; Lorenzo J. Greene, "Slave-Holding New England and Its Awakening," *Journal of Negro History* 13 (October 1928): 524–525.

51. Blackstone, *Commentaries,* vol. 1, 411. For the natural jurists and slavery, see David Brion Davis, *The Problem of Slavery in Western Culture* (Ithaca, N.Y., 1966), 111–121.

52. Hugo Grotius, *The Rights of War and Peace, in Three Books* (London, 1738), book iii, chap. iv, § 5, ¶ 1 (pp. 603–604).

53. Charles Molloy, *De Jure Maritimo et Navali: Or, a Treatise of Affairs Maritime and of Commerce,* 5th ed. (London, 1701), book iii, chap. 1, § iv (p. 354). The edition published in 1778 was the tenth. On slavery's gradual disappearance from Europe, see Eltis, "Rise and Fall of African Slavery," 1400–1401.

54. John Locke, *The Second Treatise of Government* (1681), in *Political Writings of John Locke,* ed. David Wootton (New York, 1993), chap. iv, §§ 23–24 (p. 273).

55. Molloy, *De Jure,* 355.

56. Blackstone, *Commentaries,* vol. 1, 411.

57. Vattel, *Law of Nations,* book iii, chap. viii, § 152 (p. 556).

58. The phrase "pure and proper slavery" comes from Blackstone, *Commentaries,* vol. 1, 411. As with Locke's use of "perfect" slavery in the *Second Treatise* (see above), the phrase is a reminder that slavery formed one part of a wider system of servitude, some versions of which were more involuntary than others.

59. Vattel, *Law of Nations,* book iii, chap. viii, §§ 141, 150, 152 (pp. 544, 553, 556). The passage from which the last quoted lines are taken continues: "We extol the English and French, we feel our bosoms glow with love for them, when we hear the accounts of the treatment which prisoners of war, on both sides, have experienced from those generous nations. And what is more, by a custom which equally displays the honour and humanity of the Europeans, an officer, taken prisoner in war, is released on his

parole, and enjoys the comfort of passing the time of his captivity in his own country, in the midst of his family; and the party who have thus released him, rest as perfectly sure of him, as if they had him confined in irons."

60. [Samuel Johnson], "Introduction," *Proceedings of the Committee . . . for Cloathing French Prisoners of War* (1760), in Greene, *Political Writings,* 288. See also *A Letter from a Gentleman in Town to His Friend in the Country, Concerning the Cloathing of the French Prisoners Now in the Castle of Edinburgh* (Edinburgh, 1759).

61. Long, *History of Jamaica,* vol. 1, 5.

62. [Rush], *An Address to the Inhabitants of the British Settlements,* 17–18.

63. Cugoano, *Thoughts and Sentiments,* in Gates and Andrews, *Pioneers,* 104–106.

64. [Anthony Benezet], *Observations on the Inslaving, Importing and Purchasing of Negroes* (Germantown, Pa., 1760), 3.

65. [Susanna Willard] Johnson [Hastings], *A Narrative of the Captivity of Mrs. Johnson. Containing an Account of Her Sufferings, During Four Years with the Indians and French* (Walpole, N.H., 1796), 4.

66. Ibid., 22.

67. Ibid., 73, 75, 82, 106.

68. [Benezet], *Observations,* 3.

69. Linda Colley, *Captives* (New York, 2002), 64.

70. Pownall to William Pitt, Boston, January 2, 1758, in Gertrude Selwyn Kimball, ed., *Correspondence of William Pitt, When Secretary of State, with Colonial Governors and Military and Naval Commissioners in America* (New York, 1906), 1:156.

71. Johnson [Hastings], *Narrative,* 40 [1797].

72. Elizabeth Hanson, *God's Mercy Surmounting Man's Cruelty, Exemplified in the Captivity and Redemption of Elizabeth Hanson* (Philadelphia, 1728), in *Puritans among the Indians: Accounts of Captivity and Redemption, 1676–1724,* ed. Alden T. Vaughan and Edward W. Clark (Cambridge, Mass., 1981), 242.

73. Johnson [Hastings], *Narrative,* 35–36 [1797]. For British settlers and soldiers who remained with the Indians, see James Axtell, *The European and the Indian: Essays in the Ethnohistory of Colonial North America* (Oxford, 1981), chap. 7; John Demos, *The Unredeemed Captive: A Family Story from Early America* (New York, 1994); Stephen Brumwell, *Redcoats: The British Soldier and War in the Americas, 1755–1763* (Cambridge, 2002), 173–179.

74. For the relative brevity of Indian captivity, see the editors' introduction, in Vaughan and Clark, *Puritans,* 17; Axtell, in *The European and the Indian,* 173, who notes that "Indians who raided New England tended to take captives more for their ransom value than for adoption," which tended to shorten the period of captivity. Occasionally, settlers and soldiers abducted by the Indians spent a longer time in captivity—John Giles, who was taken at Pemaquid, Maine, in 1689, spent six years with his native captors (Vaughan and Clark, *Puritans,* 93)—and captives adopted by Indians sometimes never returned (see discussion above). On the other hand, Linda Colley says that British and Irish captives redeemed by either the government or private charities "often found themselves held in North Africa for five years or more; and, before 1700, ten years was not exceptional": Colley, *Captives,* 55.

75. David Richardson, "The British Empire and the Atlantic Slave Trade, 1660–1807," in *The Eighteenth Century*, ed. P. J. Marshall, vol. 2 of *The Oxford History of the British Empire*, ed. William Roger Louis (Oxford, 2000), table 20.1 (p. 442); Colley, *Captives*, 43–72, esp. 55 (British numbers); Robert C. Davis, "Counting European Slaves on the Barbary Coast," *Past & Present* 172 (2001): 117 (European numbers). Davis's figures are for the period 1680 to 1780; according to his calculations, the European figures for 1580 to 1680 were significantly higher, possibly as many as a million.

76. *A Description of the Nature of Slavery among the Moors. And the Cruel Sufferings of Those That Fall into It* (London, 1721), 4–5.

77. Vattel, *Law of Nations*, book ii, chap. vii, § 78 (p. 301).

78. For the growing protection that Britain and Europe's other maritime powers (especially Spain and France) afforded their subjects and the corresponding tendency of the Barbary corsairs to concentrate their efforts on the inhabitants of weaker European states, see M. S. Anderson, "Great Britain and the Barbary States in the Eighteenth Century," *Bulletin of the Institute of Historical Research* 29 (1956): 87–107; Davis, "Counting European Slaves," 117. For the debate over whether British protection should be extended to the German subjects of its dynastic ally, Hanover, see Nicholas B. Harding, "North African Piracy, the Hanoverian Carrying Trade, and the British State, 1728–1828," *Historical Journal* 43 (2000): 25–47.

79. Thomas Troughton, *Barbarian Cruelty; or, an Accurate and Impartial Narrative of the Unparallel'd Sufferings and Almost Incredible Hardships of the British Captives, Belonging to the Inspector Privateer, . . . From January 1745-6, . . . December 1750* (London, 1751), 10, 18–20. Both officials privately encouraged the crew to escape, at one point supplying them with a ladder for this purpose, but they insisted that, in terms of publicly assisting their cause, there was little they could do.

80. James Sutherland, *A Narrative of the Loss of His Majesty's Ship the Litchfield . . . On the Coast of Africa. With an Account of the Sufferings of the Captain, and the Surviving Part of His Crew, in Their Slavery under the Emperor of Morocco* (London, 1761), 26, 33–34.

81. Vattel, *Law of Nations*, book ii, chap. vii, § 78 (p. 301).

82. Jean Louis Marie Poiret, *Travels through Barbary, in a Series of Letters, Written from the Ancient Numidia, in the Years 1785 and 1786* (London, [1791]), iv–v.

83. Vattel divided the "positive law of nations" into three parts, each based on a different form of consent between governments: "conventional" (express), "customary" (tacit), and "voluntary" (presumed): Vattel, *Law of Nations*, preliminaries, §§ 24–27 (pp. 77–79).

84. Ibid., book iii, chap. xiii, § 196 (p. 595–596). In the passage quoted, Vattel referred only to ships taken by corsairs. From his subsequent comments on the right of "postliminium"—that is, the right of belligerents to recover property seized in time of war—Vattel seems to have regarded slaves as somewhat different from other forms of "movable property"; the Romans, he noted, allowed for the restitution of slaves but not other movables (book iii, chap. xiv, § 209 [p. 606]). However, this case only applied to individuals who were already slaves when hostilities commenced, not to

captives (like the Europeans held in North Africa) who were enslaved in the course of warfare.

85. J[oseph] Morgan, *A Complete History of Algiers. To Which Is Prefixed, an Epitome of the General History of Barbary, from the Earliest Times,* 2d ed. (London, 1731 [orig. pub. in 2 vols., 1728–1729]), 517.

86. "An Act for Extending and Improving the Trade to Africa" (23 Geo. II. c. 31), in *The Eighteenth Century,* vol. 2 of *Documents Illustrative of the History of the Slave Trade to America,* ed. Elizabeth Donnan (Washington, D.C., 1931), 482.

87. Company of Merchants Trading to Africa, Instructions to Messrs. James Skinner and Frederick Smith, James Fort, April 6, 1751, T 70/143, 76, BNA, quoted in ibid., vol. 2, 482, n7.

88. *The Detector Detected: Or, State of Affairs on the Gold Coast, and Conduct of the Present Managers Consider'd. . . . By J. S. G. Last Commandant of Commenda, under the Royal African Company* (London, 1753), 32–34.

89. Francis Moore, *Travels into the Inland Parts of Africa: Containing a Description of the Several Nations . . . Up the River Gambia* (London, 1738), 42.

90. Cugoano, *Thoughts and Sentiments,* in Gates and Andrews, *Pioneers,* 92–94.

91. Thomas Clarkson, *An Essay on the Comparative Efficiency of Regulation or Abolition, as Applied to the Slave Trade. Shewing That the Latter Only Can Remove the Evils to Be Found in That Commerce* (London, 1789), 11 (account of "sixth" witness, emphasis in original).

92. Ibid., 10–11 (source identified as "fifth" witness).

93. *Detector Detected,* 34.

94. John Ranby, *Observations on the Evidence Given before the Committees of the Privy Council and House of Commons in Support of the Bill for Abolishing the Slave Trade* (London, 1791), 82–83.

95. John Matthews, *A Voyage to the River Sierra-Leone, on the Coast of Africa; Containing an Account of the Trade and Productions of the Country, and of the Civil and Religious Customs and Manners of the People,* 2d ed. (London, 1791 [orig. pub., 1788]), 149, 167–168.

96. Falconbridge, *Two Voyages,* in Coleman, *Maiden Voyages,* 135–136.

97. *Report on the Slave Trade,* in Lambert, *House of Commons,* vol. 69, 15.

98. Matthews, *Voyage,* 147.

99. Ibid., 148.

100. Somerset v. Stewart, in Lofft, *Reports,* 18.

101. Paley, "After *Somerset,*" in Landau, *Law, Crime, and English Society,* 165–184; Randy J. Sparks, *The Two Princes of Calabar: An Eighteenth-Century Atlantic Odyssey* (Cambridge, Mass., 2004), 101, 146–147.

102. Andrews, *Journal of a Lady of Quality,* 130.

103. Gould, "Zones of Law, Zones of Violence," 508. For Equiano's London, see Gerzina, *Black London;* Vincent Carretta, *Equiano, the African: Biography of a Self-Made Man* (Athens, Ga., 2005). For blacks in urban settings elsewhere in Britain and in British America, see Philip D. Morgan, "British Encounters with Africans and African-Americans, circa 1600–1780," in *Strangers within the Realm: Cultural*

Margins of the First British Empire, ed. Bernard Bailyn and Philip D. Morgan (Chapel Hill, N.C., 1991), 157–219; Ira Berlin, "Time, Space, and the Evolution of Afro-American Society on British Mainland North America," *American Historical Review* 85 (1980): 44–78.

104. Locke, *Second Treatise,* chap. iv, § 24 (p. 273).

105. Vattel, *Law of Nations,* book i, chap. ii, § 15 (p. 86). In a passage that seems to prefigure the language used in the Declaration of Independence, Vattel described these qualities as "the necessities, the conveniences, the accommodation of life, and, in general, whatever constitutes happiness." Vattel's comments elsewhere in the chapter make clear that civil society could only be "perfected" when all of a nation's citizens partook of such benefits (book i, chap. ii, § 14 [p. 86]). Although Vattel would not have considered slaves to be citizens, the remarks suggested that there were significant obstacles to moral progress in slaveholding societies; they also help explain why Vattel thought that slavery was "happily" absent from Europe.

106. David Hume, "Of the Populousness of Ancient Nations" (1752), in David Hume, *Essays: Moral, Political, and Literary,* ed. Eugene F. Miller (Indianapolis, 1985), 384.

107. *An Essay Concerning Slavery, and the Danger Jamaica Is Expos'd to from the Too Great Number of Slaves* (London, 1746), 51.

108. Quoted in O'Shaughnessy, *Empire Divided,* 51.

109. Richard James Hooker, ed., *The Carolina Backcountry on the Eve of the Revolution: The Journal and Other Writings of Charles Woodmason, Anglican Itinerant* (Chapel Hill, N.C., 1953), 93–94. Woodmason said in a note appended to the sermon that he wrote it in response to an invitation from the Rev. William Richardson, the minister at Old Waxhaw Church, to speak on "Christian Love and Peace." According to Woodmason, Richardson told him that "his People were very desirous of hearing an Episcopal Minister, as they had never heard an English Preacher (they being all Scotch-Irish Presbyterians)," but some of the church elders were not "agreeable," so it was "never deliver'd" (p. 93, 23n).

110. Jill Lepore, *New York Burning: Liberty, Slavery, and Conspiracy in Eighteenth-Century Manhattan* (New York, 2005), esp. xvi–xvii.

111. Extract from letter of Governor George Thomas to Board of Trade, Leeward Islands, February 25, 1757, CO 152/41, 86. In 1745, Governor Trelawny rejected a proposal for a convention from the marquis de l'Arnage, governor of Saint-Domingue: Trelawny to Newcastle, n.d., CO 137/57/2, 109–110, BNA, containing l'Arnage's letter of February 2, 1745.

112. Governor William Mathew to duke of Newcastle, St. Kitts, July 20, 1744, CO 152/44, 254, BNA.

113. Long, *History of Jamaica,* vol. 2, 309.

114. "Diary of the Earl of Egmont," January 17, 1738/39, in *The Border Colonies and the Southern Colonies,* vol. 4 of Donnan, *Documents Illustrative of the History of the Slave Trade to America* (Washington, D.C., 1935), 592. For the development of plantation slavery in Cuba, see Herbert S. Klein, *Slavery in the Americas: A Comparative Study of Virginia and Cuba* (Chicago, 1967); Thomas, *Slave Trade,* 272–273; Robin Blackburn, *The Making of New World Slavery: From the Baroque to the*

Modern, 1492–1800 (London, 1997), 497–499; Evelyn Powell Jennings, "War as the "Forcing House of Change": State Slavery in Late-Eighteenth-Century Cuba," *William & Mary Quarterly*, 3rd ser., 62 (2005): 411–440.

115. Gilbert Fleming to Don Augustine Pareja, May 21, 1751, CO 152/45, 256, BNA. See also Lords of Trade to the earl of Holdernesse, May 22, 1754, CO 152/41, 63–68, BNA.

116. Ira Berlin, *Many Thousands Gone: The First Two Centuries of Slavery in North America* (Cambridge, Mass., 1998), 73. See also Jane Landers, *Black Society in Spanish Florida* (Urbana, Ill., 1999), 34, 37, 112–113; John K. Thornton, "African Dimensions of the Stono Rebellion," *American Historical Review* 96 (1991): 1101–13; Philip D. Morgan, *Slave Counterpoint: Black Culture in the Eighteenth-Century Chesapeake and Lowcountry* (Chapel Hill, N.C., 1998), 454–455.

117. [Daniel Horsmanden], *A Journal of the Proceedings in the Detection of the Conspiracy Formed by Some White People, in Conjunction with Negro and Other Slaves, for Burning the City of New-York in America, and Murdering the Inhabitants* (New York, 1744), 11. See also Lepore, *New York Burning*, 160–164, 165–167.

118. Orlando Patterson, "Slavery and Slave Revolts: A Sociohistorical Analysis of the First Maroon War, 1665–1740," in *Maroon Societies: Rebel Slave Communities in the Americas,* ed. Richard Price, 3rd ed. (Baltimore, 1996), 260–275; Mavis C. Campbell, *The Maroons of Jamaica, 1655–1796: A History of Resistance, Collaboration and Betrayal* (Trenton, N.J., 1990), chaps. 4, 5; for slave resistance and rebellion elsewhere in British America, see Michael Craton, *Testing the Chains: Resistance to Slavery in the British West Indies* (Ithaca, N.Y., 1982); David Barry Gaspar, *Bondsmen and Rebels: A Study of the Master-Slave Relations in Antigua* (Baltimore, 1985); Marcus Rediker and Peter Linebaugh, *The Many-Headed Hydra: Sailors, Slaves, Commoners, and the Hidden History of the Revolutionary Atlantic* (Boston, 2000), chap. 6.

119. Mavis Campbell, *The Maroons of Jamaica, 1655–1796: A History of Resistance, Collaboration and Betrayal* (Granby, Mass., 1988), 155.

120. O'Shaughnessy, *Empire Divided,* 40–41; Douglas Hall, *In Miserable Slavery: Thomas Thistlewood in Jamaica, 1750–1786* (Kingston, Jamaica, 1999 [orig. pub., 1989]), 244; Richard B. Sheridan, "The Jamaican Slave Insurrection Scare of 1776 and the American Revolution," *Journal of Negro History* 61 (1976): 290–308. For trends in planter-slave relations generally, see J. R. Ward, "The British West Indies, 1748–1815," in Marshall, *The Eighteenth Century,* 436–438.

121. Campbell, *Maroons of Jamaica,* 115.

122. [John Lind], *An Answer to the Declaration of the American Congress,* 4th ed. (London, 1776), 107. For black soldiers during the Revolutionary War, see Philip D. Morgan and Andrew Jackson O'Shaughnessy, "Arming Slaves in the American Revolution," in *Arming Slaves: From Classical Times to the Modern Age,* ed. Christopher Leslie Brown and Philip D. Morgan (New Haven, Conn., 2006), 180–208; Benjamin Quarles, *The Negro in the American Revolution* (Chapel Hill, N.C., 1961), 19–32; Sylvia R. Frey, *Water from the Rock: Black Resistance in a Revolutionary Age* (Princeton, N.J., 1991); Woody Holton, *Forced Founders: Indians, Debtors, Slaves, and the Making of the American Revolution in Virginia* (Chapel Hill, N.C., 1999), 133–163; John E. Selby, *Dunmore* (Williamsburg, Va., 1977), 36–44.

123. Morgan and O'Shaughnessy, "Arming Slaves," in Brown and Morgan, *Arming Slaves,* 192–194.

124. Trelawny to the duke of Newcastle, Jamaica, May 17 and August 29, 1741, CO 137/57/1, 62, 101, BNA.

125. Falconbridge, *Two Voyages,* in Coleman, *Maiden Voyages,* 135. On the growth of planter paternalism, see Morgan, *Slave Counterpoint,* 284–296

126. Ibid.

127. Geraldine Mozley, ed., *Letters to Jane from Jamaica, 1788–1796* (London, 1938), 40 (Letter XV, Mount Pleasant, September 16, 1792).

128. Andrews, *Journal of a Lady of Quality,* 129.

129. Ibid., 199. For similar rumors in Charleston, South Carolina, see Harris, *Hanging,* chap. 4.

3. PAX BRITANNICA

1. Samuel Flagg Bemis, "British Secret Service and the French-American Alliance," *American Historical Review* 29 (1924): 484–488; Gordon E. Kershaw, "Wentworth, Paul," in *American National Biography Online,* February 2000, http://www.anb.org/articles/01/01-00947.html, (accessed September 12 2011); Gordon S. Wood, *The Americanization of Benjamin Franklin* (New York, 2004), 190–191.

2. Wentworth to William Eden, Paris, January 7, 1778, BL Add. MSS 34, 415, 48–49.

3. [Edward Gibbon,] "The Justifying Memorial of the King of Great Britain, in Answer to the Exposition, &c., of the Court of France," in *Annual Register* 22 (1779): 397.

4. Alexander Carlyle, *The Justice and Necessity of the War with Our American Colonies Examined. A Sermon, Preached at Inveresk, December 12, 1776* (Edinburgh, 1777), 46.

5. Ebenezer Radcliff, *A Sermon Preached at Walthamstow, December 13, 1776* (London, 1776), 12.

6. Thomas Lewis O'Beirne, *A Sermon Preached at St. Paul's, New-York, September 22, 1776* (Maidstone, 1776), 15. The British blamed the fire on "rebels, who lurked about the town," in the words of Ambrose Serle, General Howe's secretary: Harry M. Ward, *The American Revolution: Nationhood Achieved, 1763–1788* (New York, 1995), 98.

7. William Blackstone, *Of the Rights of Persons,* vol. 1 of *Commentaries on the Laws of England,* ed. Stanley N. Katz (Chicago, 1979 [orig. publ., 1765–1769]), 405–409; Thomas Parker, *The Laws of Shipping and Insurance, with a Digest of Adjudged Cases* (London, 1775), 265–267; John Trusler, *A Concise View of the Common Law and Statute Law of England, Carefully Collected from the Statutes and Best Common Law Writers, and Systematically Digested* (London, 1781), 79–80.

8. Charles M. Andrews, "The Acts of Trade," in *The Old Empire: From the Beginnings to 1783,* vol. 1 of *The Cambridge History of the British Empire,* ed. J. Holland Rose et al. (Cambridge, 1929), 296–299; Carl Ubbelohde, *The Vice-Admiralty Courts and the American Revolution* (Chapel Hill, N.C., 1960), 3–22.

9. "Examination of Benjamin Franklin" (February 13, 1766) in *A Collection of Papers Relative to the Dispute between Great Britain and America, 1764–1775,* ed. John Almon (New York, 1971), 73.

10. Philip V, king of Spain, "The Assiento, Adjusted between Their Brittanick and Catholick Majesties" (1713), in [Casimir Freschot], *The Compleat History of the Treaty of Utrecht [Histoire Du Congres Et De La Paix D'utrecht]* (London, 1715), vol. 1, part 2, 155–182; for the Acadian cession in the Anglo-French treaty, see ibid., vol. 2, part 1, 107.

11. "Treaty of Navigation and Commerce between Britain and France" (1713), in ibid., vol. 2, part 1, 139.

12. Daniel A. Baugh, "Maritime Strength and Atlantic Commerce: The Uses of a 'Grand Marine Empire,'" in *An Imperial State at War: Britain from 1689 to 1815,* ed. Lawrence Stone (London, 1994), 196.

13. Charles Jenkinson [earl of Liverpool], *A Discourse on the Conduct of the Government of Great-Britain, in Respect to Neutral Nations, During the Present War* (Dublin, 1759 [orig. publ., London, 1758]), 54.

14. In 1775 the tonnage of sailing vessels in the Royal Navy displacing at least 500 tons was 327,300 tons, against 190,100 tons for France and 188,800 tons for Spain; Russia and the Dutch Republic had the next largest navies in Europe, with 77,900 and 67,500 tons, respectively: Michael Duffy, "World-Wide War and British Expansion, 1793–1815," in P. J. Marshall, ed., *The Eighteenth Century,* vol. 2 of *The Oxford History of the British Empire* (Oxford, 2000), table 9.1 (p. 185).

15. N. A. M. Rodger, "Sea-Power and Empire, 1688–1793," in ibid., 169–183; Paul M. Kennedy, *The Rise and Fall of British Naval Mastery* (London, 1976; reprint, 1983), 101.

16. [Jenkinson], *Discourse,* 42, 46.

17. *A Letter from a Member of Parliament to His Grace the Duke of* ***** *Upon the Present Situation of Affairs* (London, 1755), 15–16.

18. "Memorial delivered by Major Gen. Yorke to the Deputies of the States General" (December 22, 1758), in *Annual Register* 2 (1759): 205.

19. Nicolas Magens, *An Essay on Insurances, Explaining the Nature of the Various Kinds of Insurance Practised by the Different Commercial States of Europe* (London, 1755), vol. 1, 434–435; for the war in the West Indies as a war of attrition, see Walter Louis Dorn, *Competition for Empire, 1740–1763* (New York, 1940), 172–173.

20. The best account of the plunder of Saint Eustatius is in Andrew Jackson O'Shaughnessy, *An Empire Divided: The American Revolution and the British Caribbean* (Philadelphia, 2000), 214–227.

21. *Annual Register* 24 (1781): 105.

22. See, for example, [James Marriott], *A Letter to the Dutch Merchants in England* (London, 1759), 6: "Every Subject of Holland, [who] acts as a real Dutchman, will . . . be treated as such, but the Dutchman who puts upon himself a borrowed Character, has little Reason to complain, if he is treated like what he appears to be, the Deserter of his own Country, and the Enemy of its Ally."

23. *Annual Register* 24 (1781): 101.

24. Copy of a letter from Admiral Rodney to the marquis de Bouillé, in *American Journal* (May 23, 1781): 2.

25. Report of House of Commons debate on Saint Eustatius, May 14, 1781, in *Pennsylvania Packet*, August 23, 1781.

26. [Jenkinson], *Discourse*, 8.

27. Captain Jacob Roome et al., v. St. Fernando and Lading (July 7 and August 25, 1758), in Charles M. Hough, ed., *Reports of Cases in the Vice Admiralty of the Province of New York and in the Court of Admiralty of the State of New York, 1715–1788* (New Haven, Conn., 1925), 131–132.

28. *Before the Lords Commissioners of Appeals in Prize Causes. Koninghen Esther, John Gardner, Master. Appendix to the Respondent's Case* ([London], [1760]), 3.

29. Holmes to Pitt, on board *Cambridge*, Port Royal, Jamaica, February 14, 1761, CO 137/60, 339–340, BNA.

30. Long to Gov. Moore, Spanish Town, Jamaica, December 31, 1760, and extract from letter of Richard Mercer to Messrs. Wm. & Jacob Walton & Co., and Messrs. Greg & Cunningham at New York, November 6, 1760, ibid., 307, 309–310. See also the judgment of high treason against the Philadelphia merchant William Pickles on Antigua in January 1759, which alleges, among other things, that colonial merchants carried "stores of ammunition and provisions" to France's colonies in the West Indies, "sometimes under convoy of English privateers from N° America" (CO 152/46, 66, BNA).

31. Long to Moore, December 31, 1760, ibid., 306–307.

32. J. Franklin Jameson, ed., *Privateering and Piracy in the Colonial Period* (New York, 1970), 531, n3. By contrast, in remarks on the same case, Richard Pares followed his countrymen in casting Judge Morris as the main culprit, writing, "There is not room, even in a book of this length, to relate the pettifogging villainies by which Judge Morris of New York tried to avoid bringing to book the privateer" who seized Ybañez's cargo: Richard Pares, *Colonial Blockade and Neutral Rights, 1739–1763* (Oxford, 1938), 48, n2. In his ruling of June 27, 1761, on the separate question of whether Richard Haddon, captain of the privateer that made the capture, had violated the terms of his commission in taking *La Virgen del Rosario*'s cargo, Morris stuck to his view that the "circumstances" of the Spanish schooner were "very suspicious": Hough, *Reports of Cases*, 128.

33. Moore to the earl of Holdernesse, [Jamaica], August 31, 1757, CO 137/60, 262, BNA. See also Moore to Holdernesse, Spanish Town, October 4, 1757, and Moore to Holdernesse, [Jamaica], February 6, 1758, ibid., 264, 270.

34. "Libel of Felipe Ybañez," September 27, 1758 (no. 188), in Jameson, *Privateering*, 547–548.

35. Moore to Holdernesse, [Jamaica], February 6, 1758, CO 137/60, 270, BNA; "King v. Thomas Miller and Sampson Simpson," July 14, 1758, to June 26, 1761, in Hough, *Reports of Cases*, 122–130. For the charges against Haddon, see Lt. Gov. James de Lancey, "Proclamation," November 3, 1758, in *New York Gazette* (November 20, 1758): 2; see also Jameson, *Privateering*, no. 184, n3, and no. 187, n1 (pp. 531, 535–536).

36. Morris's opinion in "King v. Miller and Simpson," June 26, 1761, in Hough, *Reports of Cases,* 127, 130.

37. Lords of Admiralty to Vice-Admiral Holburne, December 1758, quoted in N. A. M. Rodger, *The Wooden World: An Anatomy of the Georgian Navy* (New York, 1996 [orig. publ., 1986]), 161.

38. *"Prince Frederick* vs. *Postilion,"* October 27, 1746, in *Records of the Vice-Admiralty Court of Rhode Island, 1716–1752,* vol. 3 of *American Legal Records,* ed. Dorothy S. Towle (Washington, D.C., 1936), 397.

39. "John Williams, et al., vs. Sloop Prosperous Polly, Her Lading, and One Negro Man Joseph" (September 10, 1762), in Hough, *Reports of Cases,* 200–201.

40. Thomas to Pitt, Antigua, March 20, 1760, CO 152/46, 203, BNA; Deposition of Edward Bull, Antigua, March 15, 1760, ibid., 207.

41. Rodney to Stephen, February 12, 1781, quoted in O'Shaughnessy, *Empire Divided,* 220.

42. "Petition of Abraham Mendés," [n.d.], CO 246/1, 213–215, BNA.

43. "To their Excellencies the Commanders in Chief of his Britannic Majesty's Navy and Army in the West Indies," February 16, 1781, in *North American Intelligencer,* April 25, 1781.

44. [Thomas Whately], *Considerations on the Trade and Finances of This Kingdom, and on the Measures of Administration, with Respect to Those Great National Objects since the Conclusion of the Peace* (London, 1766), 74–75.

45. Opinion of Judge Richard Morris in "Andrew Elliot qui tam vs. Peter Dorey" (August 28, 1772) in Hough, *Reports of Cases,* 240. For Britain's postwar attempts to tighten the regulation of colonial trade as a continuation of the wartime efforts to prevent colonial merchants from trading with France, see Richard Pares, *War and Trade in the West Indies, 1739–1763* (Oxford, 1936; reprint, 1963), 467–468; Oliver M. Dickerson, *The Navigation Acts and the American Revolution* (Philadelphia, 1951), 168–170; Ubbelohde, *Vice-Admiralty Courts,* 38–44.

46. [Thomas Whately], *The Regulations Lately Made Concerning the Colonies, and the Taxes Imposed Upon Them, Considered,* 3rd ed. (London, 1775 [orig. publ., 1765]), 92.

47. Bernard to Pitt, Boston, May 5, 1761, in Gertrude Selwyn Kimball, ed., *Correspondence of William Pitt, When Secretary of State, with Colonial Governors and Military and Naval Commissioners in America* (New York, 1906), 2:428.

48. Edward Long, *The History of Jamaica. Or, General Survey of the Antient and Modern State of That Island* (London, 1774), 1:307.

49. "Reform of the Customs Service: Order in Council" (October 4, 1763), in *Colonies to Nation, 1763–1789: A Documentary History of the American Revolution,* ed. Jack P. Greene (New York, 1975), 16.

50. William Allen, *The American Crisis: A Letter, Addressed . . . To the Earl Gower, . . . On the Present Alarming Disturbances in the Colonies* (London, 1774), 15.

51. [Whately], *Considerations,* 24.

52. John Bonar, *A Discourse on the Advantages of the Insular Situation of Great-Britain; Delivered at Spithead, on Occasion of the Preparations for His Majesty's Review of the Fleet* (London, 1773), 21–22.

53. Ubbelohde, *Vice-Admiralty Courts,* 105–114, 119–127; Jesse Lemisch, "Jack Tar in the Streets: Merchant Seamen in the Politics of Revolutionary America," *William and Mary Quarterly,* 3rd ser., 25 (1968): 371–407.

54. Joseph Harrison to the Marquis of Rockingham, June 17, 1768, in Greene, *Colonies to Nation,* 136.

55. [Jenkinson], *Discourse,* 46.

56. [Arthur Young], *Reflections on the Present State of Affairs at Home and Abroad* (London, 1759), 38–39.

57. [Benjamin Franklin], *The Interest of Great Britain Considered, with Regard to Her Colonies, and the Acquisitions of Canada and Guadaloupe. To Which Are Added, Observations Concerning the Increase of Mankind, Peopling of Countries, &c.* (London, 1760), 8–9. According to the English Short Title Catalogue (ESTC), the pamphlet is sometimes also attributed to Richard Jackson, the Pennsylvania assembly's agent in London. The pamphlet occasioned several replies, was reprinted numerous times, and was copied at least once, for which see [William Pulteney, earl of Bath], *Reflections on the Domestic Policy, Proper to Be Observed on the Conclusion of a Peace* (London, 1763).

58. Johnstone to Ulloa, Pensacola, May 3, 1766, in Dunbar Rowland, ed., *Mississippi Provincial Archives, 1763–1766: English Dominion* (Nashville, Tenn., 1911), 312.

59. See Nicholas Tracy, "The Gunboat Diplomacy of the Government of George Grenville, 1764–1765: The Honduras, Turks Island and Gambian Incidents," *Historical Journal* 17 (1974): 711–731.

60. Ibid., 716–717.

61. Pitt's speech on the army estimates for 1764, quoted in *A Letter to the Right Honourable Ch——s T——nd, Esq* (London, 1763), 20; [David Hartley], *The Budget. Inscribed to the Man, Who Thinks Himself Minister,* 6th ed. (London, 1764), 9; [John Dickinson], *Letters from a Farmer in Pennsylvania, to the Inhabitants of the British Colonies* (Philadelphia, 1768), in Paul Leicester Ford, ed., *The Writings of John Dickinson,* vol. 1, *Political Writings, 1764–1774,* Memoirs of the Historical Society of Pennsylvania, vol. 14 (Philadelphia, 1895), 360; *The Justice and Necessity of Taxing the American Colonies* (London, 1766), 10.

62. Dissent of Nicolas Foucault, French commissary, in Superior Council Minutes, October 29, 1768, quoted in John Preston Moore, *Revolt in Louisiana: The Spanish Occupation, 1766–1770* (Baton Rouge, La., 1976), 159.

63. Ibid., 173, including passage from Browne to Lord Hillsborough, February 28, 1769, which is quoted at n13. Hillsborough apparently tested the idea with the Spanish envoy to London in February 1769, only to be told, in a not-so-subtle reference to the growth of radicalism in Boston, that "the citizens of New Orleans had anticipated what the English colonies were ready to undertake, from whom they had pursued a bad example": Masserano to Grimaldi, February 24, 1769, quoted at p. 189.

64. Ibid., 171–172, 176–177, 204, 208–209.

65. Gage to O'Reilly, New York, November 18, 1769, in Lawrence Kinnaird, ed., *Spain in the Mississippi Valley, 1765–1794,* 3 parts (vols. 2–4 of *American Historical*

Association Annual Report for 1945 [Washington, D.C., 1946–1949]), part 1, *The Revolutionary Period, 1765–1781,* 107.

66. Lord Adam Gordon, "Journal of an Officer who Travelled in America and the West Indies in 1764 and 1765," in *Travels in the American Colonies,* ed. Newton D. Mereness (New York, 1961), 383. For the problems of maintaining the army's strength during the 1760s, see John W. Shy, *Toward Lexington: The Role of the British Army in the Coming of the American Revolution* (Princeton, N.J., 1965); Michael N. McConnell, *Army and Empire: British Soldiers on the American Frontier, 1758–1775* (Lincoln, Neb., 2004).

67. Robert Rogers, *A Concise Account of North America* (New York, 1966 [orig. publ., London, 1765]), iii.

68. Letter of John Stuart to the "Great Chiefs and Leaders of the Lower Creek Nation," Mobile, January 20, 1772, in Mereness, *Travels,* 547n.

69. "Journal of David Taitt's Travels from Pensacola, West Florida, to and through the Country of the Upper and Lower Creeks, 1772", in ibid., 548–549.

70. Letter to John Stephenson, New Orleans, April 22, 1769, and "The Succession of John Fitzpatrick," May 11, 1791, in Margaret Fisher Dalrymple, ed., *The Merchant of Manchac: The Letterbooks of John Fitzpatrick, 1768–1790* (Baton Rouge, La., 1978), 46, 431–432.

71. Letter to William Weir, Spanish Manchac, September 16, 1778, in ibid., 307.

72. "Journal of Captain Harry Gordon," in Mereness, *Travels,* 476.

73. On the hollowness of the British Empire in North America, see Eric Hinderaker, *Elusive Empires: Constructing Colonialism in the Ohio Valley, 1673–1800* (Cambridge, 1997); Fred Anderson, *Crucible of War: The Seven Years' War and the Fate of Empire in British North America, 1754–1766* (New York, 2000).

74. Gordon, "Journal," in Mereness, *Travels,* 443.

75. [Whately], *Regulations,* 30–32.

76. The phrase comes from a letter by the last French governor of Louisiana, Charles Philippe Aubry, May 14, 1765, quoted in John Mack Faragher, *A Great and Noble Scheme: The Tragic Story of the Expulsion of the French Acadians from Their American Homeland* (New York, 2005), 431.

77. Gordon, "Journal," in Mereness, *Travels,* 433, 439.

78. Washington to William Crawford, September 1767, in *George Washington, Writings,* vol. 91 of *The Library of America,* ed. John H. Rhodehamel (New York, 1997), 125; Colin G. Calloway, *The Scratch of a Pen: 1763 and the Transformation of North America* (Oxford, 2006), 97, quoting Brian Slattery.

79. Egremont to Amherst, January 27, 1763, quoted in Calloway, *Scratch of a Pen,* 94.

80. Thomas C. Barrow, "A Project for Imperial Reform: 'Hints Respecting the Settlement for Our American Provinces,' 1763," *William and Mary Quarterly,* 3rd ser., 24 (1967): 116. Barrow attributes the "Hints" to William Knox, a member of Ellis's circle in London who had also spent time in Georgia. The attribution to Ellis is in Calloway, *Scratch of a Pen,* 93.

81. Gen. Gage to the Governor of Rhode Island, New York, December 6, 1763, in *1757–1769,* vol. 6 of *Records of the Colony of Rhode Island and Providence Plantations, in New England,* ed. John Russell Bartlett (Providence, R.I., 1861), 376.

82. Thomas Mante, *The History of the Late War in North-America, and the Islands of the West-Indies* (London, 1772), 479.

83. Grant to Board of Trade, St. Augustine, August 3, 1766, CO 5/548, 104, BNA.

84. Letter to Peter Swanson, Manchac, September 22, 1771, in Dalrymple, *Merchant of Manchac,* 111.

85. Memorandum of Governor William Johnstone and John Stuart, Pensacola, June 12, 1765, in Rowland, *Mississippi Provincial Archives,* 186.

86. Quoted in Claudio Saunt, *A New Order of Things: Property, Power, and the Transformation of the Creek Indians, 1733–1816* (Cambridge, 1999), 51.

87. Governor Johnstone's report to [Henry Seymour] Conway, June 23, 1760, in Rowland, *Mississippi Provincial Archives,* 511.

88. Quote in Patrick Griffin, *American Leviathan: Empire, Nation, and Revolutionary Frontier* (New York, 2007), 93.

89. "Proceedings of Sir William Johnson with the Indians at Fort Stanwix to settle a Boundary Line," in Johnson to Lord Hillsborough, Johnson Hall, November 18, 1768, and Johnson to Hillsborough, Johnson Hall, August 26, 1769, in *London Documents: XLI–XLVII, 1768–1782,* vol. 8 of *Documents Relative to the Colonial History of the State of New York,* ed. John Romeyn Brodhead et al. (Albany, N.Y., 1857), 120, 184–186.

90. Edmund Burke, *Mr. Burke's Speech, on the 1st December 1783, . . . On Mr. Fox's East India Bill* (London, 1784), 16.

91. All quotes from Calloway, *Scratch of a Pen,* 78–79.

92. [Robert Rogers], *Ponteach: Or the Savages of America. A Tragedy* (London, 1766), 4, 9.

93. Shelburne to James Grant, Whitehall, February 19, 1767, CO 5/548, 137, BNA.

94. Quoted in Saunt, *New Order of Things,* 96–97. In Pennsylvania, similar concerns must have been on the minds of the authorities who arrested one Frederick Stump for murdering a party of six Indians whom he had invited into his house, after which he "barbarously put to death an Indian woman, two girls, and a young child" in their own cabin. In an apparent replay of the Paxton massacre, a party of eighty armed men came to Stump's rescue, breaking open the jail at Carlisle and forcing the magistrates to set him free; however, the colony was able to restore "the chain of peace" at a congress near Fort Pitt. "This affair has greatly alarmed the government of Pennsylvania," reported the *London Magazine,* adding that officials were "taking every measure to prevent an Indian war": *London Magazine* (1768), 230, 383.

95. Rogers, *Concise Account,* 219, 243–244.

96. J. Hector St. John de Crèvecoeur, *Letters from an American Farmer* (Dublin, [1782]), 52; The Proclamation of 1763 (October 7, 1763), in Greene, *Colonies to Nation,* 17.

97. Daniel K. Richter, "Native peoples of North America and the Eighteenth-Century British Empire," in Marshall, *The Eighteenth Century,* 365–366.

98. Long, *History of Jamaica,* vol. 1, 336–337.

99. T. H. Breen, "Ideology and Nationalism on the Eve of the American Revolution: Revisions *Once More* in Need of Revising," *Journal of American History* 84 (1997):

33. For the British view, see Eliga H. Gould, *The Persistence of Empire: British Political Culture in the Age of the American Revolution* (Chapel Hill, N.C., 2000), chap. 4.

100. [Whately], *Regulations*, 109; R. C. Simmons and P. D. G. Thomas, eds., *Proceedings and Debates of the British Parliaments Respecting North America, 1754–1783* (Millwood, N.Y., 1982), vol. 2, 169 (Norton), 568 (Mansfield).

101. Letter to Lord Camden, Lord High Chancellor, January 29, 1768, in [Thomas Hollis], ed., *The True Sentiments of America: Contained in a Collection of Letters Sent from the House of Representatives of the Province of Massachutts [sic] Bay to Several Persons of High Rank in This Kingdom* (London, 1768), 35.

102. [Dickinson], *Letters from a Farmer in Pennsylvania*, in Ford, *Writings of John Dickinson*, vol. 1, 369, 373.

103. [Benjamin Franklin], *The Causes of the Present Distractions in America Explained: In Two Letters to a Merchant in London* ([New York], 1774), 2.

104. [William Greatrakes], *An Application of Some General Political Rules, to the Present State of Great-Britain, Ireland and America. In a Letter to the Right Honourable Earl Temple* (London, 1766), 80. According to the ESTC, the attribution is from Horace Walpole.

105. [Jonathan Boucher], *A Letter from a Virginian to the Members of the Congress to Be Held at Philadelphia, on the First of September, 1774* (London, 1774 [orig. publ., Boston 1774]), 43–44.

106. [William Knox], *The Present State of the Nation: Particularly with Respect to Its Trade, Finances, &c. Addressed to the King and Both Houses of Parliament,* 4th ed. (London, 1769 [orig. publ., 1768]), 37.

107. [Whately], *Regulations*, 88; Samuel Johnson, *Taxation, No Tyranny* (1775), in *Political Writings,* vol. 10 of *The Yale Edition of the Works of Samuel Johnson,* ed. Donald Greene (Indianapolis, 2000 [orig. publ., New Haven, Conn., 1977]), 416.

108. John Dickinson, "Arguments against the Independence of the Colonies" (July 1, 1776), in Greene, *Colonies to Nation*, 293.

109. Carlyle, *Justice and Necessity*, 36.

110. Adam Smith, *An Inquiry into the Nature and Causes of the Wealth of Nations,* ed. Edwin Cannan, with a new preface by George J. Stigler (Chicago, 1976 [orig. publ., 1904]), 2:485–486.

111. Richard [Watson], Bishop of Landaff, *A Sermon Preached before the Lords Spiritual and Temporal, in the Abbey-Church, Westminster, on Friday, January 30, 1784* (London, [1784]), 18.

112. Thomas Day, *Fragment of an Original Letter on the Slavery of the Negroes Written in the Year 1776* (London, 1784), 13.

113. William Bolts, *Considerations on India Affairs* (London, 1772), 1:75.

114. Bernard to Pitt, Boston, May 5, 1761, in Kimball, *Correspondence of William Pitt,* vol. 2, 428.

4. INDEPENDENCE

1. . "Journal of André Michaux, 1793–1796" (trans. from original French), in *André Michaux's Travels into Kentucky, 1793–96, [etc.],* vol. 3 of *Early Western Travels, 1748–1846,* ed. Reuben Gold Thwaites (Cleveland, Ohio, 1904–1907), 94.

2. Michaux met Jackson in June 1795, possibly spending the night at his plantation on the fifteenth, but said nothing of the encounter except that the "soil [was] fertile": "Journal of André Michaux," in ibid., vol. 3, 61.

3. Jackson to John McKee, Poplar Grove, May 16, 1794, in *1770–1803,* vol. 1 of *The Papers of Andrew Jackson,* ed. Sam B. Smith and Harriet Chappell Owsley (Knoxville, Tenn., 1980–), 49. According to papers in the Archivo General de Indias, Seville, Spain (Cuba 2361), Jackson took an oath of allegiance to the Spanish king at Natchez on July 15, 1789: see Robert V. Remini, *Andrew Jackson and His Indian Wars* (New York, 2001), 285, n. 16.

4. "The Declaration of Independence" (July 4, 1776), in Jack P. Greene, ed., *Colonies to Nation, 1763–1789: A Documentary History of the American Revolution* (New York, 1975 [orig. pub., 1967]), 298, 300. For more on the declaration as a bid for admission to Europe's "republic of nations," see Peter S. Onuf, "A Declaration of Independence for Diplomatic Historians," *Diplomatic History* 22, no. 1 (1998): 71–83; David Armitage, *The Declaration of Independence: A Global History* (Cambridge, Mass., 2007).

5. On the United States as a republican empire, see Lord Thomas Erskine, *A View of the Causes and Consequences of the Present War with France* (London, 1797), 58. The Tenth Amendment (1791) is in Greene, ed., *Colonies to Nation,* 583. The argument here is especially indebted to Peter S. Onuf, *Jefferson's Empire: The Language of American Nationhood* (Charlottesville, Va., 2000). See also Daniel H. Deudney, "The Philadelphian System: Sovereignty, Arms Control, and Balance of Power in the American States-Union, circa 1787–1861," *International Organization* 49 (1995): 191–228; David C. Hendrickson, *Peace Pact: The Lost World of the American Founding* (Lawrence, Kans., 2003).

6. *Three Letters Addressed to the Public* (Philadelphia, 1783), 8n. Tullius, the pseudonymous author of the pamphlet in which the phrase appears, was paraphrasing Vattel on the "dignity of nations": "Every nation, every sovereign and independent state, deserves consideration and respect, because it makes an immediate figure in the grand society of the human race, is independent of all earthly power." See Emer de Vattel, *The Law of Nations, or, Principles of the Law of Nature, Applied to the Conduct and Affairs of Nations and Sovereigns,* ed. Bela Kapossy and Richard Whatmore (Indianapolis, 2008 [orig. publ. London, 1797]), book ii, chap. iii, § 35 (p. 281).

7. John Holroyd Lord Sheffield, *Observations on the Commerce of the American States,* rev. ed. (New York, 1970 [orig. pub., 1784]), 198.

8. Richard Henry Lee, "Resolves for Independence" (June 7, 1776), in Greene, *Colonies to Nation,* 285.

9. Quoted in Bradford Perkins, *The Creation of a Republican Empire, 1776–1865,* vol. 1 of *The Cambridge History of American Foreign Relations,* ed. Warren I. Cohen (Cambridge, 1993; reprint, 1995), 19.

10. Letter to James Monroe, Paris, June 17, 1785 ("Some Thoughts on Treaties"), in *Thomas Jefferson, Writings,* vol. 15 of *The Library of America,* ed. Merrill D. Peterson (New York, 1984), 808.

11. Paine, *Common Sense* (1775), in Greene, *Colonies to Nation,* 278.

12. Randolph to George Hammond, Philadelphia, May 1, 1794, in *ASP: Foreign Relations,* 1:451–452 (George Washington, "Great Britain. Communicated to Congress, May 12, 1794").

13. [Edward Gibbon], "The Justifying Memorial of the King of Great Britain, in Answer to the Exposition, &c., of the Court of *France*" (n.d.), *Annual Register* 22 (1779): 404; see also Eliga H. Gould, "American Independence and Britain's Counter-Revolution," *Past and Present* 154 (February 1997): 114.

14. Paine, *Common Sense,* in Greene, *Colonies to Nation,* 282–283.

15. [Gibbon], "Justifying Memorial," 404.

16. Edward H. Tatum, ed., *The American Journal of Ambrose Serle: Secretary to Lord Howe, 1776–1778* (San Marino, Calif., 1940), 30–31.

17. [John Lind], *An Answer to the Declaration of the American Congress* (London, 1776), 5. See also Gould, "American Independence," 115; Margaret Avery, "Toryism in the Age of the American Revolution: John Lind and John Shebbeare," *Historical Studies* 18 (1978): 24–36.

18. Tatum, *American Journal,* 35.

19. "New York, Sept. 30," *New York Gazette* (September 30, 1776); Philip Ranlet, *The New York Loyalists* (Knoxville, Tenn., 1986), 76. The British arrested two hundred individuals, including Fellows, but quickly released most. Although Washington did not order the fire, he clearly approved of the results, writing to Lund Washington that "Providence—or some good honest Fellow, has done more for us than we were disposed to do for ourselves . . . ; however, enough of [the city] remains to answer their [i.e., the British army's] purposes": Letter to Lund Washington, Heights of Harlem, October 6, 1776, in *August–October 1776,* vol. 6 of *The Papers of George Washington, Revolutionary War Series,* ed. Philander Chase (Charlottesville, Va., 1985–), 495.

20. Thomas Lewis O'Beirne, *A Sermon Preached at St. Paul's, New-York, September 22, 1776* (Maidstone, 1776), 16–17.

21. Myles Cooper, *National Humiliation and Repentance Recommended, and the Causes of the Present Rebellion in America Assigned, in a Sermon Preached before the University of Oxford, on Friday, December 13, 1776* (Oxford, 1777), 20.

22. Israel Putnam (U.S. Army—Continental Army, 1776), Untitled broadside (Head-Quarters, Philadelphia, December 13, 1776), Evans 15181.

23. Letter to Thomas Gage, Cambridge, [Mass.], August 11, 1775, in *George Washington, Writings,* vol. 91 of *The Library of America,* ed. John H. Rhodehamel (New York, 1997), 181.

24. Tatum, *American Journal,* 82. Sullivan was taken prisoner during the Battle of Long Island and acted as Lord Howe's intermediary with General Washington before being exchanged.

25. Frederick Mackenzie, *Diary of Frederick Mackenzie: Giving a Daily Narrative of His Military Service as an Officer of the Regiment of Royal Welch Fusiliers During the Years 1775–1781 in Massachusetts, Rhode Island and New York* (Cambridge, Mass., 1930), vol. 1, 111, 112–113. Despite thinking that American officers had too much freedom, Mackenzie made it clear that he did not share the views of those who favored treating them as rebels. "I am of opinion," he wrote, that "it is write [*sic*] to treat our enemies as if they might one day become our friends."

26. "Extract of a letter dated on board the Jersey, (vulgerly called HELL) PRISON SHIP, New York, August 10, 1781," *Boston Gazette,* August 20, 1781, 3.

27. *New Hampshire Gazette,* April 26, 1777, quoted in Francis D. Cogliano, *American Maritime Prisoners in the Revolutionary War: The Captivity of William Russell* (Annapolis, Md., 2001), 151.

28. *Connecticut Gazette,* July 10, 1778, 3.

29. Robert Mills, *Statistics of South Carolina: Including a View of Its Natural, Civil, and Military History, General and Particular* (Charleston, S.C., 1826), 290.

30. David Ramsay, *The History of the American Revolution,* ed. Lester H. Cohen (Indianapolis, Ind., 1990 [orig. pub., Philadelphia, 1789]), 2:483.

31. Letter to Lieut.-General Earl Cornwallis, [n.d.], in Banastre Tarleton, *A History of the Campaigns of 1780 and 1781, in the Southern Provinces of North America* (Dublin, 1787), 85; Mills, *Statistics of South Carolina,* 250. See also [Richard Johnson], *The History of North America. Containing, a Review of the Customs and Manners of the Original Inhabitants* (London, 1789), 150: "the unresisting Americans, praying for quarters, were cut in pieces. . . . Lord Cornwallis bestowed on Tarleton the highest encomiums for this enterprise, and recommended him in a special manner to royal favour and patronage."

32. Mills, *Statistics of South Carolina,* 287–288, 290.

33. "The Fugitives from the Waxhaws," *National Intelligencer,* August 1, 1845.

34. Remini, *Andrew Jackson,* 17–19.

35. "Jackson's Description of His Experiences During and Immediately Following the Revolutionary War," in Smith and Owsley, *Papers of Andrew Jackson,* vol. 1, 5; Remini, *Andrew Jackson,* 18.

36. Letter from Henry Tazewell (U.S. senator from Virginia), July 20, 1789, and letter to James Robertson, Philadelphia, January 11, 1798, in Smith and Owsley, *Papers of Andrew Jackson,* vol. 1, 165, 207. Although the first set of quotations comes from Tazewell's letter to Jackson, there is no reason to think that Jackson disagreed with the views that they expressed.

37. The best modern study of British commercial policy in the revolution's aftermath is John E. Crowley, *The Privileges of Independence: Neomercantilism and the American Revolution* (Baltimore, 1993), esp. chap. 4. See also Stanley M. Elkins and Eric McKitrick, *The Age of Federalism: The Early American Republic, 1788–1800* (New York, 1993), 69–73, 378–380.

38. Jefferson, "Report on the Privileges and Restrictions on the Commerce of the United States" (December 16, 1791), in Peterson, *Thomas Jefferson,* 439.

39. Campbell to Lord North, Jamaica, November 28, 1783, CO 137/84, 23, BNA; "Original Address Presented to the Assembly . . . in Response to the Governor's Speech at the Opening of the Sessions" [n.d.], in ibid., 26–27. For the background to (and prevalence of) British concessions to American merchant ships, see Alice B. Keith, "Relaxations in the British Restrictions on the American Trade with the British West Indies, 1783–1802," *Journal of Modern History* 20 (1948): 1–18. See also Gordon C. Bjork, "The Weaning of the American Economy: Independence, Market Changes, and Economic Development," *Journal of Economic History* 24 (1964): 541–560; Elkins and McKitrick, *Age of Federalism,* 381–383.

40. Bond to Lord Carmarthen, Philadelphia, February 21, 1787, in J. Franklin Jameson, ed., "Letters of Phineas Bond, British Consul at Philadelphia, to the Foreign Office of Great Britain, 1787, 1788, 1789," *American Historical Association Annual Report for 1896* (Washington, D.C., 1897), 1:524. For evidence of the same "collusive" practices on Jamaica, see the letter from the island's governor, Archibald Campbell, to Lord Sydney, March 28, 1785, Jamaica, CO 137/85, 113, BNA. "There are certainly fraudulent importations to a very great amount," wrote Campbell, "but it is extremely difficult, if not impossible, to ascertain the real quantity" (f. 114).

41. Nelson to Lord Sydney, Nevis, November 17, 1785, quoted in Bjork, "Weaning," 551.

42. John H. Reinoehl, "Some Remarks on the American Trade: Jacob Crowninshield to James Madison, 1806," *William and Mary Quarterly,* 3rd ser., 16 (1959): 93. In Nelson's case, his zeal in enforcing the Navigation Laws against American ships during the mid-1780s made him so unpopular with West Indian planters and merchants that he was the subject of numerous lawsuits and an arrest warrant, which he avoided only by remaining on his ship: Keith, "Relaxations in the British Restrictions," 5.

43. Higginson to John Adams, Boston, December 21, 1789, in J. Franklin Jameson, "Letters of Stephen Higginson, 1783–1804," *American Historical Association Annual Report for 1896,* vol. 1, 771.

44. Reinoehl, "Some Remarks," 95.

45. "Extract of a letter from a gentleman in Lisbon to his friend in this town, dated October 14" (Boston, December 14), [Portland, Maine] *Eastern Herald,* January 6, 1794.

46. Richard C. Knopf, ed., *Anthony Wayne, a Name in Arms: Soldier, Diplomat, Defender of Expansion Westward of a Nation* (Westport, Conn., 1975 [orig. pub., 1960]), 7.

47. Wayne to Henry Knox, Pittsburgh, August 24, 1792, in ibid., 72.

48. H. H. Brackenridge, "Thoughts on the Present Indian War," *National Gazette* [Philadelphia], February 2, 1792. See also Andrew R. L. Cayton, " 'Separate Interests' and the Nation-State: The Washington Administration and the Origins of Regionalism in the Trans-Appalachian West," *The Journal of American History* 79

(1992): 39–67; Patrick Griffin, *American Leviathan: Empire, Nation, and Revolutionary Frontier* (New York, 2007).

49. David J. Weber, *The Spanish Frontier in North America* (New Haven, Conn., 1992), 265–270, 278–279.

50. Ibid., 265–289. For Spanish intrigues and threats in the Ohio and Mississippi valleys, see A. P. Whitaker, "Spanish Intrigue in the Old Southwest: An Episode, 1788–89," *The Mississippi Valley Historical Review* 12 (September 1925): 155–176; Thomas P. Slaughter, *The Whiskey Rebellion: Frontier Epilogue to the American Revolution* (New York, 1986), 30–59, 155–163; James E. Lewis, *The American Union and the Problem of Neighborhood: The United States and the Collapse of the Spanish Empire, 1783–1829* (Chapel Hill, N.C., 1998), esp. chap. 1.

51. Griffin, *American Leviathan.*

52. Tardiveau to François Hector, baron de Carondelet, Kaskasia, July 17, 1792, in Lawrence Kinnaird, ed., *Spain in the Mississippi Valley, 1765–1794,* 3 parts (vols. 2–4 of *American Historical Association Annual Report for 1945* [Washington, D.C., 1946–1949]), part 3, *Problems of Frontier Defense, 1792–1794,* 61.

53. James White to Louisiana Governor Estevan Miró, New Orleans, April 18, 1789, in ibid., vol. 3, *Post War Decade, 1782–1791,* 268; see also "Miró's Offer to Western Americans" (April 29, 1789), ibid., 269–271.

54. Arthur Preston Whitaker, in *The Spanish-American Frontier: 1783–1795* (Boston, 1927), 68, described Spanish policy after 1783 as one of "strangling the American west."

55. Weber, *Spanish Frontier,* 284; Remini, *Andrew Jackson,* 29–32.

56. "From the Knoxville *Gazette,* dated Wednesday, October 10," *Claypoole's Daily Advertiser* [Philadelphia], November 1, 1792.

57. Weber, *Spanish Frontier,* 285–287.

58. Tardiveau to Carondelet, July 17, 1792, in Kinnaird, *Spain in the Mississippi Valley,* part 3, 65.

59. O'Fallon to Miró, Lexington, July 16, 1790, in Kinnaird, *Spain in the Mississippi Valley,* part 2, *Post War Decade, 1782–1791,* 360.

60. Fairplay, "For the Columbian Sentinel" (Cambridge, February 15), *General Advertiser* [Philadelphia], March 3, 1794.

61. "The Anas. 1791–1806. Selections" (February 4, 1818), in Peterson, *Thomas Jefferson,* 689; *Daily Advertiser* [New York], January 3, 1794.

62. "Reply to the Representations of Affairs in America by British Newspapers" (n.d. [before November 20, 1784]), in ibid., 571–574.

63. Sheffield, *Observations,* 198–199.

64. *Mr. Charles Pinckney's Speech, in Answer to Mr. Jay, Secretary for Foreign Affairs, on the Question of a Treaty with Spain, Delivered in Congress, August 16, 1786* ([New York], [1786]), unpaginated broadside (p. 4).

65. George Washington, *A Circular Letter from His Excellency General Washington, to the Several States* (Annapolis, Md., 1783), 12. A different version with minor variations in punctuation is reprinted in Rhodehamel, *George Washington,* 516–526.

66. *Three Letters Addressed to the Public,* 8.

67. For the Loyalists generally, see Keith Mason, "The American Loyalist Diaspora and the Reconfiguration of the British Atlantic World," in *Empire and Nation: The American Revolution in the Atlantic World,* ed. Eliga H. Gould and Peter S. Onuf (Baltimore, 2005), 239–259; Maya Jasanoff, "The Other Side of Revolution: Loyalists in the British Empire," *William & Mary Quarterly,* 3rd ser, 65 (2008): 205–232.

68. "The Treaty of Paris" (September 3, 1783), article V, in Greene, *Colonies to Nation,* 421.

69. *An Address from the Committee Appointed at Mrs. Vandewater's on the 13th Day of September, 1784. To the People of the State of New-York* (New York, 1784), 3.

70. *Arguments and Judgment of the Mayor's Court of the City of New-York, in a Cause between Elizabeth Rutgers and Joshua Waddington* (New York, 1784), 24–25.

71. Bond to Lord Carmarthen, Philadelphia, July 2, 1787, in Jameson, "Letters of Phineas Bond," vol. 1, 539.

72. *Debate of the Commons of Great-Britain on the Articles of Peace. Monday, Feb. 17, 1783* (London, 1783), 6.

73. [Andrew Kippis], *Considerations on the Provisional Treaty with America, and the Preliminary Articles of Peace with France and Spain* (London, 1783), 53.

74. Ibid., 54. See also Eliga H. Gould, *The Persistence of Empire: British Political Culture in the Age of the American Revolution* (Chapel Hill, N.C., 2000), chap. 6; Stephen Conway, "From Fellow-Nationals to Foreigners: British Perceptions of the Americans, Circa 1739–1783," *William and Mary Quarterly,* 3rd ser., 59 (2002): 65–110.

75. Daniel L. Schafer, "The Memoir of Mary (Port) Macklin," *Escribano* 41 (2004): 113; James G. Cusick, "John Macklin, Loyalist," *Escribano* 41 (2004): 125. See also James G. Cusick, "Two People, Two Stories," *Escribano* 41 (2004): 97–105.

76. [Joseph Galloway], *Observations on the Fifth Article of the Treaty with America. . . . To Which Is Added, an Appendix, Stating Some Important Facts Relative to the Conduct of Congress, &C* ([London], 1783), 22–25, 45.

77. Ramsay, *History of the American Revolution,* vol. 2, 622–623.

78. Adams to John Jay, Grosvenor Square, May 25, 1786, in *The Diplomatic Correspondence of the United States of America, from the Signing of the Definitive Treaty of Peace, 10th September, 1783, to the Adoption of the Constitution, March 4, 1789* (Washington, D.C., 1833–1834), 5:120–121.

79. The literature on the Articles of Confederation and the Constitution is vast. For the interpretation here and in the following pages, I am indebted to Deudney, "The Philadelphian System," 191–228; Hendrickson, *Peace Pact;* Peter S. Onuf, *The Origins of the Federal Republic: Jurisdictional Controversies in the United States, 1775–1787* (Philadelphia, 1983); Peter S. Onuf, *Statehood and Union: A History of the Northwest Ordinance* (Bloomington, Ind., 1987).

80. No. 3, in Clinton Rossiter, ed., *The Federalist Papers* (New York, 1961), 42–45.

81. No. 4, in ibid., 49.

82. Ibid., 47.

83. No. 11, in ibid., 90.

84. No. 41, in ibid., 256.

85. No. 42, in ibid., 265.

86. No. 80, in ibid., 476.

87. [Richard Henry Lee], *Letters from the Federal Farmer to the Republican* (1787–1788), in *Empire and Nation: Letters from a Farmer in Pennsylvania, John Dickinson, [and] Letters from the Federal Farmer, Richard Henry Lee,* 2nd ed., ed. Forrest McDonald (Indianapolis, 1999), 103, 110.

88. Higginson to Henry Knox, Boston, February 8, 1787, in Jameson, "Letters of Stephen Higginson," vol. 1, 745–746.

89. [Jonathan Jackson], *Thoughts upon the Political Situation of the United States of America in Which That of Massachusetts Is More Particularly Considered* (Worcester, Mass., 1788), 45–46.

90. The reference here is to Hendrickson, *Peace Pact.* See also Deudney, "The Philadelphian System," 191–228.

91. [Jackson], *Thoughts upon the Political Situation,* 19–20.

92. John Adams, *A Defence of the Constitutions of Government of the United States of America* (London, 1787), 1:362–364. The first volume, which Adams finished before the Philadelphia Convention met in June, initially appeared as a stand-alone London publication.

93. Ibid., vol.3, 505–506.

94. Elkins and McKitrick, *Age of Federalism,* 31–34, 50–75.

95. Higginson to Henry Knox, Boston, April 7, 1790, in Jameson, "Letters of Stephen Higginson," vol. 1, 782.

96. *Daily Advertiser,* May 1, 1789, 2.

97. The most thorough treatment of the insurrection is Slaughter, *Whiskey Rebellion.* See also Elkins and McKittrick, *Age of Federalism,* 461–488; Griffin, *American Leviathan,* 222–239, 244–245.

98. Hammond to Lord Grenville, New York, August 29, 1794, FO 5/5, 265–266, BNA.

99. William Findley, *History of the Insurrection in the Four Western Counties of Pennsylvania* (Philadelphia, 1796), 163. See also Slaughter, *Whiskey Rebellion,* 212–217.

100. Quoted in Elkins and McKitrick, *Age of Federalism,* 481.

101. Paul Swain Havens, *Chambersburg, Frontier Town, 1730–1794* (Chambersburg, Pa., 1975), 194–195.

102. Quoted in Elkins and McKitrick, *Age of Federalism,* 481.

103. *Philadelphia Minerva,* July 4, 1795, 3.

104. For an overview of the two agreements, see Perkins, *Creation of a Republican Empire,* 95–101.

105. *Philadelphia Minerva,* July 4, 1795, 3. For a brief account of the riots in Philadelphia and New York, see Elkins and McKitrick, *Age of Federalism,* 420–421.

106. Jackson to Nathaniel Macon, Nashville, October 4, 1795, in Smith and Owsley, *Papers of Andrew Jackson,* vol. 1, 74.

107. [William Cobbett], *A Little Plain English, Addressed to the People of the United States on the Treaty, Negociated with His Britannic Majesty, and on the Conduct of the President Relative Thereto. . . . By Peter Porcupine* (Philadelphia, 1795), 76–77,

82–83. Bache's support for impeaching Washington is mentioned throughout the pamphlet, 80.

108. "Extract of a Letter from a Gentleman of Character and Information in Vermont" (July 18, 1795), [New York] *American Minerva,* July 24, 1795.

109. [Cobbett], *A Little Plain English,* 102.

110. Ibid., 23–24, 26, 101–102.

111. Murray to James McHenry, August 21, 1796, in Bernard C. Steiner, *The Life and Correspondence of James McHenry, Secretary of War under Washington and Adams* (Cleveland, 1907), 174.

112. *Columbian Centinel,* August 3, 1796, quoted in Bradford Perkins, *The First Rapprochement: England and the United States, 1795–1805* (Berkeley, Calif., 1967 [orig. pub., 1955]), 48.

113. McHenry to Washington, June 28, 1796, quoted in Steiner, *Life and Correspondence,* 173–174. For Lewis's instructions, see McHenry to Lewis, War Office, May [10–11], 1796, Detroit Public Library, James McHenry Papers, in *Papers of the War Department, 1784–1800,* Center for History and New Media, George Mason University, http://wardepartmentpapers.org, accessed September 13, 2011.

114. Louise Phelps Kellogg, *The British Régime in Wisconsin and the Northwest* (Madison, Wisc., 1935), 235.

115. *Federal Gazette,* August 11, 1796, quoted in ibid., 234.

116. Lord Grenville to Robert Liston (no. 12), October 7, 1796, FO 5/14, 41, BNA.

117. Pickering to King, August 29, 1796, in *1784–1820,* vol. 1 of *Diplomatic Correspondence of the United States: Canadian Relations,* ed. William R. Manning (Washington, D.C., 1940), 100.

118. Bruff to William Simmons, Niagara, September 20, 1796, National Archives and Records Administration, Rev War Service Claims Files, RG217, in *Papers of the War Department.*

119. Major John Jacob Rivardi to Alexander Hamilton, April 3, 1799, Library of Congress, Alexander Hamilton Papers, in *Papers of the War Department.*

120. Bruff to William Simmons, Niagara, September 20, 1796, National Archives and Records Administration, Rev War Service Claims Files, RG217, in *Papers of the War Department.*

121. Zephaniah Swift Moore, *A Thanksgiving Sermon Delivered at Peterborough, in New Hampshire, November 17, 1796* (Keene, N.H., 1797), 13–14.

122. See, esp., Griffin, *American Leviathan.*

123. Lacassagne to Carondelet, Louisville, October 1, 1794, in Kinnaird, *Spain in the Mississippi Valley,* part 3, 351.

124. Liston to Grenville, Philadelphia, January 25, 1797, FO 5/4, 59, BNA.

125. Curtis P. Nettels, *The Emergence of a National Economy, 1775–1815* (New York, 1962), 233.

126. Ibid., 233–234.

127. Reinoehl, "Some Remarks," 92–93. Crowninshield wrote his remarks at the request of Secretary of State James Madison.

128. Quoted in Elkins and McKitrick, *Age of Federalism,* 483–484.

129. Stephen Aron, *How the West Was Lost: The Transformation of Kentucky from Daniel Boone to Henry Clay* (Baltimore, 1996).

5. A SLAVEHOLDING REPUBLIC

1. Paul Cuffe, journal entries for February 15–16, 1812, in Sheldon H. Harris, *Paul Cuffe: Black America and the African Return* (New York, 1972), 139–141. The spelling in Harris's volume has been modernized; for an account that retains Cuffe's original spelling, see Rosalind Cobb Wiggins, ed., *Captain Paul Cuffe's Logs and Letters, 1808–1817: A Black Quaker's "Voice from within the Veil"* (Washington, D.C., 1996), 196–198.

2. Paul Cuffe, *A Brief Account of the Settlement and Present Situation of the Colony of Sierra Leone* (Nendeln, Liechtenstein, 1970 [orig. publ., 1812]), 3. For black seamen generally, see W. Jeffrey Bolster, *Black Jacks: African American Seamen in the Age of Sail* (Cambridge, Mass., 1997).

3. Harris, *Paul Cuffe,* 100, 105, 176 (quoting letter of July 1, 1812, from Thomas Clarkson and William Allen).

4. Peter Williams, *A Discourse, Delivered on the Death of Capt. Paul Cuffe, Before the New-York African Institution, in the African Methodist Episcopal Church, October 21, 1817* (New York, 1817), 12–13, reprinted with Cuffe, *Brief Account.*

5. David Waldstreicher, *Slavery's Constitution: From Revolution to Ratification* (New York, 2009). See also Don E. Fehrenbacher, *The Slaveholding Republic: An Account of the United States Government's Relations to Slavery* (Oxford, 2001), 10–11, 40–47; William M. Wiecek, *The Sources of Antislavery Constitutionalism in America, 1760–1848* (Ithaca, N.Y., 1977), 15–16.

6. See, for example, the complaints about Puerto Rico's role as a sanctuary for slaves escaping British masters in the Leeward Islands in Board to Trade to Lord Holderness, May 22, 1754, CO 154/41, 63–68, BNA; see also Jane Landers, *Black Society in Spanish Florida* (Urbana, Ill., 1999).

7. Laurent Dubois, *Avengers of the New World: The Story of the Haitian Revolution* (Cambridge, Mass., 2004).

8. Board of Trade to Lord Holderness, April 22, 1757, CO 152/41, 84–87, BNA.

9. Robin Blackburn, *The Making of New World Slavery: From the Baroque to the Modern, 1492–1800* (London and New York, 1997), 303–304.

10. "Extract of a Letter from Liverpool, June 24," *London Chronicle,* June 27, 1775; see also Philip D. Morgan and Andrew Jackson O'Shaughnessy, "Arming Slaves in the American Revolution," in *Arming Slaves: From Classical Times to the Modern Age,* ed. Christopher Leslie Brown and Philip D. Morgan (New Haven, Conn., 2006), 188–190.

11. The best and most thorough treatment of black fugitives during the Revolutionary War is Sylvia R. Frey, *Water from the Rock: Black Resistance in a Revolutionary Age* (Princeton, N.J., 1991), which puts the total losses to British forces, including both runaway and "sequestered slaves," at between eighty and one hundred thousand

(211). For similar estimates, see Benjamin Quarles, *The Negro in the American Revolution* (Chapel Hill, N.C., 1961), 18–31; James W. St. G. Walker, *The Black Loyalists: The Search for a Promised Land in Nova Scotia and Sierra Leone, 1783–1870* (New York, 1976), 3; Ellen Gibson Wilson, *The Loyal Blacks* (New York, 1976), 21. Cassandra Pybus, in "Jefferson's Faulty Math: The Question of Slave Defections in the American Revolution," *William and Mary Quarterly,* 3rd ser., 62, no. 2 (2005): 243–264, has recently suggested that these figures are exaggerated and that the number of voluntary fugitives was closer to twenty to twenty-five thousand. As Frey notes (p. 211), such discrepancies are probably less important than the "general changes that [the slaves'] departures produced."

12. Evangeline Walker Andrews, ed., in collaboration with Charles McLean Andrews, *Journal of a Lady of Quality: Being the Narrative of a Journey from Scotland to the West Indies, North Carolina, and Portugal, in the Years 1774 to 1776,* 2nd ed. (New Haven, Conn., 1934), 198, 200. See also Morgan and O'Shaughnessy, "Arming Slaves," in Brown and Morgan, *Arming Slaves,* 188–190; Woody Holton, *Forced Founders: Indians, Debtors, Slaves, and the Making of the American Revolution in Virginia* (Chapel Hill, N.C., 1999). For the response in South Carolina, see J. William Harris, *The Hanging of Thomas Jeremiah: A Free Black Man's Encounter with Liberty* (New Haven, Conn., 2009), chap. 4.

13. *Public Advertiser,* May 17, 1776.

14. Andrews, *Journal of a Lady of Quality,* 200.

15. "Extract of a Letter from Philadelphia, Dec. 6," *Morning Chronicle,* January 20, 1776.

16. John Cruden, "Sketch of a Plan for Arming the Negroes" (Charles Town, January 5, 1782), in George Livermore, *An Historical Research Respecting the Opinions of the Founders of the Republic on Negroes as Slaves, as Citizens, and as Soldiers,* 3rd ed. (Boston, 1863).

17. [William Sir Draper], *The Thoughts of a Traveller Upon Our American Disputes* (London, 1774), 21.

18. Cruden to Lord Dunmore, Charles Town, January 5, 1782, in Livermore, *Historical Research,* 143.

19. David Ramsay, *The History of the Revolution of South-Carolina from a British Province to an Independent State* (Trenton, N.J., 1785), 2:3.

20. Jefferson to Gordon, Paris, July 16, 1788, in Thomas Jefferson Randolph, ed., *Memoir, Correspondence, and Miscellanies, from the Papers of Thomas Jefferson* (Charlottesville, Va., 1829), 2:334–335. According to Pybus, "Jefferson's Faulty Math," 245–246, Jefferson actually lost twenty-three slaves from three different plantations, all of whom fled on their own. Pybus estimates that the total number of voluntary fugitives in the Upper South (including Maryland) between 1775 and 1781 was six thousand (p. 258). On the sequestration of slaves captured on rebel farms and plantations, see Frey, *Water from the Rock,* 122–124.

21. Ramsay, *History of the Revolution,* vol. 2, 31–33, 67.

22. Treaty of Paris (September 3, 1783), in Jack P. Greene, ed., *Colonies to Nation, 1763–1789: A Documentary History of the American Revolution* (New York, 1975), 422.

23. Carl Leopold Baurmeister, *Revolution in America. Confidential Letters and Journals, 1776–1784,* trans. Bernhard A. Uhlendorf (New Brunswick, N.J., 1957), 569.

24. Boston King, "Memoirs of the Life of Boston King, a Black Preacher," in *The Methodist Magazine for the Year 1798; Being a Confirmation of the Arminian Magazine* (London, 1798), 21:157.

25. Walker, *Black Loyalists,* 9. See also Frey, *Water from the Rock,* 174–179; Wilson, *Loyal Blacks,* 44–47.

26. George Washington, "Letters of George Washington Bearing on the Negro," *Journal of Negro History* 2 (1917): 418.

27. Frey, *Water from the Rock,* 176.

28. Second quote in ibid., 193.

29. "Negroes, 1794–1800," Chatham Papers, PRO 30/8/344, quoted in ibid., 193.

30. Lt. General Alexander Leslie to General Sir Guy Carleton, Charleston, June 27, 1782, in Royal Commission on Historical Manuscripts [Great Britain], *Report on American Manuscripts in the Royal Institution of Great Britain* (London, 1904–1909), 2:544.

31. Leslie to Carleton, Charleston, "Secret," October 18, 1782, in ibid., vol. 3, 175–176.

32. Certificate of Joseph Clayton, May 5, 1783, quoted in Wilson, *Loyal Blacks,* 50. For the king's approbation, see North to Carleton, August 8, 1783, CO 5/110, 62–72, and December 4, 1783, CO 5/111, 92, BNA.

33. King, "Memoirs," 157.

34. Thomas Jones, *History of New York During the Revolutionary War, and of the Leading Events in the Other Colonies at That Period,* ed. Edward Floyd de Lancey (New York, 1879), 2:256–257.

35. Frey, *Water from the Rock,* 191–192.

36. Quoted in Christopher Leslie Brown, *Moral Capital: Foundations of British Abolitionism* (Chapel Hill, N.C., 2006), 311.

37. Ibid., 312.

38. "Précis relative to Negroes," CO 5/8, 112–114, BNA, quoted in Simon Schama, *Rough Crossings: Britain, the Slaves, and the American Revolution* (New York, 2006), 151.

39. Keith Mason, "The American Loyalist Diaspora and the Reconfiguration of the British Atlantic World," in *Empire and Nation: The American Revolution in the Atlantic World,* ed. Eliga H. Gould and Peter S. Onuf (Baltimore, 2005), 254–255; Schama, *Rough Crossings,* 50; Wilson, *Loyal Blacks,* 50.

40. Schama, *Rough Crossings,* 151.

41. David Walker and Henry Highland Garnet, *Walker's Appeal, with a Brief Sketch of His Life* (New York, 1848), 54. For more on Walker, see Van Gosse, "'As a Nation, the English Are Our Friends': The Emergence of African American Politics in the British Atlantic World, 1772–1861," *American Historical Review* 113 (2008): 1003.

42. Charles Bernhard Wadstrom et al., *Plan for a Free Community Upon the Coast of Africa under the Protection of Great Britain; but Intirely Independant of All European Laws and Governments* (London, 1789), xiii–xiv.

43. Thornton to Lettsom, Newport, Rhode Island, February 15, 1787, in Thomas Joseph Pettigrew, ed., *Memoirs of the Life and Writings of the Late John Coakley Lettsom, with a Selection from His Correspondence* (London, 1817), 2:515; Granville Sharp, *A Short Sketch of Temporary Regulations (until Better Shall Be Proposed) for the Intended Settlement on the Grain Coast of Africa, near Sierra Leona,* 2nd ed. (London, 1786), 3, 1–9. Although the Sierra Leone Company nullified parts of Sharp's constitution in 1792, women retained the right to vote and could occupy the local offices of Hundredors and Tythingmen until 1797: Christopher Fyfe, *A History of Sierra Leone,* 2nd rev. ed. (Oxford, 1963), 102.

44. Walker, *Black Loyalists,* 99; Cassandra Pybus, *Epic Journeys of Freedom: Runaway Slaves of the American Revolution and Their Global Quest for Liberty* (Boston, 2006), 139–140.

45. Walker, *Black Loyalists,* 137, 242.

46. Fyfe, *History of Sierra Leone,* 63, 84–85, 99.

47. Ibid., 102–103; Schama, *Rough Crossings,* 395; Pybus, *Epic Journeys,* 215.

48. Cuffe to Allen, April 22, 1811, in Wiggins, *Captain Paul Cuffe's Logs and Letters,* 118–119. For the encounters with Reid, Francis, and Simpson, see Cuffe's journal entries for March 12, April 2, and November 23, 1811, in Harris, *Paul Cuffe,* 83, 86, 113.

49. Journal entry for June 18, 1793, in Margaret Jean Trevelyan Viscountess Knutsford, ed., *Life and Letters of Zachary Macaulay* (London, 1900), 28.

50. "Manuscript Orders and Regulations from the Directors of the Sierra Leone Company to the Superintendant and Council for the Settlement" (c. 1791), in L. E. C. Evans, "An Early Constitution of Sierra Leone," *Sierra Leone Studies* 18 (1932): 60.

51. Weaver to Granville Sharp, Sierra Leone, April 23, 1788, in Prince Hoare, ed., *Memoirs of Granville Sharp, Esq. Composed from His Own Manuscripts and from Other Authentic Documents,* rev. ed., (London, 1828), 2:97. (See also James Reid to Sharp, Sierra Leone, September, 1788, ibid, 97.) For conflicts after the company assumed direct responsibility for the province's government in 1791, see Wilson, *Loyal Blacks,* 309–321.

52. Journal entry for August 3, 1793, in Viscountess Knutsford, *Life and Letters,* 43.

53. For Macaulay's account of the episode, see his journal entries in ibid., 60–65, 74. On September 8, 1794—after he had allowed the two slaves to remain at Freetown but before Newell returned with the French privateers—Macaulay wrote that a ship from the West Indies had reported that "liberty had been proclaimed to the French slaves in the West Indies; and that America had wholly abolished the Slave Trade" (p. 63). While leaving open the slave trade to the United States, Congress had prohibited American merchants from carrying slaves to foreign destinations.

54. Jay to Wilberforce, January 28, 1795, in Robert Isaac Wilberforce and Samuel Wilberforce, eds., *The Correspondence of William Wilberforce* (London, 1840), 1:118. It is unclear which of the company's reports were in the letter to which Jay was responding. From Jay's reply, in which he mentions the "pleasure" with which he read the report, and the date of his letter, it seems unlikely that the report that Wilberforce sent referred directly to Newell's role in the raid. But the Sierra Leone Company

reports for 1794 and 1795 both contain accounts of "depredations" and other acts of hostility by American traders against the settlement.

55. Representation to the American government (undated draft) and Macaulay, "Memorial" (February 9, 1795), in Grenville to Ambassador George Hammond, Downing Street, London, April 15, 1795, in FO 5/9, 14–15, 18, BNA.

56. Landers, *Black Society*, 79–80; Donald R. Hickey, "America's Response to the Slave Revolt in Haiti, 1791–1806," *Journal of the Early Republic* 2 (1982): 364

57. "Parliamentary Proceedings, House of Commons," *World,* May 13, 1789. For more on Wilberforce's parliamentary campaign, see David Brion Davis, *The Problem of Slavery in the Age of Revolution, 1770–1823* (Ithaca, N.Y., 1975), 114–118.

58. Davis, *Problem of Slavery,* 24–29; Gary B. Nash, *Race and Revolution* (Madison, Wisc., 1990), chap. 1. As discussed below, South Carolina repealed its ban between 1803 and 1804.

59. Northwest Ordinance (July 13, 1787), article VI, and the Constitution of the United States (September 17, 1787), article I, section 9, in Greene, *Colonies to Nation,* 474, 551.

60. James Forten, *Letters from a Man of Colour on a Late Bill Before the Senate of Pennsylvania* (Philadelphia, 1813), in Nash, *Race and Revolution,* 190.

61. Luther Martin, "Genuine Information," *Maryland Gazette,* January 22, 1788, in ibid., 142; for the international dimensions of American antislavery, see also Matthew Mason, "Keeping up Appearances: The International Politics of Slave Trade Abolition in the Nineteenth-Century Atlantic World," *William and Mary Quarterly,* 3rd ser., 66, no. 4 (2009): 809–832.

62. [David Cooper], *A Serious Address to the Rulers of America on the Inconsistency of Their Conduct Respecting Slavery* (Trenton, N.J., 1783), 17–18. The preamble to the Pennsylvania Act for the Gradual Abolition of Slavery (1780) justified emancipation as a natural extension of the state's struggle against "the arms and tyranny of Great Britain": *An Act for the Gradual Abolition of Slavery* (Philadelphia, 1781), 1.

63. Nash, *Race and Revolution,* 10–17.

64. See, for example, letter from Veritas, February 3, 1794, Providence, *United States Chronicle,* February 6, 1794: "If any persons . . . can invalidate the redundancy of evidence exhibited in the House of Commons . . . they are invited, they are *challenged to do it.* Let them *manfully* enter the lists against the celebrated names of Clarkson, Wilberforce, Pitt, Fox, Burke, Thornton, Sharpe, &c. of England, and against a Jay, Ramsey, Jefferson, Pinkney, Edwards, &c., &c., of America."

65. "Remarks of James Wilson in the Pennsylvania Convention to Ratify the Constitution of the United States, 1787," in *Lectures on Law,* vol. 1 of *Collected Works of James Wilson,* ed. Kermit Hall and Mark David Hall (Indianapolis, 2007), 241.

66. *Constitution of the Maryland Society for Promoting the Abolition of Slavery, and the Relief of Free Negroes, and Others, Unlawfully Held in Bondage* (Baltimore, 1789), 3. Given the date of the meeting, September 8, 1789, the delegates would almost certainly have been aware of Wilberforce's parliamentary speech of May 12, 1789, and they were surely also thinking of the Amis des Noirs.

67. Davis, *Problem of Slavery,* 24–32; Nash, *Race and Revolution,* 9–20.

68. St. George Tucker, "On the State of Slavery in Virginia," from Tucker, ed., *Black-stone's Commentaries* (Philadelphia, 1803), in St. George Tucker, *View of the Constitution of the United States, with Selected Writings,* ed. Clyde Norman Wilson (Indianapolis, 1999), 406, 411, 433n, 434. Tucker first published the plan as a stand-alone pamphlet: St. George Tucker, *A Dissertation on Slavery, with a Proposal for the Gradual Abolition of It, in the State of Virginia* (Philadelphia, 1796).

69. Jefferson, "Sixth Annual Message," December 2, 1806, in *Thomas Jefferson, Writings,* vol. 15 of *The Library of America,* ed. Merrill D. Peterson, ed. (New York, 1984), 528.

70. *Annals of Congress,* 9th Cong., 2d Sess. (1806), 171.

71. Fehrenbacher, *The Slaveholding Republic,* 143.

72. "The Slave Trade," *Washington Expositor,* January 16, 1808.

73. *Providence Gazette,* December 26, 1807.

74. Jefferson, "Sixth Annual Message," December 2, 1806, in Peterson, *Thomas Jefferson,* 528.

75. Jefferson, "Reply to the British Newspapers" (1784), in ibid., 572. For the later estimate, see Jefferson to Gordon, July 16, 1788, in Randolph, *Memoir,* vol. 2, 335. In 1784 the Virginia General Assembly adopted a resolution tying repeal of the laws inhibiting the recovery of British debts to reparation for the slaves that Carleton carried off; in 1787 it passed an act suspending the laws against British debtors, but it specified that the law would not go into effect until Britain compensated the masters of the former slaves. See *A Message of the President of the United States to Congress Relative to France and Great-Britain, Delivered December 5, 1793, with the Papers Therein Referred To* (Philadelphia, 1793), nos. 30 and 39 (pp. 86–87, 91).

76. Ramsay, *History of the Revolution,* vol. 2, 66–67, 384. The war's costs in both Virginia and the Carolinas were significant. In South Carolina the British occupation and slave unrest that accompanied it dealt the economy a blow from which the Low Country never recovered, ending the region's dominance of the Atlantic rice trade and opening the way for a growing dependence on northern bankers and merchants: see Frey, *Water from the Rock,* 208–211; Robert Olwell, *Masters, Slaves, and Subjects: The Culture of Power in the South Carolina Low Country, 1740–1790* (Ithaca, N.Y., 1998), 271–283.

77. For the controversy over how many slaves fled to British lines or were taken by British and Loyalist forces during the Revolutionary War, see the discussion above. Part of the disagreement among modern scholars turns on how much credence to give the estimates advanced by slaveholders like Jefferson and Ramsay.

78. "Extracts from Mr. Adams' Journal respecting peace" (entries for November 17 and 29, 1782), and "Extracts of Letters from Doctor Franklin, to the honorable R. R. Livingstone, Esq., Secretary for foreign affairs" (October 14 and December 5, 1782), in *Message of the President,* nos. 9 and 10 (pp. 72–73, 75).

79. Adams to John Jay, Westminster, June 6, 1785, in *The Diplomatic Correspondence of the United States of America, from the Signing of the Definitive Treaty of Peace, 10th September, 1783, to the Adoption of the Constitution, March 4, 1789* (Washington, D.C., 1833–1834), 4:206.

80. Adams to Jay, Westminster, August 25, 1785, in ibid., vol. 4, 336.

81. "At a meeting of a number of the Citizens of Savannah . . . Saturday, the 25th of July, 1795," *Georgia Gazette,* August 6, 1795.

82. Randolph to Jay, Philadelphia, December 15, 1794, in *ASP: Foreign Relations,* 1:510. Randolph based his argument on the principles of postliminy (or postliminium), which he appears to have taken from Vattel: see Emer de Vattel, *The Law of Nations, or, Principles of the Law of Nature, Applied to the Conduct and Affairs of Nations and Sovereigns,* ed. Bela Kapossy and Richard Whatmore (Indianapolis, 2008; [orig. publ., London, 1797 [Thomas Nugent, trans.]), book iii, chap. xiv, §209 (pp. 605–606). Noting the difficulty of proving ownership of anything but fixed property, Vattel exempted most movables from the rights of postliminium because of "the endless disputes which would arise from the prosecution of the owners' claims to them." Because it was always "easy to recognize a slave and to ascertain to whom he belonged," however, slaves were an exception. Ironically, the right of postliminium extended to prisoners of war, who were entitled to their liberty once the war was over; in this capacity, it represented one of the chief bulwarks against enslaving prisoners from civilized nations (§217 [p. 610]).

83. Worthington C. Ford et al., eds., *Journals of the Continental Congress, 1774–1789* (Washington, D.C., 1904–1937), vol. 31, *August 1—December 31, 1786,* 863, 866–867. During the Jay Treaty negotiation, Lord Grenville suggested that Britain could claim a property right to fleeing slaves in wartime analogous to the right that a belligerent might claim to a stray horse that had wandered into its lines. In so doing, of course, Grenville affirmed the position of both Carleton at New York in 1783 and the American government into the 1790s that the black Loyalists owed their freedom, in part, to their status as property of the British Crown: Jay to Randolph, London, February 6, 1795, in *ASP: Foreign Relations,* 1:517. See also the summary of the American view of Carleton's position in Egbert Benson, William S. Smith, and Daniel Parker, Commissioners, to Washington, New York, January 18, 1794, in *Message of the President,* part 2, 8–9.

84. Jay to Randolph, London, September 13, 1794, in *ASP: Foreign Relations,* 1:486.

85. Randolph to Jay, Philadelphia, December 15, 1794, in ibid., 1:510.

86. Ibid.

87. Jay to Randolph, London, September 13, 1794, in *ASP: Foreign Relations,* 1:485.

88. [William Loughton Smith], *The Eyes Opened, or the Carolinians Convinced, by an Honourable and Eloquent Representative in the Congress of the United States* (New York, 1795), 16.

89. [Brockholst Livingston], "Decius," no. 4, in *The American Remembrancer; or, an Impartial Collection of Essays, Resolves, Speeches, &Tc. Relative . . . To the Treaty with Great Britain,* ed. Mathew Carey (Philadelphia, 1795–1796), vol. 2, no. 6, 133. In arriving at the higher figure, Livingston assumed that Carleton's officers had removed more former slaves than the ones named in his "Book of Negroes." By contrast, South Carolina Federalist Robert Goodloe Harper put the total number of former slaves at two thousand and assumed that Carleton's records were accurate. See Robert Goodloe Harper, *An Address from Robert Goodloe Harper, of South-Carolina,*

to His Constituents, Containing His Reasons for Approving of the Treaty of Amity, Commerce and Navigation, with Great-Britain (Philadelphia, 1795), 17. In calculating the total worth of the two estimates, Livingston used an average value of $250 per slave, while Harper used an average of $200. On Livingston's authorship of the five "Decius" essays, which appeared in the *New York Argus* in July 1795, see Todd Estes, *The Jay Treaty Debate, Public Opinion, and the Evolution of Early American Political Culture* (Amherst, Mass., 2006), 246, n28.

90. "Letter II, on the Treaty," *Providence Gazette,* August 8, 1795. See also Harper, *Address,* 17. The South Carolina politician, who put the value of the slaves in question at $400,000 asked: "Is this a sum for two countries to quarrel about? A war of three months would cost as much."

91. Fehrenbacher, *Slaveholding Republic,* 93; Landers, *Black Society,* 79–80.

92. Monroe and Pinkney to James Madison, London, January 3 and April 25, 1807, in *ASP: Foreign Relations,* 3:146, 173.

93. Bradford Perkins, *The Creation of a Republican Empire, 1776–1865,* vol. 1 of *The Cambridge History of American Foreign Relations,* ed. Warren I. Cohen (Cambridge, 1993; reprint, 1995), 124–125; see also, Donald R. Hickey, "The Monroe-Pinkney Treaty of 1806: A Reappraisal," *William and Mary Quarterly,* 3rd ser., 44 (1987): 65–88.

94. Madison did so in response to the English High Court of Admiralty's affirmation in 1810 of the condemnation of the South Carolina slave ship *Amedie* at the end of 1807 (discussed below). See the editorial notes in Benjamin Rush to Madison, Philadelphia, October 29, 1810, in *1 October 1809—2 November 1810,* vol. 2 of *The Papers of James Madison: Presidential Series,* ed. Robert Allen Rutland (Charlottesville, Va., 1984–), 601–602, esp. n2.

95. For naval reports of illegal American slave traders, see Secretary of the Treasury, Oliver Wolcott, to Benjamin Lincoln, Philadelphia, June 10, 1799; Secretary of the Navy, Benjamin Stoddert, to Wolcott, Philadelphia, April 18, 1800, in *Naval Documents Related to the Quasi-War between the United States and France,* 7 vols. (Washington, D.C., 1935–1938), vol. 3, *April 1799 to July 1799,* 323; vol. 5, *January 1800 to May 1800,* 426. On the navy's response to the law authorizing seizure of illegal slave ships, see Stoddert to Lt. John Smith, Washington, D.C., February 4, 1801, in ibid., vol. 7, *December 1800 to December 1801,* 116.

96. Elaine Forman Crane, ed., *The Diary of Elizabeth Drinker* (Boston, 1991), 2:1327 (entry for August 5, 1800). That same summer, it was reported that when Captain William Maley arrived at Philadelphia after capturing the Havana-bound Charleston slave ship *Betsey,* he was greeted "with the applause of all," with some people demanding death for "the monsters that planned the voyage": Captain Hodgdon to Timothy Pickering, Philadelphia, July 10, 1800, in *Naval Documents,* vol. 6, *June 1800 to November 1800,* 133.

97. Turell Tufts to Secretary of State Timothy Pickering, Paramibo, Guyana, January 31, 1800, in *Naval Documents,* vol. 5, 156–157.

98. Roger T. Anstey, "The Volume of the North American Slave-Carrying Trade from Africa, 1761–1810," *Revue française d'histoire d'outre-mer* 62 (1975): 65.

99. George Coggeshall, *Thirty-Six Voyages to Various Parts of the World, Made between the Years 1799 and 1841,* 3rd rev. ed. (New York, 1858 [orig. publ., 1855]), 524.

100. Quoted in Joseph Marryat, *Thoughts on the Abolition of the Slave Trade and Civilization of Africa, with Remarks on the African Institution* (London, 1816), 42.

101. Stoddert to Jared Ingersol, Washington, D.C., August 8, 1800, in *Naval Documents,* vol. 6, 232.

102. Robert Sutcliff, *Travels in Some Parts of North America, in the Years 1804, 1805, & 1806,* 2nd ed. (York, 1815), 222.

103. Philip Norborne Nicholas to Governor James Monroe, February 11, 1801, doc. no. 125, in *The Border Colonies and the Southern Colonies,* vol. 4 of *Documents Illustrative of the History of the Slave Trade to America,* ed. Elizabeth Donnan (Washington, D.C., 1935), 166–167. The statute law in Virginia was a bit vague about how slaves imported illegally were to be disposed of, but in the case of the ship that prompted Nicholas's letter to Monroe, Donnan cites a subsequent letter suggesting that the thirty "condemned negroes" were eventually sold "to a place where there was no danger of their returning to Virginia" (p. 167, n2). In the act of 1778 abolishing the slave trade, Virginia stipulated that all slaves brought illegally into the state, including those brought from Africa and the West Indies, became free: ibid, 164–165 (doc. no. 123). Under revisions enacted in 1792 and 1793, the Virginia legislature removed the language freeing slaves imported from Africa and the West Indies and instead stipulated that they be "apprehended immediately and transported out of this commonwealth": *Abridgment of the Public Permanent Laws of Virginia* (Richmond, Va., 1796), 276, 283. In 1806 the legislature ordered that slaves brought into the state illegally "be delivered to the overseers of the poor and sold for cash": Donnan, *Documents,* vol. 4, 172.

104. Christopher Lloyd, *The Navy and the Slave Trade: The Supression of the African Slave Trade in the Nineteenth Century* (London, 1968), 275. Although vice-admiralty courts elsewhere in the British Atlantic occasionally condemned slave ships, the vast majority of condemnations were by the court at Sierra Leone. For a list of condemned ships, see "Vessels, Cargoes, and Slaves Proceeded against in the Court of Vice Admiralty at Sierra Leone between June 1808 and March 1817" (n.d.), HCA 49/97, BNA.

105. An Act for the Abolition of the Slave Trade (47 Geo. III, c. 36, sess. 1, March 25, 1807), doc. no. 301, in *The Eighteenth Century,* vol. 2 of *Documents Illustrative of the History of the Slave Trade to America,* ed. Elizabeth Donnan (Washington, D.C., 1931), 664.

106. Thomas Coke, *An Interesting Narrative of a Mission, Sent to Sierra Leone, in Africa, by the Methodists, in 1811* (London, 1812), 40.

107. Cuffe, journal entries for March 1 and 9, 1811, and January 4, 1812, in Harris, *Paul Cuffe,* 81–83, 126.

108. Allen and Clarkson to Cuffe, London, July 1, 1812, in ibid., 177–178. See also Fyfe, *History of Sierra Leone,* 106, 118–120; Tara Helfman, "The Court of Vice Admiralty at Sierra Leone and the Abolition of the West African Slave Trade," *Yale Law Journal* 115, no. 5 (2006): 1143.

109. Helfman, "The Court of Vice Admiralty at Sierra Leone," 1143; Fyfe, *History of Sierra Leone,* 136.

110. Robert Thorpe, *A Letter to William Wilberforce, Esq. . . . Containing Remarks on the Reports of the Sierra Leone Company, and African Institution, with Hints Respecting the Means by Which an Universal Abolition of the Slave Trade Might Be Carried into Effect,* 3rd ed. (London, 1815), 23–24.

111. Coke, *Interesting Narrative,* 39–40.

112. *Amedie,* 2 Acton 250–251 (1810) [Thomas Harman Acton, ed., *Reports of Cases Argued and Determined before . . . The Lords Commissioners of Appeals in Prize Causes,* vol. 1, *June 1809 to July 1810* (London, 1811), 250–251]. In the ruling, Grant noted that British judges had believed that the slave trade was illegal for some time, but as long as it was sanctioned by the laws of their own country, they had no right to take notice of violations of this principle by other countries.

113. Vattel, *Law of Nations,* book iii, chap. viii, §152 (p. 556); Thorpe, *Letter to William Wilberforce,* 27.

114. U.S. Secretary of State Robert Smith to Pinkney, June 16, 1810, in Rutland, *Papers of James Madison: Presidential,* vol. 2, 602, n2; see also Madison's Annual Message to Congress, December 5, 1780, in ibid.,vol. 3, *3 November 1810—4 Novemeber 1811,* 52–53.

115. See discussion at p. 121 (above); see also George Hammond to Lord Grenville, February 22, 1794, FO 5/4, 50, BNA.

116. Russell to Secretary of State James Monroe, London, September 17, 1812, in *ASP: Foreign Relations,* 3:594.

117. Henry Wheaton, *A Digest of the Law of Maritime Captures and Prizes* (New York, 1815), chap. vii, §16 (p. 229): "The first prohibits the traffic in men, the second prohibited the carrying of slaves from Africa to the West Indies and American colonies [of foreign nations], and the latter enabled a British prize court to enforce this double prohibition against an American citizen." A National Republican and protégé of Joseph Story, Wheaton did not elaborate on what he meant by the decision's "anomalous tendency"; in the preface, however, he made clear that he did not accept the "peculiar doctrines maintained by the British government" regarding the maritime rights of neutral powers (p. vi). Significantly, the foremost British statement of the doctrine that Wheaton depicted as "peculiar" (James Stephen, *War in Disguise; or, the Fraud of the Neutral Flags,* 3rd ed. [London, 1806]) distinguished between the American slave trade, which violated the laws of the United States, and the American trade with Britain's enemies, which did not.

118. [Charles Brockden Brown], *The British Treaty* (Philadelphia, 1807), 68, 70.

119. Charles Francis Adams, ed., *Memoirs of John Quincy Adams, Comprising Portions of His Diary from 1795 to 1848* (Philadelphia, 1874–1877), 6:37.

120. William Pinkney, *The Life of William Pinkney* (New York, 1853), 318.

121. Edward Rushton, *Expostulatory Letter to George Washington, of Mount Vernon, on His Continuing to Be a Holder of Slaves* (Lexington, Ky., 1797), 14.

122. Calhoun, "Speech on the Reception of Abolition Petitions" (1837), in *Speeches . . . Delivered in the House of Representatives and in the Senate of the United States,* vol. 2 of *The Works of John C. Calhoun,* ed. Richard K. Crallé (New York, 1864), 626.

123. Journal entries for April 29 ("southward man"), May 1 ("great knowledge"), May 5 ("power-headed man" and refusal of service at Baltimore tavern), May 13 (New York tavern), and May 14 (Methodists), 1812, in Harris, *Paul Cuffe,* 148–155. Cuffe followed up the chance encounter with the Methodists by arranging a meeting with Bishop Francis Asbury, leader of the American conference, and presenting a letter with his observations on slavery to the General Conference. According to Cuffe's journal, the delegates "seemingly treated [his observations] with rather a coolness" (p. 155 [May 16]).

124. Boston *Independent Chronicle,* July 18, 1808. For accounts of black celebrations elsewhere, see "At a numerous and respectable meeting of the Africans and their descendants . . . held the 2d day of Dec., 1807, at the African School Room," *Providence Gazette,* December 26, 1807; "Slave Trade," *Poulson's American Daily Advertiser* [Philadelphia], January 1, 1808; "Slave Trade," Boston *Columbian Centinel,* January 30, 1808; "At a general meeting of the People of color, held at Gilman's Tavern, the 3d of August," New York *Oracle,* August 5, 1808.

125. "National Jubilee of the Abolition of the Slave Trade," *New York Commercial Advertiser,* December 28, 1808.

126. Jeremiah Gloucester, *An Oration, Delivered on January 1, 1823, in Bethel Church: On the Abolition of Slave Trade* (Philadelphia, 1823), 6, 13.

127. See the introductory remarks of Joe Lockhard, Gloucester, *Oration,* Antislavery Literature Project, http://antislavery.eserver.org/religious/gloucesteroration.

128. "Declaration on the Slave Trade," Vienna, February 8, 1815, *Morning Chronicle* [London], November 13, 1815. For Britain's post-1815 campaign to suppress the slave trade, see Jennifer S. Martinez, "Anti-Slavery Courts and the Dawn of International Human Rights Law," *Yale Law Journal* 117 (2008): 550–641.

129. Brian Schoen, *The Fragile Fabric of Union: Cotton, Federal Politics, and the Global Origins of the Civil War* (Baltimore, Md., 2009).

130. Treaty of Peace and Amity, December 24, 1814, in *U.S. Statutes at Large* 8:218; Fehrenbacher, *Slaveholding Republic,* 96.

131. "The French Slave Trade," *Examiner,* September 5, 1815.

132. John Dodson, ed., *A Report of the Case of the Louis, Forest, Master: Appealed from the Vice-Admiralty Court at Sierra Leone and Determined in the High Court of Admiralty, on the 15th of December 1817* (London, 1817), 45.

133. *Amedie,* 2 Acton 250 (1810).

134. Dodson, *Report,* 34, 38, 48.

135. Wheaton, *Digest of the Law,* chap. vii, §16 (p. 230).

136. Fehrenbacher, *Slaveholding Republic,* 157–161.

137. For a brief discussion of the two cases, see Fehrenbacher, *Slaveholding Republic,* 192–194.

138. Ibid., 156.

139. Walker and Garnet, *Walker's Appeal,* 94. The reason, as a British writer explained in 1839, was that no nation had a unilateral right "to take the execution of the municipal law of another nation into its own hands," even if it was to prevent something as "abhorrent" as the slave trade: *The African Slave Trade* (London, 1839), 467, 501.

140. James Smith, *The Winter of 1840 in St. Croix, with an Excursion to Tortola and St. Thomas* (New York, 1840), 7–8: "We . . . passed her in great silence," wrote Smith, adding that he "would have given anything to see an English man-of-war."

141. Coggeshall, *Thirty-Six Voyages*, 524–525.

142. Philip Drake, *Revelations of a Slave Smuggler: Being the Autobiography of Capt. Rich'd [I.E., Philip] Drake, an African Trader for Fifty Years—from 1807 to 1857*, ed. Blyden Jackson (Northbrook, Ill., 1972 [orig. publ., 1860]), 98–99.

143. Calhoun, "Speech on the Reception of Abolition Petitions," in Crallé, *Works*, vol. 2, 626.

144. For Britain and the nineteenth-century politics of slavery in the United States, pro and con, see. especially. Nicholas Greenwood Onuf and Peter S. Onuf, *Nations, Markets, and War: Modern History and the American Civil War* (Charlottesville, Va., 2006).

6. THE NEW WORLD AND THE OLD

1. Grant Foreman, ed., *A Traveler in Indian Territory: The Journal of Ethan Allen Hitchcock, Late Major-General in the United States Army* (Norman, Okla., 1996), entry for January 27, 1842 (pp. 102–107); "live with the Indians," (p. 104). The fullest account of Milly Francis's story comes from the journal that Major Hitchcock kept during his investigation of frauds committed by white contractors against the Cherokee Nation in Oklahoma. See also T. Frederick Davis, "Milly Francis and Duncan Mckrimmon: An Authentic Florida Pocahontas," *Florida Historical Quarterly* 21 (1943): 254–265; J. Leitch Wright, *Creeks and Seminoles: The Destruction and Regeneration of the Muscogulge People* (Lincoln, Neb., 1986), 200–201, 312.

2. For intermarriages between Indian women and European men, with particular emphasis on the manifold ways in which such relationships empowered Indian women, see Theda Perdue, "'A Sprightly Lover Is the Most Prevailing Missionary': Intermarriage between Europeans and Indians in the Eighteenth-Century South," in *Light on the Path: The Anthropology and History of the Southeastern Indians*, ed. Charles M. Hudson, Thomas J. Pluckhahn, and Robbie Franklyn Ethridge (Tuscaloosa, Ala., 2006), 165–178. See also the discussion of changing gender roles among the Creeks during the later eighteenth century in Claudio Saunt, *A New Order of Things: Property, Power, and the Transformation of the Creek Indians, 1733–1816* (Cambridge, 1999), 139–185.

3. Andrew Jackson to José Masot, governor of Florida, May 23, 1818, in *ASP: Military Affairs*, 1:713. For Jackson and the Seminole War, generally, see Robert V. Remini, *Andrew Jackson and His Indian Wars* (New York, 2001), 130–162.

4. J. C. A. Stagg, *Borderlines in Borderlands: James Madison and the Spanish-American Frontier, 1776–1821* (New Haven, Conn., 2009), 200–201.

5. Account of McKrimmon's proposal in the Midgeville, Georgia, *Journal*, November 3, 1818, in Davis, "Milly Francis," 260.

6. Johnson v. McIntosh, 21 U.S. 543 (1823). Although the southeastern Indians defy easy description, the Muscogulges were the predominantly Muskogean-speaking peoples who came to be known as the Creeks and Seminoles. The Seminoles, who lived in Spanish Florida, were sometimes also called Creeks. See Wright, *Creeks and Seminoles*, 1–21.

7. For American perceptions of the collapse of Spain's empire, see James E. Lewis, *The American Union and the Problem of Neighborhood: The United States and the Collapse of the Spanish Empire, 1783–1829* (Chapel Hill, N.C., 1998). For the crisis as seen from Europe, see Rafe Blaufarb, "The Western Question: The Geopolitics of Latin American Independence," *American Historical Review* 112 (2007): 742–763. The diplomatic background of the Monroe Doctrine is covered in Ernest R. May, *The Making of the Monroe Doctrine* (Cambridge, Mass., 1975).

8. Dominique de Pradt, *Europe and America, in 1821,* trans. J. D. Williams (London, 1822), 2:148.

9. Foreman, *Traveler in Indian Territory,* 103; Davis, "Milly Francis," 261.

10. James Winchester to Isaac Shelby and Andrew Jackson, October 9, 1818, quoted in Remini, *Andrew Jackson,* 157; Richard Rush, *A Residence at the Court of London: Comprising Incidents, Official and Personal, from 1819 to 1825* (London, 1845), 1:140. In the words of William Gore Ouseley, who served as British ambassador to the United States during the 1820s, the Seminole War underscored the difficulties of maintaining "peaceable neighbourhood with a people governed as the United States are": [William Gore Ouseley], *Reply to an "American's Examination" of the "Right of Search": With Observations on Some of the Questions at Issue between Great Britain and the United States, and on Certain Positions Assumed by the North American Government* (London, 1842), 80.

11. *Annals of Congress,* 15th Cong., 2d Sess. (1819), 643, 652, 654.

12. Ibid., 640.

13. Arsène Lacarrière Latour, *Historical Memoir of the War in West Florida and Louisiana in 1814–15,* trans. H. P. Nugent (Philadelphia, 1816), 100.

14. John Rowe et al., "Congratulatory Address," Boston, February 28, in *American Mercury,* Hartford, Conn., March 14, 1815.

15. Jefferson to Thomas Leiper, June 12, 1815, and Jefferson to Lafayette, May 14, 1817, in *The Writings of Thomas Jefferson* ed. Andrew A. Lipscomb and Albert Ellery Bergh (Washington, D.C., 1903–1904; reprint, 1907), :310, 15:115.

16. Jackson to Calhoun, April 8, 1818, *H.R. Doc. No. 65,* 15th Cong.. 2d Sess. (1819), 109.

17. Adams to Erving, November 28, 1818, in ibid., 23, 25.

18. *Annals of Congress,* 15th Cong., 2d Sess., 639.

19. Walter Bromley, *An Appeal to the Virtue and Good Sense of the Inhabitants of Great Britain, &c. In Behalf of the Indians of North America* (Halifax, N.S., 1820), 14–15.

20. For a recent discussion of the execution's legal and political significance, see Deborah A. Rosen, "Wartime Prisoners and the Rule of Law," *Journal of the Early Republic* 28 (2008): 559–595. See also Remini, *Andrew Jackson,* 145–146, 150–156; J. Leitch Wright Jr., "A Note on the First Seminole War as Seen by the Indians, Negroes, and Their British Advisers," *Journal of Southern History* 34 (1968): 565–575;

Frank L. Owsley Jr., "Ambrister and Arbuthnot: Adventurers or Martyrs for British Honor?" *Journal of the Early Republic* 5 (1985): 289–308.

21. Speech of Mr. Johnson, in *Orange County Patriot* [Goshen, N.Y.], March 16, 1819. The quote comes from letters that Jackson wrote from Florida.

22. Letter to the editor, Washington, January 7, 1819, *National Advocate,* January 14, 1819.

23. "Private Correspondence," *Caledonian Mercury,* October 15, 1818; ibid., January 16, 1819, emphasis added.

24. Adams to Erving, November 28, 1818, *H.R. Doc. No. 65*, 15th Cong.. 2d Sess., 20, 25.

25. Melissa A. Stock, "Sovereign or Suzerain: Alexander Mcgillivray's Argument for Creek Independence after the Treaty of Paris of 1783," *Georgia Historical Quarterly* 92 (2008): 149–176; Leonard J. Sadosky, *Revolutionary Negotiations: Indians, Empires, and Diplomats in the Founding of America* (Charlottesville, Va., 2009), 133–140.

26. [J. Freeman Rattenbury], *Narrative of a Voyage to the Spanish Main, in the Ship "Two Friends"* (London, 1819), 165. For Rattenbury's probable authorship of the *Narrative,* see Patrick W. Doyle, "Unmasked: The Author of 'Narrative of a Voyage to the Spanish Main in the Ship "Two Friends",'" *Florida Historical Quarterly* 78 (1999): 189–206.

27. George Stiggins, "A Historical Narration of the Genealogical Traditions and Downfall of the Ispocaga or Creek Tribe of Indians, Written by One of the Tribe," in Theron A. Nunez, "Creek Nativism and the Creek War of 1813–1814," *Ethnohistory* 5, no. 1–3 (1958): 136–137, 142.

28. Elizabeth Thèrése Baird, "Reminiscences of Early Days on Mackinac Island," in *Collections of the State Historical Society of Wisconsin*, ed. Reuben Gold Thwaites (Madison, Wis., 1898), 14:18–19.

29. Major Morrell Marston to Jedidiah Morse, Fort Armstrong, Illinois, November 1820, in *The Indian Tribes of the Upper Mississippi Valley and Region of the Great Lakes,* ed. Emma Helen Blair (Cleveland, Ohio, 1912), 2:180–181.

30. For white renegades generally, see Colin G. Calloway, "Neither White nor Red: White Renegades on the American Indian Frontier," *Western Historical Quarterly* 17 (1986): 43–66. Whereas Calloway describes the phenomenon in ethnographic terms, I would argue that renegades are better understood as a legal category.

31. Report of Zéspedes, in James A. Lewis, ed. and trans., "Cracker—Spanish Florida Style," *Florida Historical Quarterly* 63 (1984): 190–191, 202. See also Wright, *Creeks and Seminoles,* chap. 3, 4, 5, 7; Jane Landers, *Black Society in Spanish Florida* (Urbana, Ill., 1999), chap. 10.

32. Milo Milton Quaife, ed., *The Indian Captivity of O. M. Spencer* (Chicago, 1917), 163. Spencer's narrative first appeared in serialized form in the *Western Christian Advocate* during the 1830s (p. xii).

33. *Reporter,* November 24, 1810, quoted in Bradford Perkins, *Prologue to War: England and the United States, 1805–1812* (Berkeley, Calif., 1961), 284. For a cogent, if somewhat dated, discussion of the historiography on the war's origins, see ibid.,

418–437; see also J. C. A. Stagg, *Mr. Madison's War: Politics, Diplomacy, and Warfare in the Early American Republic, 1783–1830* (Princeton, N.J., 1983).

34. Hull's Proclamation to the Inhabitants of Canada, Sandwich, Upper Canada, July 13, 1812, in "Documents Relating to Detroit and Vicinity, 1805–1813," *Michigan Historical Collections* 40 (1929): 410–411.

35. For the Red Sticks and Tenskwatawa and Tecumseh's nativist movement, see Saunt, *New Order of Things,* 250–252; Daniel K. Richter, *Facing East from Indian Country: A Native History of Early America* (Cambridge, Mass., 2001), 228–232.

36. Adams to Erving, November 28, 1818; Proclamation of Lieut. Colonel Edward Nicholls, Pensacola, August 29, 1814; and Hopoithle Mico, Cappachimico, and Hopoy Mico, Declaration of the Muscogee nation, April 2, 1815, in Nicholls to Benjamin Hawkins, April 28, 1815, all in *H.R. Doc. No. 65,* 15th Cong., 2d Sess., 13, 31–34. See also Frank Lawrence Owsley, *Struggle for the Gulf Coast Borderlands: The Creek War and the Battle of New Orleans, 1812–1815* (Tuscaloosa, Ala., 2000).

37. J. Loomis to Commodore Patterson, August 13, 1816, *H.R. Doc. No. 65,* 15th Cong., 2d Sess., 65. On the destruction of the Negro Fort, see Fred Anderson and Andrew R. L. Cayton, *The Dominion of War: Empire and Liberty in North America, 1500–2000* (New York, 2005), 236–237.

38. *H.R. Doc. No. 65,* 15th Cong.. 2d Sess., 121–215.

39. The Spanish Atlantic was in the midst of the Spanish American wars of independence, but these were officially civil wars in which none of the other European powers were directly involved.

40. [Rattenbury], *Narrative,* 269.

41. Letter from Sawanee, Lower Creek Nation, January 30, 1818, *Niles Weekly Register* 15 (1819): 85.

42. Arbuthnot's Journal (excerpt), October 23 to November 10, 1817, *H.R. Doc. No. 65,* 15th Cong., 2d Sess., 208.

43. *Morning Chronicle,* January 9, 1819.

44. "Trial of Robert C. Ambrister," in *American State Trials: A Collection of the Important and Interesting Criminal Trials Which Have Taken Place in the United States,* ed. John Davison Lawson and Robert Lorenzo Howard (St. Louis, 1914), 2:900.

45. "Memorial of Andrew Jackson" (presented to the Senate, February 23, 1820), in *ASP: Military Affairs,* 1:757.

46. *Niles Weekly Register* 15, 184.

47. [Rattenbury], *Narrative,* 310: "Our doctrine of allegiance and protection is of this peculiar character, that the constitution extends its fostering care over the subject, to the remotest region."

48. The speeches of the Marquess of Lansdowne, the Earl of Bath, and the Earl of Liverpool in the House of Lords, as reported in *Morning Chronicle,* May 12, 1819. Rafe Blaufarb has recently argued that the War of 1812 gave "Americans such an apprehension of British power that they dared not undertake new conquests for another thirty years." See Blaufarb, "The Western Question," 745. Britain's muted response

to Jackson's execution of the two British prisoners suggests that the feelings were mutual.

49. Charles Francis Adams, ed., *Memoirs of John Quincy Adams, Comprising Portions of His Diary from 1795 to 1848* (Philadelphia, 1875), 4:114, 173.

50. Luis de Onís, *Memoir Upon the Negotiations between Spain and the United States of America, Which Led to the Treaty of 1819,* trans. Tobias Watkins (Washington, D.C., 1821), 22.

51. Adams to Erving, November 28, 1818, in *H.R. Doc. No. 65,* 15th Cong.. 2d Sess., 18.

52. Worthington C. Ford et al., eds., *Journals of the Continental Congress, 1774–1789,* vol. 5, *June 5—October 8, 1776* (Washington, D.C., 1906), 579.

53. Stagg, *Borderlines in Borderlands,* 38–51.

54. Yrujo to James Madison, Washington, March 7, 1804, in *1 November 1903—31 March 1804,* vol. 6 of *The Papers of James Madison: Secretary of State Series,* ed. Robert J. Brugger et al. (Charlottesville, Va., 2002), 557–558.

55. Report of Zéspedes, in Lewis, "Cracker—Spanish Florida Style," 190–191, 202. See also Wright, *Creeks and Seminoles,* chap. 3, 4, 5, 7; Landers, *Black Society in Spanish Florida,* chap. 10.

56. John R. Bedford to James Madison, Nashville, July 4, 1810, in *1 October 1809—2 November 1810,* vol. 2 of *The Papers of James Madison: Presidential Series,* ed. Robert A. Rutland et al. (Charlottesville, Va., 1992), 399; David J. Weber, *The Spanish Frontier in North America* (New Haven, Conn., 1992), 296–301. On the fine line that often separated professions of allegiance to Ferdinand from declarations of independence, see Jaime E. Rodriguez O., *The Independence of Spanish America* (Cambridge, 1998 [orig. publ., 1996]), 107–109; J. H. Elliott, *Empires of the Atlantic World: Britain and Spain in America, 1492–1830* (New Haven, Conn., 2006), 375–383. For the Spanish and European context of Napoleon's intervention, see Paul W. Schroeder, *The Transformation of European Politics, 1763–1848* (Oxford, 1994), 337–346.

57. Stagg, *Borderlines in Borderlands,* 58–69 (quoted passage on p. 60).

58. Weber, *Spanish Frontier in North America,* 297.

59. Declaration by the Representatives of the People of West Florida in Convention Assembled, September 26, 1810, in *ASP: Foreign Relations,* 3:396. For West Florida's claim to be the first lone star state or republic, see David A. Bice, *The Original Lone Star Republic: Scoundrels, Statesmen & Schemers of the 1810 West Florida Rebellion* (Louisville, Ky., 2004).

60. Presidential Proclamation, October 27, 1810, in Rutland et al., *Papers of James Madison: Presidential,* vol. 2, 595; William Cobbett, "American President's Speech Relative to the Spanish Colonies," in *Cobbett's Weekly Register* 49, no. 1 (January 3, 1824): 9–10.

61. *H.R. Doc. No. 65,* 15th Cong.. 2d Sess., 12.

62. Adams to Erving, November 18, 1818, in ibid., 14, 19.

63. Thomas Rodney to Caesar A. Rodney, Town of Washington, Mississippi Territory, December 10, 1810, in Simon Gratz, ed., "Thomas Rodney," *Pennsylvania Magazine of History and Biography* 45, no. 1–2 (1921): 201.

64. Stagg, *Borderlines in Borderlands,* 61. Despite the British alliance with Ferdinand in Spain, Albert Gallatin, for one, worried that Britain would use the collapse of Bourbon authority in America to take possession of Cuba and the Floridas: Gallatin to Madison, New York, September 17, 1810, in Rutland et al., *Papers of James Madison: Presidential,* vol. 2, 545–546.

65. [Fulwar Skipwith], "Gentlemen of the Senate and House of Representatives [of West Florida]," printed broadside (Natchez, n.d.), Library of Congress, Printed Ephemera Collection, portfolio 85, f. 3; from *Broadsides, Leaflets, and Pamphlets from America and Europe,* Library of Congress online, http://hdl.loc.gov/loc.rbc/rbpe.08500300 (accessed November 17, 2009).

66. Thomas Rodney to Caesar A. Rodney, December 10, 1810, in Gratz, "Thomas Rodney," 202.

67. "Proceedings of the First Convention of West Florida" (July 27, 1810), *Weekly Chronicle,* August 10, 1810, in *The Territory of Orleans, 1803–1812,* vol. 9 of *The Territorial Papers of the United States,* ed. Clarence Edwin Carter (Washington, D.C., 1934), 893.

68. Blaufarb, "The Western Question," 761. For Spanish Americans, the crucial event was Ferdinand's repudiation in 1814 of the liberal constitution of 1812 and his attempt to restore Spain's empire to the absolutist government that had existed before 1808. See Elliott, *Empires of the Atlantic World,* 388–389.

69. [Rattenbury], *Narrative,* 77–180, 89, 91, 95–96; Archibald Clark to William Crawford, St. Mary's Georgia, November 1, 1817, *H.R. Doc. No. 12,* 15th Cong., 1st Sess. (1818), 22–23, describes the arrival of the vessel carrying Rattenbury and another thirty British half-pay officers at Amelia Island. For Ambrister's involvement with MacGregor's Patriot Army, see the evidence presented at his trial in ibid., 192.

70. Blaufarb, "The Western Question," 753.

71. The analysis of European diplomacy here closely follows Schroeder, *Transformation,* 628–636.

72. "Private Letter from Petersburgh," *Morning Chronicle,* September 27, 1817; "From the German Papers," *Morning Chronicle,* October 7, 1817. For Alexander's interest in bringing the Spanish American crisis before the great powers, which Britain successfully parried at the Congress of Aix-la-Chapelle in 1818, see Schroeder, *Transformation,* 630–631.

73. *Caledonian Mercury,* September 25, 1817.

74. Jackson to Monroe, "Confidential," Nashville, January 6, 1818, in *May 1, 1814, to December 31, 1819,* vol. 2 of *Correspondence of Andrew Jackson,* ed. John Spencer Bassett and David Maydole Matteson (Washington, D.C., 1926–1935), 346.

75. Adams to Erving, November 28, 1818, in *H.R. Doc. No. 65,* 15th Cong.. 2d Sess., 19, 25 ("mock patriots").

76. Adams to Erving, November 28, 1818, in ibid., 27.

77. William McIntosh and Creek Delegation to Calhoun, Washington, March 9, 1819, Calhoun to Creek Deputation (a talk), War Department, March 28, 1819, McIntosh to Calhoun, Washington, December 31, 1819, in *The Papers of John C. Calhoun,* ed.

W. Edwin Hemphill et al. (Columbia, S.C., 1959–2003), vol. 3, *1818–1819,* 646, 700; vol. 4, *1819–1820,* 531.

78. Wright, *Creeks and Seminoles,* 166–167, 210–212. See also Saunt, *New Order of Things,* 217, 221; Remini, *Andrew Jackson,* 151–152.

79. *Annals of Congress,* 15th Cong., 2d Sess., 641.

80. Adams to Erving, November 28, 1818, in *H.R. Doc. No. 65,* 15th Cong.. 2d Sess., 20.

81. To the Creek Delegation, March 28, 1819, in Hemphill et al., *Calhoun Papers,* vol. 3, 700.

82. George Hammond to Grenville, Philadelphia, January 1, 1793, FO 5/1, 51, BNA, reporting substance of interview with Jefferson. Hammond's offer to mediate was in response to a formal request from the chiefs of the Iroquois Confederacy at a council with representatives of Governor Simcoe of Upper Canada at Buffalo Creek (modern Buffalo, New York). In Jefferson's eyes, the fact that British agents had convened a meeting of Indians within the territory of the United States made Britain's offer that much less acceptable. Jefferson made clear that regarding the Indians as dependent nations was as much in Britain's interest as the American republic's.

83. The British minutes of the negotiations are in FO 5/102, BNA.

84. "The Negotiations at Ghent," reprinted in *Boston Weekly Messenger,* October 21, 1814.

85. "An Exposition of the Causes and Consequences of the War with Great Britain," *Weekly Aurora,* March 22, 1815.

86. Bathurst to George Prevost, War Department, London, December 27, 1814, quoted in Wright, *Creeks and Seminoles,* 182–183.

87. [George Robert Gleig], *A Narrative of the Campaigns of the British Army at Washington and New Orleans, under Generals Ross, Pakenham, and Lambert, in the Years 1814 and 1815* (London, 1821), 269–270.

88. Codrington to Jane Codrington, December 1 and December 14, in *Memoir of the Life of Admiral Sir Edward Codrington,* ed. Jane Barbara Bourchier (London, 1873), 1:328–330.

89. Extracts of letters from Adams to the Secretary of State, London, September 9, 1815, and February 8, 1816, in *H.R. Doc. No. 65,* 15th Cong.. 2d Sess., 50, 52.

90. Bromley, *Appeal,* 15.

91. Thomas Forsyth to General William Clark, St. Louis, December 23, 1812, in Blair, *Indian Tribes,* vol. 2, 277. See also Richter, *Facing East,* 229–230; Frank L. Owsley Jr., "Prophet of War: Josiah Francis and the Creek War," *American Indian Quarterly* 9 (1985): 273–293.

92. *H.R. Doc. No. 65,* 15th Cong.. 2d Sess., 173–174.

93. "Representation of Wm Augustus Bowles," in Bowles to Grenville, January 3, 1791, FO 4/9, 9–10, BNA. For similar statements by the Creek leader Alexander McGillivray, see Stock, "Sovereign or Suzerain," 149–176.

94. Hawkins to Nicholls, May 28, 1815, in *H.R. Doc. No. 65,* 15th Cong.. 2d Sess., 38. See also J. Leitch Wright, *William Augustus Bowles: Director General of the Creek Nation* (Athens, Ga., 1967).

95. Decision of Judge John Kelsall, Juan Madraz v. Richard Power, Vice Admiralty of the Bahama Islands, March 31–May 29, 1802, both in Lyle N. McAlister, "The Ma-

rine Forces of William Augustus Bowles and His 'State of Muskogee': Illustrative Documents," *Florida Historical Quarterly* 32, no. 1 (1953): 24.

96. For Bowles's legacy among the Creeks and Seminoles, see Saunt, *New Order of Things*, 86–88, 205–213 .

97. *Lloyd's Evening Post*, October 22, 1800. See also Wright, *William Augustus Bowles*, vii, 124–158.

98. Charles Chalmers, *Remarks on the Late War in St. Domingo* (London, 1803), 79.

99. Laurent Dubois, *Avengers of the New World: The Story of the Haitian Revolution* (Cambridge, Mass., 2004), 223–226; Tim Matthewson, "Jefferson and Haiti," *Journal of Southern History* 61 (1995): 209–248.

100. Edward Stevens to Timothy Pickering, L'Arcahaye, Saint-Domingue, June 24, 1799, in "Letters of Toussaint Louverture and of Edward Stevens, 1798–1800," *American Historical Review* 16 (1910): 77.

101. Frank Cundall, ed., *Lady Nugent's Journal: Jamaica One Hundred Years Ago* (London, 1907), 254.

102. Chalmers, *Remarks on the Late War*, 78, 80. For connections between Haiti's declaration of independence and Jefferson's, see Dubois, *Avengers of the New World*, 298–300.

103. Cherokee Nation v. Georgia, 30 U.S. 1 (1831).

104. Hawkins to Col. Edward Nicholls, Creek Agency, May 28, 1815, in *H.R. Doc. No. 65*, 15th Cong., 2d Sess., 23, 38.

105. Stiggins, "Historical Narration," in Nunez, "Creek Nativism," no. 1: 32.

106. For the fort's connections to Saint-Domingue, see Anderson and Cayton, *Dominion of War*, 234–238.

107. Adams to Erving, November 18, 1818, in *H.R. Doc. No. 65*, 15th Cong.. 2d Sess., 13.

108. James Innerarity to John Forbes, Mobile, August 12, 1815, in James Innerarity, "The Panton, Leslie Papers: James Innerarity to John Forbes," *Florida Historical Quarterly* 12 (1934): 128.

109. See, for example, J. Loomis to Commodore Daniel T. Patterson, onboard U.S. Gun Vessel No. 149, Bay St. Louis, August 13, 1816, in *H.R. Doc. No. 65*, 15th Cong.. 2d Sess., 69.

110. McIntosh to William H. Crawford, Camden County (near Jefferson), Georgia, October 30, 1817, *H.R. Doc. No. 12*, 15th Cong., 1st Sess., 20–21.

111. Jackson to Calhoun, Fort Gadsden, May 5, 1818, in Bassett and Matteson, *Correspondence of Andrew Jackson*, vol. 2, 365–366. On the genesis of Jackson's support for Indian removal, see Remini, *Andrew Jackson*, 85, 114–116. According to Remini, the idea was first suggested by Thomas Jefferson while he was president.

112. Hawkins to Nicholls, Creek Agency, Georgia, May 24, 1815, *H.R. Doc. No. 65*, 15th Cong., 2d Sess., 37.

113. Jackson to Calhoun, Fort Gadsden, May 5, 1818, in Bassett and Matteson, *Correspondence of Andrew Jackson*, vol. 2, 365.

114. Hawkins to Nicholls, Creek Agency, Georgia, May 28, 1815, *H.R. Doc. No. 65*, 15th Cong., 2d Sess., 37–38, 40.

115. Doyle to John Innerarity, Prospect Bluff, July 11, 1817, in "The Panton, Leslie Papers: Concluding the Letters of Edmund Doyle, Trader," *Florida Historical Quarterly* 18 (1939): 136.

116. *Annals of Congress,* 15th Cong., 2d Sess., 634, 639, 652.

117. Johnson v. McIntosh, 21 U.S. 543 (1823), *Correspondence, Papers, and Selected Judicial Opinions, January 1820—December 1823,* vol. 9 of *The Papers of John Marshall,* ed. Herbert A. Johnson et al. (Chapel Hill, N.C., 1998), 285, 298.

118. Alan Taylor, *The Civil War of 1812: American Citizens, British Subjects, Irish Rebels, and Indian Allies* (New York, 2010), chap. 16.

119. Smith, "To the Good People of South Carolina—No. III," *City Gazette* [Charleston, S.C.], March 13, 1823.

120. James Innerarity to John Forbes, Aug. 12, 1815, in James Innerarity, "The Panton, Leslie Papers: James Innerarity to John Forbes," 124, 127, 130.

121. Thomas Roderick Dew, "Review of the Debate in the Virginia Legislature of 1831 and 1832," in *The Pro-Slavery Argument: As Maintained by the Most Distinguished Writers of the Southern States* (Philadelphia, 1853), 455, 457.

122. The Cherokee, in particular, are the subject of a vast literature; for a brief overview, see Anthony F. C. Wallace, *The Long, Bitter Trail: Andrew Jackson and the Indians* (New York, 1993), 58–62.

123. Susan Sleeper-Smith, "'[A]n Unpleasant Transaction on This Frontier': Challenging Female Autonomy and Authority at Michilimackinac," *Journal of the Early Republic* 25 (2005): 417–443.

124. Thomas Forsyth, "An Account of the Manners and Customs of the Sauk and Fox Nations," St. Louis, January 15, 1827, in Blair, *Indian Tribes,* vol. 2, 204.

125. Stiggins, "Historical Narration," in Nunez, "Creek Nativism," no. 2: 138.

EPILOGUE: MR. MONROE'S PEACE

1. George Dangerfield, *The Awakening of American Nationalism, 1815–1828* (New York, 1965), 20. The analysis here closely follows that of Bradford Perkins, *The Creation of a Republican Empire, 1776–1865,* vol. 1 of *The Cambridge History of American Foreign Relations,* ed. Warren I. Cohen (Cambridge, 1993; reprint, 1995), 148–149.

2. S. Putnam Waldo, *The Tour of James Monroe, President of the United States, through the Northern and Eastern States, in 1817,* 2nd ed. (Hartford, Conn., 1820), 153, 276, passim. On the tour's symbolic importance, see Perkins, *Creation,* 148.

3. The Adam-Onís or Transcontinental Treaty, which Spain waited until 1821 to ratify, is discussed in detail in James E. Lewis, *The American Union and the Problem of Neighborhood: The United States and the Collapse of the Spanish Empire, 1783–1829* (Chapel Hill, N.C., 1998), 120–172, passim; J. C. A. Stagg, *Borderlines in Borderlands: James Madison and the Spanish-American Frontier, 1776–1821* (New Haven, Conn., 2009), 195–202. See also David J. Weber, *The Spanish Frontier in North America* (New Haven, Conn., 1992), 298–299. On the Rush-Bagot agreement with Britain (1817), see Perkins, *Creation,* 208–209.

4. Ernest R. May, *The Making of the Monroe Doctrine* (Cambridge, Mass., 1975); Perkins, *Creation*, 165–169. See also Paul W. Schroeder, *The Transformation of European Politics, 1763–1848* (Oxford, 1994), 634–636. As Americans admitted, Britain's tacit consent was crucial. "Great Britain," wrote Jefferson in 1823, "is the nation which can do us the most harm of anyone, or all on earth; and with her on our side we need not fear the whole world": Jefferson to Monroe, Monticello, October 23, 1823, in *Thomas Jefferson, Writings*, vol. 15 of *The Library of America*, ed. Merrill D. Peterson (New York, 1984), 1482.

5. Waldo, *Tour of James Monroe*, 40.

6. In Britain's case, of course, the age of European colonialism was still alive and well in North America and the West Indies; however, it was something of a commonplace during the 1820s that Britain's remaining colonies of settlement would eventually follow the example of the Americas' other colonies and become independent.

7. "Retrospect of the Efforts and Progress of Mankind During the Last Twenty-Five Years," *Monthly Magazine* 59, no. 412 (1825): 587.

8. Although the notion that a "market revolution" displaced a subsistence agricultural economy is deeply flawed, a useful overview can be found in Charles Sellers, *The Market Revolution: Jacksonian America, 1815–1846* (New York, 1991). For a more nuanced account, see Robert H. Wiebe, *The Opening of American Society: From the Adoption of the Constitution to the Eve of Disunion* (New York, 1984).

9. "The Principles of the Holy Alliance; or Notes and Manifestoes of the Allied Powers," *North American Review* 17, no. 41 (1823): 373.

10. Waldo, *Tour of James Monroe*, 53.

11. Henry Wheaton, *Elements of International Law*, ed. Richard Henry Dana, 8th rev. ed. (Boston, 1866 [orig. publ., 1836]), part 2, §63, p. 92. For Wheaton's influence and reputation as the American successor to Vattel, see Nicholas Greenwood Onuf and Peter S. Onuf, *Nations, Markets, and War: Modern History and the American Civil War* (Charlottesville, Va., 2006), 50, 58–78.

12. Quoted in Waldo, *Tour of James Monroe*, 43, 50.

13. Brian Schoen, *The Fragile Fabric of Union: Cotton, Federal Politics, and the Global Origins of the Civil War* (Baltimore, Md., 2009), 47, table 3, 103–104, 112–126. On the U.S. government's treatment of trade between Britain and North America, see J. C. A. Stagg, *Mr. Madison's War: Politics, Diplomacy, and Warfare in the Early American Republic, 1783–1830* (Princeton, N.J., 1983), 512–514.

14. For the continued salience of English precedents in American law, see Morton J. Horwitz, *The Transformation of American Law, 1780–1860* (Cambridge, Mass., 1977).

15. Wheaton, *Elements*, part 4, §544, p. 715.

16. Don E. Fehrenbacher, *The Slaveholding Republic: An Account of the United States Government's Relations to Slavery* (Oxford, 2001), 148–150.

17. Harry Ammon, "Monroe, James," in *American National Biography Online* (Feb. 2000), http://www.anb.org/articles/03/03-00338.html (accessed September 22, 2011 [Published by Oxford University Press, with American Council of Learned Societies].

18. Judge Shaw's opinion in *Commonwealth v. Aves* (1836), as reprinted in Joseph Story, *Commentaries on the Conflict of Laws, Foreign and Domestic,* 2nd rev. ed. (London, 1841 [orig. publ., 1834]), 157n. The case involved the question of whether Massachusetts law sanctioned the continued enslavement of Med, a six-year-old slave girl who had accompanied her mistress from New Orleans to visit her father in Boston. Shaw found that it did not—though, like Mansfield in *Somerset* (1772), he made it clear that slavery was legal under both state and federal law.

19. *Report and Resolutions of the Legislature of Vermont, on the Subject of Texas, Slavery, the Slave Trade, &c., . . . Feb. 14, 1838, H.R. Doc. No. 182,* 25th Cong., 2d Sess. (1838). For the free-trade liberalism of American slaveholders, see Onuf and Onuf, *Nations, Markets, and War,* 156–277; Schoen, *Fragile Fabric,* 100–145.

20. The phrase "great nation" appeared in a panegyric in an Irish newspaper on Monroe's inauguration in 1817. See Waldo, *Tour of James Monroe,* 53. The United States' history as a great nation before the Civil War is treated with particular insight in Onuf and Onuf, *Nations, Markets, and War.*

21. Schroeder, *Transformation,* 554, 592.

22. "View of Publick Affairs," *Christian Advocate* 2, no. 1 (1824): 47.

23. Dominique de Pradt, *Europe and America, in 1821,* trans. J. D. Williams (London, 1822), 2:148.

24. Quote taken from Monroe's address to the citizens of Athens, Ga., May 20, 1819, as reported in "President's Tour," *Newport Mercury,* June 26, 1819. In Upper Canada, property was cheaper, taxes were lower (by as much as 80 percent), and military obligations were less onerous than in the United States. See Alan Taylor, "The Late Loyalists: Northern Reflections of the Early American Republic," *Journal of the Early Republic* 27, no. 1 (2007): 1–34.

25. "President's Tour," *Newport Mercury,* June 26, 1819. On the Union as a Jeffersonian empire of liberty, see Gordon S. Wood, *Empire of Liberty: A History of the Early Republic, 1789–1815* (Oxford, 2009).

26. Christopher Hodson, "Exile on Spruce Street: An Acadian History," *William & Mary Quarterly,* 3rd ser., 67 (2010): 249–278. White's Anglicization of his surname was typical of Acadians, especially those who lived in the United States outside the Acadian enclaves on the Gulf Coast. In the Canadian Maritimes, Acadians continued to use both forms, depending on the circumstances, moving between Dubois and Wood, Doucet and Sweet, or—in the case of my own family—Doiron and Duran or Gould. Sometimes, Acadian families appear in Canadian records using both, as in Gould *dit* Doiron. I am grateful to Professor Hodson for sharing insights from his forthcoming book on the Acadian diaspora.

27. Thomas S. Woodward, *Woodward's Reminiscences of the Creek, or Muscogee Indians, Contained in Letters to Friends in Georgia and Alabama* (Montgomery, Ala., 1859), 163. For more on Woodward, see J. Leitch Wright, *Creeks and Seminoles: The Destruction and Regeneration of the Muscogulge People* (Lincoln, Neb., 1986), 61, 75. On Indians in the Midwest who became American citizens, see Eric Hinderaker,

Elusive Empires: Constructing Colonialism in the Ohio Valley, 1673–1800 (Cambridge, 1997), 260–264.

28. I thank Richard Ross for suggesting this metaphor. For teaching me about key signatures and other areas of music theory, I am indebted to my late father, Glen Gould. I also benefited from several conversations with David Ervin of the Oyster River Middle School in Durham, New Hampshire.

Acknowledgments

Like many books, this one started as a hunch. While researching my first book on Britain and the American Revolution, I noticed that Congress's demand to be included among the independent powers of the earth, as Thomas Jefferson wrote in 1776, received far more attention in Parliament and the British press than the founders' experiment with republicanism and popular government. This, of course, differed from how most American historians treated the revolution. In both popular and scholarly accounts, the revolution's international dimensions usually played second fiddle to the internal struggles that accompanied independence. Because I was still working on the history of the revolution in Britain, I published my findings in the Oxford journal *Past and Present* and concentrated on finishing my book, yet it seemed to me that there was more to say. How, I wondered, would our understanding change if we revisited the Union's founding and placed more emphasis on Americans' relations with other nations and people?

Although a decade of writing and research has led me to refine the question that it seeks to answer, this book is a result of that query. I could not have written it without funded leaves from the Charles Warren Center for Studies in American History at Harvard University, the National Endowment for the Humanities, and the Center for the Humanities at the University of New Hampshire (UNH). Early on, several institutions at UNH, including the College of Liberal Arts, the university's Marine Program, and the history department's Dunfey Fund, helped finance travel to Britain and Europe, and I was fortunate to hold the Class of 1940 Professorship from 2001 to 2004. I am grateful to the benefactors whose generosity helped make this assistance possible and to the colleagues and administrators who supported me, especially Marilyn Hoskin and Ken Fuld, former and current deans of the College of Liberal Arts at UNH; Burt Feintuch, director of the Center for the Humanities; and Bill Harris, Janet Polasky, and Jan Golinski, who chaired the history department over the last decade.

While I was writing the book, I also benefited from invitations to present excerpts and synopses to audiences at the University of London, the National University of Ireland, Galway, Oxford University, the University of Liverpool, Universidad Nacional de Córdoba, Argentina, the Salzburg Seminar, Austria, Johns Hopkins University, Columbia University, Dartmouth College, New York University, Northwestern University, Harvard University's Atlantic History Seminar, the University of Maryland, Indiana University, the University of Virginia, the Omohundro Institute of Early American History and Culture, the McNeill Center in Philadelphia, the Library of Congress, the Newberry Library, UCLA's William Andrews Clark Library, the Huntington Library, and the Massachusetts Historical Society. I am grateful to the participants who attended these presentations and shared their thoughts and suggestions. I would also like to thank Kathleen McDermott at Harvard University Press, who has been a supportive and insightful editor, stepping in when necessary while giving me the time and space that every author needs. In Isabelle Lewis, I could not have asked for a better map maker, and Sophia Saeed Khan and Andrew Kinney, Harvard's editorial assistants, made the book's final stages far more pleasant than I had a right to expect.

I owe a tremendous debt to the many colleagues who brainstormed hunches, read chapters, shared insights, and offered suggestions and advice. Topping the list is my fellow editor (and co-sovereign), Peter Onuf, whose early, pathbreaking work on the law of nations and the American Revolution played a crucial role in helping me conceptualize the book's overall structure and who was an early and enthusiastic supporter of the project. Jack Greene and Amy Turner Bushnell have also been enormously helpful, as have John Pocock and my dear friends John and Tina Gillis. Here at New Hampshire, along with the people already named, my colleagues—Ellen Fitzpatrick, Jeff Bolster, Lucy Salyer, Funso Afolayan, Julia Rodriguez, Kurk Dorsey, David Frankfurter (now at Boston University), Cynthia Van Zandt, Jeff Diefendorf, Charlie Clark, Doug Wheeler, and Jessica Lepler—provided frequent and valuable feedback. My former doctoral student Ted Andrews, now on the faculty at Providence College, Rhode Island, was a diligent and perceptive reader, and the other graduate students with whom I have been fortunate to work helped in ways too numerous to list. I also thank Jeremy Adelman, Fred Anderson, David Armitage, Bernard Bailyn, Rose Beiler, Lauren Benton, Timothy Breen, Colin Calloway, Joyce Chaplin, Stephen Conway, Julie Flavell, Alison Games, David Hancock, David Hendrickson, Ron Hoffman, Daniel Hulsebosch, Maya Jasanoff, Sarah Knott, Elizabeth Mancke, Paul Mapp, Peter Marshall, Joseph Miller, Maura O'Connor, Geoffrey Plank, Andrew O'Shaughnessy, Carla Pestana, Daniel Richter, Richard Ross, Leonard Sadosky, James Sidbury, Fredrika Teute, Christopher Tomlins, John Voll, Dror Wahrman, and Gordon Wood, with a special acknowledgment to Frank Cogliano and the anonymous referee who read the manuscript for Harvard University Press. All gave generously of their time, and I am enormously grateful.

Finally, my heartfelt thanks go to the friends and family members who leavened the often-lonely task of writing with companionship and conviviality. Over the last decade, I have spent countless hours—most of them enjoyable—climbing 4,000-footers in the White Mountains with fellow peak-baggers David Frankfurter, Jan Golinski, and Charlie Forcey. David Mulhern was always up for lunch and conversation, and he read sections of the book, asking penetrating questions and offering helpful suggestions. Farther afield, my former college roommate Jeb Palmer allowed me to sleep on his couch while I was conducting research in London. Here in Durham, the many friends and neighbors who pried me away from my computer for skiing, kayaking, and golf did me more good than they probably realized—though the golf game still needs work. I am more grateful than I can say to my father, Glen Gould, who died before the book was completed, and my mother, Mildred Nisbet Gould, for their constant love and support, and to my brother, Warren Gould, and his family. Most of all, though, I want to thank three people: my wife, Nicoletta Gullace, and our two children, Charlie and Emma Hilary. Because she is also a historian and colleague, Nicky played a central part in the conceptualization and writing of this book. But she has done a great deal more than that. My love and gratitude know no limits.

Index

Harvard University Press is a member of Green Press Initiative (greenpressinitiative.org), a nonprofit organization working to help publishers and printers increase their use of recycled paper and decrease their use of fiber derived from endangered forests. This book was printed on recycled paper containing 30% post-consumer waste and processed chlorine free.